Foreword

Australia's understanding and knowledge of Asia has historically been cursory and superficial. For most of this century there has been a background awareness of various Asian countries, sometimes as a threat, more frequently as an enigma. But, as Dr Stephen Fitzgerald has put it, Australia has 'a peculiarly inescapable bond with its regional habitat … it has always been there and there is a sense in which it has always been part of our history'.

When the history of the last 10 or 15 years is written it will be seen in a very different light from the past. It has been a period of big change in Australia's relationships with the region. Political relationships have become closer: exchanges more frequent. The volume of trade has grown. Two-way tourist traffic and two-way investment has rapidly increased. Australians feel comfortable travelling in Asia. Business people have become more adept at dealing with complex and different business cultures. Negotiating styles are understood better.

Much of this new engagement has been government initiated. Mostly it has happened because it all makes sense. Australia, the largest economy in South-East Asia, is parked conveniently offshore from part of the world's fastest growing economic region. Asia, with rising incomes and high-growth economies, is our market of greatest opportunity. The countries of ASEAN are our neighbours: people with whom we should get on well. Our Asian migrant communities provide a rich source of advice and experience. The alumni of our universities have well-entrenched positions in the countries of the region. The interconnections become stronger day by day.

For obvious reasons these changes have happened faster in Australia than in other countries with predominantly European populations. My sense is that it gives us a competitive edge in understanding and knowledge. Geography, political relationships and trade suggest we should be experts on the region. We're not; but perhaps we're in front, and we should make every effort to stay there.

ASEAN Business, Trade and Development will help. It provides a well-developed picture of Australia's relationship with ASEAN as a bloc, and a detailed analysis of the business environment in each of the individual member countries of the group. A third section is devoted to supportive disciplines (such as commercial law, tax and marketing) with a description of how they operate in each country.

This is a comprehensive, factual and up-to-date book, invaluable to those seeking a more sophisticated understanding of the countries of ASEAN. For business people, academics and students, it's the equivalent of a Michelin guide to serious business in Asia. Individual Australians, and the country, will be well served by its widespread use as a reference book of quality and distinction.

John N Button
Minister for Industry, Technology and Commerce,
Australian Government, 1983–93.

ASEAN Business, Trade and Development

Edited by

Ron Edwards
BCom(Hons), DipEd, MA (Melb); GradDipCompEd

Senior Lecturer, Syme Business School – Frankston, Faculty of Business and
Economics, Monash University

Michael T Skully
BS BA (Arizona); MBA (Utah); GradDipEc (Stockholm); ASIA, ACIS, FCPA,
ACIM, AAIB (Snr)

Professor of Banking, Syme Department of Banking and Finance, Faculty of
Business and Economics, Monash University

Butterworth-Heinemann Asia

An imprint of Reed Academic Publishing Asia

A division of Reed Elsevier (S) Pte Ltd
1 Temasek Avenue
#17–01 Millenia Tower
Singapore 039192

ISBN 981 00 8235 5

Typeset in Australia by J & M Typesetting
Individual country maps by Gary Swinton
Printed in Australia by McPherson's Printing Group, Maryborough

Contents

4 Indonesia   54

Siang Ng

5 Malaysia   81

Anita Doraisami

9 Vietnam   189

Peter Schuwalow

10 Marketing in ASEAN   215

David Watson

14 Taxation planning and ASEAN   314

by Andrew McNicol

15 Future directions   332

Ron Edwards

Preface

Over the past decade, Australia has undergone a major shift in thinking. Nowadays most university students probably view Australia as being part of Asia in the full sense or at least in the economic sense. It is not clear whether most members of Australia's business community have the same view. If they do not, we are confident that reading this book will help to change their perspective.

The era of Asia–Pacific economic ascendancy, which may in the past have seemed remote and intangible, is now with us. The affluence and technological leadership of Singapore, the sustained growth of Thailand and Malaysia, the size and vibrancy of Indonesia and the potential of Vietnam and the Philippines combine to make Australia's immediate region the most exciting region in the Pacific. Australian business has started to turn its attention to the opportunities on its doorstep, and remarkable progress has been made in business development with the region. Nevertheless, achievements to date fall well short of potential. Australian businesses, large and small, are wishing to do more. For leaders who have little knowledge of the region and less confidence in it, and for leaders who need to broaden or update their knowledge, the book will provide relevant information and practical guidance.

Although studies of ASEAN (Association of South-East Asian Nations) and its constituent economies have previously been undertaken, our book contains the first comprehensive management guide. As well as presenting a series of country profiles, we explore each functional area of management in order to identify the special characteristics of business conduct in ASEAN countries. We therefore include chapters on the subjects of marketing, commercial law, trade finance, human-resource management and taxation, all of which are geared towards providing guidance for Australian companies that are planning to enter ASEAN markets.

The book presents a contemporary account of the way in which business, finance, trade and politics operate in the region. We discuss the entry of Vietnam, other countries' potential for joining ASEAN, and even Australia's potential membership – 'over the horizon', as this possibility has been described by Singaporean Prime Minister Goh Chok Tong. We analyse the ASEAN Free Trade Agreement (AFTA) and the various 'growth triangles', as well as APEC's (Asia–Pacific Economic Co-operation) implications for Australia, ASEAN and mutual trade.

We present without apology the challenges and impediments that are facing ASEAN, each of its member nations and the people who are seeking to do business with them. Political instability in Thailand and the Philippines, infrastructure shortcomings in Vietnam and Indonesia, the suffocating effect of 'red tape' in most countries and, most importantly, the existence of highly competitive local and foreign firms in most markets, all present pitfalls for newcomers. ASEAN's 'streets' are not 'paved with gold'! they are littered with the ghosts of ill-prepared foreign companies, including Australian ones, that have entered the market, have failed to find a profitable niche and have returned home, poorer for the experience.

For practical purposes, the book can be divided into three parts.

- The first part comprises the 'overview' – chapters l, 2 and 15 – that examine Australia's trade and the development of close ties within the region.
- The second part – chapters 3, 4, 5, 6, 7, 8 and 9 – the 'country' chapters that provide a brief overview of particular aspects of each comprises ASEAN member country's economy.
- The third part – chapters 10, 11, 12, 13 and 14 – comprises the 'functional management' chapters.

Although we hope the book is of help for Australian business, we believe it can also be used as an introductory textbook for universities and colleges that wish to offer a general business course on ASEAN. Most students in Monash University's Graduate Certificate in Asian Business program have found earlier versions of the book to be valuable. We welcome suggestions on how the book might better serve this purpose.

The book was initiated as part of Monash University's Asian Business Research Unit (ABRU) program in business education, and the chapters were developed from and enriched by shorter talks that were at first presented as part of ABRU's long-standing business-seminar series.

We wish to give a major vote of thanks both to the contributors and to Kerrie Bright, the latter of whom served as the main point of contact between the editors, contributors and publisher and whose wordprocessing skills have guaranteed a high-quality manuscript that follows a consistent format. We also sincerely thank Cheryl Yewers, who shared much of the wordprocessing effort during the editorial process, and Katalin Kish, who helped co-ordinate the galley and pageproof stages. The contributors give a joint vote of thanks to David Home and other people at Monash University's Library, for helping during the early stages of the contributors' research, as well as a range of officials within Australia's Department of Foreign Affairs and Trade. We personally thank Henry Carr of the ANZ Bank, Roger Donnelly of EFIC (Export Finance and Insurance Corporation), Patrick Hogdon of the Thai–Australia Chamber of Commerce, and George Viksnins of Georgetown University, for their encouragement and advice.

Ron Edwards and Michael Skully

List of contributors

Alice de Jonge
BA LLB(Hons) Melb, CertPostGradStuds Shanghai, DipAsiaLaw Melb, Barrister and Solicitor (Vic)
Lecturer, Syme Department of Banking and Finance, and Director of Asian Financial Research Unit, Faculty of Business and Economics, Monash University

Anita Doraisami
BEc(Hons) LaTrobe, BSW MCom(Hons) Melb
Lecturer, Syme Department of Banking and Finance, Faculty of Business and Economics, Monash University

Ron Edwards
BCom(Hons), DipEd MA Melb, GradDipComEd Monash
Senior Lecturer, Syme Business School – Frankston and Faculty of Business and Economics, Monash University. Co-author, *Doing Business in Thailand: Essential Background Knowledge and First-hand* Advice Thai–Australia Chamber of Commerce, 1995

Julie Edwards
BA MEd Melb
Lecturer, Faculty of Education, Monash University. Co-author, *Doing Business in Thailand: Essential Background Knowledge and First-hand Advice*, Thai–Australia Chamber of Commerce, 1995

Marilyn Fenwick
BA BBus Chisholm IT
Lecturer, Department of Business Management, Faculty of Business and Economics, Monash University

Andrew McNicol
BCom LLB Melb, GradDipTax LLM Monash, ACA Barrister and Solicitor (Vic) (High Court of Australia), CPA
Lecturer, Syme Business School – Frankston, and Director of Syme Taxation Research Unit, Faculty of Business and Economics, Monash University

Siang Ng
BCom Nan, MEc Syd, PhD Monash
Lecturer, Syme Department of Banking and Finance, Faculty of Business and Economics, Monash University

Mei-Leng Rankin
BEc(Hons) MEc Monash
Lecturer, Syme Department of Banking and Finance, Faculty of Business and Economics, Monash University

Peter Schuwalow
BEd Melb
Assistant Lecturer, Syme Business School – Frankston and Assistant Course Director, International Trade degree, Faculty of Business and Economics, Monash University

Michael Skully
BS BA Arizona, MBA Utah, GradDipEc Stockholm, ASIA ACIS FCAP AAIBF(Snr)
Professor of Banking, Syme Department of Banking and Finance, Faculty of Business and Economics, Monash University. Author, *ASEAN Finance Co-operation: Developments in Banking, Finance and Insurance*, Macmillan, 1985 and *Merchant Banking in ASEAN*, Oxford, 1986; co-author, *Financing East Asia's Success*, Macmillan, 1987

Nishi Verma
MA(Econ) GND MPhil(Econ) Punj
Assistant Lecturer, Syme Department of Banking and Finance, Faculty of Business and Economics, Monash University

David Watson
MEI Swinburne IT, BBus (Mktg) Monash
Senior Lecturer, Syme Department of Marketing, and Course Director – Marketing, Graduate Diploma in International Business, Faculty of Business and Economics, Monash University; Visiting Lecturer in International Marketing, Thammasat University, Bangkok. Formerly, Manager – Telecommunications Industry, Australian Trade Commission

Kevin Wong
BEc(Hons) Malaya, MA (EcoEd) Ohio, MA(InltEc) PhD S Calif
Senior Lecturer, Department of Hotel and Tourism Management, Hong Kong Polytechnic University, Kowloon; formerly Lecturer, Syme Business School – Frankston and Course Director, International Trade degree, Faculty of Business and Economics, Monash University

List of tables

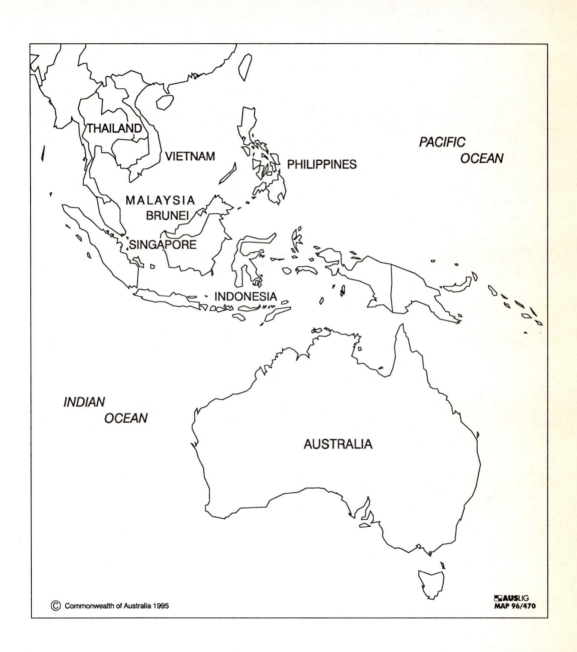

THAILAND

VIETNAM

PHILIPPINES

PACIFIC
OCEAN

MALAYSIA

BRUNEI

SINGAPORE

INDONESIA

INDIAN
OCEAN

AUSTRALIA

© Commonwealth of Australia 1995

AUSLIG
MAP 96/470

1

Regional co-operation: ASEAN, AFTA and APEC

Ron Edwards and Kevin Wong

Introduction

This chapter provides an overview of the South-East Asia region, of the countries that comprise it and of efforts to promote regional co-operation and integration. It discusses the increasing importance of intra-regional trade and the influence of this on regional integration. This provides the context for the detailed country profiles that feature in chapters further on in the book. The following two sections discuss the current and expected future state of preferential trade arrangements and the impact of these in the ASEAN and Asia–Pacific regions.

ASEAN development and structural change

The ASEAN region has a population of about 330 million people – more than six per cent of the world's population. These countries' living standards have improved dramatically; the average life expectancy has risen from 49 years in 1965 to 63 years in 1991. The people of South-East Asia are better fed and housed, better educated and better clothed than ever before. Urbanisation is proceeding quickly, and increasing consumer affluence is evident in an emerging middle class. Within ASEAN, some 15 million people enjoy OECD (Organisation for Economic Co-operation and Development) levels of affluence. Another 80 to 90 million people are approaching and should achieve that level early in the next decade. However, it should not be forgotten that extreme poverty also exists across the region.

Since the early 1980s the ASEAN countries have been restructuring their economies by adopting economic policies that have fostered exports and inward foreign investment. In 1986 the sharp fall in oil and commodity prices compelled countries such as Indonesia, that had been dependent on those products for export revenue, to promote more diversity in their economic structure. In the main, governments have been very successful. Structural change has transformed their economic profiles from being exporters of agricultural commodities and unprocessed goods to being exporters of light manufactures. Economic restructuring has transformed the region from one characterised by war and poverty to one where political co-operation and economic growth are the norm.

This success cannot be ascribed solely to government policy or even domestic economic factors. Structural change in North-East Asia, particularly in Japan, is one of the main reasons for South-East Asia's rapid growth and development. Because of Japan's increasing cost of living and the yen's rising value, labour-intensive manufacturing sectors lost their competitiveness. Many Japanese firms moved offshore to South-East Asia in order to take advantage of its large supply of cheap labour to manufacture goods that had previously been made in Japan. The ASEAN economies of Singapore, Malaysia, Thailand and Indonesia have benefited most from North-East Asian investment because their external policies made investment by foreign companies very attractive. In Malaysia, for example, inflows of foreign direct investment (FDI) have contributed around 20 per cent of gross domestic capital formation and provided access to improved technology and export markets.

Fuelled by foreign investment and focused on exports, structural change has resulted in South-East Asia undergoing an industrial revolution. ASEAN countries are among the world's fastest growing economies. With the exception of the Philippines, all members have increased their real (gross domestic product GDP) per capita by an average annual rate of at least 4 per cent. Production of goods and services for export has underpinned this economic growth.

Table 1.1   Real GDP, GDP growth and GDP per capita: selected countries

Country	Real GDP 1994 (US $billion)	GDP growth (%) 1993	GDP per capita 1994 (US$)
Australia	325.0	4.1	18,190
New Zealand	48.0	3.0	13,685
Brunei	3.8	−4.1	13,191
Indonesia	138.0	6.5	719
Malaysia	59.0	8.5	3,031
Philippines	47.0	2.0	702
Singapore	50.0	9.9	17,078
Thailand	117.0	7.8	1,965
Canada	607.0	3.5	20,756
Japan	3,139.0	0.1	25,124
South Korea	333.0	5.5	7,499
United States	6,050.0	3.1	23,213

Source: Department of Foreign Affairs and Trade, *The APEC Region Trade and Investment*. Canberra: Australian Government Publishing Service, 1995, pp 82–87.

Although ASEAN is an exciting market, especially for Australia, the size of its market should not be exaggerated. As can be noted in Table 1.1, ASEAN's GDP accounts for 2 per cent of global GDP, is slightly more than 10 per cent of Japan's GDP and is only slightly larger than that of the two Closer Economic Relations (CER) countries – Australia and New Zealand.

Direction and composition of ASEAN trade

Most ASEAN exports are directed outside the South-East Asia region. The US, Japan and the European Union (EU) have been the traditional markets. More recently, however, the destination of exports has become more broadly based. Although these countries remain very important, new markets, especially in Asia, are now also important. As can be noted from Table 1.2, exports to Japan have grown at only half the pace of total exports, but exports to Singapore, Taiwan and Hong Kong have grown strongly. On the import side, South Korea has emerged as a major supplier.

Table 1.2   ASEAN 6's regional trade 1989 and 1993

Country or region	ASEAN exports to:			ASEAN imports from:		
	1989 (US$ million)	1994 (US$ million)	Trend growth (%)	1989 (US$ million)	1994 (US$ million)	Trend growth (%)
Brunei	584	1,169	14.6	309	510	3.4
Indonesia	1,672	2,942	10.4	2,618	5,956	22.6
Malaysia	7,027	21,242	24.6	7,899	20,912	19.5
Philippines	1,274	2,794	19.8	584	1,440	23.1
Singapore	8,496	21,250	18.7	6,719	15,161	13.5
Thailand	3,667	8,193	12.5	2,263	6,926	25.3
ASEAN	**22,719**	**57,590**	**19.0**	**20,392**	**50,905**	**18.4**
Australia	2,767	4,741	13.2	3,565	6,674	10.2
Canada	1,118	2,311	16.7	1,319	1,537	−1.3
Chile	84	195	22.2	276	516	14.0
China	2,813	6,554	26.0	3,851	7,226	9.8
Hong Kong	5,293	15,112	23.9	3,299	7,748	18.0
Japan	23,194	36,110	6.9	29,918	68,993	15.7
South Korea	3,735	7,606	11.1	3,815	11,811	22.3
Mexico	157	868	34.8	190	230	0.5
New Zealand	316	745	19.8	570	911	9.0
Papua New Guinea	191	257	10.0	59	186	27.2
Taiwan	3,005	9,044	22.7	6,417	12,402	10.9
United States	25,976	51,850	17.0	19,624	39,334	13.8
APEC	**91,369**	**192,983**	**15.8**	**93,293**	**208,473**	**15.4**
European Union	17,377	37,627	13.5	16,930	40,520	12.8
Other	12,824	25,894	15.9	15,929	29,388	8.9
Total	**121,570**	**256,504**	**15.5**	**126,153**	**278,381**	**14.3**

Note: Totals and subtotals calculated from actual rather than rounded numbers
Source: Department of Foreign Affairs and Trade, *The APEC Region Trade and Investment.* Canberra: Australian Government Publishing Service, 1994, p 26.

The other change in ASEAN's trade pattern is the emergence of the ASEAN market itself. For many years, exports to the rest of the world grew at a rate much faster than that of intra-ASEAN exports, which reflected a low level of economic integration among the ASEAN members despite their geographic proximity. From 1981 to 1989, intra-ASEAN trade only just kept pace with trade with the rest of the world, maintaining a share of slightly under 20 per cent of total trade. Since 1989, the growth rate of intra-ASEAN trade has exceeded that of other exports by a small margin. In 1991, intra-ASEAN exports exceeded ASEAN exports to the US for the first time.

Although intra-ASEAN trade has increased in recent years, we should not over-state this trend. The ASEAN economies' level of integration remains well below potential. Some 75 per cent of intra-ASEAN trade originates in Singapore, the region's entrepot and most open economy, where non-ASEAN economies' goods, especially crude oil and petroleum, are re-exported to countries inside the region. If crude-oil and petroleum products are omitted, intra-ASEAN trade is only 5 per cent of total ASEAN exports.

Because of the existence of high tariff barriers among the ASEAN countries, and the fact that the countries largely export the same type of commodities and thereby compete with each other, growth and development of trade within the region have been limited. Competition, motivated by individual nation-building priorities and the consequent low level of specialisation, has created a region of low industrial complementarity. If economic integration is to progress, steps have to be taken to reverse this situation. Removal of barriers to imports from ASEAN members will foster intra-ASEAN trade. The result will be expansion of regional trade and acceleration of economic growth.

In addition, it is likely that the surge in investment from North-East Asia has and will continue to promote further economic integration. Japanese, South Korean and Taiwanese multinationals are adopting regional plans for inputs and sales in the region. Regional strategies involve subsidiaries specialising in and exchanging various elements of the product range, inputs and staff. Intra-firm trade by multi-nationals across the ASEAN region will therefore promote specialisation and push up intra-ASEAN trade.

The composition of ASEAN exports has also undergone a remarkable change over the past twenty years: there has been a big shift from agricultural commodities to manufactured goods. As shown in Table 1.3, manufactures, particularly elaborately transformed manufactures (ETMs), now dominate ASEAN's merchandise trade. Structural change has transformed a number of ASEAN economies from being exporters of agricultural commodities and unprocessed goods into exporters of light manufactures. Multinational corporations (MNCs) have also played an important role in this transformation. For example, Japanese-owned firms manufacture goods in South-East Asia that had previously been made in Japan and use the region as a manufacturing base for exporting to world markets.

Table 1.3   ASEAN 6 trade, by product type, 1994

Product type	% distribution	
	Exports	Imports
Primary products	24.3	15.5
of which processed food	6.2	3.3
Manufactures:		
Simply transformed (STMs)	4.7	9.5
Elaborately transformed (ETMs)	67.8	71.3
Total manufactures	72.5	80.8
Other	3.2	3.7

Source: Department of Foreign Affairs and Trade, *The APEC Region Trade and Investment.* Canberra: Australian Government Publishing Service, 1995, p 71.

In summary, ASEAN trade trends reflect an increasing level of integration within the group and the group's integration with North-East Asia. Japan has become ASEAN's largest supplier of imports. Manufactures are more important in ASEAN's imports and exports. Increasing standards of living and therefore demand for luxury products, together with the imports needed to serve foreign-owned factories in the ASEAN region, explain this trend. ETMs now dominate exports, whereas agriculture and fuel used to be the key elements.

ASEAN: a brief history

ASEAN was founded in Bangkok on 8 August 1967 with the signing of the ASEAN Declaration, by the foreign-affairs ministers of Indonesia, Malaysia, Singapore, Thailand and the Philippines. Brunei was not an original member but joined the Association in 1984, shortly after becoming independent. The association's purpose was mainly to strengthen the economic and social stability of the South-East Asian region and to guarantee peaceful and progressive national development.

ASEAN's basic principles of economic co-operation were based on proposals contained in a United Nations (UN) report on ASEAN economic co-operation – the Robinson, or Kansu, report. The principles were designed to achieve a balanced expansion of trade, a balanced exchange of products and a balanced allocation of 'package deal' projects.

The UN team suggested three strategies for regional co-operation: selective trade liberalisation, industrial complementarity agreements, and allocation of major industrial projects. No centralised decision-making body was formed. Policy formulation and decision-making authority were left to each ASEAN country's foreign-affairs minister, reflecting the importance members attributed to consensus decision making.

In the early years, ASEAN was slow to make progress in economic matters. The countries were concentrating their efforts on dealing with external threats such as the Vietnam War, resolving domestic tensions and addressing political instability within ASEAN itself. These events distracted the member countries from pursuing economic co-operation and development. Consequently, they rarely met during the first 10 years of ASEAN's existence.

Although geographically close, the ASEAN member countries embody diverse cultural, religious and historical traditions. The original motive for the countries coming together under the ASEAN Declaration was a common external threat: fear of communist aggression, not an economic imperative. ASEAN countries viewed themselves as being economic rivals, competing to export raw materials to the same industrialised markets and competing to attract foreign capital, technology transfer and management know-how. Consequently, individual ASEAN members were suspicious of ASEAN initiatives: they commonly viewed them as being threats to their newly won political sovereignty. They were preoccupied with the notion of nation building and industry development, protected by high tariff walls. This mindset hampered development of regional co-operation and rendered intra-regional trade and investment schemes relatively ineffective.

Another reason for the slow progress of ASEAN economic co-operation was the secretariat's lack of independent authority, limiting its ability to significantly advance regional economic co-operation. Instead, the agenda for economic development has been formulated through the member countries' consensus decision making. Although this approach has fostered unity and stability, the pace of co-operation has been dictated by the most cautious member. For many years this role was filled by Indonesia.

ASEAN Free Trade Area – AFTA

In 1977 a major commitment to joint preferential trade liberalisation was undertaken when the ASEAN foreign-affairs ministers signed an agreement on preferential trading arrangements (PTA). This was a mechanism whereby intra-ASEAN trade could be liberalised at a pace that was acceptable to all the member countries.

Tariff preferences were granted on a product-by-product basis, and each member country was to offer a set number of tariff preferences each year. Tariff cuts in the order of 10 per cent applied. However, only a limited number of commodities were approved for preferential tariff reductions.

The PTA enjoyed very limited success. Its effect on ASEAN trade was only marginal: it covered an estimated 2 per cent of intra-ASEAN trade in 1980, 5 per cent in 1986. This was due to a number of factors, as follows:

• The product-by-product approach to tariff reduction was not effective because it was too time consuming and invited the practice of 'padding' of items to be included in the list. Concessions granted were not genuine (countries could grant preferences on goods that were not traded in the region) or were of marginal significance.

• The number of products included under the PTA was relatively small in comparison with the total number of items the ASEAN countries traded.

• The member countries maintained long exclusion lists.

In 1991, the idea of having an ASEAN free-trade area (AFTA) was proposed by Thai Prime Minister Anand Panyarachun and was supported by Singaporean Prime

Minister Goh Chok Tong. Then, in January 1992, a milestone in ASEAN economic co-operation was accomplished in Singapore at the fourth ASEAN Summit Meeting, when the ASEAN heads of government signed a historic declaration for achieving a free trade area within 15 years.

AFTA's original goal was to reduce tariffs on intra-ASEAN trade in manufactured and processed agricultural goods to between zero and 5 per cent within 15 years. This was to be achieved by means of the Common Effective Preferential Tariff (CEPT) scheme comprising two programs of tariff reduction: the Fast Track and the Normal Track, with goods being assigned to one track or the other.

The Fast Track program was two tiered and involved the following:

1. Tariffs above 20 per cent to be reduced to between zero and 5 per cent within 10 years.
2. Tariffs at 20 per cent and less to be reduced to between zero and 5 per cent within seven years.

The Normal Track program was also two tiered and involved the following:

1. Tariffs above 20 per cent to be reduced in two stages: to 20 per cent within five to eight years, and subsequently to between zero and 5 per cent, according to an agreed schedule.
2. Tariffs of 20 per cent and less to be reduced to between zero and 5 per cent within 10 years.

Fifteen product groups have been designated for accelerated (or fast track) tariff reductions under the CEPT: vegetable oils, cement, chemicals, pharmaceuticals, fertiliser, plastics, rubber products, leather products, pulp, textiles, ceramic and glass products, gems and jewellery, copper cathodes, electronics, and wooden and rattan furniture.

Since its original inception a number of changes have broadened and added impetus to the scheme:

• In October 1993, the ASEAN Economic Ministers meeting (AEM) announced that 11,000 specific tariff items (around 20 per cent of total tariff lines) would be brought forward and put in place by January 1994.
• The September 1994 AEM agreed to accelerate the tariff reduction schedules from 15 to 10 years, so that 0–5 per cent was reached by 1 January 2003, rather than 2008, with fast-track items at reduced rates by 2000. Further, it agreed to include all unprocessed agricultural goods in AFTA by 2003 and to develop framework agreements on services trade and intellectual property.
• In 1995, ASEAN members declared their intention of moving to zero tariffs for as many products as possible by the year 2000 (while not taking the formal step of declaring it a new target) and established a disputes settlement mechanism. In additions, Mechanisms to strengthen ASEAN's appeal as an investment site, including simplification of investment procedures, were agreed.

Vietnam joined ASEAN in July 1995 and AFTA in January 1996, with a 10-year implementation period ending in 2006.

Free-trade areas promote trade and efficiency insofar as they entail a shift from higher cost (domestic) sources to lower cost (foreign) sources. Inefficient domestic production is replaced by imports, thereby enabling local consumers to acquire goods and services at lower prices. However, these regional trade arrangements also cause trade diversion from lower cost (non-member) sources to higher cost (member) sources, thereby resulting in inefficiency and higher prices for consumers. Free trade areas also result in importing countries losing the tariff revenue that had formerly been levied on imports from member countries.

According to economic theory regional trade arrangements are likely to improve a country's welfare by creating more trade than they divert, where

- tariffs are very high before the preferential reductions take place
- the cost disadvantage of other members of the free-trade area relative to the most efficient suppliers elsewhere is small
- the regional market created by the free-trade area is large

Like other regional trade arrangements, AFTA is expected to create a larger regional market in South-East Asia whereby increased trade flows and intra-regional investment will result. Within the enlarged, protected regional market it is expected that the expansion of output in various industries might be accompanied with economies of scale – lower costs per unit of production, translating into lower prices.

AFTA's advocates believe its successful implementation will enhance economic integration and industrial complementarity in the ASEAN region. However, AFTA remains at its early stages, and many sceptics believe it will achieve little in the long run. This scepticism is based on the fact that AFTA does not address many of the barriers that impede economic integration. Across Asia, as well as high tariff barriers, substantial non-tariff barriers are prevalent. Plans to eliminate non-tariff barriers and quantitative restrictions are still at an early stage of development. These restrictions can impede intra-regional trade and investment more significantly than tariffs. The hidden nature of many non-tariff barriers makes their identification, and the negotiation required in order to remove them, extremely challenging. Progress in these areas is essential for achievement of economic integration. (Non-tariff restrictions include import licensing, exchange controls, import quotas, health and safety regulations, and domestic support policies such as tax concessions and purchasing policies.)

Other problem areas that require attention before ASEAN can fully achieve significantly enhanced economic integration include removal of factors that obstruct intra-regional investment flows, liberalisation of capital markets, allowance of free trade in services, and harmonisation of product standards. Creation and advancement of broader integration and industrial complementarity requires a policy package that is more comprehensive than has been agreed in AFTA.

In addition to increased regional trade, AFTA will also have a positive impact on flows of foreign investment. MNCs will be attracted by the larger protected market. These firms' arrival will enlarge the regional market even more and bring greater opportunities for specialisation and economies of scale. However, attraction of foreign investment to AFTA will depend on the speed with which other reforms are undertaken in the region. These include liberalisation of local equity requirements, of laws relating to employing key expatriate workers, of restrictions on capital raising in the domestic markets, and of rules about repatriation of profits. The ASEAN members will have to be competitive in order to maintain their share of MNC investment, given the likely competition from China, India and Indochina.

In conclusion, AFTA will be a positive force for investment and trade creation but will in itself be insufficient to guarantee continued progress. Much more is needed. The AFTA members have to continue to improve their economic infrastructure, improve efficiency in their government services, and accelerate removal of government 'red tape'. Finally, the ASEAN countries should bear in mind that the nature of international trade and production is dynamic. They should therefore always be conscious of the changing matrix of investment competitiveness, production capabilities and industrial restructuring that are required for remaining at the forefront of global competition.

Growth triangles

In East Asia, the existence of formal and informal arrangements in the form of growth triangles represents yet another effort at regional co-operation whereby the Asian nations have been brought closer together, both economically and politically. The growth triangles have met with varying amounts of economic success. The most notable triangle is the Singapore–Johore–Riau Islands one, which in 1989 received formal recognition. Another, less formalised, 'triangular' trade-and-investment relationship, which has also proved to be very successful, exists between Hong Kong, Taipei and the Guangdong and Fujian provinces of Southern China. Other growth triangles that have been proposed within the Asia–Pacific Rim region include one that spans the northern states of West Malaysia, southern Thailand and Indonesia's northern Sumatra, and another spanning Brunei and parts of Indonesia, Malaysia and the Philippines.

The basic economic rationale for the growth-triangle concept is the pooling together of the vast resources and capabilities of various Asian countries that are located in close geographic proximity in order to exploit complementary economic strengths. In most cases, the economic interdependence and linkages formed between the countries have resulted in reduction of production costs, better access to capital for commercial investments and superior physical infrastructure. Through these advantages, increased production and investment are promoted and a competitive edge in export markets is provided.

The success of the Singapore–Johore–Riau arrangement has been based on the mutual gains that arise through shifting labour-intensive industries from Singapore to Johore and Riau in order to take advantage of the semi-skilled labour in Johore and the low cost of land and labour in Riau. In addition, the Riau Islands were able to benefit from the spillover effects of Singapore's rapid growth during the late 1980s and through redistribution of investments away from the overpopulated island of Java. As for Johore, its midway position between Singapore and Riau and its cheap and plentiful labour pool inspired Singapore-based companies to relocate their business operations. Even greater growth opportunities exist, though, due to exchange of technical expertise, upgrading of skilled labour, expansion of financial services and the strengthening of industrial linkages between the growth-triangle members.

The Singapore–Johore–Riau triangle has to overcome a number of problems before its full potential can be reached. More labour mobility within the triangle is required, and some land ownership issues are yet to be addressed. Also, problems exist in guaranteeing equitable distribution of gains among the participating countries.

The informal growth triangle that comprises Hong Kong, Taipei and Southern China has experienced similar gains. For Southern China, the main economic benefit has been the building of a strong, export-oriented economy based on moving goods and services through Hong Kong and Taipei, whereas for Hong Kong and Taipei it has been increased investment and production because of their access to Southern China's much cheaper labour. A study that was cited by the Asian Development Bank estimated that the average cost of standard-factory construction in Hong Kong was more than five times that in Zhuhai, a special economic zone that is located in Guangdong, Southern China. A distinguishing aspect in this growth triangle's success is the strong similarity between the countries' linguistic and cultural backgrounds. This has been of mutual benefit to the members.

Although the Hong Kong–Taipei–Southern China growth triangle has been a very successful one, some difficulties remain. These include Southern China's poor-quality economic infrastructure, despite rapid construction, and legal issues relating to direct trade and investment between Taipei and Southern China.

Asia–Pacific Economic Co-operation – APEC

The concept of APEC was first articulated by former Australian prime minister Bob Hawke in January 1989 and was launched in Canberra in November of that year with the holding of the first APEC ministerial meeting. The formation of APEC marked a new and significant stage in the evolution of Asia–Pacific economic co-operation and reflected the need for Australia to participate in the dynamism of the Asia–Pacific region.

At the time of writing APEC has 18 members, comprising the ASEAN countries; the CER countries; Papua New Guinea; Hong Kong, Taiwan and China; Japan and South Korea; the United States, Canada and Mexico (the NAFTA – North American Free Trade Agreement – countries) and Chile. Ten other countries – Argentina, Russia, India, Vietnam, Peru, Ecuador, Colombia, Mongolia, Laos and Panama – have indicated a desire to join.

The APEC group has 40 per cent of the world's population and a GDP of US$13 trillion. It accounts for 50 per cent of world GDP. In terms of their contribution to world trade, in 1993, the 18 members accounted for 46 per cent of all world exports – up from 38 per cent in 1983.

About 72 per cent of APEC-member exports went to other APEC countries in 1994 – up from 68 per cent in 1990, which reflects increased intra-regional trade flows among the smaller member countries. The greater trade volume may be attributed to a more liberal trade regime and to investment policies in ASEAN countries. Among the APEC members, Canada is the most reliant on Asia–Pacific trade: in 1994, 91 per cent of its exports were bound for member countries. Japan and Australia also significantly rely on exports to member countries: 74 per cent of Japanese and 76 per cent of Australian exports go to them.

The APEC agenda

Former Australian prime minister Paul Keating described APEC as presenting 'an extraordinary new path for the Asia–Pacific region towards extraordinary new goals'.

In the relatively short period since its foundation in 1989, APEC has evolved from being a mere concept to becoming an institution that has a secretariat and a work program aimed at liberalising trade and investment across the Asia–Pacific region.

On 15 November 1994, APEC's economic leaders came together in Bogor, Indonesia, and made the following Declaration of Common Resolve.

> [To] chart the future course of our economic co-operation which will enhance the prospects of an accelerated, balanced and equitable economic growth not only in the Asia–Pacific region but throughout the world as well ...

The economic leaders articulated a vision for the community that was based on recognition of the increasing interdependence of their diverse region. An ambitious growth strategy was expected to bring about sustainable growth, equitable development and national stability, thereby narrowing the gap in the Asia–Pacific economies' stages of development. The key element in this vision was that the developed APEC countries achieve open markets by 2010 and developing ones by 2020.

The Economic Leaders meeting opposed the creation of an inward-looking trading bloc whereby free trade in the world would be hampered. Instead, APEC was to build on the momentum generated through the agreements of the Uruguay Round of Multilateral Trade Negotiations by accelerating their implementation while refraining from increasing levels of existing protection. A commitment was made to pursue free and open trade and investment in the Asia–Pacific region in such a way as to encourage and strengthen trade and investment liberalisation among APEC countries and also between APEC nations and non-APEC nations. This is likely to be achieved by maintaining member commitments to the General Agreement on Tariffs and Trade's (GATT) 'most favoured nation' principle. Under this arrangement, all provisions liberalising trade and investment will be available to APEC members and non-members alike. This concept of 'open regionalism' distinguishes APEC from traditional, discriminatory trade blocs which restrict improvements in market access to fellow member countries.

The Bogor Declaration provided APEC with an ambitious agenda, but left largely unresolved the question of how to implement it. This task was left to the Osaka Meeting in 1995 which produced the Osaka Action Agenda, a framework for trade and investment liberalisation. The Agenda adopted a new approach, sometimes described as 'concerted liberalisation'. Under this process, APEC members agreed to prepare Individual Action Plans which set out the way in which their economies would meet the Bogor goal. Individual plans will be assessed by the APEC Ministerial Meetings but will not form legally binding commitments as used in the Uruguay Round of GATT.

An important outcome of the Osaka Meeting was that trade and investment liberalisation was to be comprehensive in its sectoral coverage. While APEC governments are left free to set their own priorities for the sequence of reforms needed to achieve free and open trade, no provision was made to exempt 'sensitive sectors' from the agreed target dates. Nevertheless, it is likely that members will postpone liberalisation of their most vulnerable sectors until near the end of the liberalisation period. Importantly, governments agreed to dismantle all impediments to international transactions, not only obstacles imposed at borders, but also those which arise from differences in domestic policies, regulatory systems and product standards.

The members agreed to make continuous contributions to liberalisation from the outset. In light of this commitment, members agreed to accelerate liberalisation by making a 'downpayment' of early reforms. Members varied in the nature and quality of their 'downpayments'. For example, among other things:

- Australia committed to bring forward, by one year, the date on which its final Uruguay Round tariff reductions.
- The Philippines introduced measures which will reduce tariffs on non-agricultural goods.
- Canada will exceed its Uruguay Round commitments by reducing tariffs on 1500 items and extend NAFTA preferential treatment of investment to all World Trade Organisation (WTO) members.
- Singapore is bringing forward and extending WTO tariff reductions and accelerating commitments on intellectual property, investment and subsidies.

'Comparable' liberalisation is expected of all members. The principle of 'comparability' reflects the intention of APEC member governments to use the evidence of liberalisation by other Asia–Pacific economies to counter domestic claims for continued protection. Such requests will be easier to deny if governments can show that other APEC members are taking comparable action and that new markets are therefore being opened. However, there is a risk that APEC may become bogged down in debates over whether individual countries have in fact offered 'comparable' liberalisation.

Chairman of the APEC Eminent Persons Group, Fred Bergsten, believes that if APEC were to act more aggressively, by not only lowering some of the tariff barriers that impede trade but by making its trade and investment rules more liberal than those required by GATT it could: 'serve as a catalyst for a whole new phase of global trade liberalisation from which the APEC countries themselves would be among the biggest gainers'. The outcome would be a regional economy where not just goods and services but capital, information and expertise would flow freely.

However, many obstacles remain in the way of achieving APEC's objectives. APEC governments remain divided about important trade matters such as the US's application of 'section 301' legislation. The US's resorting to this legislation in order to prise open the Japanese market for car parts and to press China about intellectual property rights has created disharmony in its trade relationships. This disharmony has been amplified through the US constantly criticising China's human-rights record and the unpleasant bargaining between those two countries about China's entitlement to 'most favoured nation' treatment.

Doubts also exist about the individual APEC members' level of commitment. Malaysia, for example, has expressed its preference for a smaller, non-Western, regional trade group (the East Asian Economic Caucus) and the US is sceptical about the effectiveness of the unilateral nature of APEC liberalisation.

In broad terms, APEC's attention will have to focus on six key areas, outlined as follows.

1. Achieving a comprehensive reduction in tariffs, including those which apply to 'sensitive' industries.
2. Reduction in the incidence of trade disputes between members. Threats of unilateral action against trading partners have been extremely destabilising in the past and should be eliminated. Moreover, any subregional agreements between member nations have to be made with a view to supporting and reinforcing APEC's multilateral objectives. APEC has an important role to play in monitoring subregional trade arrangements and encouraging them to develop in a direction whereby the global economic liberalisation effort is supported.
3. Highlighting of physical impediments to international trade, for example poor or congested infrastructure such as seaports, airports and telecommunication links.
4. Harmonisation of regional regulations and standards such as those relating to safety or quality: business costs would thereby be significantly reduced and access to markets would be increased.
5. Reduction of non-tariff barriers to trade such as those that apply to agriculture in North-East Asia and the US.
6. Removing the official and unofficial barriers to investment. This is best achieved by removing all discrimination against companies from APEC member countries, effectively treating them as 'national' firms.

One thing is certain: APEC offers Australia a powerful instrument for promoting non-discriminatory trade liberalisation at a time when the US and other developed APEC members continue to protect their agricultural markets and developing countries continue to protect their manufacturing sectors. Removal of these barriers will significantly help Australian exporters as they pursue new opportunities in the world economy's fastest growing region.

ASEAN: brief country profiles

As mentioned previously, the ASEAN countries are diverse in culture, language, religion and history. They are also dissimilar in their level of economic development. In order to avoid the temptation to ignore the differences between the member countries and the resulting complexities of ASEAN policy development, we provide a brief profile of the member countries.

Singapore is the most mature of the seven economies. It is technologically sophisticated and serves as an entrepot to the region; that is, it is a commercial centre for the collection, distribution and trans-shipment of goods for the region's other countries. It is commonly referred to as one of the 'Asian Tigers'.

Malaysia and Thailand are ASEAN's two fastest growing economies. They are experiencing production constraints such as inadequate infrastructure and skills shortages, and they have to overcome these problems if they are to develop into mature, industrialised economies. For example, Thailand is facing a severe water shortage because of inadequate investment in dams. With the exception of Singapore, none of the region's governments can raise enough funds for modernising infrastructure. There is therefore a growing dependence on private money. These infrastructure areas and associated skill areas offer attractive opportunities for Australian businesses.

Brunei is a small, rich, oil-dependent economy. Apart from the oil-and-gas sector, Brunei's industrial structure mainly comprises small-scale enterprises such as sawmills, brick factories, textile factories and coffee plantations. To encourage further development, the government offers investors attractive terms for developing industrial sites. Brunei's dependence on foreign expertise and investment for aiding improvement of its infrastructure represents opportunities for Australian businesses in provision of engineering, education and management services.

Economic growth in the Philippines has lagged behind that of the other member countries. The country has experienced political instability. The many attempts at formulating policies and initiatives for export-led industrialisation have proven fruitless. However, the current government of President Fidel Ramos has overcome some of the worst infrastructure shortfalls (for example 'brown-outs'), and its stable, market-oriented reforms have enabled the economy to accelerate to growth rates that approach those of its ASEAN partners.

Indonesia, which has ASEAN's largest population, is at an early stage of development. Its diverse natural resources and increasing manufacturing base have been the basis of its export drive and have served to decrease the country's reliance on oil and gas exports.

Vietnam, ASEAN's newest member, has many characteristics that are not shared by the other members. Its communist government has orchestrated rapid, market-based reform in recent times, and the economy has responded well. Although its wages are extremely low, a factor that gives it a competitive edge, its infrastructure is a shambles. The recent removal of US trade sanctions is very helpful, but bureaucratic lethargy and corruption are retarding growth.

A more detailed profile of each ASEAN country is supplied further on in the book.

REFERENCES

APEC (Asia–Pacific Economic Co-operation), *Guide to the Investment Regimes of the APEC Member Economies*. Singapore: APEC Committee on Trade and Investment, 1994.

—— *Implementing the APEC Vision*. Singapore: APEC Secretariat, 1995.

—— *Foreign Direct Investment and APEC Economic Integration*. Singapore: APEC Secretariat, 1995.

APEC Economic Leaders' Declaration of Common Resolve, Bogor, 15 November 1994.

APEC Economic Leaders' Declaration for Action, Osaka, 19 November 1995.

Asian Development Bank, *Asian Development Outlook 1993*. Hong Kong: Oxford University Press, 1993.

Asia Link, 'Asia–Pacific Economic Co-operation Members', in the *Australian*, 6 December 1993.

Bureau of Industry Economics, *Potential Gains to Australia from APEC: Open Regionalism and the Bogor Declaration*, Occasional Paper 29. Canberra: Australian Government Publishing Service, 1995.

—— *Investment Abroad by Australian Companies: Issues and Implications*, Report 95/19. Canberra: Australian Government Publishing Service, 1995.

Bora, B and Findlay, C (eds), *Regional Integration and the Asia–Pacific*. Melbourne: Oxford University Press, 1995.

Brewer, T and Green, C (eds), *International Investment Issues in the Asia–Pacific Region*. New York: Oceania Press, 1995.

Chen, E and Drysdale, P (eds), *Corporate Links and Foreign Direct Investment in Asia and the Pacific*. Pymble, NSW: Harper Educational, 1995, pp 29–55.

Department of Foreign Affairs and Trade, *The APEC Region Trade and Investment*. Canberra: Australian Government Publishing Service, 1994.

—— *ASEAN Free Trade Area: Trading Bloc or Building Block?*. Canberra: Australian Government Publishing Service, 1994.

Dobson, W and Lee, T Y, 'APEC – Co-operation Amidst Diversity', in *ASEAN Economic Bulletin*, vol 10, no 3, March 1994, pp 231–44.

East Asia Analytical Unit, *Changing Tack: Australian Investment in South-East Asia*. Canberra: Australian Government Publishing Service, 1994.

Fraser, R (ed), *The World Trade System*. London: Longman Current Affairs, 1991.

Gosper, B, Wickes, R and Feeney, J, 'APEC Progress and Implications for Agricultural Trade', Outlook 96 Conference, Canberra, 1996.

Hughes, H, 'Does APEC Make Sense?', in *ASEAN Economic Bulletin*, vol 8, no 3, November 1991, pp 125–36.

Imada, P, 'Production and Trade Effects of an ASEAN Free Trade Area', in *The Developing Economies*, XXXI–1, March 1993.

Lee, T Y, 'The ASEAN Free Trade Area: The Search for a Common Prosperity', in *Asian–Pacific Economic Literature*, vol 8, no. 1, May 1994, pp 3–7.

Pangestu, M (ed), *Pacific Initiatives for Regional Trade Liberalization and Investment Co-operation: Roles and Implications for the Private Sector.* Singapore: Pacific Economic Co-operation Council, 1992.

Pangestu, M, Soesastro, H and Ahmad, M A, 'New Look at Intra-ASEAN Economic Co-operation', in *ASEAN Economic Bulletin*, vol 8, no 3, March 1992.

Snape, R, Adams, J and Morgan, D, *Regional Trade Agreements: Implications and Options for Australia.* Canberra: Australian Government Publishing Service, 1993.

Tan, K Y, Toh, M H and Low, L, 'ASEAN and Pacific Economic Co-operation', in *ASEAN Economic Bulletin*, vol 8, no. 3, March 1992.

'APEC: The Opening of Asia', in the *Economist*, 12 November 1994.

Wallace, C and Callick, R, 'APEC Trade Means Jobs: PM', in the *Australian Financial Review*, 25 November 1993.

World Bank, 'East Asia's Trade and Investment: Regional and Global Gains from Liberalisation', cited in the *Economist*, 'APEC: The Opening of Asia', 12 November 1994.

Yeoh, C, Lau, G T, Goh, M and Richardson, J, *Strategic Business Opportunities in the Growth Triangle.* Singapore: Longman, 1992.

Yue, C S, 'Foreign Direct Investment in ASEAN Economies', in *Asian Development Review*, vol 11, no 1, pp 61–102.

2

Australia and ASEAN: a growing relationship

Ron Edwards

Introduction

This chapter is an overview of Australia's involvement in the world economy – the progressive removal of barriers to trade that commenced in the 1970s and the subsequent change to the level, composition and direction of Australia's imports and exports. The ASEAN economies' increasing importance for Australia, from a trade, investment and strategic perspective, is highlighted. The chapter therefore provides the context for the detailed 'country profiles' that follow.

Australia in the world economy

By world standards, Australia is a relatively small, affluent country. Its population is small, but its high level of income per capita means its real GDP is larger than that of any other country in the South-East Asian region. Only Indonesia's economy is comparable in size. The North American and North Asian economies are much larger than Australia's, as indicated in Table 2.1.

Although Australia enjoys a standard of living higher than that of most of its Asian neighbours, incomes have been falling in relative terms. At the beginning of the twentieth century, Australia had the world's highest income per capita. By 1920 it was second to the US, and by 1950 it was third to Canada. Since then, it has been overtaken by many countries. According to the World Bank, it has fallen to eighteenth.

Various explanations for the slow but consistent slip in Australia's income ranking can be put forward. Excessive government ownership and regulation of industry, centralised wage determination and the cost of supplying services to a population that is spread over huge distances, have all been suggested. However, it is widely agreed that two factors have been central: Australia's relatively high level of protectionism, and its distance from the world's largest markets.

Table 2.1   Real GDP and GDP per capita: selected countries, 1994

Country	Real GDP (US$ billion)	GDP per capita (US$)
Australia	325	18,190
Indonesia	138	719
Malaysia	59	3,031
Philippines	47	702
Singapore	50	17,078
Thailand	117	1,965
Canada	607	20,756
Japan	3,139	25,124
South Korea	333	7,499
United States	6,050	23,213

Source: Department of Foreign Affairs and Trade, *The APEC Region Trade and Investment.* Canberra: Australian Government Publishing Service, 1995, pp 82–7.

1.   Protectionism

At the beginning of the twentieth century, Australia's economy was one of the world's most open economies. At 6 per cent, our average tariff rate on manufacturing was markedly lower than that of Europe (20 per cent), Japan (10 per cent) and the US (73 per cent). However, over the next seven decades, Australia's protection increased whereas the rest of the world followed the opposite strategy. By 1970, only New Zealand was more protective of its industry. At 23 per cent, Australia's average protection rate was three times the European Union's (EU), double Japan's and two and a half times the US's.

Tariffs and other barriers to imports retard exports as well as imports because they focus business attention on the domestic market. Tariffs do this by making the domestic price of goods higher than prices in world markets, thereby providing domestic producers with a disincentive to incur the risk and expense of cultivating export markets. Tariffs raise the domestic price level and make production costs more expensive than those in other countries. They coddle domestic producers by keeping them safe from the rigours of competing with the world's best and enable them to maintain high costs and inefficiency.

From the early 1970s onwards, it was recognised that this inward-looking strategy was contributing to the country's relative decline. In 1973, the Whitlam Labor Government cut tariffs by 25 per cent. Although the motor-vehicle, clothing, textile and footwear industries were given respite, a sustained reduction in protection has occurred across all manufacturing sectors. With the reductions scheduled for the rest of the 1990s, the rate will be brought down to the average of other industrial countries. Lowering of protection has contributed to the 50 per cent increase in the ratio of imports and exports to GDP that has taken place since the early 1970s, which was when the reforms commenced. Freed of trade barriers, Australian firms have found both importing and exporting to be more worthwhile than was previously the case.

2.   Geographic isolation

Australia's distance from the world's leading commercial centres – Europe and the US – has also been viewed as being a factor explaining why economic growth has been retarded. South-East Asia has, in the past, been viewed as being a security threat more than a potential market. When most of the South-East Asian countries cut their colonial ties during the period that followed World War II, Australia, still considering itself to be a European outpost in the South Pacific, felt isolated and unable to deal comfortably with its newly independent, and often nationalistic, Asian neighbours. Fear of aggression, especially from Indonesia, and concern about possible erosion of the predominantly European society, which was protected through the White Australia Policy, meant South-East Asia was mainly viewed as being a military and social threat rather than a potential trading partner.

During the 1970s and 1980s, progressive refocusing of cultural ties away from Europe and towards the US as well as the boom in economic ties with North Asia, particularly Japan, coincided with increasing maturity and independence in Australia's political affiliations. All but the most conservative person now accepts that Australia is located in the Asian region. The factor that has served to sharpen Australian interest in the region has been the region's rapid economic growth. This, together with reduction in protection in most ASEAN economies, has meant that new markets for Australian businesses have been quickly developed. Australia is now within close proximity of some of the world's most dynamic economies, and a wealth of opportunities for Australian businesses are thereby presented. This has already translated into change in the composition and direction of Australia's trade.

Composition of Australia's trade

The composition of any country's imports and exports depends on its comparative advantages and its people's consumption preferences. If the country can produce goods relatively cheaply or if goods are not strongly demanded at home, it will have a source of exports. For Australia, the key to comparative advantage is our relative abundance of natural resources. We are richly endowed with agricultural land, mineral and energy resources and capital per worker. Furthermore, our labour force, although small in size, is relatively highly skilled. Therefore, Australia might be expected to be a net exporter of raw materials, food, fibre and processed primary products and a net importer of manufactures and services, especially those which call for intensive use of unskilled labour.

Australia's trade has conformed with this pattern. Agricultural and mining products have dominated exports. Manufactures have dominated imports, as indicated in Table 2.2.

Table 2.2   Australia's merchandise trade by major category and by direction

Category	World 1990–91	World 1994–95	APEC 1990–91	APEC 1994–95	ASEAN6 1990–91	ASEAN6 1994–95
EXPORTS % of total						
Unprocessed food	7	7	6	4	7	5
Processed food	12	13	11	11	7	9
Other rural	9	9	8	7	6	6
Minerals	16	12	9	7	2	–
Fuels	20	17	20	16	17	7
Total primary products	**64**	**57**	**53**	**45**	**39**	**27**
Simply transformed manufactures	10	10	11	11	14	13
Elaborately transformed manufactures	17	23	17	23	22	29
Total manufactures	**27**	**33**	**28**	**34**	**36**	**42**
Other exports	9	10	19	21	25	31
Total merchandise exports	**100**	**100**	**100**	**100**	**100**	**100**
IMPORTS % of total						
Unprocessed food	1	1	1	1	5	3
Processed food	4	4	3	3	9	7
Other rural	2	2	2	2	4	4
Minerals	1	–	–	–	–	–
Fuels	6	5	6	5	31	13
Total primary products	**14**	**12**	**12**	**11**	**49**	**27**
Simply transformed manufactures	12	11	8	8	7	9
Elaborately transformed manufactures	72	76	75	78	41	59
Total manufactures	**84**	**87**	**83**	**86**	**48**	**68**
Other exports	2	1	5	3	3	5
Total merchandise imports	**100**	**100**	**100**	**100**	**100**	**100**

Note: totals and subtotals calculated from actual numbers rather than rounded percentages
Source: Department of Foreign Affairs and Trade, The APEC Region Trade and Investment, 1995 Canberra: Australian Government Publishing Service pp 38–40.

The extent of Australia's comparative advantage in agricultural and mining products can be shown by comparing their importance in Australia's exports with their share in world trade. In 1991, for example, world trade comprised 10 per cent rural products; 12 per cent fuels, minerals and metals; 57 per cent other merchandise, and 21 per cent services. By comparing these figures with the data in Table 2.2, it can be noted that rural and mining exports were much more important for Australia than they were for the rest of the world.

Table 2.3 shows that although agriculture and mining remain very important, during the past two decades a discernible change to Australia's export focus has occurred. Since 1983–84, the share of primary exports fell 19 per cent and the share of manufactured exports rose 13 per cent.

Table 2.3 Australia's exports, by type, 1983–84 to 1994–95

Type	1983–84	1986–87	1989–90	1992–93	1994–95
Primary	76.4	71.2	65.3	61.5	57.2
Manufacturing	20.7	22.3	25.5	29.3	33.4
Others	2.9	6.5	9.2	9.2	9.4

Source: Australian Chamber of Commerce and Industry, *Australia and APEC: The Trade Relationship*. Canberra: Australian Chamber of Commerce and Industry, 1995, p 7; and Department of Foreign Affairs and Trade, *The APEC Region Trade and Investment*. Canberra: Australian Government Publishing Service, 1995, p 38.

The declining reliance on primary commodities makes Australia less vulnerable to rapid shifts in the terms of trade that are caused by the frequent changes in prices of primary products.

The trend towards added-value exports is even more extensive than is shown in the growth of manufacturing exports. This can be noted through an analysis of the components of primary and manufactured exports. Since 1983–84, unprocessed primary exports have fallen from 51 per cent to 40 per cent of total exports, whereas processed primary exports have retained a constant share. Similarly, the growth in manufactured exports has mainly come from ETMs, which have risen from 12 per cent to 23 per cent of total exports. In summary, the relative decline in primary-commodity exports has largely been due to a fall in exports of unprocessed commodities and the growth in share of manufactured exports has come mainly from ETMs.

However, this pattern is not consistently displayed in Australia's trade with all countries. For example, trends in the composition of exports to Asia over the decade to 1994 showed marked disparities.

- The share of services in exports to China fell from 20 to 10 per cent while merchandise exports grew by an average of 24 per cent per year. Exports of unprocessed food to China practically disappeared while exports of processed food, minerals and ETMs grew very strongly.
- Processed food exports to Indonesia grew by 30 per cent per year and manufactures by 14 per cent, but unprocessed food exports were stagnant and mineral sales dwindled.
- Exports to Japan are dominated by primary exports. Even so, their share has fallen from 82 per cent of merchandise exports in 1980 to 72 per cent in 1990 and 69 per cent in 1994. Exports of manufactures, especially ETMs, have become more prominent;
- Primary products are also very important in merchandise exports to South Korea, contributing 45 per cent of the total, but exports of STMs and ETMs have grown more quickly, as have exports of non-monetary gold.

- Merchandise exports to Malaysia have grown at a trend rate of 14.7 per cent over the last decade, driven mainly by exports of ETMs. Malaysia is an important services market, retaining a steady 27 per cent share of the rapidly growing total export figure.
- Services doubled their share of exports to Taiwan, and exports of unprocessed food items outpaced the growth of other primary goods, while mineral sales fell.

In summary, although great variation has occurred in trends in Australia's exports to various countries over the past 25 years, there has been noticeable growth in exports relative to production for domestic use, growth in the share of ETMs and services and decline in the share of unprocessed primary goods. Australia has therefore reversed its inward perspective and is playing a bigger role in the international economy. Although farm and quarry products remain important, exports of sophisticated, high-value manufactured products and services are taking the front position as export growth gathers pace.

Direction of Australia's trade

Australia commenced the twentieth century with its international trade focus continuing to reflect its colonial history. It mainly exported food and industrial raw materials to Britain and imported manufactured goods. Britain's gradual decline as an economic power led Australia to look to the US and later to Japan for export markets. Our exports, therefore, have been progressively redirected from Europe to the countries that make up the APEC region, as indicated in Table 2.4.

Table 2.4   Australia's merchandise exports by regional groups, % of total

Selected regions	% of total 1990–91	1994–95	Trend growth 1990–91 to 1994–95
Africa	1.2	1.4	9.5
Americas	13.6	9.9	−0.7
North Asia	43.0	45.2	8.0
South-East Asia	12.2	15.6	12.6
South Asia	1.8	2.1	10.3
Middle East (excluding Egypt)	2.7	2.0	0.6
Europe	16.5	12.7	−0.1
Oceania	7.5	9.9	14.1
Others	1.5	1.2	–
Total	**100.0**	**100.0**	6.8

Source: Department of Foreign Affairs and Trade (1995), *Composition of Trade Australia*, Australian Government Publishing Service, Canberra, p 57

APEC member countries' emerging dominance as export markets is largely a result of growth in share of exports to North-East Asia and ASEAN, as indicated in Table 2.4. The share of exports going to NAFTA members has fallen, and this has mainly been brought about through a decline in Australia's share of the US market.

South Korea has recently surpassed the US to become Australia's second-largest export market, after Japan.

In summary, over the past 35 years a marked shift has occurred in the direction of Australia's trade: away from the UK and the US and towards Japan, South Korea, Taiwan and the ASEAN countries. Australia is therefore integrated with the Asia–Pacific region much more than ever before. Although we remain Western in our main social institutions, we have become Asian in our economic focus.

Australia's trade relationship with ASEAN

The government and other commentators frequently claim we have had great success in penetrating the ASEAN market. How successful have Australian exporters truly been? In this section we will more closely examine Australia's trade with ASEAN and will judge how much credit is due. Has the increase in exports to ASEAN been the result of increased competitiveness?

Australia's trade with ASEAN grew particularly strongly over the five years to 1995. This comprises export growth of 12.6 per cent and import growth of 15.9 per cent. Exports to ASEAN now account for 15.4 per cent of total exports: a significant jump on the 9 per cent share of 1988. The Malaysian and Thai markets grew particularly quickly – 17 per cent and 23 per cent, respectively – over this time period. Imports from ASEAN have also been increasing more quickly than those from elsewhere. The trend rate of growth per year over the five years to 1995 was 15.9 per cent, which was significantly ahead of the rise in overall imports of 11.4 per cent, thereby taking imports from ASEAN from 6 per cent to 8.6 per cent of total imports.

ASEAN is a more significant trading partner for Australia than Australia is for ASEAN. In 1994, ASEAN was seven times as important a destination for Australian exports as Australia was for ASEAN exports. In fact, Australia is a small and declining export market for ASEAN exporters. Given this situation, it is important to note the demands of ASEAN business and political leaders that commerce should be free and open in all directions. If non-tariff barriers such as labelling and product specification are artificially restricting ASEAN imports, the Australian government should address the barriers in consultation with ASEAN business groups in order to maximise the benefits of trade. Integration means more than simply exporting. Furthermore, an unbalanced trade relationship can be a disadvantage when trade disputes occur. Australia has a trade surplus of $4.1 billion with ASEAN.

The growth in Australia's exports of ETMs to ASEAN has been particularly rapid. Over the five years to 1994–95, Australia's exports of these to ASEAN increased at a trend rate of 21.5 per cent and they now make up 29 per cent of all exports to ASEAN. Australia now exports more ETMs to South-East Asia than it does to the much larger market of North-East Asia. In fact, the value of Australia's ETM exports to South-East Asia is nearly double those to the far larger market of the US and three times those to Japan. This illustrates the different comparative advantages Australia has with South-East Asia and North-East Asia. Australia is able to provide manufactures to the natural-resource-rich South-East Asian countries and to provide natural-resource-intensive goods to the North-East Asian countries that have a scarcity of these resources. Despite the high tariff structures for manufactured goods, Australia's export of ETMs to the region are on the increase.

Imports of ETMs from ASEAN have also strongly increased. Imports of manufactures now make up 59 per cent of total imports from the region, up significantly from 48.5 per cent in 1988–89.

In summary, an increasing share of Australia's exports has been directed towards ASEAN markets: from 4 per cent in the early 1960s, to 8 per cent in the early 1980s, and to 15 per cent in the 1990s. As a result, most ASEAN countries are significant trading partners for us. Indonesia has jumped from being the 14th to the 10th largest export market over the past 10 years, Malaysia from 13th to 11th, the Philippines from 23rd to 18th, Singapore from 9th to 5th and Thailand from 24th to 12th. This suggests Australian exporters' marketing efforts in the ASEAN market have been very successful.

However, although these figures indicate Australian exporters are selling more to ASEAN, they do not reveal their relative performance. It may be that Australia's exports to ASEAN countries have merely matched other countries' exports to them, driven by the customers' economic growth. This is, in fact, largely the case. Although Australia has markedly increased its exports to ASEAN countries, this has not resulted in an increase in market share. Market share has, in fact, fallen in some cases.

- Although Australia's share of the Indonesian market rose from 3.5 per cent in 1980 to 5.4 per cent in 1990, it has since fallen to 4.9 per cent and Japan and the EU have retained the largest shares.
- Australia's share of the Malaysian market declined from 5.4 per cent in 1980 to 2.3 per cent in 1994 and the newly industrialising countries (NICs) experienced a large rise in their market share.
- Australia experienced a slight decline in its share of the Philippines market, falling from 2.9 per cent in 1980 to 2.8 per cent in 1994. During this period, the NICs trebled their market share.
- The rapidly growing Thai market absorbed the same share of Australian products, 2 per cent of total imports, whereas the US's share declined and the NICs' share increased markedly.
- Australia's share of the Singapore market fell slightly, from 2 per cent in 1990 to 1.5 per cent of total imports in 1994.

Taking ASEAN as a whole, Australian exporters lost market share during the period 1990–94. ASEAN's total imports increased at a trend growth of 14.3 per cent. Imports from Australia, however, increased at 10.2 per cent. Table 2.5 indicates that the major winners in the race for the ASEAN market have been Singapore and Thailand, North-East Asia and the EU. The table also highlights the dominance of the US, the EU and Japan in the ASEAN market.

Table 2.5 ASEAN imports from selected countries and regions, 1994

Country or region	US$ million	Growth rate 1990–94 (%)
Brunei	510	0.0
Indonesia	5,956	22.6
Malaysia	20,912	19.5
Philippines	1,440	23.1
Singapore	15,161	13.5
Thailand	6,926	25.3
Total ASEAN	**50,905**	**18.4**
Australia	6,674	10.2
Canada	1,537	−1.3
China	7,226	9.8
Hong Kong	7,748	18.0
Japan	68,993	15.7
South Korea	11,811	22.3
New Zealand	911	9.0
Taiwan	12,402	10.9
United States	39,334	13.8
European Union	40,520	12.8
All other countries	30,320	8.9
Total imports	**278,381**	**14.3**

Source: Department of Foreign Affairs and Trade, *The APEC Region Trade and Investment.* Canberra: Australian Government Publishing Service, 1995, p 27.

The increased level of exports to ASEAN countries has been largely driven by two factors. First, with the exception of Thailand and the Philippines, in recent years, decisive steps have been taken towards lowering ASEAN's tariff barriers, thereby facilitating expansion in imports from all countries. Second, due to ASEAN's rapid economic growth, demand for both consumer goods and factory inputs has increased. Unfortunately, little evidence exists of growth in Australia's competitiveness, thereby casting doubt on the government-claimed success story. However, we have to keep in mind that the nature of import demand will vary as countries develop. For example, import growth in Thailand and Malaysia has focused on investment items such as machinery and transport goods, items in which Australia may not have a comparative advantage. Therefore, variations in market shares are inevitable and do not necessarily reflect badly on Australian suppliers. Market realities dictate that no country will experience constant and stable growth in all exports to all countries at all times.

Examination of Australia's market performance in each ASEAN country reveals how the countries' varying circumstances and degree of complementarity with the Australian economy cause varying trade patterns. It highlights how unwise it is to generalise too broadly about the ASEAN members.

- Singapore has been an increasingly important destination for Australian exports: in 1994 it ranked as the fifth-largest export market. Our exports to it increased by an average 6.7 per cent per year between 1990 and 1994. Gold and gold coins are a large and rapidly growing component. Petroleum (crude and refined) is the next-largest export, followed by unprocessed dairy products. Singapore is Australia's third-largest market for ETMs. Agricultural exports have decreased in importance. (Data in this and the following section are taken from various editions of the Australian Bureau of Statistics (ABS) publication *Overseas Trade*.)

- For Australian exports to Malaysia, an average increase of 17.1 per cent per year was recorded from 1990 to 1994. Due to lower prices for wheat, aluminium and some minerals, export earnings were reduced from what they would otherwise have been. Australia accounts for one-fifth of Malaysia's foodstuff imports. ETM exports to the country have been on the increase and the growth in STMs has been even more rapid.

- Australia's exports to Thailand doubled in the period 1990–94, increasing at an average annual rate of 23 per cent. The growth has mainly been in ETMs and agricultural goods. Major items include aluminium, raw materials such as cotton and wool for Thailand's textile industries, and dairy products.

- Growth in Australian exports to Indonesia averaged 8 per cent per year in the period 1990–94. The most important item is crude petroleum. Cotton and wheat are also important. Fabricated iron, steel and aluminium are among the fastest growing items. Indonesia is Australia's fastest growing market for ETMs. However, a substantial decrease in agricultural exports has occurred.

- The main items exported by Australia to the Philippines include dairy products (Australia's largest market), iron and steel ingots cereals, and flour preparations. ETM exports have remained relatively constant.

In summary, Australian exports to ASEAN are determined by each member countries' particular circumstances and how these interact with Australia's competitive situation. Because of massive structural change in each country, and rapid growth, the market situation facing Australian exporters has been extremely dynamic. Although Australia has lost some market share, the market's rapid growth has meant exports to ASEAN have increased very quickly. Given the fact that ASEAN's main imports are manufactured goods (80.8 per cent) and that these goods form a minor part of Australia's exports (29.3 per cent), our exports have performed creditably.

Regional headquarters

For Australia, opportunities exist not only in increased trade. Because of ASEAN's growth and integration, we have the opportunity of becoming a regional services centre. Australia can provide a sophisticated business environment for the regional headquarters of large multinational corporations, for specialised-service suppliers and for regional telecommunications hubs. The benefits of becoming a regional services centre are considerable and include increased employment and exports. Because of these links with the region, Australia would be more integrated and involved with regional economies.

To date, Australia's success in attracting regional MNC headquarters has been limited. The major factors that influence location of an MNC's regional headquarters in Australia relate to the competitiveness of the economic environment. This depends, in part, on the quality of infrastructure and the attractiveness of the prevailing tax regimes. Other countries in the region such as Singapore, Taiwan, South Korea, Malaysia and Indonesia are much more aggressive than we are in providing tax holidays, accelerated depreciation, and so on.

Although location of regional headquarters in Australia is rare, we have had some success in attracting key service centres for Asian business. For example, Cathay Pacific, the Hong Kong-based airline, recently moved a significant part of its data-processing operations to Australia. American Express has based its regional customer-services operations in Sydney. Tax exemptions were offered in each case.

In order to attract these investments, Australia has to guarantee that a competitive tax regime is in place. Quality infrastructure, a skilled and competitively priced labour force, economic and political stability and accessibility to clients will not be enough to attract a desirable level of investment if taxation levels are uncompetitive. At the same time, cheap give-aways, and competitive bidding by the various State governments, are not likely to influence the long-term investment decisions of MNCs. Nor are they an efficient way to spend government funds.

Australian investment in ASEAN

Hardly any of Australia's FDI outflow has been directed towards ASEAN; most of it has gone to English-speaking countries. In 1994, 21.8 per cent of Australia's FDI went to the US, 39.2 per cent to the UK and 14.7 per cent to New Zealand. Australian business has not always ignored the ASEAN countries as places for investment: in the early 1980s, 39 per cent of our FDI went to the ASEAN region. However, this situation was not to last. In 1986, ASEAN's share fell to about 2 per cent of FDI. In 1987, the declining trend was reversed, and the ASEAN countries now receive 13.8 per cent of Australia's investment abroad. Nevertheless, the relatively low level of Australian investment in the area implies that few Australian companies are prepared to fully commit themselves to ASEAN by establishing business operations in its markets. Because they maintain an 'outsider' role in ASEAN, participating mainly by exporting, Australian businesses put themselves at a disadvantage against other countries' firms that are prepared to 'take the plunge' by becoming 'locals'.

Many researchers have tried to identify the reasons why Australian firms choose the UK and the US for their foreign operations. The lack of interest in Asia cannot be attributed to poor rates of return on investment capital. Research has, in fact, revealed that returns from direct investments in Asia–Pacific countries are much higher than from those in the US and Europe. Instead, it seems Australian firms are attracted to the markets of the US, the UK and New Zealand because of those countries' familiar language, cultures, histories, social systems and legal systems.

Another reason for Australian FDI's concentration in the geographically distant markets of the UK and the US seems to relate to transportation costs. Asia is closer, and transportation costs associated with exporting to it are less than when exporting to the UK and the US. Australian firms can minimise their transportation costs by exporting to regional markets in Asia but investing and manufacturing locally in the more distant European markets.

A survey conducted by the East Asia Analytical Unit of the Department of Foreign Affairs and Trade found that the prevalence of foreign MNCs in Australia was another factor that helped to explain the lack of Australian investment in Asia. Australian subsidiaries of MNCs reported that their international strategies did not allow for them to invest in Asia. 'Parent-company policy does not permit investment offshore' was therefore a common response to the questionnaire. Other reasons included a preference for concentrating on Australian operations, higher risk, lack of opportunity, difficulty with Asian business culture, difficulty obtaining finance, lack of business contacts offshore, insufficient protection for intellectual property, difficulty repatriating profits, restrictive business environment, and expectation of lower profit.

Many of these reasons seem to be misplaced: they reflect a lack of understanding of Asia and its business opportunities. The same factors have not precluded US investment in Asia. Companies, both indigenous and foreign owned, therefore have to acquire expertise in Asian business practices or to at least recruit staff members who have the expertise, in order to overcome their lack of familiarity with ASEAN business practices. If Australian firms are to maintain their current progress in ASEAN markets, they cannot afford to be pushed to the sidelines by international competitors who are prepared to submerse themselves in the region and become 'locals'.

Conclusion

Over the past thirty years there has been a marked change in Australia's attitude towards and involvement in the international economy. At first protective of our domestic industry and inwardly focused, we have progressively opened our markets to foreign producers and sold more goods and services overseas. We have moved on from our 'farm and quarry' export pattern and now export more manufactured goods and services, thereby aligning our export pattern more closely with the export patterns of other advanced industrial countries. At the same time, our direction of trade has become more complex, is no longer as Eurocentric and is now dominated by Asia, especially for exports.

The ASEAN market has played a significant role in Australia's shift towards value-added exports, especially in recent times. The market remains relatively small, but rapid growth, lower tariffs and industrialisation have meant Australia now sells significant amounts of manufactured goods and services in the regional market. Sales of processed primary goods, both rural and mining, have also expanded.

Because it is predicted that economic growth in ASEAN will continue to lead the world, Australian businesses have a great opportunity to capitalise on their geographic closeness to the region and to profit from the region's growth. To do this, though, Australia will have to integrate more fully with the ASEAN economies. Doing this involves establishing business links and commitments at many levels and in many ways. A narrow focus on exports will not be enough to maximise the opportunities the region offers. Importing, establishing production facilities in ASEAN countries, acting as a regional headquarters and as a service centre for other countries' firms are only four of the possibilities. A multidimensional role is essential if Australia is to grow to become a full member of the regional economy.

REFERENCES

Allen Consulting Group, *The Benefits of Regional Headquarters and Factors Influencing their Location in Australia*. Canberra: Department of Industry, Science and Technology, 1994.

Anderson, K, 'Australia's Changing Trade Pattern and Growth Performance', in Pomfret, R (ed), *Australia's Trade Policies*. Melbourne: Oxford University Press, 1995, pp 29–52.

Australian Bureau of Statistics, Catalogue No. 5305, *Foreign Direct Investment*. Various issues.

Australian Chamber of Commerce and Industry, *Australia and APEC: The Trade Relationship*. Canberra: Australian Chamber of Commerce and Industry, 1995.

Booz, Allen and Hamilton Inc, *Globalization – Implications for Australian Business*. Sydney: Committee for the Development of Australia, 1990.

Centre for the Study of Australia–Asia Studies, *The Asia–Australia Survey 1994*. Melbourne: Macmillan, 1994.

Department of Foreign Affairs and Trade, *Composition of Trade Australia*. Canberra: Australian Government Publishing Service, 1995.

—— *The APEC Region Trade and Investment*. Canberra: Australian Government Publishing Service, 1994.

East Asia Analytical Unit, Department of Foreign Affairs and Trade, *ASEAN Free Trade Area: Trading Bloc or Building Block?*. Canberra: Australian Government Publishing Service, 1994.

—— Affairs and Trade, *Australia's Business Challenge: South-East Asia in the 1990s*. Canberra: Australian Government Publishing Service, 1992.

—— Affairs and Trade, *Changing Tack: Australian Investment in South-East Asia*. Canberra: Australian Government Publishing Service, 1994.

Edwards, R, 'Foreign Direct Investment: Complements or Substitutes?', in *Proceedings of the Academy of International Business, Asian Region Conference*, Hong Kong, 1993.

Edwards, R, Edwards, J and Muthaly, S, *Doing Business in Thailand: Essential Background Knowledge and First-Hand Advice*. Melbourne: Thai–Australia Chamber of Commerce, 1995.

Lee, T Y, 'The ASEAN Free-Trade Area: The Search for a Common Prosperity', *Asian–Pacific Economic Literature*, vol 8, no. 1, May 1994, pp 3–7.

Ramasamy, B, 'Trade Diversion in an ASEAN Free-Trade Area', in the *ASEAN Economic Bulletin*, vol 12, no 1, July 1995, pp 10–17.

World Bank, *World Tables 1992–93*. Baltimore: John Hopkins Press, 1993.

3

Brunei

Nishi Verma

Introduction

Although Brunei is a small country – its population is no larger than that of a provincial city in Australia – its people enjoy a high standard of living and have South-East Asia's highest per-capita income,[1] a wealth that is largely based on the country's petroleum reserves. Exports of oil and natural gas generate a considerable portion of foreign exchange, which the government has invested throughout the world. It is hoped that this portfolio of assets will be enough to support the country once the oil reserves are eventually depleted. Its high per-capita income and abundant capital, combined with its strategic location in ASEAN, relatively close to Australia, mean Brunei, or Negara Brunei Darussalam, as it is officially known, has great potential as a business opportunity for Australian companies. This chapter outlines the nature of this small but attractive market and highlights some of its potential for Australian businesses.

The setting

Located 443 kilometres north of the equator on the north-west coast of the island of Borneo, Brunei Darussalam has a total area of 5765 square kilometres and – due to its major oil and gas reserves – is one of the world's 'richest' countries, for its size. Bounded in the north by the South China Sea, on all other sides it is surrounded by Sarawak, which is part of Malaysia. Brunei Darussalam is divided into four districts: Brunei–Muara, Tutong and Belait in the western section and Temburong in the eastern section. Its capital is Bandar Seri Begawan, and Seria and Kuala Belait are the two other major urban centres. The coastline, covered by mangrove swamps and sandy beaches, extends about 162 kilometres along the South China Sea. The climate is tropical: the mean monthly temperature is about

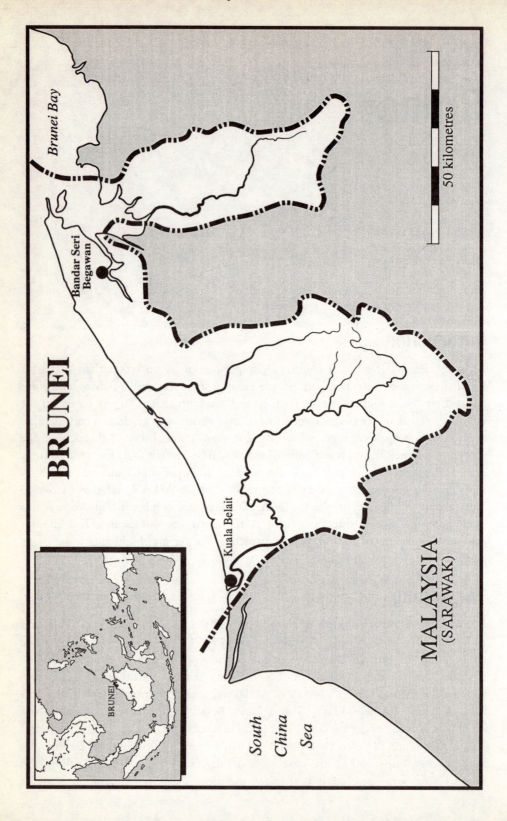

27 degrees Celsius, and the heavy annual rainfall of more than 2500 millimetres is well distributed throughout the year. Except for the coastal areas that have been cleared for permanent cultivation, about 70 per cent of the country remains covered by dense equatorial forest.

According to government estimates, in 1994 Brunei had a population of 292,266. This included 66.9 per cent Malays, 15.6 per cent Chinese, 6 per cent 'other indigenous' and 11.5 per cent as 'others'. 'Other indigenous' includes non-Muslim tribal groups such as Ibans and Penans. The population is relatively young: 53 per cent of people are less than 25 years of age. It is projected that by the year 2001 the total population will increase to 348,200. Although Malay is both the official and the dominant language, English and various forms of Chinese are also spoken.

Political history

Brunei Darussalam is one of South-East Asia's oldest sovereign States: its history stretches back to the sixth and seventh centuries AD. By the tenth century, Brunei Darussalam had emerged as a kingdom of the Buddhist Srivijaya Empire of Sumatra, which was subsequently the Hindu Majapahit Empire of Java. When the Majapahit Empire was destroyed by Muslim invaders in the fifteenth century, the sultans of Borneo became independent rulers in their own right. By the sixteenth century, Brunei Darussalam was the centre of a major empire that covered not only the island of Borneo but parts of mainland Malaysia and the Philippines (it even briefly controlled Manila, the Philippines capital). By the nineteenth century, however, piracy, wars and European nations' spread into East Asia had reduced Brunei's standing. Slowly, the Portuguese, Spanish, Dutch and English acquired parts of Brunei's empire for their own.

Brunei nevertheless maintained nominal control of most of what is now the Malaysian states of Sarawak and Sabah until the mid-1800s. Brunei's first contact with British government itself came on 18 December 1846 when the country was forced to cede Labuan Island to the Royal British Navy. On 17 September 1888, Brunei became a British protectorate, and in 1906 it accepted its first British resident for 'advising' the sultan.

Although this protectorate status was interrupted briefly during the period 1941–45 due to Japanese occupation, British control continued until 1959 when Britain's withdrawal from Malaysia forced the issue. At first, it was suggested that like Singapore, Sarawak and Sabah, Brunei would become part of the Federated States of Malaysia. However, in 1962 when Brunei's first and only elections were held, the people who were opposed to entry won 54 of the 55 seats. When the sultan indicated he continued to prefer to join with Malaysia, a local rebellion resulted. The sultan retained power with the help of British forces but subsequently decided, in 1963, that Brunei would retain its independence. The latter decision also reflected the sultan's concern about Malaysia's interest in sharing the benefits of Brunei's extensive oil and gas reserves.

As mentioned, the Brunei Darussalam Constitution and self-government were introduced in 1959. The Constitution was amended in 1971 and 1984, whereby the UK retained responsibility for Brunei's foreign affairs, security and self-defence. The country regained full independence from Britain on 1 January 1984.

Although it is seemingly a peaceful place to visit, Brunei has been operating under a state of emergency since 1962, under the provisions of the 1959 Constitution. The sultan, His Majesty Paduka Seri Baginda Sultan Haji Hassanal Bolkiah Mu'izzaddin Waddaulah, rules by decree and is advised by an eleven-member Council of Cabinet Ministers. The sultan is also prime minister and minister of defence.

In January 1984, Brunei became ASEAN's sixth member. It is also a member of the British Commonwealth, the Organisation of Islamic States, the APEC Forum, the Non-Aligned Movement and, since 1995, the World Trade Organisation, the International Monetary Fund and the World Bank.

Economic development

Given Brunei's considerable wealth of natural gas and petroleum, one might think there is not much need for the country to be concerned about development issues. Brunei's interest is that the reserves' life is finite: once they are depleted, it will have to survive without their support. Although a large portfolio of income-producing assets will do much to soften the impact, the country will also have to develop its own internal economic resources.

The government has been working towards that end and has implemented six major national development plans, for the periods 1953–58, 1962–66, 1975–79, 1980–84, 1986–90 and 1991–96. Effective development planning commenced with the launching of the Second Plan (1962–66), which was oriented towards providing the country's economic and social infrastructure as the foundation for future development. Due to the shortcomings in its implementation and the deficiencies in the economy's absorptive capacity, the plan slipped with reference to its timing and some of its activities. However, the targeted 5 per cent rate of growth of nominal per-capita income was achieved.

The main objectives of the third and fourth development plans were to maintain a high level of employment and to diversify the economy through accelerated development of agriculture, forestry, fisheries and industry (manufacturing). These plans delineated proposals for promoting the private sector's participation in accelerating development of agriculture and non-oil-based-manufacturing industries. However, the resulting diversification was far from satisfactory. During the Third Plan, the minimum targeted real-GDP growth rate of 6 per cent per year was achieved due to increased oil prices and production. In contrast, due to falling oil prices and production, the Fourth Development Plan was marked by a decline in GDP of 4.4 per cent per year and a decline in real per-capita income of 8.35 per cent per year.

The Fifth Development Plan (1986–90) was intended to strengthen Brunei's economic alternatives and wean the economy from its heavy dependence on oil and gas. The plan declared the following.

Brunei Darussalam has always been dependent on oil and gas. However, the recent situation in the oil market which has been unfavourable is expected to continue. The worsening situation of the oil market clearly signals for immediate action in the diversification programs. The area earmarked for rapid development is in the field of industry. Such development will necessitate further improvement in infrastructure and an acceleration in human resource development. Hence, the 5th Plan must therefore be seen as a watershed in the economic development of the country and the thrust of the development efforts during the 5th Plan will be a revitalising and enhancing of growth in the productive sectors.

In the plan, development of an export-oriented industry and import-substitution industries, full employment and an increased level of productivity, and emergence of Malays as leaders in industry and commerce, were envisaged. Its Br$3.73 billion budget was allocated: 10 per cent went to industry and commerce, 20 per cent to transport and communications, 20 per cent to social services, 20 per cent to public utilities, 10 per cent to public buildings, 10 per cent to security, and the remaining 10 per cent to other purposes.

In the Fifth Plan, four major industries were also identified for intensive development: agriculture, fisheries, forestry and animal husbandry. The government also sought to promote private foreign investments. Its financial incentives continue to include no personal income tax, no capital gains tax and no tax on remittances of foreign income, as well as a standard corporate-tax rate of 30 per cent. Companies that have been awarded 'pioneer status' can be exempted from paying the corporate tax for between two and five years as well as from paying taxes on imported capital goods and raw materials. Pioneer-status investments include pharmaceuticals, cement, metal fabrication, industrial chemicals, paper and textile products, and food processing. In order to facilitate more foreign-capital formation, a 'one-stop agency' was established in May 1989.[2]

The current Sixth Development Plan (1991–96) has a budget of Br$5.5 billion and its objectives are to accelerate human-resources and industry development and to sustain the oil and gas industries and growth of the private sector.

Unfortunately, the industrial diversification that was emphasised in previous plans has not been very successful. Because of the small market, the shortage of skilled labour, the administrative obstacles and the poor co-ordination between government departments, change has been inhibited.

Therefore, as indicated in Table 3.1, the petroleum sector (dominating the second item) remains the foundation of Brunei's economy; the country's economic growth is therefore inextricably linked to the global oil markets. Because of the fall in oil prices that occurred during the mid-1980s, GDP declined in real terms at that time. However, in the late 1980s, GDP turned around because of firmer oil prices and modest growth in the non-oil sector. GDP growth of 5 per cent in 1990 resulted from increased oil revenues and growth of 15 per cent in the non-oil and gas sector. Total GDP at current prices rose slightly in 1991. It then fell by 3.6 per cent in 1992 and again by 4 per cent in 1993.

Table 3.1 Brunei's GDP by sector, current market prices, 1983, 1988 and 1993

Sector	1983 Br$ million	% of GDP	1988 Br$ million	% of GDP	1993 Br$ million	% of GDP
Agriculture, forestry and fishing	79.6	1.0	120.5	2.2	207.2	3.2
Mining, quarrying and manufacturing	5,999.2	73.8	2,592.0	47.9	2,416.6	37.3
Electricity, gas and water	15.8	0.2	42.8	0.8	67.3	1.0
Construction	265.5	3.3	195.3	3.6	341.1	5.3
Wholesale	672.4	8.3	448.0	8.3	408.7	6.3
Retail trade	156.7	1.9	207.6	3.8	290.9	4.5
Restaurants and hotels	51.0	0.6	52.1	1.0	88.3	1.4
Transport, storage and communication	143.8	1.8	244.8	4.5	331.5	5.1
Banking and finance	120.3	1.5	185.8	3.4	262.1	4.0
Insurance	11.2	0.1	31.1	0.6	78.0	1.2
Real-estate and business services	107.9	1.3	61.6	1.1	74.0	1.1
Ownership and dwellings	28.2	0.4	42.7	0.8	73.1	1.1
Community, social and personal services	612.7	7.1	1,292.9	23.9	2,000.2	30.9
Less bank charges	−101.1	−1.3	−102.7	−1.9	−164.3	−2.5
GDP	8,163.2	100.0	5,414.8	100.0	6,474.7	99.9

Source: *Brunei Darussalam Statistical Yearbook*, Statistics Division, Economic Planning Unit, Ministry of Finance Negara Brunei Darussalam, 1994, p 175.

From 1980 to 1988, a period of declining real GDP, the non-oil and gas sector's share of GDP rose from about 20 per cent to 36 per cent in constant-price terms. Slight negative real growth in the oil and gas sector over the following two years was matched by another rise in the non-oil sector's share of real GDP, to 40 per cent in 1990. The fastest growing component of the non-oil and gas sector during this period was the government sector, which expanded by 29 per cent, thereby reflecting higher levels of expenditure under the Fifth National Development Plan as well as expansion of the public service as it absorbed increasing numbers of school leavers. The non-oil and gas private sector grew by 11 per cent over the same period; it had benefited from the increase in government demand.

Despite increased oil-production levels in 1991 and the policy of producing 'to availability' in 1992, the oil sector's contribution to GDP has continued to decrease. In current-price terms, the oil sector's share of GDP declined from 54 per cent in 1990 to an estimated 44 per cent in 1992.

As Table 3.2 indicates, the trend in GDP has not been particularly favourable. Given the importance of the government's efforts to maximise the benefits from the energy sector and to expand Brunei's involvement in energy; construction; manufacturing; agriculture, forestry and fishing; and communications and transport, these five sectors are now addressed specifically.

Table 3.2   Brunei's GDP, 1982–93

Trend	1984	1985	1986	1987	1988	1989	1990	1991	1992	1993
Total (Br$ milion)										
At current prices	8,068.5	7,752.3	5,227.2	5,858.4	5,915.8	6,440.5	6,508.6	6,604.3	6,372.0	6,474.7
Per head (Br$)										
At current prices	37,354	34,920	23,129	25,036	24,547	25,865	25,726	25,401	23,865	23,459

Source: *Brunei Darussalam Statistical Yearbook*, Statistics Division, Economic Planning Unit, Ministry of Finance, Negara Brunei Darussalam, 1994, p 177.

1.   Energy

Brunei is South-East Asia's third-largest petroleum producer (after Indonesia and Malaysia) and the world's second-largest exporter of liquefied natural gas (LNG). At the beginning of 1992, Brunei's hydrocarbon reserves were estimated to be 1.4 billion barrels of oil and 320 billion cubic metres of gas. Oil reserves are conservatively estimated to be sufficient for another 30 to 40 years at current production levels, and the oil field's productive life may well be extended due to recent discoveries.

In Brunei, all oil and gas activities are controlled by the Brunei Shell group of companies. Until recently, Brunei Shell had a monopoly on oil and gas production, processing and sale.[3]

Although Brunei Shell dominates Brunei's energy sector, France's Elf Aquitaine, in partnership with a local company, Jasra International Petroleum, has recently discovered oil in a number of fields. If this company is given approval to move to develop these fields first and they prove commercial, Elf Aquitaine will become the sultanate's second oil producer.

In 1979, oil production peaked at about 250,000 barrels per day, but it was then cut back in order to conserve resources. In the mid-1980s, a production ceiling of 150,000 barrels per day was introduced. During the 1990 Gulf crisis, production was allowed to rise to 152,000 barrels per day. In 1991, production continued to increase to 162,000 barrels per day, and in 1995 more than 173,000 barrels per day were produced. Table 3.3 shows the relative position in terms of cubic metres.

Table 3.3   Brunei's oil and natural gas production, 1984–94

Substance	1984	1985	1986	1987	1988	1989	1990	1991	1992	1993
Oil[a]	24.64	23.69	23.69	22.10	21.15	21.05	21.35	23.43	26.29	24.97
Gas[b]	8,644	8,494	8,224	8,654	8,544	8,661	8,972	9,208	9,850	9,959

Note: [a] crude petroleum 1000 cubic metres per day; [b] natural gas million (normal) cubic metres
Source: *Brunei Darussalam Statistical Yearbook*, Statistics Division, Economic Planning Unit, Ministry of Finance Negara Brunei Darussalam, 1994, p 67.

Brunei's LNG sales of 5 million tonnes per year are as important as its oil exports. The LNG plant at Lumut is one of the world's largest plants and is jointly owned by the Brunei government (50 per cent), Royal Dutch Shell (25 per cent) and Mitsubishi (25 per cent). Although some LNG is used domestically, most of it is purchased by three companies: Tokyo Electric, Tokyo Gas and Osaka Gas. Seven 75,000 cubic metre tankers, owned and operated by Brunei Shell Tankers, ship 152 LNG cargoes to Japan each year.

During Brunei's first twenty-year contract for supply of LNG to Japan, not one shipment was missed or late. Shipments were often completed ahead of schedule and in excess of contractual requirements. In March 1993, this reliability helped Brunei Shell secure a new twenty-year contract with the Japanese buyers for supply of 5.54 million tonnes of LNG per year: an increase of 7.8 per cent over the amount for the previous twenty-year contract. Brunei Shell is also reported to have secured a satisfactory increase in the pricing structure.

This rosy picture of Brunei's oil industry may have a dampening effect on government plans for diversification. However, discussions with Brunei Shell Petroleum (BSP) and the government about downstream processing have recently taken place and may lead to the establishment of chemical or related industries in Brunei.

2. Construction

Although construction, Brunei's second-largest industry, is of key importance for the economy, the sector heavily depends on government spending patterns. Poor management, lack of labour and materials, government departments' payment delays, and lack of an escalation clause in construction contracts (commonly used in other countries in order to allow for unforeseeable cost increases), are major constraints on the industry.

About 95 per cent of construction employees are guest workers from other ASEAN countries and the Indian subcontinent; locals usually take only clerical and management positions in construction firms. A number of Japanese, South Korean, Singaporean, Malaysian and Middle Eastern firms, as well as a few local companies, are active in the sector.

As mentioned, government spending drives the industry. For example, the 1984 run-up to independence meant a construction boom was produced: many public buildings were constructed, including the sultan's palace. In 1990, construction collapsed due to government cutbacks, shortages of materials and payment delays. The sector recovered again in 1991–92, due partly to projects for the sultan's silver-jubilee celebrations. In the Sixth National Development Plan (1991–96), more funds have been allocated to State housing projects, schools, hospitals, government ministry buildings, roads and mosques.

3. Manufacturing

By the end of the 1980s, the production and export of hydrocarbons was the main component of Brunei's industrial development. Other manufacturing remains in its infancy and is limited to small firms that produce furniture, building materials and other products, such as ice cream and biscuits, for local consumption. Small logging and saw-milling industries also produce timber for local use. Since 1989, textile-manufacturing companies from Hong Kong and Malaysia have established operations.

In recent development plans, five strategies have been used for developing an industrial base: re-siting existing small industries in an industrial estate so they can expand and restructure; creating new industries such as textiles, furniture, food processing and food manufacturing, and timber products; providing adequate housing for industrial workers; guaranteeing adequate power and other ancillary services; and nurturing entrepreneurship through encouraging local business managers to upgrade their skills and technological knowledge.

4. Agriculture, forestry and fishing

Before petroleum was discovered in the late 1920s, agriculture and forestry were Brunei's main economic activities. Development of the hydrocarbon sector and of urban areas resulted in the rural population migrating to the towns, and there was consequently a shortage of labour in agriculture.

Although at present the country imports 90 per cent of its food requirements, in 1990 the area under cultivation accounted for about 15 per cent of all land. Much potential agricultural land remained undeveloped. Despite the government's goals of self-sufficiency in food and reduced dependence on oil, agriculture remains of limited significance. The most successful farm ventures have been undertaken by Chinese vegetable growers. Now, Brunei is self-sufficient in locally grown vegetables for two months of the year but can also meet a significant proportion of its needs during the rest of the year. Attempts to promote local rice production have also had some success: Brunei's tropical climate makes twice-yearly cropping possible. This has resulted in the country now meeting more than 20 per cent of its domestic requirements. Although it also produces some tropical fruits for domestic consumption, it relies on temperate-climate fruits and vegetables imported from Australia, New Zealand and the North American west coast.

Efforts in the poultry industry have had more impact. Free advisory services, loans at concessional interest rates and customs-duty exemption on baby chicks have aided Brunei's self-sufficiency in local egg production. In the near future, the domestic requirements for chickens may also be fully met by local producers.

The prospects for development of other large-scale agricultural projects are not promising. Brunei's purchase of cattle stations in Australia's Northern Territory may be a more economical means of controlling its food supplies.

Like agriculture, the fisheries industry is underdeveloped, and many fishers operate at subsistence level. However, scope for commercial fishing exists (the fisheries limit extends to 322 kilometres), especially in Brunei Bay, where the aquaculture of fish (in cages) might be viable. Prawn farming in ponds is another possibility. In order to increase fish production, the government has promoted the establishment of a small, modern, offshore fishing industry.

Although in the mid-1980s forestry was not economically significant, it has been important in terms of soil conservation, water, wildlife and the environment. In 1994 more than 70 per cent of Brunei's total land area was covered with tropical forest; 60 per cent of this was primary rainforest. Brunei's mostly urban population, and the wealth attained through hydrocarbons, have meant the country has not had to turn to timber for revenue. Because no timber is exported, large-scale forest destruction has not occurred.

In 1989, a National Forestry Policy was issued that provided guidelines for maintenance of forestry resources and that outlined forestry programs and practices. In the policy it was emphasised that forestry could no longer be equated simply with timber extraction – forests had important environmental, biotechnological, economic and social functions. Government policy at present is to restrict timber exports so there are enough resources for future exploitation and domestic consumption.

The tourism potential of Brunei's forest areas has so far not been realised. In 1995 it was hoped that development of a national park incorporating the Temburong jungles would attract foreign visitors. If developed properly, such tourist-related ventures could become important to Brunei's economuy. Given Australians' interest in 'ecotourism', Australian investors as well as tourists may be attracted.

5.   Communications and transport

In Brunei, communications are reasonably reliable. The domestic telephone network is relatively advanced: in 1993 there was a ratio of 1 telephone per 3.5 people. Two government-financed satellite–earth communications stations provide direct international telex and telephone links. Since the late 1980s the telephone service has been considerably upgraded: a digital switching exchange and mobile-phone-and-paging network, as well as an optical fibre submarine network, links Brunei with Malaysia, Singapore, Thailand and the Philippines. Telephone and facsimile lines to Australia are generally good, as is the mobile-telephone system. Although Brunei's international calls have been much more expensive than Australia's, as part of its development program Brunei has attempted to reduce long-distance charges for calls to its neighbouring States. These improvements are part of the Ministry of Communication's plan that by 2003, Brunei will become the Service Hub for Trade and Tourism (SHuTT) within the Brunei, Indonesia, Malaysia and the Philippines–East ASEAN Growth Area (BIMP–EAGA).

At present, the road network has a total length of 2417 kilometres. In 1994 it serviced 135,641 private cars, so that almost one in every two Bruneians owned a motor vehicle. A recently introduced steep rise in custom duties in 1995 greatly increased local car prices. The main road is 135 kilometres long and links Bandar Seri Begawan with Muara and Kuala Belait.

The main port is at Muara, which is 27 kilometres from the capital. Freight services are regularly conducted from Muara to Singapore and Malaysia as well as to

Hong Kong, Thailand, Taiwan, the Philippines, Indonesia and the US west coast. Plans are underway to expand Muara's capacity. A much smaller port, Kaula Belait wharf, services the south-western oil fields. However, because the area's water is too shallow for ocean-going tankers, crude oil is pumped through a pipeline to an offshore loading platform. International shipping services link Brunei with Australia, Japan, Malaysia, the Philippines and Singapore.

The government-owned Royal Brunei Airlines was established in 1974. Regular services are operated to each of the ASEAN countries: Indonesia (Jakarta, Denpasar and Baliktapan), Malaysia (Kuala Lumpur, Kola Kinabalu, Kuching, Labuan and Muri), the Philippines (Manila), Singapore, Thailand (Bangkok) and approval for Vietnam is expected. As part of its support of the development of BIMP–EAGA, Royal Brunei Airlines has also extended the frequency of its services to neighbouring Malaysia, Indonesia and the Philippines. It also services Abu Dhabi, Bahrain, Beijing, Calcutta, Dubai, Frankfurt, Jeddah, London, Osaka, Taipei, Tokyo and Zurich. For Australia, it has twice-weekly flights to Brisbane, Darwin and Perth. Despite Brunei's airlines' extension to the world, Brunei International Airport (used by Royal Brunei Airlines and four other airlines) remains under-used.

Financial development

Given Brunei's small population and geographic size, its financial sector is relatively less developed than ASEAN neighbours' financial sectors.[4] As Table 3.4 indicates, Brunei has no central bank: most financial functions are performed by the Ministry of Finance. The currency is issued by a currency board, and the exchange rate is pegged at parity with the Singapore dollar. The financial sector instead comprises a number of commercial banks, finance companies, insurance companies and the specialist Islamic development agency the Tabung Amanah Islam Brunei.

Table 3.4 Brunei's financial institutions, 1994

Institution	Number of Institutions
Brunei Currency Board	1
Commercial banks	8
Brunei Development Bank	1
Finance companies	4
General insurance companies	18
National Superannuation Fund	1
Other provident funds	–
Life-insurance companies	3
Composite-insurance companies	2*
Securities companies	1
Tabung Amanah Islam Brunei	1
Total	**40**

*These companies deal in both life and general insurance.
Source: Industry interviews, 1995.

Of Brunei's eight commercial banks, only two are locally established: the Islamic Bank of Brunei (IBB) Bhd (formerly the International Bank of Brunei), which commenced operations on 13 January 1993 and follows Islamic banking principles, and Baiduri Bank Bhd, which was established in 1994. The other six banks are three large Western international banks (the Hongkong and Shanghai Banking Corporation, the Standard Chartered Bank and Citibank) and three ASEAN-country banks (Malayan Banking Berhad, the Overseas Union Bank and United Malayan Banking Corporation Berhad).

Although interest rates are fixed by the Brunei State Association of Banks, due to the exchange parity between the two countries the interest rates are usually in line with those prevailing in Singapore. The banks usually have enough cash deposits for credit to be easily available for business purposes. No restriction applies on borrowing by non-residents, and non-residents can deposit money in Brunei banks and maintain accounts.

Many local nationals may have their main borrowing needs filled directly by the State. This is because public servants, who comprise a major portion of Brunei's workforce, are entitled to participate in special government-funded lending schemes whereby concessional finance for housing and car-purchase loans are provided.

Brunei's four finance companies include Mortgage and Finance Berhad (owned by the Hongkong and Shanghai Bank) and Standard Chartered Finance (owned by Standard Chartered Bank).

Established in 1995, the government-owned Development Bank of Brunei may provide project finance for appropriate industrial projects, as do commercial banks and finance companies. Its loans are typically granted in conjunction with the existing commercial banks.

Another potentially important government financial institution is the national superannuation fund the Tabungan Amanah Pekerja. The fund commenced operations in 1994, for employees who were not already covered by the government-employees pension fund or a private pension fund. The employee and the employer are required to contribute an amount equal to 5 per cent of the employee's salary. These moneys and any accumulated interest are payable to the employee at age 55, on death, on becoming an invalid or on emigrating.

The Tabung Amanah Islam Brunei (Brunei Islamic Fund) is another government financial agency. It was established in October 1991 in order to promote local investment and trade and to participate in Brunei's economic development in an Islamic way.

Twenty-three insurance companies are active in Brunei. Although some of them are locally incorporated, most are branches of international insurance groups. One of them operates on an Islamic basis.

Brunei has no stock exchange, but Baiduri Securities, which was established with the help of the Banque Paribas, provides brokerage and investment services for local investors. Baiduri Securities is wholly owned by Baiduri Bank, of which Paribas is a 15 per cent shareholder.

Brunei's most important institution, the Ministry of Finance's Brunei Investment Agency, is reasonably unimportant in terms of local finance. Its impact is in international investments, where, in conjunction with a consortium of eight US, British and Japanese financial institutions, it manages a large and growing portfolio of foreign assets of an estimated US$25 billion to US$80 billion. These foreign reserves have been invested in North American, European and Asian markets, mainly in low-risk investments, including government securities, bonds, blue-chip equities, gold and real estate. They already yield returns that are comparable with Brunei's annual income earned from oil and gas exports, and are sufficient to pay for the country's imports. Brunei's wealth has also enabled it to assume the role of merchant banker for granting concessionary loans to other ASEAN countries, particularly the Philippines and Indonesia. Brunei has also recently invested in Indocement, Malaysian Airlines and Philippines Airlines.

Brunei's government is also a major investor, with Singapore's government, in the American International Group's, Bechtel's and General Electric Corporation's Asian Infrastructure Fund. It is interested in promoting major infrastructure-development projects within the region.

The sultan of Brunei has considerable personal wealth and investments.[5] He owns luxury hotels such as the Dorchester in London and the Hyatt in Singapore, as well as other real estate. Besides prestigious international property, the sultan has invested in precious metals such as gold and, with his family members, is involved in many Brunei-based enterprises.

Prince Mohammed, the sultan's brother, has control of (for example) QAF Holdings, a Singapore-listed company. The company invests in a wide range of ventures, including Gardenia Bread; the SMART supermarket chain in Brunei, Malaysia and Singapore; printing and newspapers; industrial gases; and equipment leasing, and has an interest in some department stores in China. Through its many subsidiaries and associated companies, QAF Holdings is the country's third-largest employer, after Brunei Shell and the government.

Brunei has invested in four cattle stations in Australia's Northern Territory that cover an area much larger than Brunei itself, as well as a cattle-export company that provides most of the country's beef.

Foreign investment

Brunei welcomes foreign investments. Indeed, because it has no personal income tax, payroll tax, export levies or sales tax, it offers investors an attractive fiscal environment. Individuals don't have to pay any capital gains tax, and profits that arise from individuals' sale of capital assets are also not taxable. Although company tax, the main source of government revenue, is set at 30 per cent of taxable profit, many investment incentives exist whereby its impact is reduced during a new project's start-up and expansion phases. Companies that have 'pioneer status', which is determined by the Economic Development Board, can obtain 'tax holidays' of up to eight years as well as custom-duty exemptions on import of their related capital equipment and any raw-material imports that are not available locally.

Formed in 1994, the Muara Export Zone also has special incentives for investment: no duty on raw materials that are used for export production, low-cost warehousing, and port facilities. Although not a specific financial incentive, Brunei's energy supply is guaranteed to be secure for the country that is a major oil and gas producer. These various incentives are considered to be competitive when compared with those of other South-East Asian countries. More specific details on Brunei's taxation system are set out in Chapter 14.

In practice, these investors face considerable administrative hurdles due to the slow and inefficient working of the Brunei government's bureaucracy. Each investment application has to proceed through a range of government ministries. First, endorsement from the Project Implementation Committee within the Ministry of Industry and Primary Resources is necessary. Second, the Prime Minister's Department has to approve the land use. Third, three other ministries – the Ministry of Finance, the Ministry of Home Affairs and the Ministry of Development – have to approve the project.

Also, potential investors require a local partner, preferably a Brunei-Malay. Foreign investors or consultants may find this requirement difficult to meet. Some pioneer industry investments, though, may be granted 100 per cent foreign ownership.

Another troublesome aspect involved in doing business in Brunei is a shortage of qualified staff. 'Brunei-sation' of the workforce policy means qualified Brunei-Malay staff members are keenly sought. Unfortunately, these people are rarely interested in private-sector work and often demand high salaries, especially in specialist areas such as business, banking and computing. Companies that wish to employ expatriate staff members have to plan several months in advance, because labour-quota applications take some time to process.

Foreign trade

Although Brunei had a growing, favourable balance of trade from 1972 to 1986, the trade balance started declining thereafter. This trend was reversed briefly in 1990–91 due to the Middle East Crisis and the Gulf War, but the trend has since continued: the trade surplus dropped from Br$1.95 billion in 1992 to Br$1.67 billion in 1993 and Br$1.108 billion in 1994.

Table 3.5   Brunei's external trade, 1988–93

| | Br$ million | | | | | |
	1988	1989	1990	1991	1992	1993
Exports (including re-exports)	3,463	3,694	4,036	4,292	3,863	3,684
Imports	1,451	1,723	1,848	1,875	1,917	2,042
Balance of trade	2,012	1,971	2,188	2,417	1,946	1670

Source: *Brunei Darussalam Statistical Yearbook*, 1994.

Brunei's major exports include crude oil and gas. Imports comprise food, machinery, transport equipment, building materials and chemicals.

Table 3.6   Brunei's imports and exports, by product type 1984–91

IMPORTS	1984	1985	1986	1987	1988	1989	1990	1991
COMMODITY SECTION								
Food and live animals	15.4	14.5	14.4	17.6	16.5	14.4	15.3	12.9
Beverages and tobacco	5.3	5.2	5.8	5.9	4.6	3.8	3.5	2.4
Crude materials, inedible	0.9	1.2	1.2	1.1	1.1	1.2	1.3	1.2
Mineral fuels	1.6	1.8	1.0	1.2	0.9	0.9	1.0	0.6
Animal & vegetable oils and fats	0.7	0.6	0.4	0.4	0.5	0.5	0.3	0.3
Chemicals	7.7	7.1	7.0	6.9	6.6	6.1	6.7	6.3
Manufactured goods	20.3	21.5	21.0	24.5	23.7	25.9	27.0	27.4
Machinery and transport equipment	35.0	33.8	37.8	29.8	32.8	35.7	34.4	38.3
Miscellaneous manufactured articles	8.9	10.8	10.5	11.3	11.7	10.7	10.2	10.1
Miscellaneous	4.2	3.5	1.0	1.3	1.6	0.8	0.3	0.5
TOTAL	100.0	100.0	100.0	100.0	100.0	100.0	100.0	100.0
EXPORTS								
COMMODITY SECTION								
Food and live animals	0.1	0.1	0.4	0.4	0.6	0.5	0.6	0.4
Beverages and tobacco	0.1	0.1	0.1	0.2	0.2	0.1	0.0	0.2
Crude materials, inedible	0.0	0.0	0.1	0.0	0.1	0.1	0.1	0.0
Mineral fuels	98.8	98.5	97.2	97.5	97.5	96.9	96.5	96.7
Animal & vegetable oils and fats	0.0	0.0	0.0	0.0	0.0	0.0	0.0	0.0
Chemicals	0.1	0.1	0.1	0.0	0.1	0.1	0.1	0.1
Manufactured goods	0.1	0.2	0.4	0.3	0.4	0.4	0.5	0.4
Machinery and transport equipment	0.5	0.8	1.4	1.0	0.8	1.3	1.4	1.3
Miscellaneous manufactured articles	0.3	0.2	0.3	0.4	0.3	0.6	0.8	0.9
Miscellaneous	0.0	0.0	0.0	0.0	0.0	0.0	0.0	0.0
TOTAL	100.0	100.0	100.0	100.0	100.0	100.0	100.0	100.0

Source: *Brunei Darussalam Statistical Yearbook*, 1993, p 86.

Brunei's future trade surpluses will therefore continue to depend on the country's ability to produce, and the prices it achieves for, its oil and gas exports. Because its dependence on imports of manufactured goods, machinery and equipment, as well as of food, is unlikely to decline, it will have to carefully plan its future economic development.

With reference to trade, Brunei's narrow export base means its own trading is somewhat more concentrated. In 1993, 54.2 per cent of its exports were directed to Japan, 19 per cent to Brunei's ASEAN neighbours and 17.9 per cent to EU members (the UK being the most important). This concentration of export items also makes Table 3.7's growth rates much less meaningful than the other ASEAN countries' growth rates. The international trade in gas, petroleum and petroleum products typically involves very large sales, and a successful contract in one market instead of another can greatly change market shares. Furthermore, given a finite amount of available product, a growth in one market may mean a drop in another.

Table 3.7   Brunei's major trading partners, 1989 and 1993

Country	Exports (US$ million) 1989	1993	Trend* growth (%)	Imports (US$ million) 1989	1993	Trend* growth (%)
Indonesia	0	1	–	15	48	31.2
Malaysia	22	2	–53.6	78	208	27.5
Philippines	48	54	–0.3	1	3	43.7
Singapore	90	196	22.1	231	698	38.4
Thailand	194	205	2.6	33	40	1.1
Total ASEAN	**354**	**458**	**6.7**	**358**	**997**	**33.3**
Australia	17	20	9.7	22	43	16.0
Canada	0	7	–	2	1	–4.7
China	8	0	–	20	12	–17.5
Hong Kong	0	1	–	10	30	35.1
Japan	1,095	1,287	2.9	126	140	4.0
South Korea	247	0	–	9	0	–
New Zealand	0	0	–	3	6	–
Chinese Taipei	0	61	–	0	10	–
United States	93	29	–28.3	109	526	54.2
Total APEC	**1,814**	**1,863**	**0.9**	**659**	**1,765**	**31.6**
European Union	3	425	293	167	705	51
All other countries	65	85	–	33	131	47.4
Totals	**1,882**	**2,373**	**6.0**	**859**	**2,601**	**36.4**

*This covers the period 1989–93.
Source: Department of Foreign Affairs and Trade, *The APEC Region Trade and Investment*. Canberra: Australian Government Publishing Service, 1994, pp 30–1.

However, if a number of years is examined, a marked decline can be seen to have occurred in the US and Malaysian markets since 1991. In contrast, the EU has grown even more over the same period. The overall picture of growth, an average of 6 per cent is not particularly exciting.

Because Brunei's imports cover a much wider range of products and countries, the import-trend figures are more helpful. Similarly, the import-growth figures are impressive: there was an average increase of 36.4 per cent per year. The balance-of-trade problems mentioned previously are thereby reconfirmed.

With reference to specific countries, Singapore is Brunei's main source of imports, and in 1993 it accounted for 26.8 per cent of all imports. The US, with a 20.2 per cent share is second in importance and is Brunei's fastest growing market: a growth rate of 54.2 per cent per year over 1989–93. Japan accounted for only 5.4 per cent.

Brunei's position in ASEAN is also worth more analysis. As Table 3.8 indicates, for example, Malaysia (as mentioned) dropped sharply in both nominal dollars and relative terms. Its market share therefore dropped from 1.2 per cent in 1989 to only

0.1 per cent in 1993. Thailand and the Philippines have also suffered a decline, albeit a much less significant one. In contrast, Singapore has almost doubled its market share of Brunei's exports. Overall, though, ASEAN's relative importance has increased only modestly in terms of market share, from 18.8 per cent of total exports in 1989 to 19.3 per cent in 1993, or an increase of 0.6 per cent over the period.

Turning now to imports, ASEAN shows a modest decline: it dropped from 41.6 per cent of total imports in 1989 to 38.2 per cent in 1993. This decline is in relative terms only, because the dollar amounts imported from ASEAN increased from US$358 million in 1989 to US$997 million in 1993.

Table 3.8   Brunei–ASEAN trade, 1989 and 1993

| | % of total | | | |
| | Exports | | Imports | |
	1989	1993	1989	1993
Indonesia	0	0	1.7	1.8
Malaysia	1.2	0.1	9.1	8.0
Philippines	2.6	2.3	0.1	0.1
Singapore	4.8	8.3	26.9	26.8
Thailand	10.3	8.6	3.8	1.5
Total ASEAN	**18.8**	**19.3**	**41.6**	**38.3**

Source: Department of Foreign Affairs and Trade, *The APEC Region Trade and Investment*. Canberra: Australian Government Publishing Service, 1994, pp 30–1.

Trade with Australia

Australia's trade with Brunei is a reasonably modest undertaking that in 1993 amounted to a total of A$92.6 million. The dollar amount of goods imported from Australia has continued to grow rapidly, but growth in imports from other countries was more rapid. As Table 3.9 indicates, Australia's relative importance has declined from a high 3.3 per cent share of Brunei's imports in 1987 to a low 1.7 per cent in 1993. These figures, though, may understate the true position, as some trade is conducted via Singapore. Brunei's exports to Australia have similarly increased in dollar terms, albeit more modestly. Growth in other markets has likewise resulted in a decline from Australia's peak 2.6 per cent export share in 1991 to a share of only 0.8 per cent in 1993.

Table 3.9   Australia's importance for Brunei's trade, 1984–93

Year	Brunei's exports (fob) Australia as % of total	Year	Brunei's imports (cif) Australia as % of total
1984	–	1984	3.3
1985	–	1985	2.7
1986	0.8	1986	2.6
1987	1.1	1987	3.5
1988	1.3	1988	3.3
1989	0.9	1989	2.6
1990	1.3	1990	2.6
1991	2.6	1991	2.2
1992	2.1	1992	1.2
1993	0.8	1993	1.7

Source: Department of Foreign Affairs and Trade, *The APEC Region Trade and Investment*. Canberra: Australian Government Publishing Service, 1994, p 27.

With reference to exports, Australia's major ones are concentrated across a handful of items. Motor vehicles, typically passenger cars, are the most important, followed by electrical machinery, electric-power-generation equipment, manufactures of metals (iron, steel and aluminium), live animals, and meat and meat preparations. These six categories combined accounted for 54.4 per cent of all exports. The other items and their specific dollar amounts are shown in Table 3.10.

Table 3.10   Australia's exports to Brunei for year ended 30 June 1995

Type of product	A$	%
Live animals (non-fish)	5,993,809	10.96
Meat and meat preparations	3,572,296	6.53
Dairy products and eggs	894,103	1.63
Fish and shellfish	328,739	0.60
Cereals and cereal preparations	300,628	0.55
Vegetables and fruit	2,402,963	4.39
Sugars, sugar preparations and honey	46,538	0.09
Coffee, tea, cocoa and spices and manufactures thereof	1,107,059	2.02
Feed for animals (excluding unmilled cereals)	433,061	0.79
Miscellaneous edible products and preparations	130,124	0.24
Beverages	262,978	0.48
Cork and wood	25,812	0.05
Crude fertilisers and crude minerals	468,497	0.86
Crude animal and vegetable materials	851,510	1.56
Petroleum and petroleum products	13,932	0.03
Chemicals	178,958	0.33
Dyeing, tanning and colouring materials	348,863	0.64
Medicinal and pharmaceutical products	690,388	1.26
Essential oils, perfume and cleansing preparations	62,003	0.11
Fertilisers (excluding crude ores)	66,513	0.12
Plastics	142,471	0.26
Chemical materials and products	336,633	0.62

Table 3.10 continues.

Table 3.10 (continued)

Type of product	A$	%
Rubber manufactures	37,603	0.07
Paper and paperboard	71,878	0.13
Textile yarn and fabrics	273,641	0.50
Non-metallic mineral manufactures	679,280	1.24
Iron and steel	2,477,812	4.53
Non-ferrous metals	624,775	1.14
Manufactures of metals	5,892,448	10.77
Power-generating machinery and equipment	889,077	1.63
Machinery for particular industries	1,375,488	2.51
Metal-working machinery	221,782	0.41
Industrial equipment or machine parts	1,399,730	2.56
Office and data-processing machines	374,990	0.69
Telecommunications and recording equipment	394,391	0.72
Electrical machinery and appliances (parts)	5,994,721	10.96
Road vehicles (including air-cushion vehicles)	8,309,353	15.19
Transport equipment (excluding road vehicles)	478,543	0.87
Prefabricated buildings and materials	266,834	0.49
Furniture and furnishings	152,173	0.28
Apparel and accessories	54,175	0.10
Footwear	12,183	0.02
Professional and scientific instruments	685,742	1.25
Photographic equipment, optical goods and clocks	88,982	0.16
Miscellaneous manufactured articles	4,326,391	7.91
Special transactions and commodities	654,192	1.20
Combined confidential items	300,402	0.55
Other items	15,398	0.03
Total exports	**54,709,862**	**100.00**

Source: ABS, *Foreign Trade Statistics*, 1995, pp 99–100.

Australian imports from Brunei can be discussed quickly. As Table 3.11 indicates, they almost exclusively comprise petroleum and petroleum products. Textile and apparel items and office machines are the only other significant categories.

Table 3.11   Australia's imports from Brunei for year ended 30 June 1995

Type of product	A$	%
Petroleum and petroleum products or materials	21,744,412	99.13
General industrial equipment and machine parts	6,766	0.03
Office and data-processing machines	68,773	0.31
Telecommunications and recording equipment	4,317	0.02
Apparel and clothing accessories	69,625	0.32
Professional and scientific instruments	11,659	0.05
Miscellaneous manufactured articles	27,940	0.13
Other items	1,599	0.01
Total imports	**21,935,091**	**100.00**

Source: ABS, *Foreign Trade Statistics*, 1995, p 79.

Although these statistics apply only to merchandise trade, Australia has been reasonably active in the Brunei market as a service provider, particularly in engineering, education and management.

Future prospects

Brunei may enjoy one of the world's highest levels of national per-capita income, but the country's small size means it faces many growth constraints. An exceedingly small domestic market and acute shortages of both labour and technical expertise are only three of these. In 1994 it was estimated that the working population was about 112,000, of which 35,000 were foreigners. Half the labour force is employed in the public sector, and the ethnic Brunei-Malay prefer government employment in either the civil service or the armed services to private employment. Development therefore depends on local ethnic Chinese and foreign workers. Despite the government's efforts at restructuring the workforce through having stricter immigrant-worker controls and improved vocational training facilities for Bruneians, the number of foreigners continues to rise.

Compared with its neighbours' situations, another constraint on Brunei's industrialisation and agricultural development is the country's limited domestic market. An urgent need exists for providing incentives for local as well as foreign investors to establish export-oriented industries in which the local market is not the main consideration. Brunei's wage levels are very high. This means products from lower wage countries will become increasingly competitive, thereby preventing Brunei from diversifying into other exports.

Brunei's economy is entirely dependent on oil and gas resources that will run dry in a matter of decades. Because of this dependence on oil, other areas of development such as agriculture, manufacturing and construction are constrained. Due to the decline in world oil prices over recent years, the country's economic planners have been led to review their economic strategies and embark on a diversification policy.

Although Brunei is not a major export market for Australia, its geographic position, membership of APEC and ASEAN, and rich local economy should attract increasing Australian interest. As mentioned previously, Brunei's cattle-exporting company ships live cattle from the Northern Territory to Brunei and elsewhere in the South-East Asia region. More recently, some Australian meat producers have gained permission to export *halal*-processed chilled and frozen meat to Brunei. The Northern Territory and Western Australia are particularly involved in this trade, due to the twice-weekly air connections between both Brunei and Darwin and Brunei and Perth.

With reference to services for Brunei, Australian secondary and post-secondary institutions attract Bruneian students. Brunei-government-sponsored students are also studying in Australia, in order to upgrade their skills under Brunei-government inservice scholarship schemes. This is an area where the Australian education sector should gain an increasingly larger share of this once traditionally UK-dominated market.

Australian engineering and technical consultancies that are located in Brunei advise the government and Brunei Shell about project design and tendering. Brunei's dependence on foreign expertise for aiding improvement of its infrastructure and diversification of its economy provides opportunities for Australian businesses to enter the Brunei market.

Import demand for foodstuffs and consumer goods and building materials should increase, given the country's high average per-capita income.

An Australian company has set up a ready-mixed-concrete venture in Brunei. A joint Australia–Brunei venture has also recently been established for manufacturing aluminium roofing materials.

In conclusion, hurdles exist, but patience, persistence and determination to develop good working relationships at a personal level can aid firms' entry to the Brunei market. Good communications systems within, to and from out of the country; the country's central location in South-East Asia; its cheap gas supplies; its political stability; its various tax exemptions; and its government's policy of actively supporting foreign investments, all provide sound reasons for Australian companies to venture into its market.

ENDNOTES

1 In 1993, Brunei had an estimated per-capita income of US$18,500. Although this is one of the world's highest levels of national income per-capita, a wide disparity exists in income levels. It is estimated that about half the country's labour-force, members including guest workers, earn less than US$5000 per year. This information is from the *Far Eastern Economic Review*, 29 April 1993, p 22.

2 'One-Stop Agency' was given the specific tasks of considering applications for industrial projects, negotiating on priority investment areas and providing facilities for industrial sites.

3 The Brunei Shell group of companies comprises four major firms. Brunei Shell Petroleum (BSP) is the country's main firm and largest industrial concern and is owned equally by Shell and the Brunei government. Brunei Shell Marketing, which is also owned equally by Shell and the government, distributes petroleum products throughout Brunei. Brunei LNG, (which is jointly owned by Shell, Mitsubishi and the government, operates Brunei's LNG facilities. Brunei Coldgas, which is also owned by Shell, Mitsubishi and the government, markets and transports Brunei's LNG to Japan.

4 A more detailed discussion of this development is in the 'Brunei' chapter in Skully, Michael T (ed), *Financial Institutions and Markets in Southeast Asia*. London: Macmillan, 1984, p 47.

5 *Fortune* magazine estimates his wealth to be US$37 billion. This information is from the *Far Eastern Economic Review*, 29 April 1993, p 22.

REFERENCES

Arief, S, *The Brunei Economy*. East Balmain, New South Wales: Rosecons, 1986.

Burton, B, 'Brunei Darussalam in 1989: Coming of Age within ASEAN', in *Asian Survey*, vol 30, no. 2, February, 1990, p 196.

Chan, K S and Jin, N K, 'Currency Interchangeability Arrangement Between Brunei and Singapore: A Cost–Benefit Analysis', in the *Singapore Economic Review*, vol 37, no 2, October, 1992, p 21.

Cleary, M and Wong, C Y, *Oil, Economic Development, and Diversification of Brunei Darussalam*. New York: St Martin's, 1994.

Crosbie, A, 'Brunei in Transition', in *Southeast Asian Affairs*, 1981, pp 75–88.

—— 'Brunei: The Constraints on a Small State', in *Southeast Asian Affairs*, 1970, pp 67–79.

Doshi, T, 'Brunei: The Steady State', in *Southeast Asian Affairs*, 1991, pp 71–7.

Economic Intelligence Unit, *Country Profile: Malaysia, Brunei*. London: Economic Intelligence Unit, 1992–93.

Hamzah, B A, 'Brunei Darussalam: Continuity and Tradition', in *Southeast Asian Affairs*, 1989, pp 99–102.

—— *The Oil Sultanate: Political History of Oil in Brunei Darussalam*. Negari Sembilan: Mawaddah Enterprise, 1991.

Kling, Z, 'The Changing International Image of Brunei', in *Southeast Asian Affairs*, 1990, p 89.

KPMG Peat Marwick, *Investment in Brunei Darussalam*. Bandar Seri Begawan: KPMG Brunei Darussalam, 1993.

Leake, D, *Brunei: The Modern Southeast-Asian Islamic Sultanate*. Jefferson, NC: McFarland, 1989.

Mani, A, 'Negara Brunei Darussalam in 1992: Celebrating the Silver Jubilee', in *Southeast Asian Affairs*, 1993, p 95.

Menon, K U, 'Brunei Darussalam in 1986: In Search of the Political Kingdom', in *Southeast Asian Affairs*, 1987, pp 85–91.

Mulliner, K, 'Business As Usual After the Gala', in *Asian Survey*, vol 25, no 2, February 1985, pp 217–19.

Rogers, A and McCampbell, M, 'The Billionaires List', in *Fortune*, vol 127, no 13, 28 June 1993, p 44.

Saunders, G E, *A History of Brunei*. Kuala Lumpur: Oxford University Press, 1994.

Siddall, N, 'Brunei: The Foreign Relations of Wealth', in *Journal of Southeast Asia Business*, no 19, Winter, 1989.

Siddique, S, 'Brunei Darussalam 1991: The Non-Secular State', in *Southeast Asian Affairs*, 1992, p 91.

—— 'Brunei Darussalam in 1985: A Year of Nation Building', in *Southeast Asian Affairs*, 1986, pp 48–51.

Mong, T O T, 'Modern Brunei: Some Important Issues', in *Southeast Asian Affairs*, 1983, pp 74–80.

Vatikiotis, M, 'Lord of the Rigs', in *Far Eastern Economic Review*, 21 April 1993, p 22.

APPENDIX 3.1:   *Australian and Bruneian Representation*

Australian addresses

High Commission of Brunei Darussalam
16 Bulwarra Close
O'Malley 2606, ACT, Australia
Telephone: (61 6) 290 1801
Facsimile: (61 6) 286 1554

Addresses in Brunei

Australian High Commission
Teck Guan Plaza
Jalan Sultan
Bandar Seri Begawan 1929, Brunei Darussalam
Telephone: (673 2) 229 435
Facsimile: (673 2) 221 652

Australian Trade Commission
Fourth Floor, Teck Guan Plaza
Jalan Sultan
Bandar Seri Begawan 1929, Brunei Darussalam
Telephone: (673 2) 241 121
Facsimile: (673 2) 221 652

4

Indonesia

Siang Ng

Introduction

Indonesia is South-East Asia's most populous country and therefore Australia's largest close neighbour. Given its government's main objective of achieving economic prosperity through liberalisation, and a GNP growing at about 6.5 per cent, it offers Australian business tremendous trade and investment opportunities. This chapter provides an overview of Indonesia's burgeoning economy, its economic and financial structure, foreign investment and trade as well as its trade relations with Australia and future prospects.

The setting

Indonesia is the world's largest archipelago. It comprises 13,667 islands with a total land area of 1.9 million square kilometres. The five main islands – Java, Sumatra, Kalimantan, Sulawesi and Irian Jaya – account for 92 per cent of this land and about 94 per cent of its estimated 203 million people. It is the world's fifth-most populous nation, but the population is very unevenly dispersed; 60 per cent live in Java, but that island accounts for only 6.7 per cent of the land. In contrast, another 20 per cent of people live in Sumatra, which accounts for 25 per cent of the total land area.

These peoples are equally dispersed in terms of cultures with more than 300 ethnic groups (45 per cent Javanese, 14 per cent Sundanese, 7.5 per cent Madurese, 7.5 per cent Malays and 26 per cent others) and 250 languages and dialects are spoken throughout the archipelago. The ethnic Chinese, although only 2.5 per cent of the population, are extremely important in Indonesia's commerce and industry. For example, of the 33 guests who reportedly attended a key President Suharto

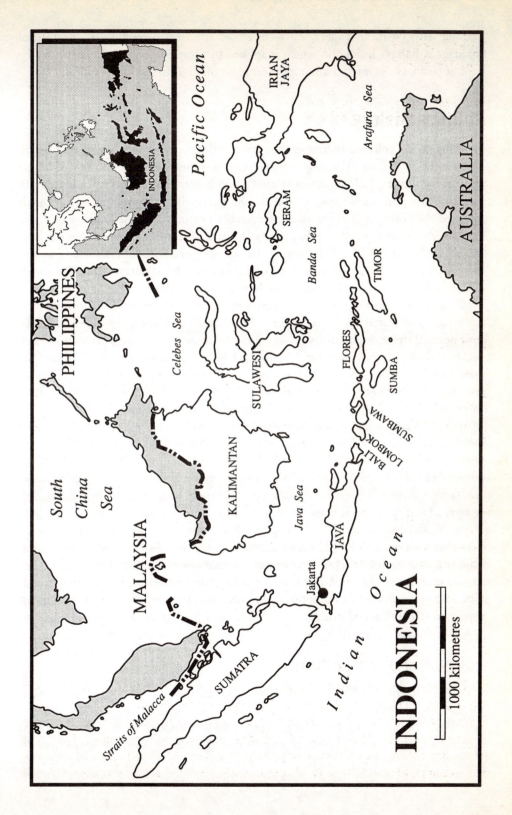

INDONESIA

1000 kilometres

meeting with business leaders, 29 were ethnic Chinese. Nevertheless, the official language is Bahasa Indonesia which is spoken by almost everyone; English may be used in business circles and among government officials in the larger cities.

Political history

In terms of its culture, Indonesia has been influenced by Hinduism, Buddhism, Islam and Christianity. The first three cultures were introduced by Indian, Chinese and Arabic traders. Indonesia's early contact with Western culture and Christianity was through Portuguese traders during the early sixteenth century. The Dutch replaced the Portuguese in the early seventeenth century with the Dutch East India Company gaining control of what is now Jakarta. Indonesia became a Dutch government colonial in 1799. This control was not accepted without resistance (such as the Java War 1825–30) and this in turn helped foster local nationalism; the Dutch did not gain full control of present-day Indonesia until 1910.

This nationalism was strengthened even more due to the relative ease with which the Japanese defeated the Dutch during World War II. When in 1945 the Japanese surrendered, the Indonesians were unwilling to resume their colonial status. They declared their independence on 17 August 1945 and named Achmed Sukarno as president. The Dutch, though, did not recognise the new republic and sought to re-establish their ownership. Although several years of armed struggle followed, in 1949 the Dutch finally withdrew politically from the archipelago.

Independence was not achieved without its costs, however, and inexperienced management resulted in many unsuccessful government-conducted economic experiments. Proper fiscal management was lacking, and the government turned to the printing presses in order to cover its deficits. Inflation soon became hyper-inflation and the economy's Westernised sector ground slowly to a halt. Political instability resulted. Finally, in 1965, after an unsuccessful coup attempt, political power was gradually transferred to General Suharto. Under President Suharto's government over the last two and a half decades, political and economic stability have been achieved. In March 1993, Suharto was once again re-elected president.

Government of the country has since independence been guided by five principles, known as 'Pancasila': belief in God, humanity, nationalism, democracy (based on consensus) and social justice.

Economic development

Endowed with rich and fertile land, Indonesia is mainly an agriculture-based and a resources-based country. Agriculture and mining are the economy's major sectors – combined, the two account for 36 per cent of GDP. Although oil and gas have been the major contributors to government revenues and export earnings (more than 80 per cent during the oil boom), manufacturing has gradually replaced them in importance. Manufactured goods' contribution to GDP has increased from 13 per cent to more than 20 per cent, as indicated in Table 4.1.

Table 4.1   Indonesia's GDP by industry, 1991–93*

	Rp billion		
Industry	**1991**	**1992**	**1993**
Agriculture, including livestock, forestry and fisheries	22,657.0	24,003.7	24,802.0
Mining	19,341.4	19,064.5	19,027.6
Manufacturing	24,481.6	26,856.1	27,812.8
Electricity, gas and water	842.8	928.2	928.0
Construction	10,594.7	11,420.3	11,997.6
Retail trade and hotels and restaurants	19,572.8	21,029.6	23,639.6
Transportation and communication			
Banking and financial	6,869.4	7,595.0	4,117.8
Public sector	5,561.0	6,257.8	6,401.8
Services	9,052.1	9,320.0	9,934.8
	4,191.8	4,433.5	4,494.8
Total	**123,164.8**	**130,908.7**	**133,156.8**

* figures stated in 1983 prices
Note: total calculated from actual not rounded numbers
Source: Biro Pusat Statistik, *Statistik Indonesia*, various issues.

Since 1969 Indonesia has been implementing a series of Five-Year Plans, or *Repelita*, with great success: it has achieved an annual average growth rate of 4.5 per cent in per-capita income and of 6.5 per cent in GDP. Its economic performance over 1968–81 was even more remarkable: it averaged almost 8 per cent. This rapid growth was partly due to increased investment, improved productivity and the government's expansionist policy. Although in the first half of the 1980s there was a slowdown in growth, in the late 1980s the average real annual economic growth remained at about 5 per cent, as indicated in Table 4.2. This slower growth may have resulted from the government's contractionist policy, which it adopted in response to the falling oil revenues that were due to the oil-price decline and OPEC-imposed oil quotas. The government responded by reducing its expenditure on salaries and wages in the public administration sector, and this in turn had a contractionary impact on the whole economy. Another government response, though, has been to continuously, but gradually, devalue the currency – rupiah – in order to stimulate the export and domestic import-substitute industries.

Table 4.2   Indonesia's real-GDP growth, 1986–94

Year	%
1986	5.9
1987	4.9
1988	5.8
1989	7.5
1990	7.2
1991	6.9
1992	6.3
1993	6.5
1994	7.3

Source: Biro Pusat Statistik, *Statistik Indonesia*, various issues.

More efficient use of resources has been promoted through implementation of the outward-oriented strategy: investment, both domestic and foreign, has been stimulated during this phase of economic expansion. However, Indonesia has also encountered inflationary pressure and rising foreign debt. Price increases over the past decade, though, have been effectively controlled through having tight monetary policy (implemented by Bank Indonesia) supplemented by less expansionary fiscal budgets. Although in the first nine months of 1993 inflationary pressure (8.24 per cent) was higher than that in the same period of 1992, this situation was partly caused by increased fuel prices and a crop-destroying flood in Java. Table 4.3 shows Indonesia's inflation situation since the mid-1980s.

Nevertheless, in order to support the economy's rapid growth, the government has raised its expenditure on basic infrastructure, transport, power and education. In particular, in the 1994–95 budget, priority was placed on roads, telecommunications and electricity generation. That budget represented a 2 per cent increase in real expenditure over the 1993–94 budget.

Table 4.3   Indonesia's inflation rate, 1985–95

Year	%
1985	4.31
1986	8.83
1987	8.90
1988	5.47
1989	5.97
1990	9.53
1991	9.52
1992	4.94
1993	9.80
1994	9.20
1995	8.64

Source: Biro Pusat Statistik, *Statistik Indonesia*, various issues.

Financial development

Indonesia's financial sector was once a labyrinth of direct controls and other government intervention. Since the late 1980s, though, this position has changed considerably and nowadays Indonesia's financial intermediaries operate under a much less restricted regulatory regime; one that fosters a more competitive and market-oriented environment. This has allowed the private foreign exchange banks to expand rapidly and, as shown in Table 4.4, they now control more assets in aggregate than previously dominant state banks. Besides more operational freedoms, the government has also taken a liberal approach to new entry and, as shown in Table 4.5, the number of banks has increased sharply. The foreign exchange system has been similarly liberalised. Today the rupiah is subject to a managed float with the central bank, Bank Indonesia, setting the daily reference rate based on a 'basket' of currencies of Indonesia's major trading partners.

Table 4.4   Assets of Indonesia's financial institutions, 1991–94

	Rp billion			
Institution	1991	1992	1993	1994
Bank Indonesia	55,220	63,885	68,440	66,504
State banks	70,158	83,291	91,333	93,544
Private FX banks	45,654	55,340	76,092	95,436
Foreign banks	12,070	15,175	18,419	21,334
Non-FX private banks	12,868	11,009	12,674	14,758
Development banks	14,505	17,251	19,916	18,622
Rural banks	6,243	–	–	–
Total	**216,718**	**245,951**	**286,874**	**310,198**

Source: Bank Indonesia, *Report for the Financial Year 1993–1994*, 1994, p 64.

Table 4.5   Indonesia's financial institutions, 1991–94

	Number			
Institution	1991	1992	1993	1994
State commercial banks	5	5	5	5
Foreign and joint-venture banks	29	30	39	39
Private commercial banks	126	141	158	166
Development banks	29	29	29	29
Savings banks	3	3	3	3
Rural banks	6,296	8,520	8,717	8,897
Total	**6,488**	**8,728**	**8,951**	**9,139**

Source: Bank Indonesia, *Report for the Financial Year 1993–1994*, 1994, p 64.

Before the financial reform of 1986, the banking sector was dominated by five State-owned banks. However, these banks were under the direction of Bank Indonesia, credit decisions and interest-rate controls. Besides serving as the central bank, Bank Indonesia was a major commercial lender. Because of restrictions placed on branching and imposition of a credit ceiling, competition in the banking and finance sector was hampered. Due to the concern expressed about inflation, though, Indonesia's open capital account policy led to unrestricted movement of capital, into and out of the country, by the non-financial private sector in the 1970s.

Table 4.6   Indonesia's major domestic commercial banks, 1994

Bank	Assets* US$ million
Bank Negara Indonesia (12/94)**	13,964
Bank Degang Negara (12/94)**	12,591
Bank Bumi Daya (12/93)**	11,933
Bank Rakyat Indonesia (12/94)**	11,693
Bank Central Asia (12/94)	8,744
Bank Ekspor Impor Indonesia (12/94)**	8,819
Bapindo (12/94)**	6,361
Bank Danamon (12/94)	4,779
Bank Internasional Indonesia (12/94)	4,241
Lippo Bank (12/94)	3,146
Bank Tabungan Negara (12/94)	3,117
Bank Umum Nasional (12/94)	2,521
Bank Bali (12/94)	2,265
Bank Dagang Nasional Indonesia (12/92)	2,145
Panin Bank (12/94)	1,550
Bank Duta (12/94)	1,105
Co-operative Bank of Indonesia (12/94)	788

* Figures for the year ended are noted in parentheses.
** These are Indonesian state-government banks.
Source: The *Banker*, October 1995, p 65.

As well as its banking system, Indonesia has a range of financial institutions that include securities companies, finance companies, life and general insurers, pension funds and pawnshops. Of these, the pension funds are the most interesting. For example, as of mid-1995 there were some 521 licensed pension funds with assets estimated to be 19 trillion rupiah. So far, most of these assets have been placed in fixed deposits. Considerable scope seems to exist for more active portfolio management, and Australian firms, like the AMP Society, Lend Lease and National Mutual, have all established local joint-venture companies for servicing that area.

As well as the financial institutions mentioned, Indonesia has an active money market, the start of a corporate-debt market and a share market. The Jakarta Stock Exchange, which commenced operations in 1977, serves as an important source of equity funds for larger Indonesian companies and also provides a secondary-trading market in support of the government's privatisation program. At the end of 1994, 147 domestic companies were listed on the exchange. Companies that do not fulfil the exchange's listing requirements may approach another exchange: the Indonesian Stock Exchange.

In the late 1980s, due to the rapid growth enjoyed by the export, manufacturing, forestry and tourist sectors, as well as the increased investment in infrastructure and the liberalisation of finance and trade, Indonesia's economy improved considerably. The strong growth in GDP continued into the 1990s and averaged about 6.4 per cent. Given the government's main objective of achieving economic prosperity and liberalisation, strong growth may be expected to continue during the rest of the 1990s. The World Bank has estimated an average real-output growth of 7 per cent for Asian economies during the period 1995–98. As for other Asian NICs, the 'trade as an engine of growth' strategy has proved to be very successful. The World Bank has reported a sharp fall in the percentage of Indonesia's poor: in 1970, 60 per cent of people were living in poverty, whereas in 1990 the figure was only 16 per cent.

In this section of the chapter, some mention of the Indonesian rupiah should be made. As part of economic policy, the government, via Bank Indonesia, has instigated a gradual depreciation of the rupiah against the US dollar. As Table 4.7 indicates, more rupiah is required each year to purchase one US dollar. Over 1990–95, the rupiah also declined against the Australian dollar but not to the same magnitude.

Table 4.7   Indonesian rupiah against the US dollar and the Australian dollar, 1990–95

Year	US$ High	Low	Close	A$ High	Low	Close
1990	1901.00	1808.00	1901.00	1541.73	1377.19	1439.00
1991	1992.00	1912.00	1992.00	1578.46	1482.81	1519.00
1992	2062.00	2004.00	2062.00	1552.49	1421.24	1493.00
1993	2110.00	2066.00	2110.00	1478.28	1362.77	1416.00
1994	2200.00	2122.00	2200.00	1713.23	1506.99	1709.00
1995	2308.00	2207.00	2308.00	1734.80	1595.15	1719.00

Source: Australia and New Zealand Banking Group (ANZ) and Bank Indonesia, 1996.

Foreign investment

Apart from its rich natural resources, Indonesia is endowed with an abundant labour force with a wage structure considerably lower than that of Australia. This makes it particularly attractive for foreign companies, especially those that produce labour-intensive goods, to invest in Indonesia. Under President Suharto's New Order government, foreign investments have been promoted and welcomed in order to complement Indonesia's abundant natural wealth. Although unskilled labour is abundant, Indonesia does not have enough highly skilled workers, especially in technical and managerial areas. Consequently, foreign-investment projects that promote these two areas are particularly desirable. As can be noted from Table 4.8, foreign investment has expanded during recent years. From 1987 to 1992, approved foreign investment has increased from US$1480.6 million to US$10,313.2 million. Due to the enormous increase in the late 1980s, for the period 1988–92 the accumulated approved foreign investment amounted to US$36,986.3 million. This figure very much exceeds the total foreign investment for the preceding two decades, 1967 to 1987.

Table 4.8   Approved foreign investment in Indonesia (excluding crude oil and gas), 1967–95

Years	US$ million
1967–80	368.4
1981–86	1,389.3
1987	1,480.6
1988	4,425.9
1989	4,718.9
1990	8,750.1
1991	8,778.2
1992	10,313.2
1993	8,100.0
1994	23,700.0
1995	39,900.0

Source: Investment Co-ordinating Board (Badan Koordinasi Penanaman Modal), 1996.

East Asian economies have been growing rapidly, thereby increasing that region's importance in the world economy. For the past two decades, foreign capital has been flowing to Indonesia. Since 1967, more than 50 per cent of Indonesia's total approved foreign investment was from elsewhere in East Asia. As can be noted from Table 4.9, Japan's role as Indonesia's largest foreign investor has since been taken over by Asia's four 'little dragons' – Hong Kong, South Korea, Singapore and Taiwan. Although the range of investor interests from these four economies is very wide, the countries invest mostly in labour-intensive, export-oriented manufacturing industries. They have therefore become the main source of Indonesia's economic development capital and provide efficient use of Indonesia's mass labour force. Whereas Taiwanese investors are investing in manufacturing, mining and transportation, Singaporeans focus on the property and housing sector and Koreans concentrate on manufacturing and forestry. Hong Kong investors are interested in almost everything: the property, forestry, construction and hospitality industries.

Table 4.9   Approved foreign investment in Indonesia, by source, 1987–93

Country or region	US$ million						
	1987	1988	1989	1990	1991	1992	1993
Japan	531.8	247.0	678.7	2,240.8	929.3	1,509.3	836.1
Hong Kong	134.9	239.5	406.8	993.3	277.7	1,021.3	384.1
South Korea	23.0	199.5	466.1	722.9	301.3	618.3	661.4
Singapore	6.0	240.2	166.1	264.3	346.4	454.1	1,460.2
Taiwan	7.9	910.2	155.2	618.3	1,056.5	563.3	131.4
United States	72.2	671.0	348.0	153.4	275.6	922.6	444.5
Rest of the world	680.7	1,900.0	2,408.0	3,757.1	5,591.4	5,224.4	4,226.5
Total	**1,456.5**	**4,407.4**	**4,628.9**	**8,750.1**	**8,778.2**	**10,313.3**	**8,144.2**

Source: Investment Co-ordinating Board (Badan Koordinasi Penanaman Modal), 1995.

Australia's position as a foreign investor is also worth noting. As can be noted from Table 4.10, with reference to Indonesia's total approved foreign investment, up to December 1994 the cumulative approved Australian investment was 1,587.1 billion rupiah (A$1 equalled 1,718.7 rupiah at the end of 1995), which represented 1.7 per cent of Indonesia's total approved foreign investment. Australian businesses can contribute in a range of areas. Telecommunications, for example, is a likely winner: given Indonesia's population and emerging purchasing power, its demand for telephone lines is enormous. Another example is life insurance, which analysts estimate to be growing at 30 per cent per year. Due to the strong economic growth, more Indonesians will be able to afford overseas travel, and tourism therefore has great potential.

Table 4.10   Total foreign investment in Indonesia from January 1967 to December 1994

Place	US$ million
United States	4,650.1
Rest of America	799.9
Europe	
Belgium	294.5
France	466.8
Germany	2,058.2
Netherlands	2,764.3
United Kingdom	5,644.0
Switzerland	643.3
The rest of Europe	1,440.4
Asia	
Japan	15,665.4
Hong Kong	12,005.0

Table 4.10 continues.

Table 4.10 (continued)

Place	US$ million
Malaysia	598.1
Philippines	50.7
Singapore	5,568.6
South Korea	5,448.5
Taiwan	6,570.4
Thailand	110.8
Rest of Asia	556.2
Australia	1,587.1
Rest of the world	24,740.4
Total	**92,379.1**

Source: Biro Pusat Statistik, *Statistik Indonesia*, various issues.

Foreign trade

During the 1990s the total value of Indonesia's imports has increased significantly, as indicated in Table 4.11. This is due to the rising demand for manufacturing goods, chemicals, raw materials and food. The imported value of fuel, however, has decreased. In 1995 the value of imports was 26.8 per cent higher than that in 1994: it rose from US$32.0 billion to US$40.6 billion.

Exports, increased from US$40.1 billion in 1994 to US$45.4 billion in 1995 and the foreign-exchange reserves were thereby significantly raised. In January 1993, foreign-exchange reserves increased by 1.4 per cent, and at the end of 1992 a 17.7 per cent increase over 1991 was recorded. The increase in exports, mainly in non-oil and gas products, was 27.6 per cent, whereas the figure for oil and gas exports dropped by 2.1 per cent. Excluding crude oil and gas, the balance of trade was at a deficit of US$1.9 billion. However, if crude oil and gas are included, the surplus was about US$6.7 billion.

Table 4.11   Indonesia's trade, 1986 to 1995

Year	US$ billion		Balance of trade
	Exports	Imports	
1986	14.8	10.7	4.1
1987	17.1	12.4	4.7
1988	19.2	13.2	6.0
1989	22.2	16.4	5.8
1990	25.7	21.8	3.9
1991	29.1	25.9	3.2
1992	34.0	27.3	6.7
1993	36.8	28.3	8.5
1994	40.1	32.0	8.1
1995	45.4	40.6	4.8

Source: Biro Pusat Statistik, *Statistik Indonesia*, various issues.

Indonesia's major trading partners are Japan, the United States and the ASEAN countries. Table 4.12 shows the direction of Indonesia's international trade.

Table 4.12   Indonesia's trade, 1992 and 1993

	US$ million			
	Imports		**Exports**	
Country or region	**1992**	**1993**	**1992**	**1993**
Malaysia	524.6	491.5	487.5	720.4
Thailand	344.7	244.9	352.8	484.1
Philippines	52.2	58.2	181.3	324.0
Singapore	1,670.7	1,820.7	3,313.5	3,854.4
Brunei	0.7	1.2	25.3	44.4
Hong Kong	229.0	240.7	881.1	942.1
Japan	6,013.7	5,981.8	10,760.5	11,862.0
Rest of Asia	5,496.1	5,842.1	6,566.9	7,532.8
Africa	213.2	138.7	418.9	551.3
United States	3,822.4	3,266.5	4,419.1	5,309.5
Canada	459.3	410.6	289.0	275.2
Rest of North America	488.0	616.8	328.1	512.0
Australia	1,413.0	1,321.5	746.1	778.7
Europe	6,415.9	7,352.8	5,144.2	6,037.3
Rest of the world	136.1	167.9	52.7	77.2
Total	**29,872.5**	**30,572.4**	**38,327.4**	**44,732.7**

Source: Biro Pusat Statistik, *Statistik Indonesia*, various issues.

As might be expected, Indonesia's more specific trade relations vary from country to country. The major items exported or imported can therefore be quite different even within Asia. The details of Indonesia's major export and import products, as well as each of its larger trading partners, are provided in Appendix 4.2 and Appendix 4.3.

As ASEAN's largest country and a powerful APEC player, Indonesia has a significant influence over the region's economic co-operation and trade relationships. One of these activities is its involvement in the East ASEAN growth triangle. The growth-triangle concept, whereby Indonesia and Malaysia provide land and labour, and Singapore supplies technological and managerial know-how, is manifested in an economic co-operation manufacturing project that is located on Batam Island. This project has already attracted investments from countries that are outside the region, such as the United States, Japan and Hong Kong, and is proving to be a success. Two other triangles that link Thailand, northern Malaysia and Sumatra on one side and eastern Malaysia, the Philippines and Sulawesi on the other have been proposed. In the late 1980s the average growth rate for the ASEAN countries was slightly more than 6.5 per cent, and this strong growth is expected to continue. Expansion of intra-regional trade strengthens this optimistic picture even more.

Indonesia's active involvement in intra-regional economic co-operation reflects the emphasis the country places on trade and openness.

Trade with Australia

Because it pursues an outward-oriented strategy, Indonesia, one of Australia's closest neighbours, offers Australian businesses with many opportunities. The relationship between the two neighbouring countries is at present reasonably good, and it should continue to be so. As former prime minister Paul Keating stated on 16 March 1994,

> No country is more important to Australia than Indonesia. If we fail to get this relationship right, and nurture and develop it, the whole web of our foreign relations is incomplete.

Indonesia's fundamental importance to Australia has been reconfirmed in 1996 by the Howard Liberal/National Party government.

With reference to culture, language, religion, population, political environment and economic environment, the two countries are very different. However, because of the cultural differences, tourists have been attracted from both sides. The Australian Bureau of Statistics has reported that more than 30,400 Indonesian tourists visited Australia during the first half of 1993 – an increase of more than 50 per cent – and that 88,100 Australian tourists visited Indonesia – 16 per cent more than in the same period of 1992.

In 1993 Indonesia was Australia's tenth-largest export market. For the first three years of the 1990s, Australia's exports to Indonesia increased by 27 per cent. As indicated in Table 4.13, about 2.1 per cent of Indonesia's total exports went to Australia, whereas 4.9 per cent of its total imports came from us. Trade between Indonesia and Australia therefore remains in Australia's favour.

Table 4.13   Australia's importance for Indonesia's trade, 1984–94

Year	Australia as % of total exports	Australia as % of total imports
1984	1.3	2.7
1985	0.8	4.5
1986	1.1	3.9
1987	1.8	3.6
1988	1.5	4.3
1989	1.7	5.7
1990	1.6	5.5
1991	2.2	5.3
1992	2.2	5.2
1993	2.1	4.9
1994	2.0	5.2

Source: Department of Foreign Affairs and Trade, *The APEC Region Trade and Investment.* Canberra: Australian Government Publishing Service, 1995, p 29.

With reference to specific trade, Australia's exports to Indonesia have been dominated by our traditional primary products. As indicated in Table 4.14, non-ferrous metals (notably aluminium, copper and zinc) have been the most important of these, followed by petroleum and petroleum products, textile fibres, live animals and dairy products. However, this pattern is gradually changing to include more manufactured items. Indeed, in Indonesia's booming manufacturing industry there is much higher demand for industrial inputs and capital goods in order to supplement the country's abundant labour input. Besides being an abundant source of labour, Indonesia's large population makes the country an attractive market for Australian consumer goods. Although the current per-capita GDP is only about US$650, Indonesia's fast economic growth will be responsible for creating an increasingly large group of affluent consumers who demand more and better quality imported goods. The existence of an increasing middle-income group that is at present the size of Australia's total population has been reported. Some of Indonesia's newly rich people earn an annual income of US$75,000 or more. Indonesia's dynamic growth and extended deregulation in trade, investment and financial sectors provides Australia with greater opportunity for expanding its export of goods and services (especially financial and technological consultancy services and educational services) to Indonesia. Given its comparative advantage, Australia should benefit from these new developments, because strong complementarities exist between the two countries.

Table 4.14   Australian exports to Indonesia for year ended 30 June 1995

Type of product	A$	%
Meat and meat preparations	34,526,586	1.72
Dairy products and eggs	51,480,108	2.57
Fish, shellfish and preparations thereof	1,999,897	0.10
Cereals and cereal preparations	7,450,449	0.37
Vegetables and fruit	36,540,195	1.82
Sugars, sugar preparations and honey	9,731,332	0.49
Coffee, tea, cocoa, spices and manufactures thereof	4,273,495	0.21
Feed for animals (excluding unmilled cereals)	10,045,963	0.50
Miscellaneous edible products and preparations	3,973,237	0.20
Beverages	5,608,161	0.28
Raw hides, skins and furskins	4,129,071	0.21
Crude rubber (including synthetic and reclaimed)	2,981,315	0.15
Cork and wood	2,301,886	0.11
Pulp and wastepaper	24,401,438	1.22
Textile fibres	161,651,644	8.06
Crude fertilisers	3,978,705	0.20
Metalliferous ores and metal scrap	4,225,930	0.21
Crude animal and vegetable materials, nes*	1,391,036	0.07
Coal, coke and briquettes	12,137,809	0.61
Petroleum and petroleum products	240,779,089	12.00

Table 4.14 continues.

Table 4.14 (continued)

Type of product	A$	%
Chemicals	17,074,248	0.85
Dyeing, tanning and colouring materials	27,335,072	1.36
Medicinal and pharmaceutical products	5,930,333	0.30
Essential oils, perfumes and cleansing preparations	16,307,634	0.81
Fertilisers (excluding crude)	1,523,405	0.08
Plastics	32,565,541	1.62
Chemical materials and products	22,836,966	1.14
Leather, leather manufactures and dressed furskins	6,652,751	0.33
Rubber manufactures	4,483,455	0.22
Cork and wood manufactures (excluding furniture)	5,741,013	0.29
Paper and paperboard	5,738,283	0.29
Textile yarn and fabrics	8,167,812	0.41
Non-metallic mineral manufactures, nes*	16,971,379	0.85
Iron and steel	103,447,200	5.16
Non-ferrous metals	268,134,506	13.37
Manufactures of metals	95,477,026	4.76
Power-generating machinery and equipment	14,226,280	0.71
Machinery specialised for particular industries	69,293,815	3.45
Metalworking machinery	9,399,322	0.47
Industrial equipment and machine parts	44,945,018	2.24
Office and data-processing machines	9,063,340	0.45
Telecommunications and sound-recording equipment	6,237,114	0.31
Electrical machinery and appliances	79,412,781	3.96
Road vehicles (including air-cushion vehicles)	26,129,520	1.30
Transport equipment (excluding road vehicles)	9,843,594	0.49
Prefabricated buildings and fittings	3,037,484	0.15
Furniture and similar stuffed furnishings	1,830,252	0.09
Travel goods, handbags and similar containers	1,676,604	0.08
Apparel and clothing accessories	3,545,105	0.18
Professional and scientific instruments	6,068,267	0.30
Photographic equipment, optical goods and clocks	12,662,211	0.63
Miscellaneous manufactured articles	9,733,416	0.49
Non-monetary gold (excluding gold ores and concentrates)	182,581	0.00
Confidential trade and commodities	430,260,669	21.45
Other items	6,427,899	0.32
Total exports	**2,005,969,242**	**100.00**

* not elsewhere specified
Source: ABS, *Foreign Trade Statistics*, 1995, pp 606–8.

This complementarity is also beginning to be reflected in the nature of our imports from Indonesia. Again, we have traditionally been an importer of Indonesian petroleum and petroleum products even though this is also one of our major export items. The reason is that Australia and Indonesia produce slightly different types of petroleum, each of which has its own advantages. Australia's other imports from Indonesia are more diverse: textiles and footwear, furniture, wood and wood products, coffee, tea and other food products account for much of the remainder. More specific details are provided in Table 4.15.

Table 4.15   Australian imports from Indonesia for year ended 30 June 1995

Type of product	A$	%
Fish, shellfish and preparations	9,543,281	0.80
Cereals and cereal preparations	2,527,994	0.21
Vegetables and fruit	6,560,400	0.55
Sugars, sugar preparations and honey	2,248,075	0.19
Coffee, tea, cocoa, spices and manufactures thereof	39,803,264	3.32
Feed for animals (excluding unmilled cereals)	674,011	0.06
Miscellaneous edible products and preparations	3,257,852	0.27
Tobacco and tobacco manufactures	454,217	0.04
Crude rubber (including synthetic and reclaimed)	33,357,060	2.79
Cork and wood	31,319,852	2.62
Textile fibres	3,547,534	0.30
Metalliferous ores and metal scrap	33,037,612	2.76
Crude animal and vegetable materials	930,984	0.08
Petroleum and petroleum products	378,879,229	31.63
Gas (natural and manufactured)	9,932,448	0.83
Vegetable fats and oils or preparations	18,451,198	1.54
Chemicals	8,642,282	0.72
Dyeing, tanning and colouring materials	3,671,517	0.31
Essential oils and cleansing preparations	1,868,517	0.16
Plastics	11,242,624	0.94
Chemical materials and products, nes*	3,584,074	0.30
Rubber manufactures, nes*	9,917,820	0.83
Cork and wood manufactures (excluding furniture)	54,130,528	4.52
Paper and paperboard	43,732,188	3.65
Textile yarn, fabrics and related products	147,611,471	12.32
Non-metallic mineral manufactures	27,975,211	2.34
Iron and steel	2,569,888	0.21
Non-ferrous metals	5,225,769	0.44
Manufactures of metals	13,271,189	1.11
Machinery specialised for particular industries	1,791,376	0.15
Industrial equipment and machine parts	4,898,550	0.41
Office and data-processing machines	2,118,509	0.18
Telecommunications and recording equipment	9,336,711	0.78
Electrical machinery and appliances	20,081,450	1.68
Road vehicles (including air-cushion vehicles)	4,254,877	0.36
Prefabricated buildings and fittings	1,059,845	0.09
Furniture and stuffed furnishings	44,157,561	3.69
Travel goods, handbags and similar containers	3,137,859	0.26
Articles of apparel and clothing accessories	28,522,643	2.38

Table 4.15 continues.

Table 4.15 (continued)

Type of product	A$	%
Footwear	42,436,666	3.54
Miscellaneous manufactured articles, nes*	38,124,608	3.18
Combined confidential items of trade and commodities nes*	87,407,183	7.30
Other items	2,382,252	0.20
Total imports	**1,197,678,179**	**100.00**

* not elsewhere specified
Source: ABS, *Foreign Trade Statistics*, 1995, pp 368–9.

Future prospects

No one can dispute that East Asia will become more politically and economically influential in the twenty-first century. Given that Australia's domestic market is relatively small, the world's fastest growing lucrative markets such as China and Indonesia will be the markets that provide Australian businesses with room for expansion. Although Australia has benefited from Indonesia's trade, the level of Indonesia's importance remains relatively low. Indeed, a negative perception of Indonesia may remain in force in Australia. It will be a great loss if Australia, through its business activities, fails to participate in East Asia's rapidly growing economies and to take advantage of the more open and liberalised economic policies the countries have made. Australia has to make a shift, away from its traditional links with English-speaking or European-culture-based countries and towards the Asian region.

It goes without saying that, internationally, Australia has to be cost efficient: many other countries are also looking towards the world's most populous, fastest growing region. Although it remains culturally different, Australia can be part of Asia with reference to geography and economy. It can provide the capital, expertise and technology required by these 'new' Asian economies, such as China and Indonesia. However, the existence of language and cultural barriers may prevent Australia from breaking into this dynamic and expanding market, and higher risks may also thereby be presented. This perhaps explains the reasons for Australian companies' low level of investment in Asian countries. A greater corporate presence might provide better linkages. Australia could also benefit if the northern part of the country became more involved in the newly formed East ASEAN Growth Area (Brunei, Indonesia, Malaysia and the Philippines), which is an area that has a daily regional trade value of about US$1.5 million.

In order to achieve closer economic ties with its Asian neighbours, Australia has to become more understanding about and sensitive to its neighbours' cultures, languages and ways of doing business. The risk would thereby be lowered and Australia would be able to take full advantage of these booming markets right on its doorstep. In recognition of this, immediate actions should be taken for placing more emphasis on Asian languages, Asian-culture studies and professional business-dealing skills. In order to promote Australia as a sophisticated, technologically advanced export country, in June 1994 the country launched 'Australia Today', a major trade and cultural promotion, in Indonesia. Undertaking more of this type of promotion would help generate greater business and investment contacts and strengthen links between Australia and Indonesia.

In order to attract additional foreign capital, Indonesia has deregulated foreign-investment control for some industries and joint ventures, whereby 100 per cent foreign equity has been permitted. Due to increased relaxation, investment opportunities in areas such as port developments, railways, production and transmission of power, telecommunications and the mass media were also opened. Australian companies that have the appropriate technical know-how and management expertise are therefore well placed to position themselves in this dynamic economy.

At the time of writing, Indonesia required an amount of US$330 billion in investment over the forthcoming five-year period to April 1999. In fact, the Australia and Indonesia Working Group on Trade, Industry and Investment has identified several areas – shipbuilding, power generating, construction, automotive, textiles, and clothing and footwear – for potential co-operation. The areas in which Australian companies may have a competitive edge include food, telecommunications, transport infrastructure, mining and energy, and building and construction. Moreover, Indonesia has reduced tariffs on manufacturing items, agricultural items, raw materials and capital goods. Tariffs on a wide range of food items, including wheat, have been reduced to zero. Great potential for Australian exports is thereby offered.

It is evident that the Indonesian government's outward-oriented economic policy has been a great success, and this currently strong growth could well be sustained for the rest of the 1990s. Macro-economic stability having now been achieved, Indonesia's focus should be on maintaining efficiency and improving infrastructure (having better utilities, communications and transportation) and on creating better human-resource-development programs. One of President Suharto's twenty-five year economic plan targets is to quadruple the current per-capita GDP and to achieve an average growth of 7 per cent. The increased government expenditure on infrastructure should in turn stimulate domestic sectors such as building and manufacturing. However, the government has to be careful and avoid overheating of the domestic economy. The current economic boom is already likely to add inflationary pressures. Also, because of deregulation and the increased number of financial institutions, prudential supervision cannot be neglected. Provided that in the course of its evolution the relationship between the military and the president remains stable, during the 1990s Indonesia will remain South-East Asia's largest and strongest economic force.

In recent years, Indonesia's economic liberalisation has gathered momentum. With the removal of tariffs on more than 6000 items, Australian businesses with the appropriate technical know-how and management expertise have an exciting opportunity for building trade and investment relationships with this dynamic economy. The prospect for mutually beneficial Australia–Indonesia economic relations can hardly be overstated.

REFERENCES

Anwar, Dewi Fortuna, *Indonesia in ASEAN: Foreign Policy and Regionalism*. New York: St Martin's Press, 1994.

Asian Development Bank, *Key Indicators*.

Badan Koordinasi Penamanan Modal (Investment Co-ordinating Board).

Ball, D and Wilson, H (eds), *Strange Neighbours: The Australia–Indonesia Relationship*. North Sydney: Allen & Unwin, 1991.

Bank Indonesia, *Report for the Financial Year 1993–1994*, 1994.

Biro Pusat Statistik, *Statistik Indonesia*, various issues.

Booth, A (ed), *The Oil Boom and After: Indonesian Economic Policy and Performance in the Soeharto Era*. Singapore: Oxford University Press, 1992.

Bresnan, J, *Managing Indonesia: The Modern Political Economy*. New York: Columbia University Press, 1993.

Dorling, P (ed), *Diplomasi: Australia and Indonesia's Independence*. Canberra: Australian Government Publishing Service, 1994.

Faulkner, G, *Business Indonesia: A Practical Insight into Doing Business in Indonesia*. Chatswood, New South Wales: Business & Professional Publishing, 1995.

Herderschee, H and Hughes, H, *Aid, Investment and Trade within the Australian, Indonesian and Papua New Guinean Triangle*. Nathan, Queensland: Centre for the Study of Australian–Asian Relations, 1986.

Hill, H (ed), *Indonesia's New Order: The Dynamics of Socio-economic Transformation*. Sydney: Allen & Unwin, 1994.

Hooker, M V (ed), *Culture and Society in New Order Indonesia*. Kuala Lumpur: Oxford University Press, 1993.

Institute for Economic and Financial Research, *Indonesia Capital Market Directory*, 1994.

Joint Standing Committee on Foreign Affairs, Defence and Trade, *Australia's Relations with Indonesia*. Canberra: Australian Government Publishing Service, 1993.

MacIntyre, A, *Business and Politics in Indonesia*. North Sydney, New South Wales: Asian Studies Association of Australia, in Association with Allen & Unwin, 1991.

Pangetsu, M, 'ASEAN Free Trade Area (AFTA): An Indonesian Perspective', in the *Indonesian Quarterly*, vol 23, no. 1, 1995, p 38.

Ramasamy, B, 'The ASEAN Free Trade Area: Implications for Indonesia's Imports', in *Bulletin of Indonesian Economic Studies*, vol 30, no. 2, 1994, p 149.

Schwarz, A, *A Nation in Waiting: Indonesia in the 1990s*. St Leonards, New South Wales: Allen & Unwin, 1994.

APPENDIX 4.1: *Australian and Indonesian representation*

Australian addresses

Bank Internasional Indonesia
Level 29, The Chifley Tower
2 Chifley Square
Sydney 2000, NSW, Australia
Telephone: (61 2) 9375 2168
Facsimile: (61 2) 9375 2121

Embassy of the Republic of Indonesia
8 Darwin Avenue
Yarralumla 2600, ACT, Australia
Telephone: (61 6) 250 8600
Facsimile: (61 6) 250 8666

Indonesian Trade Promotion Centre and
Indonesian Commercial Office
17th Floor, National Mutual Centre
Corner Market and York Streets
Sydney 2000, NSW, Australia
Telephone: (61 2) 9299 7741
Facsimile: (61 2) 9262 2857

Lippo Finance Australia Ltd
Level 12, Lippo House
210 George Street
Sydney 2000, NSW, Australia
Telephone: (61 2) 9251 1178
Facsimile: (61 2) 9251 1174

Indonesian addresses

Australia and New Zealand Banking Group Limited
Representative Office
17th Floor, BNI Building
Jalan Jendrel Sudirman Kav. 1
Jakarta Pusat 10220, Indonesia

Telephone: (62 21) 570 1204
Facsimile: (62 21) 570 5138

Australian Trade Commission
5th Floor, World Trade Centre
Jalan Pemuda No. 27–31
Surabaya, East Java, Indonesia
Telephone: (62 31) 519 191
Facsimile: (62 31) 519 288

Australian Trade Commissioner
Australian Embassy
3rd Floor
Jl HR Rasuna Said Kav. C15–16 Kuningan
Jakarta Selatan 12940, Indonesia
Telephone: (62 21) 522 7111
Facsimile: (62 31) 522 7103

Commonwealth Bank of Australia
11th Floor, World Trade Centre
Jalan Jendral Sudirman Kav. 29–31
Jakarta 12920, Indonesia
Telephone: (62 21) 522 4424/4425/4426
Facsimile: (62 21) 522 4427

Investment Co-ordinating Board (BKPM)
Jalan Gatot Subroto 44
Jakarta 12190, Indonesia
Telephone: (62 21) 525 2008
Facsimile: (62 21) 525 49445

National Australia Bank
9th Floor, Bank Bali Tower
Jalan Jendral Sudirman Kav. 27
Jakarta 12920, Indonesia
Telephone: (62 21) 250 0685
Facsimile: (62 21) 250 0690

Westpac Banking Corporation
9th Floor, Lippo Plaza
Jalan Jendral Sudirman No. 25
Jakarta, Indonesia
Telephone: (60 21) 520 3904
Facsimile: (60 21) 520 3893

APPENDIX 4.2: *Indonesia's major imports, by country of origin, 1993*

Country and import/s	US$ thousand
Malaysia	
Cement	6.4
Thailand	
Rice	2,545.0
Singapore	
Fertilisers	0.1
Cement	1.3
Crude petroleum	419.2
Iron and steel	9.0
Motor vehicles	0.1
Machinery	28.1
Japan	
Fertilisers	0.2
Cement	135.9
Crude petroleum	26.8
Iron and steel	131.6
Motor vehicles	107.4
Machinery	531.1
Taiwan	
Crude petroleum	5.4
South Korea	
Crude petroleum	10.8
China	
Crude petroleum	3.7
United States	
Rice	2,218
Fertilisers	0.5
Cement	74.1
Crude petroleum	109.3
Iron and steel	22.6
Motor vehicles	6.0
Machinery	216.6
Australia	
Cement	81.4
Crude petroleum	86.2
Machinery	28.9
Iron and steel	3.2
Motor vehicles	0.2
Europe	
Fertilisers	33.1
Crude petroleum	37.0
Iron and steel	24.8

APPENDIX 4.2 continues.

APPENDIX 4.2 (continued)

Country and import/s	US$ thousand
Motor vehicles	21.7
Machinery	446.6
Saudi Arabia	
Crude petroleum	101.3
Iran	
Crude petroleum	308.3
The rest of the world	
Rice	32.0
Fertilisers	38.4
Cement	418.6
Crude petroleum	96.4
Iron and steel	40.5
Motor vehicles	6.7
Machinery	674.0

Source: Biro Pusat Statistik, *Statistik Indonesia*, 1994.

APPENDIX 4.3: *Indonesia's major exports, by country of destination, 1993*

Country and export/s	US$ thousand
Malaysia	
Tobacco	519.8
Shrimp	677.6
Tin	0.2
Plywood and laminated wood	3,499.7
Fertilisers	6.4
Thailand	
Quinine, quinine crundum and quinine salt	421.8
Copper	13.7
Fertilisers	11.8
Philippines	
Petroleum and petroleum products	115.3
Gas	1.8
Fertilisers	1.6
Singapore	
Petroleum and petroleum products	210.4
Gas	5.6
Rubber	168.9
Coffee	24.1
Tea	6.4
Shrimp	47,524.8

APPENDIX 4.3 continues.

APPENDIX 4.3 (continued)

Country and export/s	US$ thousand
Pepper	19,961.8
Sawn wood	32.2
Tin	97.7
Copper	1,196.1
Weaving yarns and textiles and their products	996,882.8
Clothes	792,988.7
Plywood and laminated wood	39,923.2
Fertilisers	1.6
Hong Kong	
Gas	1.9
Shrimp	11,472.5
Pepper	0.3
Sawn wood	24.6
Copper	4,544.4
Weaving yarns and textiles and their products	182,711.2
Clothes	14,594.0
Plywood and laminated wood	199,542.9
Japan	
Petroleum and petroleum products	6,438.5
Gas	3,314.7
Rubber	38.7
Coffee	65.5
Tobacco	1,614.3
Shrimp	597,415.7
Sawn wood	154.3
Copper	352,673.4
Weaving yarns and textiles and their products	88,219.5
Clothes	349,335.0
Plywood and laminated wood	1,582,436
Palm oil	0.8
Taiwan	
Petroleum and petroleum products	263.0
Gas	365.2
Swan wood	37.6
Plywood and laminated wood	293,347.7
South Korea	
Gas	629.3
Sawn wood	13.2
Copper	36,823.3
Plywood and laminated wood	649,182.6
Petroleum and petroleum products	603.2
China	
Coffee	0.1
Fertilisers	13.6

APPENDIX 4.3 continues.

APPENDIX 4.3 (continued)

Country and export/s	US$ thousand
United States	
Petroleum and petroleum products	825.8
Gas	24.0
Rubber	534.5
Coffee	27.8
Tea	11.3
Tobacco	18,060.2
Shrimp	100,542.0
Pepper	6,352.0
Sawn wood	4.1
Weaving yarns and textiles and their products	154,971.2
Clothes	1,058,833.9
Plywood and laminated wood	408,242.4
Palm oil	6.9
Canada	
Weaving yarns and textiles and their products	32,675.4
Palm oil	0.4
Australia	
Petroleum and petroleum products	708.7
Tea	10.1
Shrimp	2,675.5
Quinine, quinine crundum and quinine salt	106.7
Weaving yarns and textiles and their products	6,951.5
Clothes	21,421.5
Europe	
Rubber	101.5
Coffee	119.7
Tea	36.8
Tobacco	33,218.0
Shrimp	54,128.7
Pepper	9,587.9
Quinine, quinine crundum and quinine salt	535.2
Sawn wood	90.1
Tin	12.7
Weaving yarns and textiles and their products	502,445.8
Clothes	1,095,744.7
Plywood and laminated wood	254,520.5
Palm oil	364.7
Saudi Arabia	
Weaving yarns and textiles and their products	167,664.7
Clothes	254,994.1
Plywood and laminated wood	148,597.1
Rest of the world	
Petroleum and petroleum products	1,943.7

APPENDIX 4.3 continues.

APPENDIX 4.3 (continued)

Country and export/s	US$ thousand
Gas	8.1
Rubber	153.1
Coffee	154.6
Tea	40.1
Tobacco	16,779.6
Shrimp	8,995.3
Pepper	4,170.9
Quinine, quinine crundum and quinine salt	1,204.2
Sawn wood	5.1
Tin	0.3
Weaving yarns and textiles and their products	886,483.6
Copper	233,186.7
Clothes	462,572.8
Plywood and laminated wood	848,976.3
Palm oil	271.7
Fertilisers	112.0

Source: Biro Pusat Statistik, *Statistik Indonesia*, 1994.

APPENDIX 4.4: *Australia's strategic priorities for Indonesian trade and investment*

- Expand Australia's exports of manufactures, particularly industrial and aviation supplies and equipment (building and construction, defence and mining).
- Expand Australia's exports of primary products, particularly wheat, cotton, fruit, live cattle, horticulture, dairy foods and other processed foods. Promote opportunities for wool, hides and skins.
- Promote Indonesia's awareness of and improve access conditions for Australia's services exports (financial; telecommunications; professional, including legal and medical; construction; engineering; airport development; power generation and transmission, and water supply; environmental technology; education, and tourism).
- Promote protection of Australia's intellectual-property-right holders (for technology transfers and copyright on sound recordings).
- Promote expansion of Australia's investment in Indonesia, particularly through joint ventures.
- Promote expansion and diversification of Indonesia's investment in Australia.
- In Australia, promote awareness of bilateral trade and investment opportunities and of business practices in Indonesia.
- Promote awareness in Indonesia of Australia's technological capabilities and of its research and development capabilities.

- Promote Australia–Indonesia collaboration in the commercial application of science and technology.
- Develop strategic complementarities in food and fibre processing.
- Promote Australia as a destination for Indonesian tourists.

Source: Department of Foreign Affairs and Trade, *Australian Trade and Investment Development*. Canberra: Australian Government Publishing Service, 1994, p 82.

5

Malaysia

Anita Doraisami

Introduction

Malaysia's modern and vibrant economy is quickly acquiring NIC status. Given the country has had seven years of growth rates of about 8 per cent, it is one of the world's fastest growing economies. The pace is observable, particularly in the thriving capital, Kuala Lumpur. Since 1957 when it became independent, Malaysia has been successfully transforming from a commodity-based economy to a manufacturing one. It has also succeeded in reducing poverty among its multi-ethnic population of about nineteen million. These successes have been achieved with political stability. This chapter examines the success story in more detail by addressing Malaysia's geographic setting, political history, economic and financial development, incentives for foreign investment, foreign trade, and Australian trading relations and their prospects for more growth.

The setting

Malaysia is located in South-East Asia in the 'square' formed by the longitudes of 100 degrees east and 120 degrees east and the latitudes of the equator and 7 degrees north. Its land mass comprises two parts: Peninsular Malaysia, at the southern tip of the Asian mainland, and East Malaysia, on the northern part of the island of Borneo.

Peninsular Malaysia has an area of 131,598 square kilometres and extends 740 kilometres from the Thai border in the north, to the causeway to the island of Singapore in the south. At its widest point, the peninsula measures 322 kilometres. East Malaysia, which is 644 kilometres to the east of the peninsula, across the South China Sea, has an area of 198,160 square kilometres.

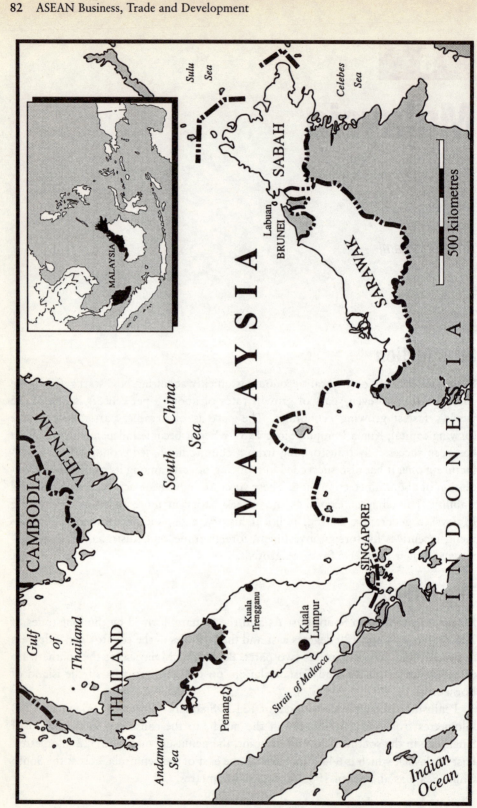

Political history

On 31 August 1957 the country then known as Malaya achieved independence from Britain. The head of the Alliance Party, Tunku Abdul Rahman, was named as the first prime minister. The Alliance Party comprised the Malay community (the indigenous people, known as *bumiputeras*, or 'sons of the soil'), through the United Malay National Organisation (UMNO), the Chinese community, through the Malaysian Chinese Association (MCA), and the Indian community, through the Malaysian Indian Congress (MIC). The last two ethnic groups had arrived during the late-nineteenth century and the twentieth century due to British encouragement of them as tin- and rubber-industry workers. The Chinese soon established themselves as the major entrepreneurial community and today comprise almost 35 per cent of the population; the Indian community comprises another 10 per cent.

While self-government was evolving in Malaya, Singapore was also moving towards independence. The prospect of an independent Singapore (which was and is predominantly Chinese) caused some concern among some of Malaya's political leaders who feared that the delicate racial balance would be tilted in favour of the Chinese.

Consequently Tunku Abdul Rahman promoted the idea of creating a federation that would incorporate Malaya, Singapore, Brunei, Sarawak and Sabah in the hope that the Malay-speaking Muslim population of these territories would serve to balance Singapore's Chinese. On 16 September 1963, the Federation of Malaysia was born, comprising Malaya, Singapore, Sarawak and Sabah. Brunei with its large oil reserves declined to join. In August 1965, Singapore left the Federation and subsequently became an independent republic.

Malaysia's delicate racial balance – Chinese running of the economy and Malay political domination – held firm for most of the 1960s. However, this *modus operandi* was shattered when violence erupted after the May 1969 federal election was held. In that election, the MCA lost ground to two Chinese opposition parties that sought to end the Malay political domination. The 'victory party' held in the streets of Kuala Lumpur degenerated into a bloody riot in which hundreds of people died. In the aftermath, the Constitution was suspended and it became illegal to openly discuss Malays' special rights, Islam's status as the official religion or the sultans' powers. The ruling Alliance Party then expanded to take in seven opposition parties, including the fundamentalist Party Islam Semalaysia (PAS), and was renamed the National Front (Barisan Nasional).

In the book *A Question of Class: Capital, the State and Uneven Development in Malaya*, Jomo asserts that the riots provided the opportunity for the so-called 'new turks' within the ruling party to replace the incumbent prime minister, Tunku Abdul Rahman, with Tun Abdul Razak. Dominated by the UMNO, the National Front quelled much of the social tension. Razak went on to introduce his twenty-year New Economic Policy (NEP), which was designed to eradicate poverty and eliminate identification of race with economic function.

When Razak died, in 1976, he was replaced by then deputy prime minister Datuk Hussein Onn. The new prime minister faced two major crises during his first year in office: the resurgence of communist-guerrilla activities in northern Peninsular Malaysia and the expulsion of the fundamentalist PAS from the National Front.

When Hussein Onn resigned due to poor health, in July 1981, he was replaced by then deputy prime minister Datuk Seri Dr Mahathir Mohamad. Dr Mahathir has remained prime minister since that time. He had a landslide victory in April 1995 and has retained a comfortable two-thirds majority in the parliament – a prerequisite for making amendments to the Constitution. The National Front is in power in every state except the traditionally maverick Kelantan, which is ruled by a highly conservative Islamic government led by the PAS. The National Front and its predecessor, the Alliance Party, have therefore held a majority in parliament as a result of every election since Independence.

Dr Mahathir has not been reticent about his plans for Malaysia. Soon after gaining office he launched his 'Look East' policy, in which the economic achievements of Japan and South Korea were extolled and Malaysians were exhorted to be efficient and hardworking and to emulate the East Asian model. Mahathir also spearheaded the drive into heavy industry, and launching of the national car, the Proton Saga, is widely believed to have been his long-cherished dream. He has also presided over comprehensive and broad-ranging privatisation programs and fostered the concept of 'Malaysia Inc.': close co-operation between the government and the private sector. This approach is evident in the range of consultative mechanisms that exist between business, the Ministry of Finance and the Ministry of International Trade and Industry. Furthermore, the Malaysian Business Council's meetings include both key government and key private-sector groups.

More recently, Mahathir has been associated with 'Vision 2020', whereby developed-country status is boldly aimed to be achieved by the year 2020. Mahathir has also taken Malaysia to new frontiers in international affairs by promoting the developing countries' interests at international forums and by hosting several significant international meetings, including the 1989 Commonwealth Heads of Government Meeting (CHOGM) and the forthcoming (1998) Commonwealth Games and APEC meetings.

Malaysia has been active in establishing the Commission of the South and pioneered within the establishment of the 'Group of 15' (G15) developing countries to advance south–south co-operation. It has also supported developing countries' calls for a new international economic order, particularly as a member of the Cairns Group of countries that seek liberalisation of agricultural trade. In recent years, Malaysia has increasingly emphasised its relations with the Organisation of the Islamic Conference, the non-aligned movement, and countries in the wider South Pacific region. Finally, it upholds the South Pacific's zone of peace, freedom and neutrality, whereby great-power rivalry is sought to be excluded from the South-East Asia region.

It is ASEAN, though, that is fundamentally important for Malaysia's foreign policy and that forms the basis of the country's approach to the region's independence and resilience. At the 1991 ASEAN summit, Malaysia presented its proposal for an East Asia Economic Caucus (EAEC). In that caucus, ASEAN and other East Asian economies are sought to be included but the United States, Canada, Australia and New Zealand are palpably sought to be excluded in preference to APEC – giving rise to its nickname, 'the caucus without the Caucasians'.

Although, in the 'Third World', Mahathir is viewed as being a 'champion of the underdog' and something of a hero, he has recently emerged as being a vocal critic of the West on matters of the environment, protection and human rights. Some in the West have retaliated by describing Malaysia as a 'modified democracy' – a place in which democratic practices are permitted only as long as they do not actually undermine the ruling elite and are quickly modified or abolished when elite interests are threatened (see Crouch's article 'Authoritarian Trends, the UMNO Split and the Limits to State Power'). Also, the Western media frequently makes references to human-rights infringements, lack of freedom of the press, curtailment of the judiciary, and 'money politics' (see Mills's article, 'Malaysia').

Anwar Ibrahim, the man who is destined to succeed seventy-year-old Dr Mahathir in the prime-ministerial stretched Proton Saga, has called for more dialogue and rapprochement between East and West and appears to have many admiring acolytes. Ellis enthuses in the article 'Mahathir's Busy Year':

> Mobile Anwar is all things to all people; action man on jet-ski, pious Muslim, super salesman to foreign investors, the safe pair of hands for stewarding the economy.

Anwar has not always been viewed in this way, however. A one-time Islamic firebrand who was gaoled under Malaysia's draconian Internal Security Act, he has had close links with PAS's outspoken leaders, particularly its president. He is undeniably an asset for a government that frequently asserts its Islamic credentials while seeking to convince both non-Malays and foreign investors that in Malaysia, Islam is a moderate force that is compatible with economic development. This has been achieved through linking the conservative social values of frugality and diligence with economic productivity and through developing Islamic banking practices.

During 1994 the government sought to ensure it is viewed as being a tolerant Islamic-majority State. It has banned the messianic Islamic movement Al Arqam and blocked PAS's attempts to establish Islamic-fundamentalist laws in Kelantan. Also, concern that ethnic tension will emerge as a source of instability in the short to medium term, hardly exists, due to rapid growth including redistribution. Malays are now included in all areas of the economy, and a generation of so-called 'new Malays' are now senior corporate figures and successful entrepreneurs. Political stability is guaranteed for the future.

Economic development

In Malaysia, planning commenced during the 1950s through the simple philosophy of equating revenue with expenditure. More sophisticated techniques evolved during the 1960s when the development program was directed towards growth through infrastructural and rural developments (see Lim's article 'Malaysian Development Planning'). The commonly accepted reason for the making of this decision relates to the political influence of the rural, mainly Malay and indigent population. As Rudner explains in the book *Nationalism, Planning and Economic Modernisation in Malaysia: The Politics of Beginning Development*, under the Malaysian Constitution rural areas are given a disproportionately large representation in parliament, the rural Malays, due to their dominant political franchise, effectively determined the government of the day.

When planning commenced, 80 per cent of Malays resided in rural areas and two-thirds of them were below the poverty line, earning incomes that were only half the average income of non-Malays (see Bussink's article 'Employment and Income Distribution in Peninsular Malaysia'). In the article 'The Economic, Political and Social Background for Development Planning in Malaysia', Lim asserts that in the 1960s planning involved application of decentralised, market-based policies in a dual economy, whereby an advanced, monetised export sector (mainly rubber and tin mining) operated alongside but independently of a mainly subsistence agricultural sector. Due to lack of spread effects from the modern sector, some drastic and immediate changes in the economy's structure were warranted, particularly because this demarcation paralleled ethnic divisions. In spite of high growth rates, unemployment rose and the incidence of poverty increased.

The serious shortcomings involved in pursuing these policies, especially in a multiracial country in which economic inequality occurs along ethnic lines, became evident in May 1969 when serious race riots broke out. The civil disturbance resulted in a new development ideology, the New Economic Policy (NEP), which became the blueprint for all subsequent development plans from 1970 to 1990. The NEP's ultimate goal was to foster national unity through eradication of poverty, regardless of race, and to restructure society in order to eliminate identification of race with economic function and geographic location.

In operational terms, the target was reduction of the incidence of poverty from the 1970 level of 49 per cent of households to 17 per cent by 1990. In the case of restructuring goals, four areas were given specific attention: reduction of income imbalance among various ethnic groups and regions, restructuring of employment patterns (by sector and by occupation), ownership and control of corporate-sector limited companies' share capital, and creation of a *bumiputera* commercial and industrial community.

With reference to the firstmentioned area, the government's main concern was raising the income level of *bumiputeras* to match those of non-*bumiputeras* and raising the less developed states' income levels through implementing various public-sector activities and programs. In terms of the second area, operational targets for employment, by sector, a pattern of employment that reflected the population's racial make-up – 54 per cent Malay and other indigenous peoples, 35 per cent Chinese, 10 per cent Indians, 1 per cent others – was called for. In terms of the targets for employment, by occupation, a greater share of *bumiputera*, particularly in the higher earning professional and technical group, was envisaged, in order to reflect the *bumiputeras*' share in the total population.

The third main restructuring area was increasing the share of Malay corporate-sector ownership to at least 30 per cent (compared with the 1970-level 2.4 per cent share). The share that was owned and operated by other Malaysians was targeted to increase from 34.3 per cent to 40 per cent, whereas the share that was owned and operated by foreigners was to drop from 63.3 per cent to 30 per cent.

The fourth restructuring objective was to increase *bumiputeras*' ownership of and participation in non-corporate economic activities, particularly in the small-scale commercial and service sectors. This was to be achieved through proprietorships and partnerships whereby, together with the anticipated increase in the corporate sector, the way would be paved for establishment of the *bumiputera* commercial and industrial community.

These changes were planned over a twenty-year Outline Perspective Plan (OPP) period from 1971 to 1990. The Second Malaysia Plan was the first in a series of medium-term developmental plans to be formulated and implemented over this period. The plan targets were to be achieved not through a disruptive redistribution of the 'cake' but through enlarging the 'cake'. The emphasis placed on growth was intended to ensure that no particular group experienced any feeling of deprivation.

In order to achieve the first NEP objective – eradication of poverty – the strategy embarked on was acceleration of land-development schemes, guaranteed-minimum-price schemes for many commodities, improved provision of agricultural extension services, job-creation schemes for unemployed people, and greater provision of social overhead.

In order to achieve the NEP's restructuring objective – *bumiputeras*' participation in the modern sector and creation of a *bumiputera* bourgeoisie – ethnic employment and education quotas were instituted. Several special agencies that used public funds for investing in *bumiputera* enterprises and that provided a range of technical and consultancy services were also established. Furthermore, in the article 'The Role of the State in Economic Development and Theory: The East Asian Experience and the Malaysian Case', Brown asserts that the State-controlled banking system operated a quota system whereby *bumiputera* enterprises were given preferential access to funds.

The NEP was a paradigm shift in that development was defined in terms of growth and an equitable distribution of wealth. A greater role for the public sector was envisaged for meeting the NEP's objectives. Accordingly, development planning became increasingly interventionist, thereby resulting in the rise of Stateist capitalism in Malaysia. For the NEP's first 15 years, Malaysia remained a largely 'traditional' developing country that exported raw materials and built up heavy industry with large-scale State involvement. In 1985–86, a brief but serious growth hiatus, which was caused by a collapse in the prices of Malaysia's main export commodities (tin, rubber and crude oil), sparked a marked shift in policy.

In response to economic crisis, the State, which was suffering plummeting revenues due to recession, commenced an extensive privatisation program and adopted the strategy of emulating the East Asian NICs. Increased foreign investment in manufacturing was courted through creation of attractive incentive packages. This quest proved highly successful: a massive tenfold increase in investment occurred between

1986 and 1991. However, investors were also attracted by Malaysia's political stability, good infrastructure, abundant raw materials and cheap but well-educated labour force.

In the article 'A Vision for the Future', Liden and Sargent maintain Malaysia quickly recovered from the mid-1980s crisis and that on the basis of easy credit, investor confidence and optimism in the Asia–Pacific region it achieved high growth rates and massive structural transformation. In 1987 it reached a symbolic milestone in its transition towards being an industrialised nation when manufacturing surpassed agriculture as the major sector of its economy. Underscoring the country's rapid success has been its ability to reduce the incidence of poverty from its 1970 level of 50 per cent to its level at present of 15 per cent. The pace and extent of poverty reduction has been unprecedented in any country since the 1940s.

The NEP expired in 1990 and was replaced in 1991 with the National Development Policy (NDP). The policy is embodied in the Sixth Malaysia (1991–95) Plan and the Second Outline Perspective Plan (OPP2) 1991–2000. Although the NDP upholds the basic framework of its predecessor, it places much more emphasis on growth through the private sector.

The National Development Policy's spirit seems to have been captured in the concept of Wawasan 2020, or Vision 2020. The local media coined this term in order to summarise the gist of a paper that Prime Minister Dr Mahathir delivered to the Malaysian Business Council, in which he outlined his hope to have a fully developed industrial Malaysia by the year 2020.

'Vision 2020' is now painted in giant letters on two-storey posters plastered on public buildings. It is written in floral letters for National Day parades and has become a household word in Malaysia. Apart from spawning a huge growth in the number of optical aids shops named 'Vision 2020', it has become a central reference point for the whole nation by usefully putting the people into future mode.

Vision 2020's goal is to have an industrialised Malaysia the citizens of which will have purchasing power equivalent to that of US citizens. This means the national income has to be doubled every 10 years: an eightfold increase by 2020. In other words, the country has to have a 7 per cent per year growth rate, year after year, for the next three decades.

The challenges that confront Vision 2020 are enormous. The momentum involved in national income growth will become increasingly difficult simply by nature of the fact that economies slow as they mature. More formidable challenges are likely to stem from transforming the relatively fragile manufacturing sector as well as from changing the destination of manufactured exports.

Malaysia's manufactured-export performance has been heavily influenced by the country's relative competitiveness with neighbouring East Asian countries. Buffeted by currency appreciation, rising labour costs and the US's withdrawal of the generalised system of preferences (GSP), the NICs have been forced to relocate because of increasing foreign investment in the ASEAN countries.

In this context, Malaysia has been extremely successful in attracting foreign investment from East Asia through having a bevy of investment incentives, including tax, tariff and financial incentives. However, as labour markets tighten and wages rise, the country is likely to be undercut by a new generation of lower cost producers. With reference to East Asian investment, Southern China and Vietnam are now emerging as an attractive destination for investment. If this trend continues, Malaysia may not be in a position to sustain the high rate of capital flow.

Furthermore, although manufactured exports now account for more than 70 per cent of total exports, Malaysia's manufacturing base is somewhat narrow. It is dominated by two large sectors: electrical and electronics, and textiles. Increasing development of technology, particularly in the electrical-and-electronics sector, will mean many labour-intensive processes will become automated. The need for cheap labour could thereby be reduced, and developed countries' competitiveness could be enhanced, even in traditionally labour-intensive industries. It is therefore urgent that the manufacturing base be diversified.

Equally urgent is the need to diversify manufactured-export destinations. In order to circumvent the constraints imposed through the existence of a small market, Malaysia adopted an outward-looking industrial policy. Although the NICs' success might indicate this strategy is worth pursuing, the strategy may be a decade too late. The NICs were aided due to the preferential access treatment the US was according at the time and due to the generally more benign world trading climate. The US's current economic woes, particularly its current-account deficit, suggest increased penetration of US markets is highly unlikely and that Malaysia's GSP preference given by the US is likely to be withdrawn as the country's GDP rises. At present, the US is the destination of more than 25 per cent of Malaysia's manufactured exports. There is an urgent need to seek out new export markets, given that bilateralism and protectionism are undergoing a resurgence.

The Malaysian manufacturing sector's structural weaknesses will also have to be remedied. The manufacturing sector's main stimulus has been inflow of foreign capital and the public sector's active intervention through direct equity and government involvement in large industrial projects. A major weakness in this structure is its notable lack of technology transfer or economic linkages, whether backwards or forwards, with reference to small-scale and medium-scale industries (SMIs).

This lack of linkages has led to a dualistic structure that is characterised by transnational and foreign firms that are located in modern enclaves (free-trade zones) and SMIs that are dominated by domestic investors. Compared with transnational companies, SMIs tend to be characterised by inadequate capital, managerial, marketing and production capabilities, and a low level of use of modern technology. The need exists to upgrade Malaysian SMIs and facilitate technology transfer if Malaysia is to gain NIC status before 2000.

In this period, the major macro-economic policy challenges arise from the problems involved in having a high growth rate. As production accelerates, several characteristics are becoming more evident: shortage of both skilled and unskilled indigenous labour, infrastructure bottlenecks, inflation, escalation of foreign debt, and lack of research and development. Of much greater concern, though, are environmental issues. As Jomo states in the article 'Beyond the New Economic Policy? Malaysia in the Nineties', the rate at which limited non-renewable resources, particularly forestry and petro-leum reserves, are being exhausted for a temporary acceleration in economic growth, is worrisome, as is the lack of attention given to occupational health and safety standards, waste disposal and environment hazards caused by environmentally irresponsible investors.

Although several barriers have to be surmounted, we have every reason to be optimistic that Vision 2020 will be achieved. Foremost among the reasons are Malaysia's high savings–investment ratios, natural resources wealth and early success in moving on to manufacturing's higher value areas. Equally important is the fact that the government and the new generation of leaders have recognised the economy's shortcomings and are systematically addressing the problems through implementing the Sixth Malaysia Plan. Furthermore, Malaysia is playing a leading role in fostering greater economic co-operation in one of the world's fastest growing regions, through its association with AFTA. Although AFTA is at present committed to having free trade between ASEAN's member countries within 15 years, every indication exists that this timeframe will be shortened if the need emerges. In Malaysia, intra-ASEAN trade-and-growth triangles may increasingly become a path to prosperity. They have been responsible for driving down costs (particularly transaction costs) and may be increasingly used as a means of raising productivity, thereby enabling Malaysia to compete with countries that have lower labour costs. Growth triangles are being developed in order to take advantage of the complementarities that exist between neighbouring countries, in response to the increasingly evident gaps between labour costs, capital flows, land and technology. Malaysia now has the potential to be involved in triangles that incorporate Thailand, Singapore, Indonesia and the Philippines.

Although the road towards achieving the 'holy grail' of 'NIC-dom' will be a long and winding one, it is almost certain Malaysia will join the ranks of the NICs by the turn of the century.

In Malaysia in 1970 (the year the NEP was proclaimed), poverty was overwhelmingly rural in terms of location and Malay in terms of ethnicity. Although this remains true, the situation of large growth of economic output has been accompanied with remarkable progress in reducing the incidence of absolute poverty. In Peninsular Malaysia between 1970 and 1993, the incidence of poverty fell from about half the population to 10.5 per cent. This rate corresponds to a fall in the total number of poor households from 829,300 to 517,200. Rural poverty decreased from 58.7 per cent to 14.4 per cent of households, urban poverty from 21.3 per cent to 4.4 per cent. The urban–rural poverty ratio fell from 2.14 in 1970 to 1.75 in 1993.[1]

In 1970, furthermore, 74 per cent of Malays, 26 per cent of Chinese and 39 per cent of Indians were living in poverty, whereas in 1990 the corresponding figures were 23.8 per cent, 5.5 per cent and 8 per cent. This resulted in a decrease in the Chinese–Malay[2] poverty ratio, from 2.25 to 1.78, and in the Indian–Malay[3] ratio, from 1.75 to 1.29.

The government succeeded in many ways in achieving poverty eradication targets and, in some cases, in overachieving them. This was accomplished through having massive increases in both government-sector and private-sector employment by way of quotas and targets, and through having subsidies for education, agriculture and housing. However, this success has been won at a cost: intra-ethnic income inequality has been exacerbated, particularly within the Malay community, between the so-called new-Malay entrepreneurs, who benefited greatly from the NEP and rural dwellers.

Concern is now focused on removing hard-core poverty regardless of ethnicity. Concern also exists about disparities in per-capita GDP among the various states. For example, in 1993, whereas state GDP per capita as a percentage of the national average was 1.46 in Selangor, it was a paltry 0.37 in Kelantan. So that this problem would be addressed, regional development strategies that were outlined in the Sixth Malaysia Plan include incentives for firms to locate in less developed regions and in growth triangles, and development of six specialisation zones in these two areas for specific industry groups.

The agricultural sector used to be the Malaysian economy's 'engine of growth'. Due to the runaway success of Malaysia's manufacturing sector, however, agriculture's contribution to overall GDP has diminished. As Table 5.1 indicates, in 1994 agriculture was estimated to account for about 15 per cent. It makes up about the same percentage of export volume. It employs about a quarter of the workforce, though. In the article 'New Techniques Needed', Cooke argues the government has maintained its commitment to the agricultural sector because more than half the agricultural workers are *bumiputeras* and because agricultural policy dovetailed well with the government's overall aims in poverty eradication.

Table 5.1 Malaysia's GDP, by sector: 1955, 1965, 1975 and 1985, and 1990–94

	1955	1965	1975	1985	1990	1991	1992	1993	1994*
					% of GDP				
Agriculture	40.2	31.5	27.7	20.8	18.6	17.2	16.6	15.9	14.8
Mining	6.3	9.0	4.6	10.5	9.7	9.2	8.7	8.0	7.5
Manufacturing	8.2	10.4	16.4	19.7	26.8	28.1	28.9	30.1	31.5
Construction	3.0	4.5	3.8	4.8	3.6	3.8	3.9	4.0	4.2
Services	42.3	44.6	47.5	44.2	42.6	43.3	43.8	44.4	44.6
Less Imputed Bank Service Charges, plus import duties	–	–	–	–	–1.3	–1.6	–1.9	–2.4	–2.6

*The 1994 figures are estimates only.
Source: Malaysian Ministry of Finance, 1995.

Over the past 20 years, the main policy thrust has been massive supporting of smallholders and sponsoring of State farms. Either through ownership restrictions or financial constraints, the old foreign-owned plantation companies have declined in importance. By 1992, smallholder units were responsible for more than 70 per cent of rubber production. However, the government now admits that the heavily subsidised smallholders and the State farm systems have been inefficient and excessively bureaucratic.

The Sixth Malaysia Plan states agriculture has reached a watershed and emphasises economies of scale and need for improved productivity and marketing. The government proposes a return to estate-type structures whereby equity-holding smallholders would be consolidated into private, corporate entities. The need to improve production techniques is crucial for combating acute labour shortages that are occurring even though there is heavy reliance on foreign labour. In spite of the agricultural sector's decline, Malaysia remains the world's leading palm-oil producer and its third-largest rubber producer.

High economic growth rates and rapid industrialisation have led to severe environmental degradation. In industrial and heavy-traffic areas, particularly the Klang Valley, air quality is a source of concern. Increasing affluence has led to great expansion of car ownership, and the resultant smog and noise pollution now present a health hazard. In Malaysia, though, unlike neighbouring Singapore, the government is unwilling to curtail car ownership because of its support for the local car industry. Some hope exists, however, that the light-rail transit and the suburban network of electric-powered trains will aid easing of the problem.

According to the Sixth Malaysia Plan, in urban areas, lack of understanding exists of the environmental hazards of having unorganised waste disposal. This is especially the case with reference to wrappers, packaging materials and domestic refuse, a substantial proportion of which are plastics or aluminium based and are neither biodegradable nor recyclable. Other concerns are based on open burning and management of toxic and hazardous wastes.

River-water quality has also deteriorated, due to its being polluted with heavy metals such as mercury, with industrial and domestic discharge, with untreated domestic sewage and animal wastes, and in watercourses, with silt. Coastal and marine water remain contaminated with oil traces. Pollution is also rapidly threatening the tourism sector: beach resorts such as Penang and Port Dickson have become unsafe as recreational beaches or recreational watersport locations.

The government's responses have included public awareness campaigns, reafforestation programs, promotion of use of biodegradable and recyclable products, increasing of research and development projects in order to produce safer processes and products, and increasing the use of legislation in order to control pollution. The general idea that growth is to be placed above the environment unfortunately persists, though.

Due to the consistently high growth rates that have been occurring since 1988, inflationary pressures have increasingly been placed on the economy. The government's track record in this area nevertheless remains excellent. When in 1992 inflation peaked at 4.7 per cent as indicated in Table 5.2, a special prime-minister-chaired Cabinet committee on inflation was set up. The prime minister has argued that with the support of all sectors, Malaysia should set a target of zero inflation.

Table 5.2   Malaysia's real GDP growth and inflation: 1960–70, 1970–80, 1980–85, 1986–90, and 1991–94

					%			
	1960–70	1970–80	1980–85	1986–90	1991	1992	1993	1994
Real GDP growth	6.5	7.9	5.7	6.7	8.7	7.8	8.3	8.7
Annual inflation	0.9	5.9	4.7	2.0	4.4	4.7	3.9	4.5

Source: Bank Negara Malaysia, *Quarterly Economic Bulletin*, various issues.

In January 1994, Bank Negara Malaysia (Malaysia's central bank) increased the statutory reserve requirement by 1 per cent to 9.5 per cent, in order to withdraw excess liquidity from the system, which had been due to a deluge of foreign speculative funds. It also announced monetary measures for moderating liquidity growth and discouraging people from undertaking excessive currency speculation. These included having controls on foreign participation in local financial markets and curbing local banking and financial institutions' foreign-currency transactions. Most of these controls were later removed in response to a slowing of short-term capital inflows. It demonstrates, however, the extent to which the reserve bank will go in order to combat inflation.

In May 1994, the government launched an anti-inflation campaign. Two million ringgit were set aside to pay for increasing consumer awareness and anti-inflation measures such as 'fair-price shops'. Before the 1995 budget was released, 25 food staples were placed under price supervision. The 1995 budget, though, was an extremely generous 'election budget': there was not a single tax rise, only tax breaks. Company taxes fell to 30 per cent, 30 per cent of low-income Malaysians were removed from the tax net, and a bonus of one month's salary was announced for all civil servants and security-force members. This was accompanied with tariff reductions on 2600 items – mostly consumer products and foodstuffs.

The 1995 budget's expansionary stance has fuelled fears of an escalating inflation rate. This is particularly the case because Malaysia has entered a period of labour scarcity and rising wages. Wages in all sectors have surged, and concern is rightly focused on labour productivity's failure to keep pace with wage increases. The productivity gap is now estimated to be about 6 per cent. Given this scenario, and at the time of writing, the burden of the government's anti-inflation policy will largely be placed on monetary policy in 1995, for which a 4 per cent inflation rate has been forecast.

In 1994 the labour market continued to firm and the unemployment rate was pushed down to 2.9 per cent, which is considered to be over-full employment. Job creation was strongest in the manufacturing sector, which accounted for almost two-thirds of all jobs generated in that year. At present, acute shortages exist of unskilled and semi-skilled workers. This has to a large extent been temporarily solved through the employment of about a million foreign workers and thousands more illegal workers.

The government has responded to the unskilled-worker shortage by attempting to accelerate the shift from low-skill, labour-intensive activities. With reference to the skilled workforce, resources have been committed for vast increases in the quantity and quality of technical, vocational and professional workers.

Financial development

The financial structure shown in Table 5.3 is often dichotomised into the banking system (commercial banks through discount houses), which is under the direct supervision of Bank Negara Malaysia – the central bank, and the non-banking system (provident funds given to other institutions), which is under the supervision of various government departments and agencies.

Table 5.3   Malaysia's financial institutions, 1994

Institution	Number of institutions	Assets (M$ billion)
Central Bank (Bank Negara Malaysia)	1	92.8
Commercial banks	37	242.5
Finance companies	40	73.5
Merchant banks	12	23.6
Discount houses	7	9.3
Employees' Provident Fund (EPF)	1	84.5
Other provident funds	5	12.3
Life-insurance funds	18	14.9
General insurance funds	53	6.1
Development-finance institutions	7	9.7
Savings institutions	4	15.7
Other institutions*	168	43.3
TOTAL	353	628.2

* These do not include agricultural credit institutions, urban credit co-operatives, Pilgrim Management and Fund Board or venture-capital companies.
Source: Bank Negara Malaysia, as cited in *Asiamoney*, September 1995, p 26.

Like all national central banks, Bank Negara Malaysia is entrusted with the country's financial health. Its main objectives are issuing of currency and keeping of reserves, safeguarding the currency's value, acting as banker and financial adviser to the Malaysian government, promoting monetary stability and a sound financial structure, and influencing the credit situation to the country's advantage. It acts as agent in the raising and managing of the government's internal and external loans, undertakes credit operations whereby the banking system is a last-resort lender, discounts and rediscounts bills, operates in foreign exchange, and administers exchange-control regulations. The bank also supervises and regulates the activities of commercial banks, merchant banks and finance companies.

Bank Negara's role with reference to the ringgit is of particular importance to people who seek to do business with Malaysia. Although the ringgit maintained parity with the Singapore dollar and the Brunei dollar some years ago, the government has since then allowed it to decline against those currencies. As indicated in Table 5.4, the ringgit has also declined somewhat against the US dollar between 1984 and 1991. In the 1990s, though, the gradual decline has been reversed and the ringgit is now worth more: as of 15 December 1995. It took 2.54 ringgit to equal one US dollar. The ringgit's performance against the Australian dollar is quite different: the ringgit strengthened from 1988 onwards. As of 15 December 1995, it took only 1.89 ringgit to equal one Australian dollar.

Table 5.4   Malaysian ringgit against the US dollar and the Australian dollar, 1984–1995*

Year	US dollar			Australian dollar		
	High	Low	Close	High	Low	Close
1984	2.4290	2.2910	2.4290	1.7710	1.4380	1.6540
1985	2.5830	2.4190	2 4200	1.9350	1.3860	1.6090
1986	2.6260	2.5750	2.5990	1.9410	1.6430	1.8760
1987	2.5355	2.4765	2.4890	2.2350	1.7240	2.1260
1988	2.7100	2.5500	2.7100	2.2970	1.8510	2.1350
1989	2.7350	2.6895	2.6960	2.3120	1.9880	2.0770
1990	2.7270	2.6858	2.6995	2.2621	2.0680	2.0840
1991	2.7857	2.6970	2.7235	2.2069	2.0644	2.0644
1992	2.6240	2.4925	2.6140	2.0720	1.7148	1.8021
1993	2.6935	2.5455	2.6935	1.8687	1.6541	1.8283
1994	2.7660	2.5520	2.5520	2.0100	1.8577	1.9778
1995*	2.5647	2.4305	2.5430	1.9900	1.7260	1.8853

*The 1995 figures are up to 15 December of that year.
Source: Australia and New Zealand Banking Group Ltd, 1995.

Commercial banks

In Malaysia, the commercial banks are the largest and most important group of financial institutions. Since 1970 the group has experienced one of the economy's fastest growth rates: an average of 20 per cent per year over the past two decades. At present, Malaysia has 39 operating commercial banks, 23 of which are locally incorporated, 16 foreign incorporated. Combined, the commercial banks operate 716 banking offices throughout the country. Reflecting a well-developed and modern financial system, Malaysia's commercial banks offer a comprehensive range of banking services for both the corporate and the individual customer. The names and relative importance of the major locally incorporated commercial banks are shown in Table 5.5. As well as the domestic institutions listed, a number of local and foreign commercial banks exist that now offer major companies and wealthy individuals offshore banking services through subsidiaries or offshore branches that are established on Labuan, Malaysia's international, offshore financial centre.

Table 5.5   Malaysia's major domestic commercial banks, 1994

Bank*	Assets US$ million
Malayan Banking (6/94)	27,843
Bank Bumiputra Malaysia (3/95)	14,872
Public Bank (12/94)	10,938
DCB Bank (12/94)	8,028
AMMB Holdings (3/95)	7,505
United Malayan Banking Corporation (1/95)	6,510
Bank of Commerce (M) (12/94)	4,465
Perwira Affin Bank (12/94)	2,795
Southern Bank Berhad (12/94)	1,946
Oriental Bank (3/95)	1,841
Hock Hua Bank (12/94)	1,642
Pacific Bank (12/94)	1,512
Ban Hin Lee Bank (12/94)	1,372
Malaysian French Bank (12/94)	1,247
Hong Leong Bank (12/93)	1,116
Bank Islam Malaysia (6/93)	779

*The figures in parentheses indicate the month and the year ended.
Source: The *Banker*, October 1995, p 67.

Merchant banks

Licensed under the Banking Act 1973, Malaysia's 12 merchant banks contributed towards the modernisation of the financial structure in many ways, particularly through the increase in the sophistication of the money and capital markets that gradually occurred. Merchant banks specifically offer wholesale-banking services and specialised financial services. These include all aspects of corporate financing and investment banking and complement and supplement the activities and services offered by existing financial institutions. The merchant banks mainly function as intermediaries in the short-term money market and the capital markets. They also help in promotion of new investments in Malaysia in order to sustain growth of the country's production capacity. Along with commercial banks, they use their wide network of international banking contacts and foreign shareholders, and their indepth knowledge of domestic markets, to satisfy their clients' corporate needs and aspirations. So that their funding base would be broadened to service the industry more effectively, from 1982 merchant banks were allowed to accept deposits that were denominated in foreign currencies. They were also permitted to grant foreign-currency loans to residents and to aid financing of new domestic production capacity and purchase of Malaysian assets that were owned by non-residents. They were also permitted to invest in corporate equity ('venture capital', or 'seed money') – up to 10 per cent of the paid-up capital reserves in the shares of any single enterprise.

Finance companies

Licensed under the Finance Companies Act 1969, the finance companies are Malaysia's second-largest group of deposit-taking financial institutions: there are 45 of them located throughout the country.

Finance companies offer short-term to medium-term credit facilities, including hire-purchase loans, leasing, housing loans and short-term to medium-term loans for businesses. They are prohibited from accepting demand deposits, from dealing in gold or foreign exchange and from granting loans in the form of overdrafts, including unsecured loans of more than M$5000. They also offer their customers savings and fixed-deposit facilities and usually pay interest rates that are higher than the commercial banks. More than 90 per cent of money deposited with the finance companies is in the form of fixed deposits of varying maturity – from three to 60 months. It is important to note that finance companies are also playing an increasingly important role in Malaysia's development. Their lending direction has changed from the traditional role of lending to private individuals for purchase of consumer durables to more development-oriented financing, which includes loans granted to the priority sectors such as the *bumiputera* community, small-scale enterprises, and individuals, for purchase of houses.

Development-finance institutions

Development-finance institutions have been set up in order to extend promotion of development in agriculture and industry through mobilising savings and providing capital and expertise to enterprises in these two sectors.

Apart from offering medium-term and long-term capital, they specialise in providing financial, technical and managerial advice during establishment of new projects. They also participate in venture capital and underwriting and act as issuing houses for public share issues and as loan guarantors. Their role complements the major financial institutions' role of providing specialised services that are not usually provided by commercial banks and finance companies. The major institutions include the Malaysian Industrial Development Finance (MIDF) Berhad, the Agricultural Bank of Malaysia and the Development Bank of Malaysia. A number of specialised public development statutory agencies also exist that provide some types of finance, such as the Federal Land Development Authority (FELDA), the Urban Development Authority (UDA), the Rubber Industry Smallholders Development Authority (RISDA), various state economic-development corporations, and other development authorities.

Savings institutions

Savings institutions are established with the main objective of promoting and mobilising savings among the lower income groups, most of which are located in rural areas. The most important institution is the National Savings Bank (NSB). Through its extensive network of post offices and mobile postal vans, the NSB has become easily accessible to people who live in areas that are not adequately serviced by the banks and finance companies. Co-operative societies are also active in providing small-scale savings services and lending services.

Other financial services

New instruments such as currency-portfolio management, mutual funds, discretionary trading in currencies, equities and so on, as well as trust services, are entering the market. It is in this connection that the island of Labuan is to be developed as an international offshore centre.

Foreign investment

Malaysia's manufactured-export success has been underpinned by high levels of foreign investment. The government's key priorities in this area now focus on increasing domestic investors' role in the economy and on developing a more technology-intensive manufacturing sector.

Malaysians are increasingly recognising the benefits of investing abroad. The government is promoting this trend, and the largest Malaysian investment accrues to Singapore, the US, Hong Kong and Australia, in that order, and is mostly concentrated in manufacturing and services. However, in recent years a noticeable increase has occurred in the flow of investment to the US (the electronics and aviation industries) and to Japan (services sector). Although Malaysia's investment in Australia has traditionally focused on the property sector, this situation is diversifying to include significant new investment in finance, manufacturing and tourism.

Foreign investment has been critical for Malaysia's manufacturing-export success. Japan, Taiwan, Korea, the US and the UK are the country's largest foreign investors; Australia is in tenth place. Australia's investment has largely been concentrated in a few industries: textile and textile products, non-metallic mineral products, rubber, electrical and electronic products, and fabricated products. However, as Brent argues in the article 'Healthy Trade in Misunderstanding', Australia's investment is projected to increase as Australian investors recognise Malaysia's proximity, the two countries' compatible legal and administrative systems fostered through their shared British-colonial past, and the common usage of English. In the 1995 budget, significant resources were allocated to increasing the efficiency of domestic investment and to developing basic infrastructure for small-size and medium-size industries. The objective is to achieve a 60:40 ratio between domestic and foreign investment; at present the ratio is 46:54. The government has also announced full income-tax exemption for profits earned by Malaysian firms abroad if the profits are reinvested in Malaysia.

Although Malaysia continues to provide generous incentives for attracting foreign investment, the incentives are now targeted at a more sophisticated technology investor. The government is also committed to increasing the level of research-and-development expenditure to 2 per cent of GDP by 2000 in order to help achieve this objective.

Malaysia's investment incentives are designed to provide total or partial relief from payment of income and development taxes for companies investing in new enterprises or expanding new ones. The main Act that regulates these investment incentives is the Promotion of Investments Act 1986 (the POI). The Act provides a wide range of incentives for investments in the manufacturing, agricultural and tourism sectors. The tax incentives provided for under the POI include 'pioneer status', investment-tax allowances, abatements for exports, double-export-expense deductions and other incentives.

'Pioneer status'

Companies that intend to participate in 'promoted' activities or to produce 'promoted products' are eligible to apply for the 'pioneer status' incentive, which entitles them to a 'tax holiday' of five years for profits that are derived from the promoted activity or product. Dividends that are paid to shareholders out of tax-exempt income are also exempted from tax. The tax-relief period can be extended from five to ten years for manufacturing companies that produce particular promoted products and that have invested M$25 million in fixed assets (excluding land) or employ 500 full-time Malaysian workers.

Investment Tax Allowance (ITA)

A minimum percentage of the ITA is not specified in the POI. Instead, the POI provides for a percentage, as approved by the Ministry of Trade and Industry (MITI), of not more than 60 per cent of the total qualified capital expenditure (QCE) incurred. It is calculated by referring to qualifying expenditures incurred within five years of the date of approval for the ITA.

Abatements of adjusted income for exports

This incentive is for provision of tax relief for the manufacturing industry in the form of abatements of adjusted income (that is gross income *less* allowable expenses). This abatement is granted to resident manufacturing companies that export directly or through agents, products that are manufactured in Malaysia, with few exceptions. The amount of the adjusted income abated is an amount equal to 25 per cent of export sales.

Double deduction for promotion of export expenses

This incentive has the effect of granting a double deduction for approved export-promotion expenses in arriving at adjusted business income. Companies that are resident in Malaysia can claim a double deduction for all qualifying outlays and expenses that have mainly been incurred while they were seeking opportunities for, or creating or increasing demand for, export of goods or agricultural produce that were manufactured, produced, assembled, processed, packed, graded or sorted in Malaysia.

Other more specialised foreign-investment incentives include schemes for approved operational headquarters, venture-capital companies, unit trusts, the industrial adjustment allowance, the reinvestment allowance, research-and-development incentives, and the research allowance.

Other incentives

Approved-operational-headquarters program

An Approved Operational Headquarters (OHQ) company is a company the entire equity of which is held by foreign companies or individuals who are not Malaysian citizens and whose business consists of providing services to its offices or related companies outside Malaysia. Tax incentives that are enjoyed by companies who have been granted OHQ status include a concessionary tax rate of 10 per cent on management fees that have arisen from services rendered, interest in loans raised through Malaysian financial institutions, and royalties that have arisen from research-and-development work undertaken in Malaysia. The after-tax income can be distributed to shareholders as tax-exempt dividends. The concessionary tax on management fees, interest and royalty income are for a minimum period of five years and a maximum period of ten years.

Venture-capital-companies scheme

A venture-capital company is a resident company incorporated in Malaysia that holds shares in companies that are involved in high-risk ventures and new technology that would promote or enhance Malaysia's economic or technological development. Any gains that accrue from a disposal of the shares (within two years of the listing date) and dividends are exempted from tax. A portion of specific expenses such as directors' fees, rent, management fees and advisory fees is also allowed as a deduction.

Unit trusts

Unit trusts may enjoy a number of advantages. Gains that arise from realisation of shares and property are not treated as income of a unit trust. Unit trusts are allowed a special deduction for capital expenditure incurred on machinery and plant installed for the purpose of deriving income from letting of real property. The deduction is in the form of an allowance that is equal to 10 per cent of the expenditure. A unit trust will be allowed to deduct a portion of expenses that are not usually allowable, subject to a minimum 10 per cent and a maximum 25 per cent. These expenses include managers' remuneration and share-registration expenses. When income distributed by a unit trust is chargeable to tax on a unit holder, the tax chargeable on the unit trust will be set off against the tax charged on the unit holder.

Industrial adjustment allowance

'Industrial adjustment' is defined as any activity that is undertaken by a particular manufacturing-industry sector for restructuring by way of reorganisation, reconstruction or amalgamation. A company that is undertaking an approved industrial adjustment is entitled to a tax exemption of up to 100 per cent of the capital expenditure it incurs on a factory or plant or machinery used in Malaysia in connection with and for the purpose of the manufactured product.

Re-investment allowance

This incentive is granted to companies that are engaged in manufacturing whereby qualifying capital expenditure is incurred for the purpose of approved expansion. An allowance of 50 per cent of company-incurred capital expenditure for expansion of production capacity, modernisation of production facilities and diversification into related products is claimable.

Research-and-development incentives

The following incentives are designed to promote research and development in industry.

1. Person-incurred expenses for scientific research that is related to the person's business and that is directly undertaken by him or her or on his or her behalf are eligible for deduction.
2. A double deduction is available for research expenditure that is incurred during participation in an industrial adjustment program.
3. An industrial building allowance is available for buildings that are used for approved research or employees' training, even though the research may not be related to the business.
4. Plant and machinery that are used for approved research are eligible for capital allowances.
5. A double deduction is given for
   a in-cash contributions given to approved research institutions by individuals and corporations
   b expenses that are incurred by companies that are undertaking to use approved research institutions' facilities and services.

Research allowance

So that Malaysia's objective of being an industrialised country, in line with Vision 2020, may be achieved, and so that local producers' competitiveness is maintained as well as strengthened, a research allowance is claimable under the POI. Approved research companies that are undertaking research-and-development projects for their holding, subsidiary and associated companies are granted a research allowance of 100 per cent of the qualifying capital expenditure that is incurred within a ten-year period.

Foreign trade

Malaysia's strongly export-oriented trade policy is responsible for it becoming the world's nineteenth-largest exporter. Because exports are moving at more than 132 per cent of GDP, Malaysia has naturally been a strong supporter of trade liberalisation and the multilateral trading system.

The government is strongly committed to open regionalism, and Malaysia has been active in making regional economic agreements, particularly in the context of AFTA. Within AFTA, Malaysia has pushed for early implementation of the CEPT scheme and development of ASEAN agreements with reference to services and intellectual property rights.

In recent years, Malaysia has embarked on a trade-diversification policy whereby non-traditional markets, particularly ones in developing countries, are emphasised. The government has initiated trade missions to countries such as China, Vietnam and Zimbabwe and has concluded a number of bilateral trade and investment agreements with developing countries.

Table 5.6   Malaysia's trading partners, 1989 and 1993

Country or region	Exports (US$ million)			Imports (US$ million)		
	1989	1993	Trend %*	1989	1993	Trend %*
Brunei	82	188	24.9	1	3	33.5
Indonesia	415	543	9.7	346	718	24.1
Malaysia	–	–	–	–	–	–
Philippines	325	480	10.2	159	219	11.3
Singapore	4,948	10,228	19.5	3,059	6,955	22.4
Thailand	615	1,695	27.0	678	1,134	14.8
Total ASEAN	**6,385**	**13,134**	**19.4**	**4,243**	**9,029**	**21.0**
Australia	573	629	5.2	858	1,293	9.1
Canada	188	456	24.7	217	233	0.6
Chile	51	37	17.1	58	81	10.2
China	481	1,204	22.8	609	1,096	18.9
Hong Kong	770	1,942	26.6	463	921	20.4
Japan	4,016	6,113	10.8	5,438	12,533	22.8
South Korea	1,254	1,614	5.4	563	1,391	25.9
Mexico	24	245	72.7	14	13	–3.6
New Zealand	41	200	54.7	161	242	11.4
Papua New Guinea	12	51	49.1	2	21	88.0
Chinese Taipei	566	1,511	30.4	1,126	2,447	20.6
United States	4,684	9,580	20.3	3,803	7,725	18.1
Total APEC	**19,045**	**36,716**	**17.9**	**17,555**	**37,025**	**20.2**
European Union	3,858	6,832	15.7	3,137	5,291	12.7
All other countries	2,146	3,541	13.2	1,897	3,236	14.4
Total exports	**25,049**	**47,080**	**34,405**	**22,589**	**45,552**	**17.2**

*The trend growth is for the period 1989–93.
Source: Department of Foreign Affairs and Trade, *The APEC Region Trade and Investment*. Canberra: Australian Government Publishing Service, 1994, pp 34–5.

Table 5.7   Malaysian–ASEAN trade, 1989 and 1993

| | % of total | | | |
| | Exports | | Imports | |
Country or region	1989	1993	1989	1993
Brunei	0.3	0.4	0.0	0.0
Indonesia	1.7	1.2	1.5	1.6
Philippines	1.3	1.0	0.7	0.5
Singapore	19.8	21.7	13.5	15.3
Thailand	2.5	3.6	3.0	2.5
Total ASEAN	**25.5**	**27.9**	**18.8**	**19.8**

Note: total calculated separately rather than a simple addition of the above percentages
Source: Department of Foreign Affairs and Trade, *The APEC Region Trade and Investment*. Canberra: Australian Government Publishing Service, 1994, p 34–5.

On the domestic front, Malaysia has implemented unilateral measures for liberalising trade, and wide-ranging tariff reductions have become a regular feature of the budget process. The government's objective is encouragement of industries that can compete without having significant protection. However, Malaysia's levels of protection for infant industries in the manufacturing sector and the agricultural sector as a whole remain high.

The country's main exports are manufactured goods, particularly electrical products, electronic products, textiles and weaving apparel, as well as rubber products – in aggregate, these comprise 78.3 per cent of total exports. Other exports include crude petroleum, timber, palm oil, liquid-nitrogen gas, rubber and tin. Malaysia is Australia's sixteenth-most important source of imports, and wooden products are the largest import. Also important for Australia are Malaysia's manufactured goods, such as radio-broadcast receivers, video recorders, sound systems, television monitors and computers, which account for another 25 per cent of Malaysian imports.

Trade with Australia

Because of Malaysia's high economic growth rates, scope is offered for an increase in Australian exports and investment. Australia's exports to Malaysia total A$1.75 billion, and Malaysia is Australia's eleventh-most important export market. From a Malaysian viewpoint, though, Australian business has not kept pace with this growth. For example, over the period 1983–94, Malaysia's exports grew by an average of 15.1 per cent per year whereas its exports to Australia grew at only 12.9 per cent. As indicated in Table 5.8, this has resulted in a decline in our market share: this was only 1.3 per cent in 1993, having reached a peak of 2.4 per cent in 1988. Although they have increased significantly in dollar terms, Malaysia's imports from Australia have also grown at a slower rate – 13.2 per cent per year over the period 1984–93 – than that of Malaysia's total imports over the same period – 18.9 per cent. Our relative importance has also decreased – from a peak of 4.2 per cent of total Malaysian imports in 1986 to 2.3 per cent in 1993.

Table 5.8   Australia's importance for Malaysian trade, 1984–93

	Malaysia's exports (fob)		Malaysia's imports (cif)
Year	Australia as % of total	Year	Australia as % of total
1984	1.5	1984	4.0
1985	1.7	1985	4.1
1986	2.0	1986	4.2
1987	2.2	1987	4.1
1988	2.4	1988	4.1
1989	2.3	1989	3.8
1990	1.7	1990	3.4
1991	1.7	1991	3.2
1992	1.7	1992	2.7
1993	1.3	1993	2.8

Source: Department of Foreign Affairs and Trade, *The APEC Region Trade and Investment*. Canberra: Australian Government Publishing Service, 1994, p 27.

Australia's main exports to Malaysia are primary commodities, particularly wool, dairy products, fruit and beef, and ores and base metals, particularly gold, copper and aluminium. These two categories make up about a third of all Australia's exports to the country.

Table 5.9   Australian exports to Malaysia for year ended 30 June 1995

Type of product	A$	%
Non-fish live animals	22,073,030	1.09
Meat and meat preparations	34,663,593	1.71
Dairy products and eggs	142,922,892	7.04
Fish and shellfish	12,979,059	0.64
Cereals and cereal preparations	9,492,527	0.47
Vegetables and fruit	72,176,487	3.55
Sugars, sugar preparations and honey	2,351,962	0.12
Coffee, tea, cocoa and spices	6,483,799	0.32
Feed for animals (excluding unmilled cereals)	9,789,423	0.48
Miscellaneous edible products and preparations	6,265,096	0.31
Textile fibres and their wastes	134,354,023	6.62
Crude fertilisers and crude minerals	3,419,486	0.17
Metalliferous ores and metal scrap	34,427,146	1.70
Crude animal and vegetable materials	3,297,896	0.16
Coal, coke and briquettes	25,936,377	1.28
Petroleum and petroleum products	23,772,348	1.17
Chemicals	6,225,377	0.31
Dyeing, tanning and colouring materials	16,339,792	0.80
Medicinal and pharmaceutical products	32,791,212	1.61
Essential oils, perfume and cleansing preparations	14,060,452	0.69

Table 5.9 continues.

Table 5.9 (continued)

Type of product	A$	%
Fertilisers (excluding crude)	2,492,143	0.12
Plastics	16,838,445	0.83
Chemical materials and products, (nes)	15,820,425	0.78
Leather, leather manufactures and dressed furskins	3,172,618	0.16
Rubber manufactures	1,691,221	0.08
Cork and wood manufactures (excluding furniture)	2,472,193	0.12
Paper and paperboard	30,773,641	1.52
Textile yarns and fabrics	12,150,502	0.60
Non-metallic mineral manufactures	10,266,101	0.51
Iron and steel	138,493,313	6.82
Non-ferrous metals	166,664,063	8.21
Manufactures of metals	47,994,144	2.36
Power-generating machinery and equipment	10,738,960	0.53
Machinery specialised for particular industries	58,607,018	2.89
Metalworking machinery	7,950,184	0.39
General industrial equipment and machine parts	55,087,254	2.71
Office and automatic data-processing machines	20,491,674	1.01
Telecommunications and recording equipment	14,242,611	0.70
Electrical machinery and appliances	54,547,182	2.69
Road vehicles (including air-cushion vehicles)	40,289,163	1.98
Transport equipment (excluding road vehicles)	26,681,999	1.31
Prefabricated buildings and fittings	1,255,470	0.06
Furniture and stuffed furnishings	1,733,424	0.09
Apparel, footwear and clothing	1,460,328	0.07
Professional and scientific instruments	6,609,814	0.33
Photographic equipment, optical goods and clocks	3,419,585	0.17
Miscellaneous manufactured articles	17,859,678	0.88
Gold	283,379,603	13.95
Confidential trade and commodities	357,179,088	17.59
Other items	6,676,473	0.33
Total exports	**2,030,860,294**	**100.00**

Source: ABS, *Foreign Trade Statistics: 1994–95*. 1995, pp 848–50.

These figures do not reflect Australia's increasing income that is derived from sale of services, particularly education but also consulting and tourism. Many of Australia's exports to Singapore also 'move across the causeway' and are recorded as imports from Singapore, not from Australia. For example, the Austrade organisation estimates 25 per cent of Australia's Singapore-bound fruit and vegetable exports find their way to Malaysia. Increases in consumption of food and services can be expected as GDP grows and preferences change. Australian firms are increasingly becoming involved in Malaysia's building-and-infrastructure boom as its government acts to help clear the severe infrastructural bottlenecks that have emerged due to the high growth rates.

Future prospects

Businesses planning to target the Malaysian market must carefully assess their specific product area on first estimation, due to the composition of Malaysia's imports – machinery, capital and transport equipment comprise about 55 per cent of total imports – not much room seems to be left for Australia to increase its exports to Malaysia in these areas, in which Australia is basically an importer, not a large-scale producer.

As foreshadowed in the Seventh Malaysia Plan, the government plans a major investment in human resource development. Whereas in the past Malaysia has sent many students to study in Australia, its promotion of local 'twinning' arrangements with overseas tertiary institutions will gradually slow this outflow. The opportunity for Australian institutions is just not maintaining their market share but also to expand these arrangements particularly in the areas of technical and vocational training. Services that can be provided not just to Malaysians but to students from elsewhere within ASEAN.

Malaysia's ASEAN potential should not be understated. With the creation of AFTA and Malaysia's location in the heart of this trading region, direct investment in the country could provide an opportunity to 'jump tariff hurdles' and thereby access the rapidly growing ASEAN economies' markets. Malaysia's own major infrastructure projects offer similarly attractive opportunities.

However, Australian companies have to remember that although many similarities exist between the two countries, key cultural differences are also evident. Because of the need to appreciate the broader political environment when securing government contracts, as well as the government's current focus on domestic investment, local equity requirements and the importance of *bumiputera* participation, it is advisable that Australian companies seek out joint ventures with Malaysian firms. If they have the right partners and a carefully chosen and well-managed entry strategy, Australian firms will profit through the inclusion of this relatively affluent neighbour in their global strategies.

ENDNOTES

1 That is, in 1970, for every person who experienced urban poverty, there were 2.14 persons who experienced rural poverty, whereas in 1993, for each person who experienced urban poverty, 1.75 persons were in rural poverty.

2 In 1970 for every Chinese in poverty 2.25 Malays were in poverty, while in 1990 this ratio had declined to 1.78.

3 In 1970 for every Indian in poverty 1.75 Malays were in poverty, while in 1990 this ratio had declined to 1.29.

REFERENCES

Bank Negara Malaysia, *Quarterly Report*, various issues.

Brent, P, 'Healthy Trade in Misunderstanding', in *Australian Business Monthly*, August 1993.

Brookfield, H (ed), *Transformation with Industrialization in Peninsular Malaysia*. Singapore: Oxford University Press, 1994.

Brown, J, 'The Role of the State in Economic Development and Theory: The East Asian Experience and the Malaysian Case', in *Asian Development Economics Staff Paper*, no. 52, Asian Development Bank, December 1993.

Bussink, W, 'Employment and Income Distribution in Peninsular Malaysia', in Young, K, Bussink, W and Hassan, P (eds), *Malaysia: Growth and Equity in a Multiracial Society*. Baltimore: John Hopkins Press, 1980, pp 97–126.

Camroux, D, *Looking East and Inwards: Internal Factors in Malaysian Foreign Relations During the Mahathir Era*. Griffith, Queensland: Griffith University Press, 1994.

Cooke, K, 'New Techniques Needed', in the *Financial Times*, 28 August 1992.

Crouch, H, 'Authoritarian Trends, the UMNO Split and the Limits to State Power', in Kahn, J S and Loh, F (eds), *Fragmented Vision: Culture and Politics in Contemporary Malaysia*. Sydney: Allen & Unwin, 1992.

Ellis, E, 'Mahathir's Busy Year', in the *Australian Financial Review*, 30 May 1994.

Gomez, E T, *Politics in Business: UMNO's Corporate Investments*. Kuala Lumpur: Forum, 1990.

Jomo, K S, *A Question of Class: Capital, the State and Uneven Development in Malaysia*. Singapore: Oxford University Press, 1986.

—— 'Beyond the New Economic Policy? Malaysia in the Nineties', in *The Sixth James C Jackson Memorial Lecture*, presented at Griffith University, Malaysia Society of the Asian Studies Association of Australia, July 1990.

Liden, J and Sargent, S, 'A Vision for the Future', in *Euromoney*, August 1992.

Lim, D, 'The Economic, Political and Social Background for Development Planning in Malaysia', in Lim, D (ed), *Readings in Malaysian Economic Development*. Kuala Lumpur: Oxford University Press, 1975, pp 2–10.

—— 'Malaysian Development Planning', in *Pacific Affairs*, vol 55, no 4, 1982, pp 613–39.

Malaysian Government, *Sixth Malaysian Plan (1991–1995)*. Kuala Lumpur: Malaysian Government Printer, 1991, pp 104–5.

Mills, S, 'Malaysia', in Mills, S (ed), *Asian Business Insights*. Sydney: John Fairfax Press, 1994.

Muthaly, S K K and Cree, M, *Business Investment In Malaysia: the Australian Experience*. North Melbourne: Australia–Malaysia Business Council – Victoria, 1993.

Rudner, M, *Nationalism, Planning and Economic Modernisation in Malaysia: The Politics of Beginning Development*. London: Sage Publications, 1975.

APPENDIX 5.1: *Australian and Malaysian representation*

Australian addresses

High Commission for Malaysia
7 Perth Avenue
Yarralumla 2600, ACT, Australia
Telephone: (61 6) 273 1543
Facsimile: (61 6) 273 2496

Australia–Malaysia Business Council
PO Box E14, Queen Victoria Terrace
Canberra 2600, ACT, Australia
Telephone: (61 6) 273 2311
Facsimile: (61 6) 273 3196

MBfi Australia Limited
Level 5, 261 George Street
Sydney 2000, NSW, Australia
Telephone: (61 2) 251 7033
Facsimile: (61 2) 251 7062

Malaysian addresses

Australian Trade Commission
Suite 5.06, Fifth Floor
Menara PSCI
39 Jalan Sultan Ahmad Shah
10050 Pulau Penang, Malaysia
Telephone: (60 4) 229 6606
Facsimile: (60 4) 229 6608

Australian Trade Commission
6 Jalan Yap Kwan Seng
50450 Kuala Lumpur, Malaysia
Telephone: (60 3) 242 3122
Facsimile: (60 3) 248 8870

Malaysia–Australia Business Council
6 Jalan Yap Kwan Seng
50450 Kuala Lumpur, Malaysia
Telephone: (60 3) 240 6659
Facsimile: (60 3) 241 7747

Malaysian Industrial Development Authority (MIDA)
Wisma Damansara
Jalan Semantan
PO Box 10618
50720 Kuala Lumpur, Malaysia
Telephone: (60 3) 255 3633
Facsimile: (60 3) 255 7970

Australia and New Zealand Banking Group Limited
Fourth Floor, Wisma Genting
Jalan Sultan Ismail
50250 Kuala Lumpur, Malaysia
Telephone: (60 3) 261 6088/6790
Facsimile: (60 3) 261 3210

National Australia Bank
Sixth Floor, Wisma Genting
Jalan Sultan Ismail
50250 Kuala Lumpur, Malaysia
Telephone: (60 3) 263 6545/6546/6548
Facsimile: (60 3) 263 6559

Westpac Banking Corporation
Eleventh Floor, Menara Bank, Pembang
Jalan Sultan Ismail
Kuala Lumpur, Malaysia
Telephone: (60 3) 292 0650
Facsimile: (60 3) 298 0016

APPENDIX 5.2: *Australia's strategic priorities for Malaysian trade and investment*

- Encourage Australian businesses to establish partnerships with Malaysian companies.
- Maintain, and when possible increase, Australia's market share in key commodities.
- Improve access for Australian agricultural and food products, particularly value-added product, and market increasingly sophisticated food exports.
- Promote and expand trade in services, particularly in the telecommunications, professional and aviation sectors.

- Improve access for, and expand exports to, Malaysia of STMs, ETMs and construction–engineering services, particularly ones that are related to infrastructure.
- Maintain and increase Australia's existing market share in education services, particularly vocational training, and have better targeted niche marketing that is based on a long-term, market-development perspective by Australian providers.
- Promote recognition of Australia as a main source of defence-equipment supply, servicing and support.
- Promote Australia–Malaysia collaboration in development of commercial applications of science and technology, including environmental management.
- Derive mutual commercial benefit for both Australia and Malaysia from development-co-operation programs that are operating in Malaysia and other ASEAN countries.
- Promote links between Australia's and Malaysia's business communities, including through the two countries' business councils and the business-skills migration program.
- Provide on-the-ground trade-development assistance in northern Malaysia in order to capture opportunities that are related to the BIMP–EAGA.
- Develop sporting and cultural ties in order to maximise commercial opportunities for Australian business, being particularly mindful of the forthcoming 1998 Commonwealth Games in Kuala Lumpur and Sydney Olympics 2000.
- Promote greater networking and co-operation between Australian companies that are already represented in Malaysia.

Source: Department of Foreign Affairs and Trade, *Australia Trade and Investment Development.* Canberra: Australian Government Publishing Service, 1994, p 94.

6

The Philippines

Mei-Leng Rankin

Introduction

Traditionally, the Philippines has been viewed as being a politically, socially and economically mismanaged country. Scarred through having suffered years of social and economic disparities and political instability, and through being heavily reliant on the US for economic and political support, in the 1990s the country is finally addressing the problems of its colonial heritage. It has 'cut its apron strings' with the US and, under President Fidel Ramos, regained some political stability. The Philippines therefore has an excellent opportunity to address its past economic and social problems, and this in turn means significant opportunities are offered for Australian business. To understand the factors behind this transformation, this chapter examines the Philippines' political history, economic development, resource endowments, current economic experiences and potential for Australian exporters and investors.

The setting

The Philippines is an archipelago that comprises 7101 islands and has a land mass of 298,170 square kilometres. This area is mostly accounted for by 11 islands, of which Luzon and Mindanao are the most important. These islands, which extend about 2015 kilometres and are located about 1127 kilometres off the south of China, have been subject to migration of many peoples and occupation by many countries.

All these factors have had an effect, and what used to be mainly a Malay population (Malays comprise 95 per cent of the Philippines' population of 72.3 million) now contains a culture that has significant Chinese, Spanish and American influences and, to a lesser extent, Arab, Japanese and Polynesian ones. The American

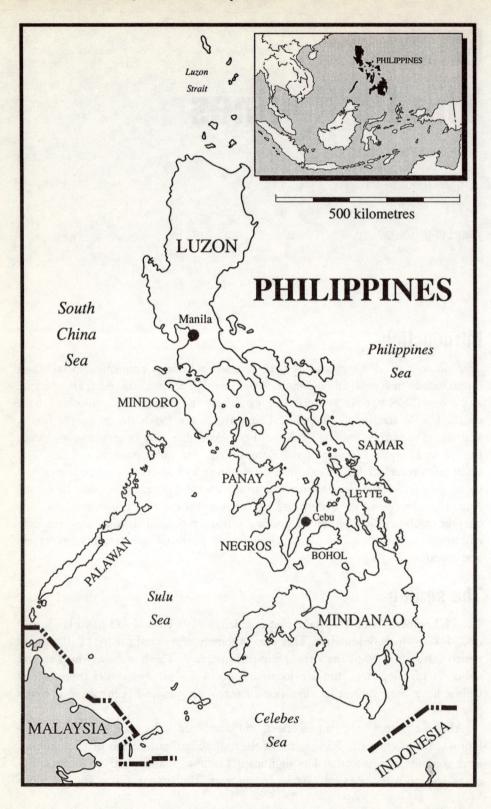

influence remains particularly strong within the urban culture, and although Tagalog is the national language, English remains important in most business environments. The Spanish influence continues to be reflected in the importance placed on the Roman Catholic Church: about 83 per cent of Filipinos belong to that faith. Another 9 per cent are Protestant Christians. Although Muslims account for 5 per cent of the population, this is concentrated in the southern islands.

The country is well endowed with a wide range of abundant natural resources, including fertile land, minerals and timber, as well as a range of other resources, all of which are discussed further on in the chapter. Its endowment with reference to weather is somewhat less fortunate though: it is located in the 'typhoon belt', so an excellent water supply is guaranteed, but at least half a dozen or more major cyclones that frequently cause havoc occur each year. Landslides, fire, volcanic eruptions and earthquakes all confirm that nature can be both kind and damaging to a country.

Political history

The Philippines' socio-cultural structure is similar to that of Latin America, with which it shares more than four centuries of history. Its many ethnic groups have been unified through this common history, and its distinct contemporary culture reflects these historical influences, particularly Spanish and American colonialism.

Spanish colonialism: 1521–1898

The Spanish came to the Philippines in 1521 and used it as a base for spreading the Catholic religion throughout the rest of Asia. Filipinos today remain predominantly Roman Catholic. The economic impact of the early Spanish-colonial social structure also remains prevalent to this day. The Spanish *encomienda* (feudal) system aided creation of a landlord class. The *encomienderos* (elite landlords) expanded their landholdings and political power through use of a hierarchical political structure that was characterised by reciprocal obligations: a system whereby lower officials sought superior officials' protection in exchange for the officials' allegiance. This patronage system continues to dominate the country.

Spain's early economic successes in the country were responsible for attracting other entrepreneurial foreigners, especially the Chinese. These settlers intermarried with Catholic Filipinos and created a new elite class, the *mestizo*, who looked to Spain for their culture. Through them, Spanish nationalism became part of Filipino society. By 1896, massive poverty, deteriorating landlord–tenant relations, high unemployment and labour exploitation had unfortunately left the Philippines in turmoil.

American colonisation: 1898–1946

In 1898 when the US declared war on Spain, it helped the Filipinos to resist their Spanish rulers. On 12 June 1898 the Philippines declared independence, only to have the US assume control under the Treaty of Paris. The US declared its intention that the Philippines eventually become independent and promoted local self-government, mainly by the land-owning class. English became the language of education and business, and American culture became firmly embedded in Philippine society.

During this period the Philippines' economy enjoyed one of South-East Asia's highest growth rates, and Philippine agricultural exports and American products both had free entry into the two countries' markets. Although a new, affluent middle class emerged, nationalistic Filipinos believed the Americans were exploiting the Philippines' natural resources. Tenancy problems, deteriorating landlord–tenant relationships, excessive taxes, a high level of rural unemployment, and wealth disparity, led to peasant unrest. Rebellions were led by the communist-guerrilla group the *Hukbalahaps* (*Huks*), the *Partido Komunista ng Pilipina* (the Communist Party of the Philippines) and Muslim guerrillas.

Independence

Following the country's Japanese occupation of 1941–44, although the US at first resumed local control, it granted independence on 4 July 1946, and Manuel Roxas was named as president. The US nevertheless continued to be a significant political and economic influence – it maintained 23 military bases and continued the free-trade arrangement. The Philippines even granted US citizens and corporations the same rights as Filipinos for exploitation of local natural resources.

With independence came a growing discontentment and disillusionment as the gap widened between the poor working class and the elite minority. Communists and Muslim secessionists resumed their protests and threatened a political system that was marred by fraud, bribery and intimidation. By 1965 when Ferdinand Marcos came to power, the Philippines' economy had stagnated. In September 1972, Marcos declared martial law and himself sole ruler. Due to improved political stability, the crime rate declined and foreign investment returned. However, the economy's former performance level was never recaptured.

Filipinos were dissatisfied with the Marcos Administration's corruption, political intimidation and economic mismanagement. In 1986, Marcos was overthrown due to a popular civilian–military revolt, and Corazon Aquino was officially sworn in as president. Aquino inherited an abused political structure and a crumbling economy. Her efforts at restoring law and order, though, were hampered by guerrilla insurgencies and dissatisfied military factions that attempted five unsuccessful coups.

When Fidel Ramos was elected as president on 11 May 1992, the Philippines turned over a new page in its political history. Also, the US's withdrawal from the Subic Naval Base and Clark Air Base has given the country a new, more independent stature in regional affairs. On the domestic front, Ramos has sought to work closely with the communist rebels and the Muslim secessionists and to restore law and order. The Philippines understands well the value of stable government.

Economic development

Historically, the Philippines' economy was predominantly agricultural. It was based on the *encomienda*, or *hacienda*, system, whereby peasant farmers worked for the elite landlords, or *encomienderos*. The landlords in turn encouraged foreign entrepreneurs to provide the capital and technical expertise for the mining and forestry industries and to expand agricultural exports.

When independence was declared in 1946, the Philippines initially adopted an import-substitution, labour-intensive industrialisation-development program in order to diversify the economy, away from its over-dependence on agricultural exports, and to promote faster economic growth and higher employment. However, this attempted transition was responsible for producing recurring economic instability. Domestic savings and foreign-exchange resources fell short of investment requirements, and protective quotas and high tariffs were required for protection of the infant-stage domestic manufacturing industries that resulted. Unfortunately, the protected infant-stage industries never became competitive in the world market – most remained small, inward looking, inefficiently managed and mainly owned by the oligarchs or 'cronies' who had significant influence over a corrupt government.

In 1987, the Aquino Administration drew up a medium-term development plan (1987–92) in order to alleviate poverty, generate productive employment, promote equity and social justice and attain sustainable economic growth. Due to economic liberalisation, monopolies in the sugar and coconut markets were dismantled, agricultural prices and grain imports were liberalised and many tax exemptions were eliminated. The government also attempted to have privatisation in order to raise more funds. Shareholdings worth some 140,000 million pesos, including six commercial banks, were put up for sale.

In 1988, Aquino introduced the Comprehensive Agrarian Reform Program (CARP) in order to redistribute land to the landless farmers and farm workers. However, policies for stimulating economic growth conflicted with the need to repay the huge foreign debt. Indeed, foreign-debt interest repayments amounted to more than 46 per cent of budgetary expenditure.

The brief economic history presented in this chapter leads to a review of the Philippines' natural resource endowments and their associated industries and of the Ramos government's contemporary economic policy.

Although the characteristics of the Philippines' political history have not always been conducive to the country's economic development, nature has been much kinder and endowed the land with a wealth of natural resources, particularly with reference to products related to the areas of forestry, agriculture, minerals and energy.

Production of forestry products such as logs, lumber, veneer and plywood provides substantial export earnings. However, the forests have been depleted significantly since the early 1970s, due to illegal logging, shifting cultivation, population pressure and an inadequate reafforestation program. As part of the government's reafforestation and conservation policy, logging bans are now imposed in some areas and control of timber licensing is stricter.

The Philippines' tropical monsoon climate and topography are conducive to growing a wide variety of crops such as *palay* (rice), corn, coconuts, sugar cane, bananas, pineapples, coffee, mangoes, and *abaca* (manila hemp). Rice and corn are the main crops. The Philippines exports rice, *abaca*, coconuts and coconut products (such as copra and coconut oil), sugar, pineapples, tobacco and bananas. It is also the world's largest exporter of coconuts and coconut products. Rice, coconuts, sugar and maize are grown in large holdings, or *haciendas*, that are usually farmed by agricultural tenants or workers. Non-traditional export crops such as bananas and pineapples are grown mainly on 'agri-business' plantations; food crops are grown in smallholdings.

The Philippines has extensive marine and inland fishing resources. Fishing accounts for about 6 per cent of GDP per year. Since 1986, although an increase has occurred in the volume of fish production, productivity has been low due to over-fishing and destructive fishing methods.

About 14 known metallic and 29 non-metallic mineral resources have been iden-tified in the Philippines. Metallic minerals such as nickel, copper, gold, iron, cobalt and chromite are produced commercially. The Philippines is South-East Asia's largest copper producer, and copper concentrates account for more than 30 per cent of annual mineral production. The Philippines is the world's eighth-largest gold producer.

Non-metallic mineral resources such as cement, clay, marble, sand and gravel, gypsum salt, limestone, clay, felspar, dolomite, carbide-rock phosphate, guano and pyrite are also produced on a commercial basis.

About 40 per cent of the country's total energy consumption comes from natural sources such as hydro-electric power (which provides about 10 to 11 per cent of total needs), geothermal energy, coal and domestic oil. In the 1970s the Philippines was importing more than 90 per cent of its energy requirements (mainly petroleum and oil). However, due to more effective use of domestic energy substitutes, it now imports about 60 per cent of its total energy requirements.

In mid-1992 the country was faced with a power crisis whereby continued eco-nomic growth was jeopardised. The shortage of electric power resulted in cessation of power supply, or 'brown-outs', for up to 12 hours per day. Production in the growing manufacturing sector was thereby severely hampered. In order to deal with the crisis the government set up a department of energy, for developing a substantial energy base and examining alternative power supplies such as use of coal and geo-thermal energy. In 1993 the government managed to reduce the number of brown-outs to two hours a day.

In summary, although the Philippines has a wealth of natural resources at its dis-posal, political instability and economic mismanagement have long been respon-sible for preventing it from making the most of its economic development opportunities. This situation may fortunately now have changed under the leader-ship of President Ramos, who has introduced a plan, 'Philippines 2000', to make the Philippines an industrialised nation. The plan gives top priority to rural infra-structure through initiatives such as lowering seed and fertiliser prices, expanding irrigation, redistributing land and providing incentives for having farms that are efficient and of an economical size. Despite these measures, agriculture now comprises a reasonably small share of GDP.

Table 6.1 The Philippines' GDP, by sector, 1970 and 1993

	%	
Sector	1970	1993
Agriculture	30	22
Manufacturing	25	24
Other industry	7	9
Services	38	45
TOTAL	**100**	**100**

Source: World Bank, *World Development Report.* 1994, p 166.

The National Economic and Development Authority (NEDA) is responsible for the formulation, implementation and co-ordination of the country's long-term and short-term development programs. Its key aims include restoring and restructuring the economy through attaining sustainable economic growth and reducing the enormous debt, thereby creating productive employment and redressing social and regional disparities.

The Ramos government has enjoyed considerable success in tackling the country's economic problems. The Philippines has had one of the ASEAN countries' highest inflation rates. In order to curb inflation and reduce debt, the government implemented tight monetary policies that included having high and positive real interest rates. It has enjoyed marked success in tackling this problem. In 1994, inflation stood at only 7.1 per cent, compared with its 1991 level of 18.7 per cent. The price, though, has been a relatively high unemployment rate. Interest rates on basic loans have now fallen from their 1991 level of about 21 per cent to about 8 per cent. Reforms have also been introduced for improving efficiency of the government's financial institutions.

Table 6.2 The Philippines' key economic indicators, 1989–94

	%					
Indicator	1989	1990	1991	1992	1993	1994
GDP growth	6.2	2.7	−0.5	0.6	2.0	4.3
Inflation	12.2	14.1	18.7	8.9	7.6	7.1
Unemployment	8.4	8.1	9.0	8.6	9.3	9.3

Source: Department of Foreign Affairs and Trade, *The APEC Region Trade and Investment.* Canberra: Australian Government Publishing Service, 1994, pp 84, 96 and 100.

The Philippines' fiscal policy has long been driven by attempts at paying interest on the huge national debt and at complying with the International Monetary Fund's

(IMF's) demands that the country reduce its budget deficit. In 1986, when Aquino came to power, the budget deficit amounted to about 4.6 per cent of Gross National Product (GNP). The Philippines had the ASEAN countries' worst debt problem, and in 1987 servicing the debt required 38 per cent of government spending.

Although the country continues to have South-East Asia's highest foreign debt, the IMF has agreed to reschedule the payments. Pressure on fiscal policy has thereby been reduced, and the government has been freed to concentrate on the economy's rebuilding instead of on debt repayment.

Despite this development, the government continues to face deficiencies in its tax-revenue structure. Although the government hoped revenue would be increased through revising the tax structure and implementing the privatisation program, it has been faced with setbacks such as widespread tax evasion, administration inefficiency and political opposition. As a result, the government's expenditure continues to outpace its income. In order to improve the inadequate infrastructure, the government is considering foreign help and participation in 'build–operate–transfer' schemes.

The government, in an attempt at reducing the budget deficits and at stimulating private investments, has initiated a privatisation program that permits sale of State-owned corporations and enterprises. In 1984, 303 government-owned or government-controlled enterprises existed. Most of them were inefficiently managed and have been responsible for contributing to the deficit blow-out as well as high inflation. At the time of writing, 123 of the corporations had been approved for sale.

The Philippines continues to receive foreign aid for helping to alleviate the debt problem and to develop its infrastructure. The main contributors are the World Bank, the Asian Development Bank, Japan, the US and Germany. Australia is the sixth-largest contributor to the Philippine Assistance Programme (PAP).

Financial development

As in the case with other aspects of the Philippines' economy, the banking system was first developed under the Spanish – what is now the Bank of the Philippine Islands was established in 1851. In practice, today's financial system shows hardly any influence from that early period. Instead, the system verys much reflects the more recent American-colonial period. In more recent year it has been modified to follow a somewhat more European approach, particularly with reference to introduction of universal banking, which has been adapted to suit local conditions.

The financial sector comprises a wide range of financial institutions, of which the types and their relative importance are shown in Table 6.3. Of the institutions, the commercial banks are the most important and offer most of the usual services that are expected in Australia. Although the government has been responsible for restricting foreign access to the local banking market, in 1994 a major change occurred in this policy: 10 new foreign banks were granted local licences. Importantly, from an Australian perspective, the ANZ Bank was included in the group of 10. Foreign entry had previously been directed towards opening of an

Offshore Banking Unit (OBU) and towards operation in Manila's equivalent of Singapore's Asian-dollar market. These OBU licences, though, had provided more access to the domestic market than Singapore had and therefore had enabled the institutions to provide some financial help for foreign firms and joint ventures.

Table 6.3   The Philippines' financial institutions, 1995

Institution	Number of institutions as at 30 June 1995	Total assets (million pesos)
Central Bank	1	458,314.5[a]
Commercial banks	3,026	1,137,482.0[a]
Savings and mortgage banks	366	
Private development banks	277	117,683.0[b]
Stock savings and loan associations	226	
Specialised government banks	77	68,284.8[b]
Rural banks	1,297	29,734.0[c]
Offshore banking units	17	US$1,654.01m[d]
Non-banks that have quasi-banking functions	n/a	10,689.9[e]
Investment houses	56	9,196.2[e]
Finance companies	204	23,293.7[e]
Investment companies	64	18,616.0[e]
Securities dealers and brokers	129	9,027.3[e]
Pawnshops	3,965	6,070.8[e]
Lending investors	1,911	4,289.5[e]
Non-stock savings and loan associations	115	10,595.3[e]
Mutual building and loan associations	7	134.1[e]
Private insurance companies	127	51,380.9[e]
Government non-banks	5	214,376.1[e]
Venture-capital corporations	10	90.6[e]
Total	**11,880**	**not applicable**

Note: [a]These figures are as at 30 June 1995. [b]These figures are as at 31 July 1995. [c]This figure is as 31 March 1995. [d]This figure is as at 30 September 1995. [e]These figures are as at 31 December 1994.
Source: Bangko Sentral ng Philipina, 1995 correspondence.

Because, in practice, the foreign-bank offices are concentrated in greater Manila, the banking services located in other areas may require accessing of the country's larger domestic commercial banks. The 15 largest of these institutions are listed in Table 6.4.

The Philippines also has an active stock exchange – the Philippines Stock Exchange. It was founded in 1994 through a merger of the longstanding Makati and Manila stock exchanges. At the end of 1994, 189 domestic companies were listed in the Philippines. A futures market in commodities and foreign currencies also exists that is conducted by the Manila International Futures Exchange.

Table 6.4   The Philippines' major domestic commercial banks, 1994

Bank*	Assets US$ million
Metrobank (12/94)	4,916
Philippine National Bank (12/93)	4,434
Land Bank Philippines (12/94)	3,981
Philippine Commercial International Bank (12/94)	2,973
Far East Bank & Trust Company (12/94)	2,835
Bank of the Philippine Islands (12/94)	3,924
United Coconut Planters Bank (12/94)	2,080
Allied Banking Corporation (12/94)	1,730
Rizzal Commercial Banking Corp (12/94)	2,161
China Banking Corp (12/94)	1,189
Equitable Banking Corp (12/94)	1,249
Security Bank Corp (12/94)	832
Solidbank (12/93)	653
City Trust Banking Corporation (12/94)	837
Prudential Bank (12/94)	720

*The month and year ended are in parentheses.
Source: The *Banker*, October 1995, p 68.

Foreign investment

Historically, the Philippines has not been a popular FDI destination. FDI accounts for only 6 per cent of total investment in the country, a figure that is well short of the shares received by other ASEAN member nations. The country's volatile political system, inadequate and inefficient infrastructure facilities, sluggish economic performance, restrictive regulations, bureaucratic delays and problems of law and order have been responsible for restricting investment. However, because of deregulation of the market and implementation of various trade-liberalisation and investment-liberalisation policies such as floating of the peso, lowering of tariffs in various industries, making long-term leases available to foreign investors and expansion of the role of the country's foreign banks the Philippines has been helped to become more attractive as a place for foreign trade and investment.

In order to promote foreign-equity investments, the government has introduced a number of reforms through the Board of Investments (BOI). Drafted in 1987, the Omnibus Investments Code has been responsible for provision of new incentives and more efficient and speedy processing of investment applications, and the Council of Investments has been helping foreign investors to obtain the necessary approvals. The Foreign Investment Act 1991 (the FIA) removed all foreign ownership restrictions on export enterprises and on domestic markets' firms except when listed on the Foreign Investment Negative List (FINL), where a maximum of 40 per cent foreign equity is permitted.

Since 1993, foreigners have been allowed to lease private land for up to 75 years. Foreign-exchange controls that involve exports and imports, dollar remittances and sale of gold to foreign buyers were also deregulated in that year, and restrictions on foreign investment in the services, banking and finance sectors were reduced. This measure included permitting more foreign banks to enter the Philippines' domestic market.

Since 1992, a marked increase has occurred in foreigner interest in Philippine investment opportunities. Japan has become the largest source of new foreign equity. As indicated in Table 6.5, the US, the second-largest investor, retains the largest value of assets because of its having invested over a much longer term. Other major foreign investors are Hong Kong, Taiwan and Bermuda.

Table 6.5   The Philippines' FDI, by major source, 1994

Investor	US$ million
United States	689
Hong Kong	298
Taiwan	274
Bermuda	206
Malaysia	164
Virgin Islands	151
Japan	106

Source: Philippines Board of Investment, 1995.

In the Philippines' economy, apart from Australian-government joint ventures, many Australian firms feature in the private sector. About 100 Australian companies are operating in the Philippines at present. Three companies that are significant contributors in Australia–Philippines trade relations are BHP Engineering, BTR Nylex and ACI.

Development of the former US Clark Air Base and Subic Naval Base as well as of the Baguio export-processing area has meant many opportunities have opened up for local and foreign investments. Subic Bay is being developed as a centre for commercial, financial and investment activity. In order to promote foreign investment in the Subic Bay Special Economic and Freeport Zone, the government has offered very generous tax incentives, including 5 per cent income tax on gross income as well as exemptions from all other taxes, including tariffs. Taiwanese investors have responded by developing a 300 hectare industrial site in the Zone. A third of the site's allotments have been taken by Taiwanese companies, including the computer maker Acer.

Foreign trade

As indicated in Table 6.6, the Philippines' main exports comprise ETMs, including cathode valves, semi-conductors, integrated circuits and telecommunications equipment. Agricultural products, including fruit and nuts, vegetable fats and oils, are the second-most important export.

Table 6.6   The Philippines' exports and imports, by product type, 1993

Product type	% distribution	
	Exports	*Imports*
Primary products,	20.8	23.3
of which processed food	8.7	3.7
Manufactures		
simply transformed	2.6	11.7
elaborately transformed	40.9	49.0
Other	35.7	16.0
Total	**100.0**	**100.0**

Source: Department of Foreign Affairs and Trade, *The APEC Region Trade and Investment*. Canberra: Australian Government Publishing Service, 1994, p 69.

Table 6.7   The Philippines' pattern of trade, 1993

Country or region	Exports %	Trend* %	Imports %	Trend* %
Brunei	0.0	34.2	0.3	−8.1
Indonesia	0.4	−17.1	1.8	0.2
Malaysia	1.4	0.4	2.0	−1.9
Singapore	3.4	2.8	5.7	3.8
Thailand	1.5	−11.8	1.0	1.8
Australia	1.0	−8.6	2.7	−6.4
Canada	1.7	2.0	0.8	−12.7
Chile	0.2	36.3	0.2	−9.2
China	2.0	30.5	1.2	−12.7
Hong Kong	4.8	6.1	5.4	5.0
Japan	16.3	−5.5	22.8	4.7
Korea	1.7	−7.7	4.6	5.1
Mexico	0.3	11.5	0.0	−20.0
New Zealand	0.1	−3.6	0.7	−7.1
Papua New Guinea	0.0	17.2	0.4	−0.2
Taiwan	3.0	3.5	5.7	−2.4
United States	38.3	0.6	19.8	−0.1
TOTAL APEC	**76.3**	**−0.7**	**75.2**	**1.0**
European Union	16.9	0.4	10.3	−1.1
Other	6.9	9.1	14.5	−3.6
Total	**100.0**		**100.0**	

*The trend growth is for the period 1989–93.
Note: totals and subtotals calculated from actual numbers not rounded percentages
Source: Department of Foreign Affairs and Trade, *The APEC Region Trade and Investment*. Canberra: Australian Government Publishing Service, 1994, p 36.

The US and Japan are the Philippines' main trading partners, and trading relations are sustained through having trade concessions on Philippine products, aid, and substantial private-investment inflows. In recent years trade with other countries has substantially increased, as indicated in Table 6.7. Through adopting a more liberal policy, the government has been responsible for increasing the country's trade relations with other countries. This trend does not yet involve other ASEAN member countries, though: the level of trade with them is relatively low.

In order to make the economy more competitive, the government has adopted a simplified four-tier tariff structure, which is shown in Table 6.8.

Table 6.8   The Philippines' four-tier tariff structure, 1993

Item	Tariff %
Raw materials	0,* 3 and 10
Intermediate goods	20
Finished products	30
213 items (mainly luxury goods)	50 (temporary)

*Zero per cent is granted for 'exceptionally meritorious cases'.

At present, the overall effective protection rates are 25 per cent and 35 per cent in the manufacturing sector. These figures represent a significant reduction when compared with the 44 per cent overall effective rate and the 73 per cent rate that was in place in the manufacturing sector during the Marcos era.

So that greater incentives are provided in the export sector, measures have been taken to remove what was termed the 'anti-export bias of local trade policies'. The policies include provision of better export-finance credits, simplification of exporting procedures, provision of marketing and promotion help and reduction of restrictions on raw-material imports. At the same time, though, taxes are imposed on the export of raw materials in order to create incentives for them to be processed locally.

Due to growth of the export-oriented industries, the economy's structure has significantly changed from the one that resulted from the import-substitution 'Filipinos First' ideology that was pursued so diligently by the Marcos government. This has been a major accomplishment for what used to be South-East Asia's most restrictive trade and foreign-investment regime.

Trade with Australia

The Philippines has for many years enjoyed good bilateral trade relations with Australia. Apart from the fact it is geographically close and presents no language barriers, Australia has been recognised by the Ramos Administration as being a significant contributor to the Philippines' assistance and development projects. The Philippines is the third-largest recipient of Australia's foreign aid. Through the assistance program, Australia hopes to not only help to alleviate the Philippines' level of poverty but to foster closer bilateral relations with the country. Today, the Philippines is Australia's 25th-largest trading partner.

The Philippines seems to have had more difficulty exporting its products to Australia than finding Australian products to import. This is reflected in the 5 per cent per year average increase in its exports to Australia compared with a growth rate of 15.7 per cent. Because the Philippines' exports to all countries grew at an average of 10 per cent per year and its imports by 15.7 per cent between 1984 and 1993, Australia's relative importance as a trading partner declined during the same period. As indicated in Table 6.9, Australia's 1.7 per cent share of Philippine exports in 1984 had dropped to only 1 per cent by 1993. Its share of the Philippine import market did better, though: it actually rose slightly, from 2.4 per cent in 1984 to 2.7 per cent by 1993.

Table 6.9   Australia's importance for Philippine trade, 1984–93

Year	Australia as % of total Philippine exports (fob)	Year	Australia as % of total Philippine imports (cif)
1984	1.7	1984	2.4
1985	1.7	1985	3.4
1986	1.4	1986	3.1
1987	1.6	1987	3.2
1988	1.6	1988	3.6
1989	1.6	1989	3.5
1990	1.2	1990	3.1
1991	1.2	1991	3.2
1992	1.1	1992	2.8
1993	1.0	1993	2.7

Source: Department of Foreign Affairs and Trade, *The APEC Region Trade and Investment*. Canberra: Australian Government Publishing Service, 1994, p 28.

The Philippines is Australia's 32nd-largest supplier of exports. Products include consumer manufactured goods such as clothing and textiles, housewares and furniture, sporting goods, industrial manufactures such as telecommunication equipment, food products (fresh and processed fruit and nuts) and fertilisers. The details about the types of Australia's imports from the Philippines are listed in Table 6.10.

Table 6.10   Australian imports from the Philippines for year ended 30 June 1995

Product type	A$	%
Fish and shellfish	4,362,952	1.68
Cereals and cereal preparations	387,381	0.15
Vegetables and fruit	9,302,117	3.59
Sugars, sugar preparations and honey	251,909	0.10
Coffee, tea, cocoa and spices	4,262,865	1.65
Miscellaneous edible products and their preparations	1,361,993	0.53
Beverages	580,846	0.22
Cork and wood	1,409,216	0.54
Textile fibres	171,293	0.07
Crude fertilisers and crude minerals	213,139	0.08
Metalliferous ores and metal scrap	1,093,446	0.42

Table 6.10 continues.

Table 6.10 (continued)

Product type	A$	%
Crude animal and vegetable materials (nes)	6,299,006	2.43
Chemicals	5,355,473	2.07
Dyeing, tanning and colouring materials	133,566	0.05
Medicinal and pharmaceutical products	3,198,387	1.24
Essential oils, perfume and cleansing preparations	746,235	0.29
Fertilisers (excluding crude)	828,285	0.32
Plastics	396,901	0.15
Chemical materials and products	6,141,636	2.37
Rubber manufactures	524,955	0.20
Cork and wood manufactures (excluding furniture)	3,217,410	1.24
Paper and paperboard	2,939,779	1.14
Textile yarns and fabrics	10,680,235	4.12
Non-metallic mineral manufactures	7,363,062	2.84
Non-ferrous metals	24,231,897	9.36
Manufactures of metals	2,808,473	1.08
Machinery specialised for particular industries	306,810	0.12
General industrial equipment and machine parts	5,664,525	2.19
Office and data-processing machines	7,766,065	3.00
Telecommunications and sound equipment	20,453,494	7.90
Electrical machinery and applicances	63,492,497	24.52
Road vehicles (including air-cushion vehicles)	1,402,428	0.54
Transport equipment (excluding road vehicles)	431,307	0.17
Prefabricated buildings and fittings	1,577,174	0.61
Furniture and similar furnishings	15,741,537	6.08
Travel goods, handbags and similar containers	4,206,309	1.62
Articles of apparel and clothing accessories	15,882,655	6.13
Footwear	2,172,872	0.84
Professional and scientific controlling instruments	387,078	0.15
Photographic equipment, optical goods and clocks	1,550,410	0.60
Miscellaneous manufactured articles (nes)	18,157,205	7.01
Combined confidential items and commodities	1,055,230	0.41
Other items	434,133	0.17
Total imports	**258,944,186**	**100.00**

Source: ABS, *Foreign Trade Statistics: 1994–95*, 1995, pp 647–8.

The Philippines' main imports from Australia include food (mainly dairy produce such as milk and cream, and cereals), iron and steel products (in primary form and flat, rolled sheets), zinc, aluminium and live cattle; the Philippines is in fact Australia's main live-cattle buyer. Specific details of these exports and their relative importance are listed in Table 6.11.

Table 6.11   Australian exports to the Philippines for year ended 30 June 1995

Product type	A$	%
Non-fish live animals	69,917,702	8.33
Meat and meat preparations	26,340,582	3.14
Dairy products and eggs	195,824,083	23.34
Cereals and cereal preparations	40,140,638	4.78
Vegetables and fruit	11,346,469	1.35
Sugars, sugar preparations and honey	5,035,510	0.60
Coffee, tea, cocoa spices, and their manufactures	5,444,504	0.65
Feed for animals (excluding unmilled cereals)	5,444,731	0.65
Miscellaneous edible products and preparations	3,053,938	0.36
Pulp and wastepaper	1,285,986	0.15
Textile fibres	40,018,927	4.77
Crude fertilisers and crude minerals	876,383	0.10
Coal, coke and briquettes	7,802,903	0.93
Petroleum, petroleum products and related materials	7,122,204	0.85
Animal oils and fats	1,185,731	0.14
Fats and oils (processed), waxes and inedible mixtures or preparations	432,040	0.05
Chemicals	4,014,537	0.48
Dyeing, tanning and colouring materials	21,671,503	2.58
Medicinal and pharmaceutical products	32,055,049	3.82
Essential oils, perfume and cleansing preparations	2,694,414	0.32
Plastics	15,297,968	1.82
Chemical materials and products	8,703,833	1.04
Leather, leather manufactures and dressed furskins	1,409,214	0.17
Rubber manufactures	2,608,704	0.31
Cork and wood manufactures (excluding furniture)	1,233,046	0.15
Paper and paperboard	1,979,925	0.24
Textile yarns, fabrics and related products	5,812,777	0.69
Non-metallic mineral manufactures	2,937,754	0.35
Iron and steel	45,503,789	5.42
Non-ferrous metals	140,788,715	16.78
Manufactures of metals	11,744,043	1.40
Power-generating machinery and equipment	3,487,781	0.42
Machinery specialised for particular industries	21,276,179	2.54
Metalworking machinery	949,427	0.11
General industrial equipment and machine parts	16,669,739	1.99
Office and data-processing machines	8,643,013	1.03
Telecommunications and recording equipment	4,835,659	0.58
Electrical machinery and appliances	8,723,702	1.04
Road vehicles (including air-cushion vehicles)	1,488,789	0.18
Transport equipment (excluding road vehicles)	7,617,420	0.91
Furniture and stuffed furnishings	969,848	0.12
Professional and scientific instruments	2,297,696	0.27
Photographic equipment, optical goods and clocks	2,708,050	0.32
Miscellaneous manufactured articles	8,218,274	0.98
Combined confidential items of trade and commodities	22,398,380	2.67
Other items	9,063,179	1.08
Total exports	**839,074,738**	**100.00**

Source: ABS, *Foreign Trade Statistics: 1994–95*, 1995, pp 1231–3.

Historically, Australia has enjoyed a balance-of-trade surplus with reference to the Philippines. This is because Australia has a relative advantage in food production, particularly dairy products, and also because Australian imports feature significantly in the Philippines' input base. The Philippines, however, has had difficulty in penetrating Australian markets. For example, Australia's strict quarantine laws are of concern with reference to the Philippines' food products and cane products, which form a substantial portion of the country's exports to Australia. Also of concern is Australia's lack of accreditation of Philippine inspection agencies.

The Philippines is a country that is rich in natural resources but unfortunately lacks the technological and management expertise and capital funds necessary for fully using them. In the pursuit of economic growth, the government's trade-liberalisation and investment-liberalisation policies have been responsible for opening up many opportunities for foreign investment. Because political stability has been restored and business confidence is increasing, many avenues are open for increasing bilateral trade between the two countries. Through the Australian Aid Development program, the number of joint government and private ventures and projects undertaken by the countries has increased substantially, especially in development of the Philippines' infrastructure, health equipment and services, environmental management and education-service provision. Other opportunities for Australian expertise exist in development of primary commodities and farm machinery, mining exploration, power generation, building and construction, transportation, management consultancy, telecommunications and tourism. Due to the reduction of restrictions in the banking sector, Australia has also increased its influence and market share.

Future prospects

The Philippines has to lift its image as the 'poor person of Asia'. Because debt rescheduling has been successfully renegotiated and the power crisis dealt with, the country is on the path towards economic recovery. Its ability to stimulate growth will depend on its ability to continue to lower its foreign debt while simultaneously managing macro-economic policies.

As part of President Ramos's 'Philippines 2000' vision to kick-start the economy, the government has implemented various strategies that include an expansionary fiscal policy, a more flexible monetary policy, privatisation, and continued trade and investment liberalisation. The country's ability to attract foreign investments and business will depend on the success of the government's policy of lowering restrictions on foreign equity as well as on its ability to sustain a stable political climate. As part of his commitment to stimulate foreign trade and investment, Ramos has taken a more active role in developing better ties with his ASEAN neighbours and with other countries located in the Asia–Pacific region.

The Philippines will continue to rely on and benefit from foreign aid. Japan's role is likely to significantly increase as more investment ventures are established. The US, though, has decreased its contribution since 1991 when it withdrew its military facilities, and the EU countries are likely to focus their political and economic efforts on Eastern Europe.

If Ramos is to succeed in transforming the Philippines into a newly industrialised nation, he will have to concentrate on reducing the deficit, upgrading the infrastructure and managing sustainable economic growth. The pace at which economic development advances will depend on his ability to implement more economic and political reforms while maintaining a stable political environment. His task involves gaining support for his policies from the traditionally slow-moving Senate.

In conclusion, six years into the 1990s, signs exist of some positive outcomes of the Ramos-introduced reforms. These outcomes include elimination of the 'brown-out hours' that crippled the economy for almost a year, reduction of the debt–service ratio to 16 per cent of GNP, reduction of inflation and the trade deficit, an increase in revenue from the successful privatisation programs and an increase in foreign investment.

Indeed, if the Philippines continues on this steady growth path, the not too distant future may witness the country's emergence from its 'poor person of Asia' image to join its ASEAN neighbours as a 'young tiger' economy.

REFERENCES

Alburo, F A, *Political Economy in Liberalizing Foreign Trade: Philippine Experiences*. Quezon City: School of Economics, University of the Philippines, 1993.

Buss, C, *The United States and the Philippines*. Washington, DC: American Enterprise Institute for Public Policy Research, 1977.

George, L, *The East–West Pendulum*. London: Woodhead-Faulkner Ltd, 1992.

Gochoco-Bautista, M and Faustino, J, *AFTA and the Philippines: National Economic Policy-making and Regional Economic Co-operation*. Diliman: Institute for Strategic and Development Studies, 1994.

International Monetary Fund, *International Financial Statistics Yearbook*. International Monetary Fund, 1995.

Lyons, J and Wilson, K, *Marcos and Beyond: The Philippines Revolution*. Kenthurst, New South Wales: Kangaroo Press, 1987.

Rivera, T C, *Landlords and Capitalists: Class, Family and State in Philippine Manufacturing*. Diliman: University of the Philippines Press, 1994.

Shibusawa, M, Ahmad, Z and Bridges, B, *Pacific Asia in the 1990s*. London: Routledge, 1992.

Wong, J, *ASEAN Economies in Perspective*. London: The Macmillan Press, 1979.

World Bank, *World Development Report*. 1994.

Yoshihara, K, *The Nation and Economic Growth: The Philippines and Thailand*. Singapore: Oxford University Press, 1994.

APPENDIX 6.1: *Australian and Philippine representation*

Australian addresses

Australia–Philippines Business Council
PO Box E14, Queen Victoria Terrace
Canberra 2600, ACT, Australia
Telephone: (61 6) 273 2311
Facsimile: (61 6) 273 3196

Embassy of the Philippines
1 Moonah Place
Yarralumla 2600, ACT, Australia
Telephone: (61 6) 273 2535
Facsimile: (61 6) 273 3984

Philippine addresses

Australia and New Zealand Banking Group Limited
Sixth Floor, Salustiana Dee Ty Tower
104 Paseo De Roxas (corner Perea Street)
Legaspi Village
Makati, Metro Manila, The Philippines
Telephone: (63 2) 812 7293/7291
Facsimile: (63 2) 812 7294

Australian Trade Commissioner
Australian Embassy
Third Floor, Salustiana Dee Ty Tower
104 Paseo de Roxas (corner Perea Street)
Legaspi Village
Makati, Metro Manila, The Philippines
Telephone: (63 2) 817 7911
Facsimile: (63 2) 810 2895

APPENDIX 6.2: *Australia's strategic priorities for Philippine trade and investment*

- Advance Australia's reputation of being a reliable and competitive supplier of quality products.
- Update Australian exporters' perceptions of the Philippine market and increase their awareness of increasing opportunities.
- Expand Australia's involvement in infrastructure projects, especially in the energy and telecommunications sectors.

- Overcome market-access barriers, notably for agricultural products, and continue to encourage the Philippines' government in its stated intention to move away from Horne Consumption Value (HCV) as the method for calculating customs duties.
- Increase exports of higher value processed foods.
- Pursue commercial opportunities in the following priority sectors.
    - Livestock, mining and building–construction
    - Telecommunications and energy systems
    - Environmental control and pollution-control technology
    - Industrial technology such as sugar-mill rehabilitation equipment.
- Actively strengthen commercial links between the APBC and the PABC.

Source: Department of Foreign Affairs and Trade, *Australia Trade and Investment Development*. Canberra: Australian Government Publishing Service, 1994, p 112.

7

Singapore

Kevin Wong and Ron Edwards

Introduction

Singapore is often presented as being a model of successful economic development and is now hailed as being the most powerful of the Asia–Pacific region's 'mini-dragons'. It has had phenomenal economic success over the past two decades, is based on sound economic management and social and political stability. This has been responsible for the transformation of the island metropolis, which has limited natural resources, into a modern industrial State. It has a burgeoning economy and is recognised as being an international financial centre.

Singapore's economy has grown as fast as, and in some cases even faster than, the other NIC economies. Its 1995 per-capita income, estimated at US$21,361, was the highest of the NICs. In 1995, its GDP increased at a rate of 8 per cent, similar to its growth rate over the previous five years. Because of this performance, Singapore is an ideal target for Australian exports and investment. Not surprisingly, perhaps, it is already one of Australia's most popular ASEAN markets. This chapter examines the country's position in detail through an examination of its, economic and financial development, its foreign-investment incentives, foreign trade, trade with Australia and its future prospects.

The setting

Located at the tip of the Malaysian peninsula, Singapore occupies an extremely important strategic position between Malaysia and Indonesia, on the main sea route from Europe to East Asia. Although modern warfare capabilities have been responsible for reducing much of its previous military importance, it remains strategic in terms of location. Twenty-five per cent of the world's shipping passes close to its port facilities.

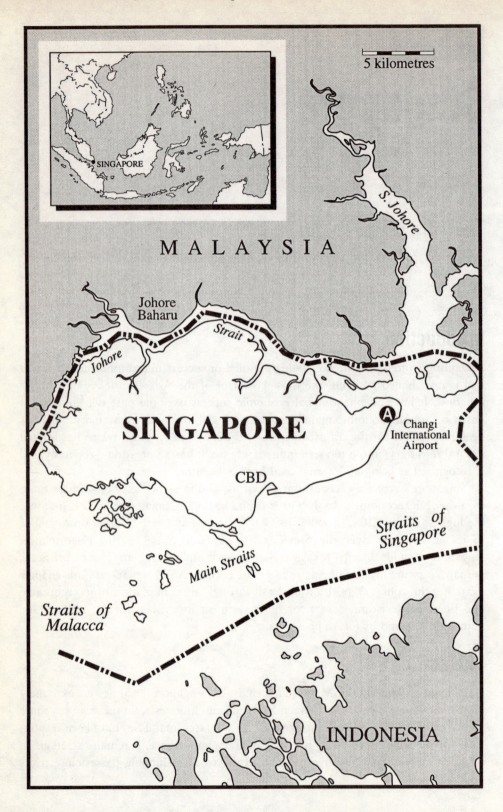

Although many visitors think of Singapore as being an island country, it is more technically an 'islands country' because the republic also includes a number of smaller islands within its 632.6 square kilometres of land. Some of these, such as Sentosa, now seem to be part of the main island in the future. Land reclamation may be responsible for connecting other relatively close islands.

Despite its relatively small land area, Singapore has a population of about 2.9 million. It comprises three main racial groups: Chinese (76 per cent), Malay (15 per cent) and Indian (7 per cent); other groups account for the remaining 2 per cent. This ethic mixture is reflected in the country having four official languages: English, Malay, Mandarin Chinese and Tamil. Malay is also the official national language, and the national anthem is sung in Malay. In practice, English is now the main language of business and of most education environments.

Given its population and small land area, Singapore is basically an urban country. Only 7 per cent of its land area is devoted to permanent crops. The country is also limited through its lack of significant natural resources. Nowadays, even its local water supply is mainly imported from Malaysia. It is often stated that Singapore's only natural resource is the Singaporeans themselves. Its economic success is therefore almost solely dependent on their efforts.

Political history

Singapore was founded on 28 January 1819 by Britain's Sir Thomas Stamford Raffles. He had been instructed to find a strategic station somewhere south of Malacca so that the East India Company's trade interests in the Malay Archipelago would be protected. In an 1824 treaty, the Sultan of Johor ceded control of the entire island, and Raffles made Singapore a free port. He decided a *laissez-faire* policy best suited the company's trading interests and limited Britain's financial commitment to the island.

In 1867, what was at that time the Straits Settlement (Penang, Malacca and Singapore) became a British Crown colony, beginning a period of British-government colonisation and dominance. The British-colonial policy basically continued the tradition of non-interference in the local community's everyday affairs.

Although Singapore was not directly involved in World War I, it was a strategically significant base and port for Western countries' monitoring of armed power in Asia. In World War II, the Japanese quickly conquered what had supposedly been 'Fortress Singapore' and occupied the island for three and a half years. This bitterly demonstrated Singapore's fragility, although the Japanese also demonstrated the role Singapore might potentially play in a Japanese-run East Asia. 'Syonan', or 'light of the South', as the Japanese called Singapore, was placed at the centre of the South-East Asia 'Co-prosperity Sphere'. The Japanese recognised the full potential of the country's strategic geographic position and the advantages of collaboration with its overseas Chinese merchants. In April 1946, following Japan's surrender, British civilian rule resumed.

Singapore's first election was held on 20 March 1948, and 13,458 of the 22,395 electors cast their votes. In 1954 the People's Action Party (PAP) was formed, expressly in order to move Singapore towards independence. In 1961 the PAP's Moderate Wing, led by Lee Kuan Yew (chief minister since the May 1959 election), faced a new onslaught from the left which split from the PAP to join the Opposition.

Meanwhile, Malaysia officially came into existence on 16 September 1963. Indonesia, though, did not recognise the 'neo-colonial' creation of Malaysia, and its President Sukarno commenced a policy of confrontation that continued from 1963 to 1966. All through 1964, Singapore was threatened by a series of Indonesian-inspired riots and bombings.

At the same time, Singapore–Kuala Lumpur relations deteriorated because the Malays accused the PAP of undermining Malaysia's Constitution. Finally, on 9 August 1965, the Malay leaders announced Singapore's official separation from Malaysia. Henceforth, Singapore would be a sovereign, democratic and independent State. The challenge for Singapore was clear. Severed from Peninsular Malaysia and a century of colonialism, it set out to prove it could nevertheless survive and prosper as an independent nation.

Under the leadership of Lee Kuan Yew and his close collaborators in the PAP, Singapore's economy grew from strength to strength and surmounted difficult physical and human-resource constraints. Some writers point out that the country's record of achievement under this first generation of leaders was the product of a small, highly intelligent, well-balanced, likeminded and cohesive Cabinet team as much as it was the work of a single person. This team formulated the ideas, plans and policies that came to provide Singapore with whereby the strong foundation that was necessary for development.

On 28 November 1990, a new chapter opened in Singapore's political history. Lee Kuan Yew handed the 'torch of leadership' to Goh Chok Tong in the expectation that the new leader would carry the nation towards continuing prosperity and security. Others hoped the transition would bring a loosening of the rigid social policy that distinguished Singapore from more liberal trends elsewhere in South East Asia.

Economic development

In 1965, as a newly independent State, Singapore was confronted with a number of economic and political crises which threatened to undermine its economic growth. The seemingly imminent confrontation with Indonesia and the separation from Malaysia threatened its traditional commercial interests in the South-East Asia region. Moreover, the economic realities of a small internal market with almost no natural resources meant the country was presented with a series of challenges.

First, separation from Malaysia meant the two countries' former symbiotic economic association was severed. One immediate result was that trade sharply declined as Malaysia redirected its primary-product exports to local ports and accelerated direct trade links with other trading partners. Malaysia's industrialisation program, which emphasised import substitution, further added to Singapore's problems. Malaysia introduced tariff protection and imposed import quotas in order to provide impetus to nascent industries. As a consequence, Singaporean products were gradually replaced by Malaysian ones.

Second, between 1963 and 1965 the confrontation with Indonesia resulted in a trade boycott by that country, reducing Singapore's total imports by 22 per cent and its total exports by 6 per cent. The boycott was responsible for closing the Indonesian market for many Singaporean goods (textiles and motor vehicles) and for depriving Singaporean traders of their main source of rubber and petroleum products – the mainstay of their entrepot trade. Accordingly, in 1964, entrepot trade shrank by 24.1 per cent.

These political and economic adversities were magnified due to Britain's decision to reduce its military presence, both air and naval, in Singapore and Far East Asia. The already ailing Singaporean economy faced being plunged into the depths of recession. British-government military expenditure and economic and business activity that had been tied to the British presence declined rapidly, causing Singapore's national income to shrink even more.

Confronted with these economic misfortunes, Singapore was determined to adapt to the changed economic and political circumstances. The city-state began to direct its people's energies, enterprise and resourcefulness towards finding alternative pathways to economic growth and development.

Traditionally, Singapore's economic success had been derived from its geostrategic location on the international trade routes: it is right in the heart of the resource-rich Asia–Pacific region. This position allowed the country to act as a channel for trade flows in goods and services between South-East Asia and the rest of the world. This entrepot trade involved, on one side, trade with the natural-resource exporters and 'workshops' of South-East Asia, North-East Asia, South Asia and the Middle East and, on the other side, trade with the industrialised countries (the US, Japan and Western Europe).

The government wanted to broaden the base of the economy and determined that a stronger manufacturing sector would provide the desired growth and security. A well-planned and executed industrialisation program, which commenced in the 1960s, laid the foundation for Singapore's strong future growth. Industrialisation was undertaken, first, to create employment for an expanding labour force, and second, to provide Singapore with an economic alternative to its excessive reliance on entrepot trade. The latter objective has been achieved. In 1993, for example, re-exports comprised only about a third of total exports, compared with about 90 per cent of these in earlier times.

The government's highly interventionist role in economic development has involved establishment of many development agencies and enterprises. Indeed, the Economic Development Board, established in 1961 as a one-stop agency, spearheaded the country's industrialisation program. This was achieved through promotion of investment in manufacturing, particularly to foreign enterprises. The board's 16 overseas offices in the US, Europe and the Asia–Pacific region continue to attract investment.

Almost 500 government-owned companies and statutory boards exist, so the government is also heavily involved in actual production of goods and services. The goods and services include a wide range of manufacturing and service activities such as steel mills, textiles, electronics, oil refining, hotels, shipbuilding and repair, shipping, financial services, air transport and property development. Education, health, public transport and utilities are similarly very much under government control.

In steering Singapore's industrial development, the government has always emphasised economic freedom, including the strong participation of private enterprise and foreign investment. This economic freedom, though, is usually practised under selective and strict State controls whereby investments are channelled into preferred areas that are deemed by the government to be appropriate for sustained economic growth.

Some writers have claimed Singapore's prosperity has been and remains due to the presence of a: 'far sighted and relentless Government rather than the sort of deal-making and quick-footedness which typifies Hong Kong and southern China'.[1]

Between 1979 and 1981, the Singapore government defined and prioritised new sectors of development that were associated with high-technology and advanced services. The sectors included precision engineering, electronics, information technology, optics, chemicals, pharmaceuticals, aeronautics, telecommunications and biotechnology. This change in emphasis was supported through development of the relevant human capital (the Skill Development Fund) and the physical infrastructure. Investment incentives for foreign investment, including technology transfer, credits for research (the Research and Development Assistance Scheme) and productivity improvement (the Mechanisation Scheme) also fostered this change.

Given the existence of changing parameters that might impact on Singapore's continuing economic growth, in 1991 the Economic Planning Committee developed a Strategic Economic Plan. This was designed to bring labour, business and government together in a collaborative effort to secure Singapore's future in the world economy. Its aims are to build on Singapore's major strengths and to initiate a national planning process that involves having a shared vision among labour, business and government. Its vision is for Singapore to catch up with the 'first league' of developed nations, on a moving-target basis, by the years 2020–2030, in four key areas: economic dynamism, national identity, quality of life and configuration of a global city.

The plan's basic strategy is to maintain and extend Singapore's international competitiveness through eight 'strategic thrusts', implemented through 17 programs. The eight strategic thrusts are as follows:

- Enhance human resources through attraction of international talents.
- Promote teamwork among the members of governments, business and the labour force.
- Increase international orientation through education of the people and alliance with the region's countries.
- Promote an innovative climate through review of government rules that hinder innovations.
- Develop specific clusters, or niches, within manufacturing and services whereby Singapore can match the capabilities of first-class developed nations.

- Help the domestic sector to redevelop economically and improve productivity.
- Improve the country's ability to maintain competitiveness through development of better monitoring systems of both short-term and medium- to long-term competitiveness.
- Minimise economic vulnerabilities by encouraging MNCs to treat Singapore as a home base and by developing local enterprises.

Singapore's rapid but balanced economic growth has continued over the first few years of the 1990s. GDP has grown: in 1993 it registered a healthy 9.9 per cent growth rate but in 1994 and 1995 it slowed slightly to an expected steady growth rate of 7.0 per cent.

Table 7.1   Singapore's key economic indicators: 1989, 1992, 1993 and 1994

	%			
Indicator	1989	1991	1993	1994
Inflation	2.4	3.4	2.4	3.1
Unemployment	2.2	1.9	2.7	2.6
Real GDP growth	9.2	7.0	9.9	7.0

Source: Department of Foreign Affairs and Trade, *The APEC Region Trade and Investment*. Canberra: Australian Government Publishing Service, 1994, pp 84, 96 and 100; 1995, pp 84, 96 and 100.

The growth momentum of the manufacturing sector and the financial services subsector was sustained in the early 1990s, particularly 1993. Led by expansion of the electronics industry and the US economy's recovery, the manufacturing sector grew by 7.6 per cent in the first quarter of 1993 and the financial services subsector registered growth of 7.9 per cent during the same period. The services sector, which as indicated in Table 7.2 now contributes about two-thirds of GDP, expanded by 10.3 per cent in 1993 – the highest rate since 1990 – and is expected to increase by almost 6 per cent in 1996. The transport-and-communications sector and the construction sector also experienced strong value-added growth.

Table 7.2   Singapore's GDP by sector, 1994

Sector	% of total
Primary	0.1
Manufacturing	25.6
Electricity, gas and water	1.6
Construction	7.1
Wholesale and retail trade	16.2
Transport and communications	11.4
Finance and business services	28.0
Other services	10.0
Total	**100**

Source: *Europa World Year Book (1995)*, Europa, London, p 2696.

Specific industries such as printing and publishing, food and beverages, and transport equipment including ship repair, are expected to grow more strongly over the next few years, despite emerging competition for Singapore's exports and the world economy's slow recovery.

External demand for goods and services has been strong over the past few years. Exports of goods and services rose by 33 per cent in 1994. Expansion of both domestic exports and re-exports contributed to high export growth. There has been strong growth in domestic export of disk drives, integrated circuits, computer parts and peripherals, as well as in radio telephonic and telegraphic receivers. Significant growth also occurred in re-exports of computer parts and related computer products, video-cassette recorders, airconditioners, calculating machines, and like products.

Over the past three decades of economic development, Singapore has painstakingly built up capabilities in a wide range of services – from financial and banking services to infrastructural services such as construction, public housing, utilities, port, telecommunications and transportation, as well as technology services such as information technology. A number of these services have significant export potential, particularly in the areas of finance and banking, telecommunications, transportation and information technology. The government is keen to build on these competitive advantages and to 'market' them as preferred industries in Singapore's industrial development.

Financial development

A key platform of Singapore's regional trade-and-investment strategy has been transformation of its traditional trade-financing role, as an entrepot, into the role of a modern, international financial centre. Since creation of the Asian-dollar market in 1968, Singapore has played an increasingly important role in the South-East Asia region as well as in general world finance – indeed, it is now often ranked fourth among the world's top financial centres.

As indicated in Table 7.3, Singapore's financial sector comprises an impressive group of financial companies that includes a wide range of institution types. This diversity is an important component of the country's international and regional success, and the government continues to encourage high-quality foreign firms to open a local office. The market therefore seems to be highly competitive.

Table 7.3 Singapore's financial institutions, 1995

Institution	Number of institutions
Monetary Authority of Singapore	1
Local commercial banks	12
Fully licensed foreign commercial banks	22
Restricted licensed foreign commercial banks	14
Offshore licensed foreign banks	92
Post Office Savings Bank	1
Merchant banks	77
Finance companies	23
Asian-currency units (ACUs)	209
Insurance companies	23
Local stockbrokers	33
Foreign stockbrokers	48
Investment advisors	136
International moneybrokers	11
Economic Development Board	1
Central Provident Fund	1
Total	**704**

Source: Monetary Authority of Singapore, *Annual Report 1994–1995*. Singapore: Monetary Authority of Singapore, 1995, p 52.

In practice, though, we should consider Singapore's financial sector from two closely connected viewpoints. The first aspect for consideration is that the country is a modern, highly internationalised offshore financial centre. We could view this as being Singapore's 'showcase'. Because almost every important international commercial or investment bank is represented there, Singapore is truly the ASEAN countries' most international financial sector. Most of its commercial banks and merchant banks are active participants, through Asian-currency-unit (ACU) authorisations, in what is commonly known as the Asian-dollar market. Due to availability of the most modern of electronic communication methods, the Singapore market is closely integrated with the key world markets of London, New York, Tokyo, Hong Kong, and Sydney–Melbourne and is the world's fourth-largest foreign-exchange market.

Singapore's government seeks to expand this foreign-exchange and international banking leadership to encompass other aspects of international finance. In the futures market, for example, the Singapore International Monetary Exchange (SIMEX) plays an important trading role for the region with reference to a range of contracts, most of which are unrelated to Singapore's domestic markets. Also with noticeably less success, it has attempted to promote the Stock Exchange of Singapore (SES) in order to have a similar international or regional role through encouragement of foreign listings and electronic trading. Another, somewhat more successful, area is international funds management. Tax incentives make it attractive for international funds managers to base their portfolios in Singapore. At the end of 1994, 113 fund-management companies were handling about 43.6 billion Singaporean dollars (S$43.6 billion) on behalf of their overseas clients. As well as being attracted by Singapore's tax incentives and other financial centre advantages, the international fund managers were attracted by the country's own domestic-market potential and the government's plans for liberalising the management choices that were available to its Central Provident Fund members.

Before we move on from the financial sector, some mention should be made of the Singapore dollar, because it has played an important role in the country's development. In general, the government has pursued a strong dollar policy as part of its anti-inflation measures. It believed any disadvantage from higher export prices would be offset by higher productivity and by lowering the price of imported raw materials. As Table 7.4 indicates, this policy is reflected in part in the Singapore dollar's gradual appreciation against the US dollar. The appreciation against the Australian dollar has been even more extreme, and the two currencies are now almost at parity.

Table 7.4   Singapore dollar against the US dollar and the Australian dollar, 1984–95*

Year	US dollar			Australian dollar		
	High	Low	Close	High	Low	Close
1984	2.1810	2.0615	2.1810	N/A**	N/A	1.4850
1985	2.3110	2.0860	2.1050	N/A	N/A	1.4352
1986	2.2450	2.0990	2.7925	N/A	N/A	1.4454
1987	2.1728	1.9825	1.9970	N/A	N/A	1.4420
1988	2.0565	1.9330	1.9450	N/A	N/A	1.6599
1989	1.9855	1.8900	1.8975	N/A	N/A	1.4952
1990	1.9157	1.7000	1.7352	1.5050	1.2960	1.3392
1991	1.8000	1.6175	1.6210	1.3984	1.2282	1.2287
1992	1.6850	1.5865	1.6950	1.2464	1.1079	1.1303
1993	1.6693	1.5540	1.6075	1.1799	1.0102	1.0912
1994	1.6148	1.4542	1.4570	1.1586	1.0746	1.1292
1995*	1.4636	1.3917	1.4135	1.1318	1.0269	1.0525

*The 1995 figures are up to 31 December.
**N/A = not applicable.
Source: Australia and New Zealand Banking Group, 1995.

The second aspect of Singapore's financial sector is the domestic finance industry. Unlike the offshore financial sector, entry to the domestic market remains restricted. No foreign banks have been given even a restricted local licence since 1977. Retail banking is dominated by four powerful financial groups: the Development Bank of Singapore (DBS), Oversea-Chinese Banking Group (OCBC), Overseas Union Bank (OBU), and the United Overseas Bank (UOB). These banks' relative asset sizes are shown in Table 7.5. Each group has an equity position in other smaller banks that are located in Singapore and overseas, as well as an equity position in affiliated finance companies, property-development firms, merchant banks and, frequently, insurance companies. While it is beyond doubt that these institutions compete keenly for business and have invested heavily in technology, this market is quite different from its Asian-dollar counterpart.

Table 7.5 Singapore's major domestic commercial banks, 1994

Bank*	Assets US$ million
DBS Bank (12/94)	30,936
Oversea-Chinese Banking Corporation (12/94)	27,075
United Overseas Bank (12/94)	25,571
Overseas Union Bank (12/94)	14,592
Keppel Bank of Singapore (12/94)	5,491
Tat Lee Bank (12/94)	5,139

*The figures for the year and month ended are in parentheses.
Source: The *Banker*, October 1995, p 68.

Foreign investment

Singapore has been a ready recipient of foreign equity. Foreign-capital inflow jumped from a meagre US$8.6 million at the end of 1962 to US$84.4 million in 1966 and then to US$252.8 million in 1969. In the 1980s, foreign ownership represented more than a third of all equity investments in the corporate sector – by far the highest level in East Asia.[3] By the end of 1991, cumulative foreign manufacturing investment in the country totalled US$26 billion. Singapore's success in attracting foreign capital has in fact given rise to some concern about the 'over-presence' of, and the over-reliance on, the MNCs that supply a third of the country's gross-capital formation.

Singapore's government has played a significant role in attracting MNCs. This has involved provision of industrial sites and establishment of an agency in order to cater for the investing firms' financial, labour and advisory needs. Legislation has been introduced so that specific investment can be promoted; two examples are introduction of the Pioneer Industries Ordinance 1959 and the Economic Expansion Incentives Act 1967, whereby qualifying investors were exempted from paying company tax for five years.

The Trade Development Board (TDB) undertakes development and expansion of Singapore's trade in goods and services through providing a market-advice service to firms that sell overseas. Globalink and TradeNet are examples of computer networks the TDB uses to provide up-to-date market and trade information to clients. The TDB may also administer tax incentives.

Tax concessions include tax 'holidays' and reduced tax rates that are used to attract new investment for the government's preferred industries. The concessions are administered by the Economic Development Board, which is also responsible for helping corporations to set up operations in Singapore, obtain land and factory space and, if necessary, obtain the appropriate skilled labour. It also helps contact potential suppliers, subcontractors and joint-venture partners if the potential investor requires those services. Seven of the more important tax incentives are listed as follows.[4]

Pioneer industries

This designation is given to approved manufacturing and service activities and takes the form of a five- to ten-year tax holiday.

Post-pioneer

This status enables approved companies' profits that are earned after completion of the pioneer period to be assessed for an extended period of up to 10 years at a rate as low as 10 per cent.

Capital investments

Businesses may claim an accelerated depreciation allowance at a rate of 33.3 per cent per year that is based on a straight-line calculation for machinery and equipment.

Pioneer service companies

This incentive is extended to service companies that promote Singapore as a centre for development and export of high-quality technical services.

Foreign-loan scheme for manufacturing and service activities

This includes exemption from paying the withholding tax on interest.

Approved royalties for approved manufacturing and service activities

These include half or full exemption of the withholding tax on royalties.

Investment allowance

This is given so that investment in new production equipment is stimulated and thereby brings about higher productivity in terms of labour use and higher value-added activities, for example mechanisation and automation.

These tax policies have been very successful, and Singapore has received the largest capital inflow of all the ASEAN members. Forty per cent of the funds have been channelled into the electrical and electronic products industry. Other than that industry, the most significant FDI has been in petroleum and petroleum products, industrial chemicals, machinery, and fabricated-metal products. In the manufacturing sector, the most significant foreign investors are from the US, Japan and various European countries. These companies feature in Singapore's import and export trade. In 1988, for example, it was estimated that foreign corporations accounted for 90 per cent of the manufacturing sector's exports.

Although Australia is not a major FDI supplier to world markets, from its very low 1970s base, it increased its investment supply at a rate of 17 per cent per year during the 1980s. In 1994 only 13 per cent of the total stock of funds was located in ASEAN member countries – Australian MNCs prefer to invest in the UK, the US and New Zealand.

Singapore and Malaysia are ASEAN's largest recipients of Australian investment: they have two-thirds of ASEAN's total stocks of Australian FDI. Although comment on the nature of the firms involved is prevented due to data restrictions, it is clear that Australian manufacturing companies, finance houses and service providers are prominent in Singapore.

Foreign trade

International trade is Singapore's lifeblood. The country has few imports barriers. It prefers to expose its domestic producers to international competition and thereby gives them unfettered access to imported raw materials and other inputs. Singapore has therefore not pursued the import-replacement strategies that have commonly been used by other ASEAN members. Because of its export growth it has been raised to a prominent position in world trade. Over the past two decades it has moved from being the world's thirty-first-largest exporter to being its twelfth-largest, which is a surprising achievement given the small size of its economy. Singapore now accounts for 2.3 per cent of total world exports. By way of comparison, Australia ranks twenty-first and contributes 1.1 per cent of world trade.

The explanation for Singapore's disproportionate importance in world trade lies in its role as an entrepot for the region. It has long used its strategic location in order to act as a distribution centre – trans-shipping goods and undertaking basic processing of raw materials for re-export. Its exports therefore exceed its GDP by more than a third. However, its industrial structure has changed over the past two decades. Manufacturing has progressed from its earlier labour-intensive nature and focuses on higher value-added products and services. Consequently, manufactures now account for 83 per cent of total exports. ETMs make up the bulk of this percentage: 79 per cent. In order of importance, the exports include automatic data-processing equipment, refined petroleum, semi-conductors and integrated circuits, and telecommunications equipment. The major imports include crude petroleum, semi-conductors and integrated circuits, parts and accessories for office machines, and telecommunications equipment.

Table 7.6   Singapore's trading partners, 1994

Country or region	Exports %	Trend* %	Imports %	Trend* %
Brunei	0.8	−5.0	0.2	−2.6
Indonesia	1.9	−6.3	3.9	5.5
Malaysia	19.4	7.7	15.7	3.8
Philippines	1.6	9.9	0.7	11.3
Thailand	5.4	−4.7	4.6	13.8
Total ASEAN	29.1	3.2	25.1	5.7
Australia	2.3	−2.2	1.5	−6.3
Canada	0.6	−8.1	0.4	−11.8
Chile	0.1	3.2	0.1	−2.5
China	2.1	13.9	2.7	−6.3
Hong Kong	8.5	7.6	3.2	1.6
Japan	6.9	−6.1	21.2	1.3
South Korea	2.6	4.7	3.7	6.1
Mexico	0.2	8.6	0.1	−12.4
New Zealand	0.3	−4.2	0.2	−5.6
Papua New Guinea	0.2	−11.5	0.0	8.6
Taiwan	4.0	2.9	3.7	−3.0
United States	18.4	−2.5	14.7	−1.4
Total APEC	**75.3**	**1.0**	**76.6**	**1.4**
European Union	13.2	−2.6	12.6	−2.2
Other	11.5	−2.8	10.8	−6.8
Total	**100.0**		**100.0**	

*The trend growth is for the period 1990–94.
Source: Department of Foreign Affairs and Trade, *The APEC Region Trade and Investment*. Canberra: Australian Government Publishing Service, 1995.

In recent years, Singapore's emergence as an international financial centre has caused manufacturing to decline as a share of GDP and has caused financial and business services to grow. This reflects the country's loss of competitiveness in labour-intensive manufacturing and its expanding role as a services supplier. It now supplies almost half of ASEAN's services exports.

Singapore has led the process of ASEAN's economic integration, and this is reflected in the trade figures. Intra-ASEAN trade, especially in manufactured goods, has been increasing. Over the past five years, exports to ASEAN members have grown faster than total exports have, and they now account for 29 per cent of total exports. Singapore's exports to Malaysia, for example, nearly doubled in 1994, thereby making Malaysia Singapore's largest market. The US nevertheless remains an important export market, taking 18 per cent of total exports in 1994.

For Singapore, ASEAN has also become more important as a source of imports and now supplies more than 25 per cent of the total. Japan is the second-largest import source: in 1994 it supplied 21 per cent of the total imports.

It is also worthwhile to examine Singapore's trade with ASEAN from a historical perspective. Between 1990 and 1994, as indicated in Table 7.6, some noticeable shifts have occurred in Singapore's trade with ASEAN. With reference to exports, for example, a decline has actually occurred in the relative importance of Indonesia and Thailand. The Philippines and Malaysia showed the most improvement. The position is slightly different with reference to imports: all ASEAN members except Brunei have increased their share of Singapore's imports, and Thailand has had the largest increase.

Trade with Australia

Singapore is the most important destination for Australia's merchandise exports to South-East Asia and is the fifth-largest in the world. This partly reflects the growing demand that exists elsewhere in South-East Asia, because many of these goods are re-exported. Growth in Australia's trade with Singapore has been very strong: each year, exports grow by about 7 per cent and imports by 11 per cent. This growth has not been enough for Australia to increase its relative importance, though. As Table 7.7 indicates, in 1984 Australia accounted for 3.4 per cent of Singapore's exports but by 1994 our importance had declined to only 2.3 per cent. Our share of Singapore's imports have likewise declined, from 2.5 per cent in 1984 to only 1.5 per cent in 1994.

Table 7.7 Australia's importance for Singaporean trade, 1984–94

	Singapore's exports (fob)		Singapore's imports (cif)
Year	Australia as % of total	Year	Australia as % of total
1984	3.4	1984	2.5
1985	3.3	1985	2.6
1986	3.1	1986	1.7
1987	2.7	1987	1.9
1988	2.7	1988	2.0
1989	2.9	1989	1.7
1990	2.5	1990	2.0
1991	2.5	1991	1.9
1992	2.4	1992	1.7
1993	2.3	1993	1.7
1994	2.3	1994	1.5

Source: Department of Foreign Affairs and Trade. *The APEC Region Trade and Investment*. Canberra: Australian Government Publishing Service, 1995, pp 38–9.

It should again be emphasised that in absolute dollar terms, Singapore's exports to and imports from Australia have increased significantly. It is simply that Singapore's trade with other countries (notably Malaysia) has grown even more rapidly. Even so, Australia has done reasonably well from its relationship with

Singapore and enjoys a substantial trade surplus. In 1994, the surplus amounted to more than A$1.4 billion.

Non-monetary gold and manufactures dominate our exports to Singapore. Gold and gold coins account for more than 40 per cent of exports, despite the occurrence of a decline from A$1.9 billion of export sales in 1992–93 to A$1.6 billion in 1993–94. Petroleum (crude and refined) is the second-largest export item, followed by unprocessed dairy products. Singapore ranks as Australia's third-largest ETM market, ahead of Japan, which makes it a very important market for this sector of Australia's economy.

Table 7.8   Australian exports to Singapore, 1995

Type of product	A$ thousand	%
Meat and meat preparations	39,295	1.1
Milk and cream products	73,525	2.0
Butter and other milk fats	19,645	0.5
Seafood	39,808	1.1
Vegetables	41,141	1.1
Fruit and nuts	49,539	1.4
Food and live animals	70,369	1.9
Crude petroleum and oils	150,589	4.1
Refined petroleum and oils	200,982	5.5
Inorganic chemicals	9,983	0.3
Paints, varnishes and pigments	28,517	0.8
Medicaments (including veterinary)	23,493	0.6
Chemicals and related products	67,139	1.8
Pearls and precious stones	5,974	0.2
Non-metallic mineral manufactures	23,697	0.7
Flat-rolled iron, steel coated	58,542	1.6
Iron and steel	31,417	0.9
Copper	86,457	2.4
Aluminium	62,181	1.7
Zinc	6,225	0.2
Structures of iron, steel or aluminium	16,808	0.5
Metal manufactures	22,222	0.6
Manufactures classified by material	86,100	2.4
Power generating machinery	19,705	0.5
Civil engineering equipment	18,189	0.5
Other industry-specific machinery	32,456	0.9
Heating and cooling equipment	15,884	0.4
General industrial machinery	58,993	1.6
Computers	49,231	1.4
Computers and office machine parts	108,559	3.0
Electrical equipment for circuits	43,165	1.2
Electrical machinery and appliances	51,590	1.4
Road vehicles	37,982	1.0
Ships, boats and floating structures	7,976	0.2
Machinery and transport equipment	66,680	1.8

Table 7.8 continues.

Table 7.8 (continued)

Type of product	A$ thousand	%
Measuring and checking equipment	14,200	0.4
Photo and cinematographic supplies	77,501	2.1
CDs, tapes, software and musical instruments	7,431	0.2
Miscellaneous manufactures articles	83,325	2.3
Gold, monetary and non-monetary	1,573,359	43.0
Confidential items	124,269	3.4
Other	35,113	1.0
Total	**3,639,251**	**100**

Note: total calculated from actual not rounded numbers

Source: Department of Foreign Affairs and Trade, *Composition of Trade, Australia 1994–95*. Canberra: Australian Government Publishing Service, 1995.

Table 7.9   Australian imports from Singapore, 1995

Type of product	A$ thousand	%
Seafood	13,166	0.6
Cocoa	30,726	1.4
Edible products and preparations	10,850	0.5
Food and live animals	13,622	0.6
Crude materials	12,489	0.6
Crude petroleum and oils	7,524	0.3
Refined petroleum and oils	301,577	13.4
Animal and vegetable oils, fats and waxes	9,909	0.4
Organo-inorganic and heterocyclic compounds	54,076	2.4
Medicinal and pharmaceutical products	7,392	0.3
Polymers of ethylene, primary forms	20,633	0.9
Prepared additives for mineral oils, etc	16,609	0.7
Chemicals and related products	45,887	2.0
Cork and wood manufactures	4,485	0.2
Paper cut to size and paper articles	12,913	0.6
Metal manufactures	16,912	0.8
Manufactures classified by material	57,803	2.6
Other industry-specific machinery	10,746	0.5
Gas pumps, centrifuges and purifiers	27,221	1.2
General industrial machinery	26,860	1.2
Computers	654,504	29.1
Computers and office machine parts, etc	191,887	8.5
Television monitors and projectors	3,883	0.2
Radio-broadcast receivers	67,511	3.0
Telecommunications equipment	26,794	1.2
Electrical equipment for circuits	33,512	1.5
Household equipment	8,384	0.4
Cathode valves and tubes, integrated circuits, etc	113,526	5.1
Electrical machinery	25,554	1.1
Aircraft and associated equipment	4,206	0.2
Ships, boats and floating structures	10,961	0.5

Table 7.9 continues.

Table 7.9 (continued)

Type of product	A$ thousand	%
Machinery and transport equipment	39,946	1.8
Furniture, mattresses, etc	2,717	0.1
Measuring and checking equipment	46,679	2.1
Photo optical equipment and clocks	9,948	0.4
Printed matter	59,184	2.6
Plastic articles	18,794	0.8
CDs, tapes, software and musical instruments	77,870	3.5
Miscellaneous manufactured articles	26,583	1.2
Confidential items	119,169	5.3
Other	3,953	0.2
Total	**2,246,914**	**100.0**

Note: total calculated from actual not rounded numbers
Source: Department of Foreign Affairs and Trade, *Composition of Trade, Australia 1994–95*. Canberra: Australian Government Publishing Service, 1995.

In 1994–95, manufactures accounted for 77 per cent of Australia's merchandise imports from Singapore, up from the 1989–90 figure of 60 per cent. The main imports from Singapore, as shown in Table 7.9, included computers, refined petroleum, cathode valves and tubes, compact discs (CDs), tapes, computer software, musical instruments, semi-conductors and integrated circuits.

Table 7.10   Australia's merchandise trade with Singapore, 1994–95

	Exports (A$ million)	Trend* %	Imports (A$ million)	Trend* %
Unprocessed food	128.9	4.4	11.0	10.4
Processed food	212.0	12.4	68.7	1.3
Other rural	12.0	28.2	8.9	0.2
Minerals	5.8	−5.7	3.4	21.2
Fuels	353.0	−9.4	310.9	−2.2
TOTAL PRIMARY PRODUCTS	**711.6**	**−2.6**	**402.9**	**−1.2**
Simply transformed	174.0	6.3	107.4	9.9
Elaborately transformed	1,047.5	18.0	1,616.2	23.8
TOTAL MANUFACTURES	**1,221.5**	**16.0**	**1,723.6**	**22.6**
Other merchandise	1,706.1	4.5	120.4	22.0
TOTAL	**3,639.3**	**5.7**	**2,246.9**	**15.7**

Source: Department of Foreign Affairs and Trade. *The APEC Region Trade and Investment*. Canberra: Australian Government Publishing Service, 1995, p 45.

As Singapore is pursuing its drive towards becoming a high-technology and services-oriented industrial economy and a regional business hub, it will increase its investment in infrastructure, building and construction, capital equipment and business systems. Labour-intensive activities are likely to be relocated to surrounding economies. Also, because of its citizens' high average income, considerable demand for consumer goods will be generated. Accordingly, there will be demand for building materials, construction equipment and processed foods. Australian business has demonstrated its capacity to compete in the building-and-construction sector. It should be able to capitalise on the opportunities Singapore's development will generate, despite the strength of competition from local firms and other countries' firms. A good example of this was Australian firms' success in the Changi Airport project. Firms supplied landing-help equipment, lighting, drainage and sewerage-hole covers, metal ceiling systems, acoustic material, data communications, roofing and steel structures.

At present, Australia supplies 9 per cent of Singapore's food market. Competition in that market is likely to increase because Malaysia and Indonesia are expanding their interests in the area. However, Australia remains well placed to continue being a major supplier, especially of meat, dairy products, sugar and other higher added-value produce.

Singapore will maintain and expand its role as a regional headquarters, despite Australia's ambitions in that area. Singapore's specific advantages in finance, business services and research and development will continue to be responsible for its attractiveness as a foreign-affiliate location. The existence of these three strengths means opportunities are presented for Australian firms that can provide support services – for example, Australia is well placed to provide education, training and professional services. At present, Australia ranks third, behind the US and the UK, as a destination for Singaporean university students.

Future prospects

In a survey of international competitiveness, Singapore has ranked second (its score was 94.9) – behind only the US (its score was 100). Using about 380 criteria, the survey combined official statistics and a questionnaire and was sent to 16,500 business executives worldwide so that a grid of business competitiveness could be built. The report concluded that Singapore 'shines in almost every aspect of competitiveness', and ranks first in 'government' and 'people' factors. However, due to the rise of new, lower cost competitors such as China, Vietnam, Thailand and Malaysia, which are rapidly developing their capabilities and gaining a competitive edge, Singapore cannot afford to rest on its laurels. It can no longer compete on cost alone but will have to evolve a differentiated competitive strategy that is viable and sustainable in the medium to long term.

Based on a survey of more than 137 top Singaporean executives, who are working in either the government sector or the private sector, Singapore now considers its most important challenges to be as follows:
- The shortage of skilled and talented workers is responsible for discouraging viable companies from expanding or diversifying.

- The rising cost of doing business is leading to loss of competitiveness.
- The industrialised countries are experiencing recession.
- Upgrading infrastructural facilities in the region's other countries makes them more competitive.
- Political upheavals in South-East Asia have a direct impact on Singapore.[5]

As Singapore continues to undergo a structural change from being a predominantly manufacturing-oriented economy to being service-oriented labour shortages will continue to place upward pressure on wages. This implies a need for the government to enhance human-resource investment, as well as a need for review of the education system and immigration policy, particularly the aspects that relate to foreign professionals.

In order to maintain competitiveness in Asia and the world economy, Singapore will continue to restructure towards three areas: higher value-added activities, knowledge-intensive products, and technology-intensive production lines. Australian businesses are well placed to share in the growth – to 'ride on the tiger's tail'.

ENDNOTES

1 From 'The *Australian* Special Survey', in the *Australian*, 13 August, 1993, p 28.
2 From Bello, W and Rosenfeld, S, *Dragons in Distress: Asia's Miracle Economies in Crisis*. London: Penguin Books, 1992.
3 From the Government of Singapore, *Singapore: The Next Lap*. Singapore: Times Editions Ltd, 1991.
4 Compiled from Bello, W and Rosenfeld, S, *Dragons in Distress: Asia's Miracle Economies in Crisis*. London: Penguin Books, 1992; and Price Waterhouse, *Doing Business in Singapore: Information Guide*. 1993.
5 From the Government of Singapore, *Singapore: The Strategic Economic Plan – Towards a Developed Nation*. Singapore: Times Editions Ltd, 1991.

REFERENCES

Asian Development Bank, *Asian Development Outlook 1994*. Hong Kong: Oxford University Press, 1994.

Bello, W and Rosenfeld, S, *Dragons in Distress: Asia's Miracle Economies in Crisis*. London: Penguin Books, 1992.

Berger, P L and Hsiao, H M (eds), *In Search of an East Asian Development Model*. New Brunswick: Transaction Books, 1988.

Bureau of Industry Economics, *Australian Direct Investment Abroad*. Occasional Paper 26. Canberra: Australian Government Publishing Service, 1995.

Carnegie, G, and Sharpe, D, *Singapore*. Kensington, New South Wales: Asia–Australia Institute, University of New South Wales, 1993.

Chen, E K Y, *Hyper-growth in Asian Economies*. London: Macmillan, 1980.

Chia, S Y, The Role of Foreign Trade and Investment in the Development of Singapore, in Galenson, (ed), 1985.

Department of Foreign Affairs and Trade, *The APEC Region Trade and Investment*. Canberra: Australian Government Publishing Service, 1994.

East Asia Analytical Unit, Department of Foreign Affairs and Trade, *AFTA: Trading Bloc or Building Block?*. Canberra: Australian Government Publishing Service, 1994.

—— *Australia's Business Challenge: South-East Asia in the 1990s*. Canberra: Australian Government Publishing Service, 1992.

Huff, W G, *The Economic Growth of Singapore: Trade and Development in the Twentieth Century*. Cambridge: Cambridge University Press, 1994.

Josey, A, *Singapore: Its Past, Present and Future*. London: Andre Deutsch Ltd, 1980.

Lee, C Y, *Singapore: The Year in Review*. Singapore: Times Academic Press, 1994.

Lim, C Y *et al.*, *Policy Options for the Singapore Economy*. Singapore: McGraw-Hill Book Company, 1988.

Milne, R S and Mauzy, D K, *Singapore: The Legacy of Lee Kuan Yew*. Boulder: Westview Press Inc, 1990.

Monetary Authority of Singapore, *Annual Report 1994/95*. Singapore: Monetary Authority of Singapore, 1995.

Murray, G and Perera, A, *Singapore: The Global City-State*. New York: St Martin's Press, 1995.

Patrick, H (ed), *Pacific Basin Industries in Distress*. New York: Columbia University Press, 1991.

Price Waterhouse, *Doing Business in Singapore: Information Guide*. United States: Price Waterhouse World Firm Ltd, 1993.

Regnier, P, *Singapore: City-State in South-East Asia*. Malaysia: S Abdul Majeed and Co, 1992.

Rodan, G (ed), *Singapore Changes Guard: Social, Political and Economic Directions in the 1990s*. Melbourne: Longman Cheshire, 1993.

Seng, Y P and Lim, C Y, *The Singapore Economy*. Singapore: Eastern University Press, 1971.

Soon, L Y (ed), *Foreign Direct Investment in ASEAN*. Kuala Lumpur: Malaysian Economic Association, 1990.

'The *Australian* Special Survey', in the *Australian*, 13 August 1993.

The Government of Singapore, *Singapore: The Next Lap*. Singapore: Times Editions Ltd, 1991.

Wong, K, 'Singapore: A New Trade Era', in *Business Victoria*, October 1993.

World Bank, *World Development Report*. Oxford: Oxford University Press, 1994.

Yeoh, C, Theng, L, Goh, M and Richardson, J, *Strategic Business Opportunities in the Growth Triangle*. Singapore: Longman Singapore Publishers, 1992.

APPENDIX 7.1: *Australian and Singaporean representation*

Australian addresses

Bank of Singapore
Level 2, 75 Castlereagh Street
Sydney 2000, NSW, Australia
Telephone: (61 2) 9235 2022
Facsimile: (61 2) 9221 4360

Overseas Union Bank
Level 12, 53 Martin Place
Sydney 2000, NSW, Australia
Telephone: (61 2) 9233 4211
Facsimile: (61 2) 9233 6492

Singapore High Commission
17 Forster Crescent
Yarralumla 2600, ACT, Australia
Telephone: (61 6) 273 3944
Facsimile: (61 6) 273 3260

United Overseas Bank
Level 19, 32 Martin Place
Sydney 2000, NSW, Australia
Telephone: (61 2) 9211 1924
Facsimile: (61 2) 9221 1541

Singaporean addresses

Australia and New Zealand Banking Group Limited
17–01/07, Ocean Building
10 Collyer Quay
Singapore 0104
Telephone: (65) 535 8355
Facsimile: (65) 539 6111

Australian High Commission
25 Napier Road
Singapore 1025
Telephone: (65) 731 1767
Facsimile: (65) 734 4265

Australian Trade Commissioner
Australian High Commission
25 Napier Road
Singapore 1025
Telephone: (65) 731 7160
Facsimile: (65) 734 4265

Commonwealth Bank of Australia
22–04, Shell Tower
50 Raffles Place
Singapore 0104
Telephone: (65) 224 3877
Facsimile: (65) 224 5812

National Australia Bank
31–00, OCBC Centre
65 Chulia Street
Singapore 0104
Telephone: (65) 535 7655
Facsimile: (65) 534 4264

Westpac Banking Corporation
OCBC Centre
Level 42
65 Chulia Street
Singapore 0104
Telephone: (65) 530 9520
Facsimile: (65) 535 7509

APPENDIX 7.2: *Australia's strategic priorities for Singaporean trade and investment*

- Expand exports of ETMs, particularly in high-growth sectors such as information technology and communications.
- Expand exports of services, especially education, tourism, design, architecture, health, public relations, transport and project management.
- Promote two-way investment flows by identifying opportunities and bringing investment partners together.
- Continue to improve Australia's image of being a sophisticated, efficient and capable economic partner.

Source: Department of Foreign Affairs and Trade, *Australia Trade and Investment Development*. Canberra: Australian Government Publishing Service, 1994, p 76.

8

Thailand

Julie Edwards

Introduction

Over the past 25 years, Thailand's economy has undergone dramatic change. The country has moved from being an agricultural economy based on a narrow range of commody exports to a country that is gaining a reputation as being an NIC. Thailand's relationship with Australia has also shifted during this period. It has developed from being an exotic tourist destination to being an important trading partner. During the 10 years to 1993–94, Thailand rose 12 places to become the twelfth-most important destination for Australian exports. It also holds a solid position among the world's 50 top exporting nations. It ranks twenty-fifth and has a 1.0 per cent share of world exports.

Thailand's rapid growth and expanding industrial base offers substantial and exciting trade opportunities for Australian businesses. However, the enterprises first have to be prepared to invest in researching the market and building an understanding of Thai culture. Potential areas for investment include infrastructure, environmental services, agricultural equipment and rural extension services, processed food and beverages, information technology, energy and mining systems and education.

This chapter attempts to place these opportunities in their proper context through discussing Thailand's geographic setting, political history, economic development, financial development, foreign investment, foreign trade, trade with Australia and future prospects.

The setting

Geographically, Thailand is strategically well placed to access other Asian markets. It forms the gateway to Laos, Cambodia, Vietnam, Burma and parts of China. Its 514,000 square kilometre land area is flanked by the Gulf of Thailand and the

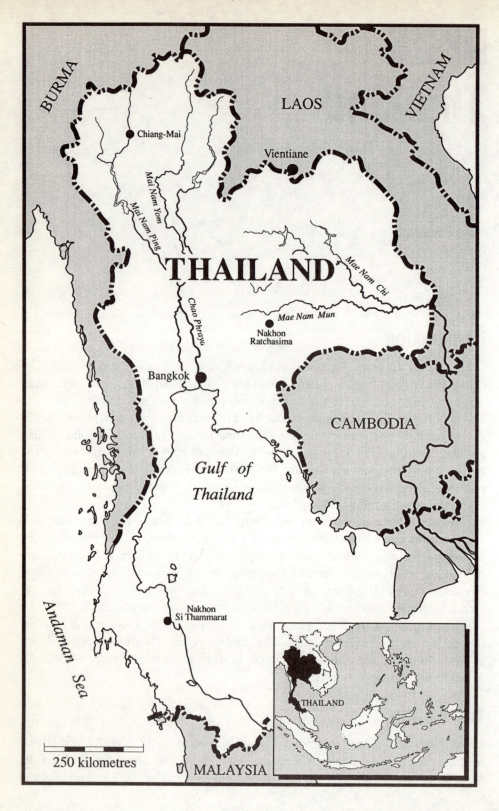

Andaman Sea and to the south is bordered by Malaysia. Due to construction of the 'Friendship Bridge' over the Mekong River to Laos, built with Australian Agency for International Development (AusAID) help, Thailand's importance as an expanding economic power within the IndoChina region has been further enhanced. Initiatives such as this aid also strengthen bilateral relations between Australia and Thailand.

Thailand is divided into four regions: the mountainous and thickly forested north; the heavily populated north-east, which has some of the country's poorest people and the additional problems of inadequate irrigation and poor soil; central Thailand's fertile, alluvial plain, which is occupied by about a third of the population; and the narrow southern peninsula, which is rich in minerals.

Although Thai culture is very strong throughout the country, it is supplemented, particularly in the north, by a variety of tribal peoples as well as Chinese and other immigrant groups. Thailand's population, estimated in mid-1995 to be 60,271,300, comprises 75 per cent Thai, 14 per cent Chinese and 11 per cent other groups. Buddhism is the dominant religion: about 95 per cent of the people are Buddhist. Islam accounts for 3.8 per cent, Christianity only 0.5 per cent. Buddhism is responsible for the ready acceptance of birth control and the population-growth rate is now 1.24 per cent per year.

Political history

Thailand's phenomenal economic growth, coupled with rapid industrialisation, has had a profound effect on all aspects of Thai society – religion, family, demography, health, education, business and politics. This growth and change has occurred against a colourful and at times very disruptive political background.

Because of the country's strategic position, it has also been a very attractive target for its neighbours. Empires that were based in Indonesia, Myanmar (Burma) and Cambodia have all controlled various parts of what is now Thailand. Some hundreds of years ago, even the Thai people themselves were located further north, extending up into Southern China. Thailand assumed something of its present-day state under the current dynasty, which in 1782 established Bangkok as the capital.

Unlike the other ASEAN countries' situations, the Thai kings were successful in playing one European power against another so that Thailand could retain its independence. The same political skills whereby Thailand's independence has been guaranteed have been put to less use on the domestic front, as political uncertainty combined with authoritarian rule has characterised Thai politics for most of the twentieth century. Thailand had an absolute monarchy until 1932 when it was overthrown in favour of a constitutional monarchy which continues up to the present. Since 1932, government has been controlled mainly by military regimes or elected governments relying heavily on the support of the armed forces. There have been 18 coup attempts, the most recent of which occurred in February 1991. Thailand achieved partial democracy during General Prem Tinsulanon's 1980–88 prime-ministership, and this progress continued in 1988 when Chartchai Choonhavan became the country's first elected prime minister in 12 years.

Following the general election in September 1992, Chuan Leekpai, leader of the Democracy Party, was elected prime minister. He headed a somewhat disparate five-party coalition that comprised his own Democracy Party, the New Aspiration Party, the Social Action Party, the Palang Dharma, and the small Solidarity Party. In May 1992 these parties opposed military suppression of pro-democracy demonstrations. In September 1993 Chuan formed his second government after expelling the troublesome 21-member Social Action Party (which planned to join with Opposition parties) and replaced it with the eight-member Serithan Party.

Many Thais were concerned about Chuan's 'low-key style' and what they perceived to be his indecisiveness. During 1993 he successfully fended off several no-confidence motions. Because of the possibility of dissent within his own Cabinet, coupled with the existence of Opposition criticism and the military's looming presence, Chuan had to be firm and confident in his ability to not only hold his government together but make strong and perhaps unpopular decisions in order to keep the economy moving.

In early 1992, Chuan's leadership position was not aided by allegations of influential politicians' involvement in a stock-market scandal nor by the disputes about revenue arrangements between the government and Bangkok Expressway investors. In September 1993 the Expressway Authority of Thailand resorted to court action so the new road could be opened. Given Bangkok's notorious traffic problems, the legal delays not only affected the government's popularity and credibility; they adversely affected the main shareholder, the Japanese construction giant Kumagai Gumi. Lack of coherent policies and procedures also makes foreign investors and financiers wary of future infrastructure arrangements. A land-reform scandal, which involved the alleged granting of land rights on the southern island of Phuket to 10 wealthy Thais, instead of the intended poor farmers, finally heralded the government's demise and was responsible for ending Chuan's term as Thailand's longest-serving elected leader.

Following the July 1995 election, Chuan was replaced by Banharn Silpa-archa, leader of the Chart Thai Party. Together with five smaller parties, Banharn has formed a somewhat precarious coalition government. He may well face problems similar to those experienced by his predecessor. As well as having to fend off potential dissent from the various parties within the coalition, he has to contend with three distinct factions within his own party. He will also have to please both the rural majority, who elected his party to office, and the vocal, urban-Bangkok minority, who seem to be sceptical of his leadership ability. Banharn's election commitment to find an urgent solution to Bangkok's infrastructure problems is aimed at appeasing the urban electorate.

Corruption charges against three of Banharn's party, including the justice minister, could also affect the government's stability. A fate similar to that of the Chuan government could well result if corruption is not kept in check. Unlike the previous government, which had instigated measures for reducing the military's power, in Banharn's government the military seems to have a stronger role. Chuvalit

Yongchaiyuth, a former army commander, concurrently holds the positions of deputy prime minister and minister for defence.

At present, an uneasy truce exists between civilian politicians, the military and the monarchy. Thailand's King Bhumibol Adulyadej is well respected by the Thai people and acts as a check on the military. Without the king's support, any push for power is likely to be met with a popular uprising. Also, in undertaking his duty of approving senior promotions, the king is able to modify the various military cliques' power and to influence the direction the military will take.

In fairness to the military, Thailand's army commander during Chuan's government, General Wimol Wongwanich, attempted to de-politicise the army's senior-officer corps through instituting a restructuring program. His policy was to promote younger and more professional generals to senior posts in place of the politically minded generals who had dominated most senior posts until May 1992. It remains to be seen whether the new government continues with this policy. The army has a track record of strong intervention, and senior army postings have attracted wealth, power and prestige – perhaps three strong temptations for some people. This is highlighted by Anek Laothamatas, a political scientist at Thammasat University:

> In the army, from the top ranks to the middle ranks . . . there is a collective memory of how people in the army can benefit from being involved in politics.

Political uncertainties of this magnitude are responsible for making not only the Thai public cautious but also potential investors. In spite of this, Thailand's sustained economic growth indicates political instability is not necessarily responsible for discouragement of business operations. This is partly because the various political parties have similar economic policies and appreciate the need for business to 'get on with the job', free of political interference.

The potential problems are not confined to the military, though. Tensions also exist with Muslim Malays in southern Thailand. This area has traditionally been the seat of complex and sensitive issues due to the large Muslim population in predominantly Buddhist Thailand. In recent times the unrest has intensified.

Economic development

In the four decades following 1950, Thailand's economy has undergone a dramatic change. In 1950 the country had zero growth of per-capita output and was one of the world's poorest countries. Since then it has changed from being an agricultural economy dependent on a narrow range of export commodities to a rapidly developing economy that is vying for NIC status. Although it remains one of Asia's main agricultural exporters, its reliance on agriculture has been reduced because of rapid growth in manufacturing and services. In 1985, manufacturing outstripped agriculture in GDP share and tourism is now the country's most important foreign-exchange source. The paradox is that following a long period of stagnation, economic progress has occurred in a rapid and stable way despite political turmoil.

Table 8.1   Thailand's GDP, by sector, 1965 and 1995

	%	
Sector	1965	1995
Agriculture	32	10
Manufacturing	23	37
Services	45	53
TOTAL	**100**	**100**

Source: World Bank, *World Development Report*. 1992, p 222;
1995, p 167.

Table 8.1 highlights a 22 per cent decline in agriculture's GDP share between 1965 and 1995. In contrast, manufacturing's GDP share increased by 14 per cent during the same period whereas services grew by only 8 per cent.

Three economic planning agencies are responsible for the Thai government's economic policies: the Bank of Thailand (BOT), the National Economic and Social Development Board (NESDB) and the Board of Investment (BOI). The BOI was established in 1960 in order to foster foreign and domestic investment and to administer, in particular, applications seeking promotional privileges. The Ministry of Industry handles other investment applications.

Government planning

The NESDB was established in 1960 to formulate the First National Development Plan (1961–66). It and the subsequent five-year plans have been intended to co-ordinate economic development. At present Thailand is in the final part of its Seventh Plan (1992–96).

The first two national development plans mainly concentrated on the rural sector and expansion of agricultural production. Heavy investment occurred in infrastructure, particularly transport and power generation (which accounted for 50.9 per cent of the plan's budget), irrigation projects and communications. These investments were responsible for opening up substantial areas of new agricultural land for cash-crop cultivation and, due to investment incentives, rapid development of an import-substitution-based industrial sector was promoted. Growth continued throughout the early 1970s because Thailand was able to find significant export markets for cassava, sugar cane and pineapple as well as for new manufactured goods, notably textiles and garments.

Foreign investment grew rapidly particularly that from MNCs. In the article 'Technocrats, Businessmen and Generals: Democracy and Economic Policy-making in Thailand', Pasuk Phongpaichit identifies a variety of reasons why Thailand was successful in attracting foreign investment, particularly from Japan:

> It was judged to be politically stable, accommodating for foreign investors, and blessed with good natural resources and a plentiful, inexpensive and relatively skilled labour force. All these factors reduced the transaction costs of incoming foreign firms.

But above all, Thailand provided a cost-efficient site for relocation of industrial processes forced out of Japan, Taiwan and elsewhere by rising currencies and rising wage and other costs. The devaluation of the baht and the reorientation of promotional policies were critical in making Thailand an attractive investment environment at the time East Asian capital needed to relocate.

By 1970, a world economic slowdown and reduced American military presence were responsible for presenting Thailand with a widening balance-of-payments and budget deficit. The Third Development Plan (1972–76) therefore emphasised both import substituting industrialisation (ISI) and export oriented industrialisation (EOI). The necessity of increasing exports and domestic capital supplies was also strongly reflected in the Fourth Plan (1977–81) under which EOI was given a central role.

By the early 1980s, a number of major threats emerged that endangered the momentum of Thailand's economic growth. Deteriorating environmental conditions meant agricultural growth was limited; the 1979–80 oil-price increases added to the import bill; Vietnamese-military activity on the borders raised security issues; and most of Thai industry's very limited export orientation meant threats were posed for continued economic progress. The balance-of-trade deficit and the balance-of-payments deficit tended to widen during the early 1980s, and foreign debt increased rapidly. For the government, finding employment for the rapidly growing labour force and dealing with the continually widening development gap between Bangkok and the rural provinces, further compounded the planning problems faced.

The Fifth National Development Plan (1982–86) attempted to address the problems. Its main emphases were reduction of rural poverty and achievement of a balance between development and conservation; improvement in the balance of payments through intensifying promotion of exports, particularly by enhancing industrial production's competitiveness; intensification of energy-conservation measures and development of alternative sources; and reduction of the budget deficit through increasing government revenues.

These policies were also continued during the Sixth Plan (1987–91) together with promotion of increased private-sector input in infrastructure and commercial agriculture.

These various national development policies have paid rich dividends. Between 1984 and 1990, Thailand's GDP growth rates averaged 11 per cent per year, which makes the country the world's fastest growing economy. Over the past five years, growth has fallen to more sustainable rates of about 8 per cent. However, some significant challenges remain. Domestic production of intermediate and capital goods is grossly inefficient. Serious inefficiency remains in resource allocation, particularly in the import-substitution industries such as oil refining, vehicle assembly, chemicals and machinery – industries that were created during the 1970s through tariff protection and investment incentives. Although Thailand's relatively low average labour costs continue to afford it a comparative advantage in labour-intensive manufactures, those industries are beginning to face more restrictive and competitive world markets. Given these factors, the new emphasis is on achieving greater efficiency and competitiveness through promotion of industries that are based on domestic resources. Thailand's government is responding to the situation by imposing fiscal and monetary discipline, limiting public external borrowing and placing more emphasis on export performance.

So that the economy can be decentralised and wealth redistributed, the Seventh Plan (1992–96) aims to:

* maintain stable economic growth, with a reasonable inflation rate and acceptable trade deficit
* emphasise more equitable income distribution and extend development to the provincial areas
* improve the quality of life and natural resource protection.

Contemporary economic performance

Inflation has varied from a peak of 20 per cent in 1980 to very low levels in the mid-1980s when it bottomed at 2 per cent. Over the past few years it has averaged 5 per cent, a creditable result in light of Thailand's rapid economic growth.

For Thailand, unemployment estimates are not as precise as those for developed countries. However current estimates place it at 3.1 per cent, of which only 1 per cent of those people may be looking for work. Although an industrial growth rate of 8 per cent over a number of years has been responsible for absorbing considerable numbers of workers, supply has also been growing quickly. Together with rapid population growth, agriculture's relative decline has meant labour supply has largely met the growing demand.

Table 8.2   Thailand's key economic indicators, by percentage growth, 1990–95

Indicator	1990	1991	1992	1993	1994	1995
Real GDP growth	10.0	15.4	7.6	7.8	8.2	8.6
Consumer prices	5.9	5.7	4.1	3.6	5.3	5.8
Exchange rate*	25.585	25.517	25.400	25.319	24.910	24.840

*The rate is of the Thai baht against the US dollar; that is, a fall denotes an appreciation against the US dollar.
Source: Department of Foreign Affairs and Trade, *The APEC Region Trade and Investment*. Canberra: Australian Government Publishing Service, 1994, pp 84, 96 and 98, and Office of the National Economic and Social Development Board (Thailand) correspondence, 1996.

For most of the past 20 years, Thailand has followed a fiscal policy whereby budget deficits have regularly been produced and at the same time has adopted a somewhat passive monetary policy. In the early 1970s, deficits ran at an average of 3.8 per cent of GDP, the bulk of them were financed from domestic sources and there was minimal foreign borrowing. From the beginning of the 1988 economic boom onwards, increased revenues allowed the government to achieve a budget surplus and thereby enjoy some early repayment of foreign debts and increase its focus on infrastructure development.

Although the budget position the government faces has remained positive, the 1994 budget returned to deficit: expenditure exceeded revenue by 25 billion baht (Bt25 billion).

The budget's key aims were pursuit of the government's decentralisation and wealth-redistribution policies. One of the largest projects that received funding was the Southern Seaboard Development Program which included construction of a four-lane highway through the southern-seaboard region. The focus was the establishment of infrastructure so that industry – both domestic and foreign – would be enticed to pursue complementary private investment.

Like many developing nation governments, Thailand's government is restricted because it has a narrow revenue base, a factor which is responsible for promoting continued reliance on import duties. Despite attempts at broadening the tax base over the past few years, the government has found it difficult to bring about the revenue increases required. More than 70 per cent of government revenues are still derived from indirect taxes which are sensitive to any slowdown in economic activity such as occurred in 1984–85. In the absence, until recently, of any marked increase in contributions from personal and corporate income taxes, the tax system is inefficient at generating extra revenues. The economic upsurge of 1987–90 produced a major increase in receipts from import duties and business taxes.

At the beginning of 1992, various business taxes were rationalised through the introduction of value-added tax, which was initially levied at 7 per cent. At the same time, the government lowered personal and corporate income-tax rates.

The government has sought to have a conservative monetary policy and to also support growth. Interest rates have varied between 10 and 16 per cent over the past six years. Credit expansion has occasionally been held in check so that price stability can be maintained and the balance-of-payments deficit can be moderated.

The Thai baht is tied to a basket of currencies that is heavily weighted in favour of the US dollar. As a result, the currency is very stable, and this is a useful backdrop for international trade.

Financial development

Given Thailand's strategic location – it neighbours the potentially dynamic economies of Myanmar (Burma), Cambodia and Laos – the country is well placed to emerge as a regional financial centre for these countries as well as for South-East Asia.

As indicated in Table 8.3, Thailand's domestic financial system is served by a wide range of institutions. These and other institutions are regulated by the Bank of Thailand, the central bank, which acts as an agent for the Ministry of Finance with reference to public debt management, exchange control and general banking supervision.

Table 8.3 Thailand's financial institutions, 1995

Institution	Number of institutions
Bank of Thailand	1
Local commercial banks	15
Foreign commercial banks	14
Bangkok International Banking Facilities (BIBF)	44
Provincial International Banking Facilities (PIBF)	10
Finance and finance-and-securities companies	91
Credit-foncier companies	13
Government Savings Bank	1
Government Housing Bank	1
BAAC	1
Export–Import Bank of Thailand	1
Industrial Finance Corp. of Thailand	1
Small Industry Finance Corporation	1
Life-insurance companies	8
Life-and-non-life-insurance companies	5
Non-life-insurance companies	62
Reinsurance companies	2
Agricultural co-operatives*	2,461
Savings co-operatives*	1,045
Pawnshops	378
Mutual funds	104
Provident funds	822
Total	**5,081**

*This information is as at 31 December 1994.
Source: Bank of Thailand correspondence, 1995.

The market is dominated by the commercial banks and the banking system itself has traditionally been dominated by four local banks: the Bangkok Bank, the Krung Thai Bank, the Thai Farmers Bank and the Siam Commercial Bank. As Table 8.4 indicates, these four institutions are the most important and together they account for almost half the local banking assets. Their level of importance is even higher because each one has affiliated finance and securities companies that are often among the largest as well as other institutions.

Although some foreign banks have been licensed for the local market, from 1955 to 1995 Thailand's government greatly restricted foreign access, a foreign bank could open only if its home country did not already have a bank that had a Thai office and if a Thai bank was seeking to open a branch in that country. Twelve foreign banks have nevertheless long been active in Thailand; the Bank of Tokyo, the Sakura Bank and Citibank are the most active.

Table 8.4   Thailand's major domestic commercial banks, 1994

Bank*	Assets US$ million
Bangkok Bank (12/94)	35,792
Krung Thai Bank (12/94)	21,781
Thai Farmers Bank (12/94)	20,197
Siam Commercial Bank (12/94)	14,502
Bank of Ayudhya (12/94)	11,330
Thai Military Bank (12/94)	9,079
First Bangkok City Bank (12/94)	7,057
Siam City Bank (12/94)	6,388
Bangkok Bank of Commerce (12/94)	5,686
Bangkok Metropolitan Bank (12/94)	5,337
Metrobank (12/94)	4,916
Bank of Asia (12/94)	3,322
Thai Danu Bank (12/94)	2,701
Union Bank of Bangkok (12/94)	1,795
Nakomthon Bank (12/94)	1,758

*The month and year ended are in parentheses.
Source: The *Banker*, October 1995, p 69.

A blueprint that Cabinet approved in February 1995 is designed to make Thailand's banking more competitive. In the plan, more licences for domestic and foreign banks are called for and it will enable finance and securities firms to go into new lines of business. Also sought is improvement of regulatory oversights and promotion of the spread of assets outside Thailand. Under a new five-year plan, licences will be issued to five new domestic banks. These banks will be required to establish their headquarters in a Thai provincial city. This caveat is designed to support the government's decentralisation policy. The government is also planning to issue new offshore-banking licences in May 1996.

The offshore banking licences, which are part of the current Bangkok International Banking Facilities (BIBF) program, represent the other side of Thailand's finance: the country's regional or international finance role. Like Singapore's Asian currency units (ACUs), BIBF authorisation permits a foreign bank to establish a separate set of accounts through which it conducts particular aspects of banking from a Bangkok office. This can be done by banks already locally licensed or by a foreign bank that has only a representative office. The BIBF does not give licence to conduct general banking in Thailand. Like the ACU, it is intended more for international banking activities such as loan syndications, foreign-exchange trading, money-market operations and investment-banking activities for firms located outside Thailand. The attraction is that the profits from these activities are taxed at a concessional rate of 10 per cent instead of the usual 30 per cent corporate tax. However, the BIBF also has some direct access to the Thai market with reference to foreign currency denominated lending.

Implementation of the BIBF is indicative of the government's commitment to continuing the financial sector's liberalisation. Indeed, in 1995 the original foreign banks that had been issued BIBFs were subsequently given permission to open a full branch in Bangkok as well as a branch in the provinces, known as Provincial International Banking Facilities (PIBF). Further liberalisation will result in both more competition and more volatility in the capital and money markets and the importance of risk management will thereby be increased.

As well as having forced more competition within the domestic financial sector, the government has encouraged Thai banks to start competition outside Thailand and establish operations elsewhere within the region. They could play an important regional role because the Bangkok Bank is not only Thailand's largest local bank it is ASEAN's largest locally owned bank. The Thai banks, led by the Bangkok Bank, have established branches, subsidiaries and representative offices throughout the region as well as in the United States and Europe. Not surprisingly, perhaps, the Bangkok Bank has been the most active bank in these efforts; it has branches in Ho Chi Minh City and Hanoi (Vietnam), Jakarta (Indonesia) and Singapore, as well as in China, Germany, Hong Kong, Japan, Taiwan, the UK and the US and subsidiaries in Malaysia.

In addition to having financial institutions, Thailand also has an active stock exchange, the Stock Exchange of Thailand (SET). This was established in 1974 and is governed by the Stock Exchange Act 1992. It processes all applications made by companies that wish to be listed to ensure that applications meet the requirements set out by the Ministry of Finance. It has also established reporting requirements for listed companies and it monitors all listed securities' trading activities. At the end of 1994, 389 domestic companies were listed. In 1992, the Public Companies Act and the Securities Exchange Act were introduced. The latter established the Securities Exchange Board so that development of the capital market, particularly the corporate-debt market, could be supervised and so that clearer separation of companies that are involved in the stock market and of those that remain outside it can be achieved. Plans also exist to develop a Thai futures and options market.

Foreign investment

Thailand's government has created two investment-service bodies to cater for foreign investment. Applications seeking promotional privileges are handled by the BOI whereas other foreign-investment applications are handled by the Ministry of Industry.

Although Thailand's rapid economic growth is responsible for creating exciting opportunities for trade and investment, Bangkok's notorious infrastructural shortcomings and pollution remain problems for businesses that are considering locating in the region. The government has implemented a number of incentives to attract businesses away from Bangkok and establish industries in specific areas the characteristics of which are consistent with national development priorities.

Table 8.5   Thailand's net FDI, by major source, 1990–95

	US$ million					
	1990	**1991**	**1992**	**1993**	**1994**	**1995**
Total	**2,528**	**2,013**	**2,114**	**1,730**	**1,322**	**1,995**
By country						
United States	240	232	464	286	155	241
Taiwan	280	108	87	49	82	96
Japan	1,091	611	337	305	123	531
United Kingdom	44	10	127	161	44	55
Germany	45	33	24	25	30	38
Hong Kong	275	453	573	193	318	264
Singapore	240	253	265	61	184	144
Others	313	313	236	650	385	626
By sector						
Industry	1,212	934	365	451	212	575
Trade and service	585	366	364	238	396	548
Construction	129	130	572	152	70	36
Mining and quarrying	45	81	123	125	52	51
Agriculture	30	23	–6	13	–6	–0.55
Financial institutions	177	267	258	65	7	25
Others	351	212	438	686	591	761

Source: Bangkok Bank, *Economy at a Glance*. Bangkok: Bangkok Bank, 1996.

As indicated in Table 8.5, Japan is Thailand's main FDI source, followed by the US, North-East Asia and Singapore. Australia is not a significant investor in Thailand, in 1993 it invested only A$90 million. However, although this figure is very small relative to Australia's investment elsewhere and to other investment in Thailand, it represents the presence of some significant MNCs including BHP, CIG, Pacific Dunlop, Powauto and the Australian Dairy Corporation.

Decentralisation of industry

Development of industry in the provinces is a government priority and industries are offered incentives to relocate or establish there. The BOI actively encourages export-oriented businesses that provide local employment, particularly employment away from Bangkok. The incentives include tax advantages (exemption of corporate income tax for up to eight years), relaxation of foreign-participation restrictions, transportation allowances and rebates on tariffs for imported materials.

Long-term development plans relate to the 'light' and 'clean' industries such as clothing and electronics and to agro-industry located around Chiang-mai, Lamphun and Lampang in the north. In the south, a major infrastructural program that is based on strategic linkages between the Andaman Sea in the west and the Gulf of Thailand in the east may also be responsible for attracting more traditional natural-resource-based industries.

For the impoverished north-east, the government hopes to boost the economy by establishing links with the country's poorer neighbours: Laos, Cambodia and Vietnam.

The BOI has divided Thailand into three zones. The relocation advantages are greatest for businesses that are locating furthest from Bangkok. In order to promote dispersal, the government has put many 'software' incentives in place or is developing them. For example, the BOI has strengthened its incentives for investors in Zone 3. One attraction is that the minimum-wage rates in Zone 3 are 20 per cent below those of Zone 1 (greater Bangkok) and Zone 2 (the province that is closest to greater Bangkok and the eastern seaboard). During the three months from April 1993 when the zoning incentives were introduced, applications for Zone 3 accounted for more than 60 per cent of the total: 66.7 billion baht (US$2.7 billion) out of a total of 106,117 million baht (US$4.2 billion).

However, in the provinces improved infrastructure is necessary if regional zoning is to be successful. The three zone areas and their associated benefits are listed as follows.

Zone 1

This covers the greater-Bangkok area[1] and has the following incentives:

- A 50 per cent reduction in import duties on machinery on which at least 10 per cent import duty is imposed, provided the project exports at least 80 per cent of its production or is located in an industrial estate or approved industrial zone.
- Exemption from corporate income tax for three years for a project that exports at least 80 per cent of its product and is located in an industrial estate or approved industrial zone.
- Exemption from import duties for one year on raw or essential materials in products that are manufactured for export by businesses that export at least 30 per cent of their production.

Zone 2

This covers the region that is within a two-hour drive from Bangkok.[2] The exemptions for businesses that are located in the area include the following:

- A 50 per cent reduction in import duties on machinery on which at least 10 per cent import duty is imposed.
- Exemption from corporate income tax for three years (extendable to seven years if the projects are located in industrial estates or approved industrial zones).
- Exemption from import duties for one year on raw or essential materials that are used in production of goods for export provided the project exports at least 30 per cent of its production.

Zone 3

This covers the rest of the country and the Laem Chabang Industrial Estate. The businesses located in this area may qualify for the following.

- Exemption from import duty on some machinery.
- Exemption from corporate income tax for eight years.
- Exemption from import duties for five years on raw or essential materials used in products manufactured for export provided the project exports at least 30 per cent of its product.
- A 75 per cent reduction in import duties on raw or essential materials that are imported for production for domestic sales for five years renewable on an annual basis.
- Special tax-deductible expenses.
- Machinery related to basic transportation systems, public utilities, conservation and environmental enhancement, technological development or primary industries is eligible for an exemption from import duty.

Promotional privileges may also be granted to companies in which more than 49 per cent of the registered capital is held by foreigners who invest or jointly invest in production for domestic consumption, and which locate in Zone 3. Approval is granted on a case-by-case basis. Established factories that wish to relocate to an outer zone are eligible for a range of exemptions.

Foreign trade

Given Thailand's locational and resource advantages, we might have expected it to devote most of its trading activities to its neighbours. In practice, this has not been the case. As Table 8.6 indicates, in 1994 Thailand's main trading partners continued to be the US, Japan, the EU member countries, and Taiwan. These same countries were also the most important trading partners in 1989. Of the ASEAN nations, only Singapore has been important. With reference to growth, though, the ASEAN members do somewhat better with Singapore being an important and rapidly growing market for Thai exports.

The ASEAN countries' position is perhaps made somewhat clearer if it is examined in percentage terms, as shown in Table 8.7. First, in overall terms, the then five-member ASEAN accounted for 13.6 per cent of Thailand's exports in 1994, compared with 11.42 per cent in 1989. AFTA has seemingly therefore had some impact with reference to Thai exports. In contrast, Thailand's imports from ASEAN have had hardly any benefit; the group's relative market share has effectively remained unchanged.

Table 8.6 Thailand's trading partners, 1989 and 1994

	Exports			Imports		
	1989 (US$ million)	1994 (US$ million)	Trend* (%)	1989 (US$ million)	1994 (US$ million)	Trend* (%)
Brunei	30	45	10.7	183	233	5.0
Indonesia	162	277	11.8	269	417	26.4
Malaysia	585	1,107	18.9	650	2,627	22.6
Philippines	95	211	11.6	94	254	26.0
Singapore	1,432	4,037	26.9	1,871	2,512	0.2
Australia	373	633	12.3	508	1,074	18.1
Canada	298	594	17.3	346	371	1.2
Chile	3	24	27.7	26	101	26.9
China	541	914	30.9	744	1,483	3.5
Hong Kong	869	2,211	20.8	336	924	13.1
Japan	3,422	7,524	16.0	7,736	16,540	12.9
South Korea	300	553	7.1	742	2,034	16.6
Mexico	31	100	3.3	71	76	1.9
New Zealand	44	76	27.3	94	149	8.4
Papua New Guinea	9	27	28.6	3	30	NM
Taiwan	316	969	29.3	1,278	2,560	11.1
United States	4,358	9,706	16.3	2,842	6,136	14.6
European Union	3,839	6,954	6.1	3,564	8,673	12.4
Other countries	3,467	5,795	16.1	4,016	8,130	12.7
Total	**20,175**	**41,757**	**15.5**	**25,373**	**54,324**	**12.4**

*The trend is for the period 1990–94.
NM = not meaningful
Source: Department of Foreign Affairs and Trade, *The APEC Region Trade and Investment*. Canberra: Australian Government Publishing Service, 1995, pp 40–1.

Table 8.7 Thailand–ASEAN trade, 1989 and 1994

	Exports %		Imports %	
	1989	1994	1989	1994
Brunei	0.15	0.10	0.72	0.40
Indonesia	0.80	0.70	1.06	0.80
Malaysia	2.90	2.70	2.56	4.80
Philippines	0.47	0.50	0.37	0.50
Singapore	7.10	9.70	7.37	4.60
ASEAN (5 countries)	11.42	13.60	12.09	11.10

Source: Department of Foreign Affairs and Trade, *The APEC Region Trade and Investment*. Canberra: Australian Government Publishing Service, 1994, pp 40–1.

With reference to specific countries the impact is even more serious. Between 1989 and 1994, Brunei's, Indonesia's and Malaysia's shares of Thailand's exports have actually declined, and the Philippines has experienced only a nominal increase.

Were it not for Singapore, ASEAN would have shown virtually no change at all. With reference to Thailand's imports from its ASEAN colleagues, the picture is even more mixed: Malaysia increased its share at the expense of Singapore, Indonesia and Brunei.

Since 1970, manufactures' share of total exports has increased and now exceeds agricultural exports' share, as indicated in Table 8.8. Processed foods, textiles, garments, electronic goods and jewellery comprise a significant proportion of Thailand's manufactured exports. Since the late 1980s, these five product groups have come to account for almost two-thirds of the country's manufactured exports.

Table 8.8   Thailand's exports and imports, by sector and product type 1993–95

	billion baht		
	1993	**1994**	**1995**
Exports classified by sector			
1. Agriculture	111	130	159
2. Fisheries	56	68	71
3. Mining	6	7	7
4. Manufacturing	753	923	1,151
5. Others	10	10	16
Total exports	936	1,138	1,404
Imports by economic classification			
1. Consumer goods	114	145	183
2. Intermediate products and raw materials	349	395	510
3. Capital goods	501	614	803
4. Fuel and lubricants	86	92	118
5. Others	117	123	158
Total imports	1,167	1,369	1,772

Source: Bangkok Bank, *Guide to Thai Economy*. Bangkok: Bangkok Bank, 1996.

Thailand's commercial policy remains highly protectionist. It sets official tariff rates at ASEAN's highest levels and supports them by having significant non-tariff barriers. Tariff rates of 50–60 per cent apply for meat, 25–40 per cent for dairy products, about 60 per cent for many vegetables, 30 per cent for wool and 5 per cent for cotton. Although most goods fall into the 50–60 per cent range, for some luxury consumer goods import duty can be as high as 150 per cent. Thailand, in fact, applies up to 200 per cent duty on foreign cars!

Because of these high tariff levels, a significant barrier is presented both to Australian companies seeking to sell into the Thai market and to Australian MNCs using Thailand as a production base. Naturally, exemptions apply to BOI-approved industrial projects, as discussed previously. Similarly, if the goods are imported for ultimate re-export, companies may qualify for a refund of duties paid. However, these measures do little to change the high tariffs' overall impact on the economy.

Apart from formal tariff barriers, many restrictions apply to imports. Many goods, which are classified under 45 categories, are subject to import licences.

Licence applications are subject to Ministry of Commerce approval and are valid for only six months. Total embargoes apply to particular industries that have been identified for protection. For import transactions, exchange-control approval is required. Each bureaucratic process can be slow and cumbersome, thereby adding to the cost of the business's operation.

Thailand, as a major agricultural exporter, is a member of the Cairns Group of agricultural exporting nations, which is chaired by Australia. The inconsistency involved in Thailand's pursuing better access to US and EU agricultural markets while remaining highly protectionist itself is often highlighted by the country's critics, and rightly so.

Trade with Australia

Thailand's impressive economic performance coupled with its ideal location in the centre of mainland South-East Asia, makes it an attractive location for businesses that are interested in extending into the Asian market. During the late 1980s the country's export growth averaged 28 per cent per year.

Australia's trading relations with Thailand have been expanding rapidly. Over the period 1990–94, for example, Thailand's exports to Australia increased in value by 70 per cent and its imports from Australia grew by 91 per cent. Unfortunately, because Thailand's overall export growth was higher and its import growth slightly lower, Australia – as indicated in Table 8.9 – has not experienced any improvement in its own relative percentages over the same period. With reference to exports, our 1.7 per cent share of 1984 had declined to 1.5 per cent in 1994. By contrast, our import share was steady at 2 per cent over the same period.

Table 8.9   Australia's importance for Thai trade, 1984–94

Thailand's exports (fob)		Thailand's imports (cif)	
Year	Australia as % of total	Year	Australia as % of total
1984	1.7	1984	2.0
1985	1.7	1985	1.7
1986	1.8	1986	1.8
1987	1.9	1987	1.8
1988	1.9	1988	1.7
1989	1.8	1989	2.0
1990	1.6	1990	1.7
1991	1.6	1991	1.7
1992	1.6	1992	2.2
1993	1.4	1993	2.1
1994	1.5	1994	2.0

Source: Department of Foreign Affairs and Trade, *The APEC Region Trade and Investment*. Canberra: Australian Government Publishing Service, 1995, p 30.

Despite the decline in market share, Thailand was Australia's twelfth-largest export market in 1994–95, a big change from its twenty-sixth position in 1984–85. At one time, our trade focused on traditional primary-commodity exports such as unprocessed food, dairy products, petroleum, minerals, cotton and wool. Today, although these items remain important, as indicated in Table 8.10, their individual growth figures over the past few years have been quite different. Manufactured items now account for more than half our exports and remain one of our fastest growing export categories. ETMs, such as computing, electrical and telecommunications equipment have grown particularly fast and now exceed exports of STMs. A more detailed picture of our export trade is shown in Table 8.11. Non-ferrous metals, particularly aluminium, is by far the most significant category: it accounted for 22.46 per cent of our exports; it was followed by gold which accounted for 15.86 per cent. Textile fibres such as wool and cotton, 7.84 per cent, and dairy products, 5.25 per cent, remain the other largest categories.

Table 8.10 Australia's merchandise trade with Thailand, by major category, 1994–95

	Exports (A$ million)	Trend* %	Imports (A$ million)	Trend* %
Primary products				
Unprocessed food	16.7	−16.7	122.7	16.2
Processed food	107.9	23.0	162.6	12.4
Other rural	168.6	24.4	21.3	18.3
Minerals	35.4	41.4	4.7	43.1
Fuels	40.0	−13.5	4.8	–
TOTAL PRIMARY PRODUCTS	**368.5**	**13.0**	**316.1**	**12.1**
Manufactures				
Simply transformed	404.8	13.8	109.0	11.0
Elaborately transformed	488.3	29.7	504.5	20.6
TOTAL MANUFACTURES	**893.1**	**21.1**	**613.5**	**18.6**
Other	296.7	73.8	40.6	19.2
TOTAL	**1,558.4**	**23.9**	**970.1**	**16.3**

*The trend growth is for the period 1990–91 to 1994–95.
Source: Department of Foreign Affairs and Trade, *The APEC Region Trade and Investment.* Canberra: Australian Government Publishing Service, 1995, p 46.

Table 8.11   Australian exports to Thailand for year ended 30 June 1995

Product type	A$	%
Non-fish live animals	4,496,224	0.29
Meat and meat preparations	3,664,422	0.24
Dairy products and eggs	81,869,422	5.25
Fish, shellfish and preparations thereof	9,983,878	0.64
Cereals and cereal preparations	4,990,687	0.32
Vegetables and fruit	3,869,895	0.25
Coffee, tea, cocoa, spices and manufactures thereof	4,968,826	0.32
Feed for animals (excluding unmilled cereals)	3,574,323	0.23
Beverages	2,179,743	0.14
Raw hides, skins and furskins	41,919,806	2.69
Pulp and wastepaper	4,939,588	0.32
Textile fibres	122,247,558	7.84
Crude fertilisers and minerals	2,003,795	0.13
Metalliferous ores and metal scrap	33,269,084	2.13
Crude animal and vegetable materials	1,762,714	0.11
Petroleum and petroleum products	39,829,843	2.56
Animal oils and fats	2,582,356	0.17
Chemicals	5,698,978	0.37
Dyeing, tanning and colouring materials	33,056,697	2.12
Medicinal and pharmaceutical products	25,382,474	1.63
Essential oils, perfumes and cleansing preparations	7,986,942	0.51
Plastics	11,543,116	0.74
Chemical materials and products	14,139,590	0.91
Leather, leather manufactures and dressed furskins	12,019,113	0.77
Rubber manufactures	7,960,222	0.51
Cork and wood manufactures (excluding furniture)	2,607,459	0.17
Textile yarns and fabrics	7,079,543	0.45
Non-metallic mineral manufactures	24,358,240	1.56
Iron and steel	48,932,618	3.14
Non-ferrous metals	350,146,514	22.46
Manufactures of metals	18,515,903	1.19
Power-generating machinery and equipment	5,189,861	0.33
Machinery specialised for particular industries	25,033,643	1.61
Metalworking machinery	8,666,724	0.56
General industrial equipment and machine parts	41,038,999	2.63
Office and data-processing machines	24,264,159	1.56
Telecommunications and sound equipment	67,818,864	4.35
Electrical machinery and appliances	34,694,025	2.23
Road vehicles	47,445,879	3.04
Transport equipment	8,123,148	0.52
Furniture and furnishings	2,271,172	0.15
Professional and scientific instruments	8,682,130	0.56
Photographic equipment, optical goods and clocks	25,841,803	1.66
Miscellaneous manufactured articles	21,016,969	1.35
Gold (excluding gold ores and concentrates)	247,268,108	15.86
Combined confidential items of trade and commodities	45,697,408	2.93
Other items	8,066,627	0.52
Total exports	**1,558,699,092**	**100.00**

Source: ABS, *Foreign Trade Statistics: 1994–95*. Canberra: ABS, 1995, pp 1602–4.

With reference to imports, our trade with Thailand has grown somewhat more slowly, thereby helping to ensure we enjoy a surplus in our balance of merchandise trade. As Table 8.6 indicated, over the past four years the overall growth rate has been 18.1 per cent. It is also worth noting processed foods' relative importance for our imports. If we examine the much more detailed set of categories in Table 8.12, it is clear that 'fish and shellfish' is the dominant item – it accounted for 17.15 per cent of all imports. These imports are mainly tinned, frozen or dried goods and represent one of Thailand's major export areas. 'Textile yarns, fabrics and made-up articles' was second in importance, followed by 'Miscellaneous manufactured articles', 'Telecommunications and recording equipment' and 'Office and data-processing machines'.

Table 8.12   Australian imports from Thailand for year ended 30 June 1995

Product type	A$	%
Fish and shellfish	166,311,359	17.15
Cereals and cereal preparations	18,123,769	1.87
Vegetables and fruit	31,802,338	3.28
Sugars, sugar preparations and honey	4,461,050	0.46
Coffee, tea, cocoa and spices	8,608,105	0.89
Feed for animals (excluding unmilled cereals)	33,595,458	3.46
Miscellaneous edible products and preparations	17,614,162	1.82
Tobacco and tobacco manufactures	2,618,440	0.27
Crude rubber (including synthetic and reclaimed)	10,575,934	1.09
Pulp and wastepaper	1,373,955	0.14
Textile fibres	3,493,804	0.36
Crude fertilisers and minerals	4,222,682	0.44
Crude animal and vegetable material	5,683,755	0.59
Petroleum and petroleum products	4,832,985	0.50
Animal or vegetable fats and oils	1,468,988	0.15
Chemicals	3,214,316	0.33
Dyeing, tanning and colouring materials	395,300	0.04
Medicinal and pharmaceutical products	3,306,406	0.34
Essential oils, perfume and cleansing preparations	606,046	0.06
Plastics	20,970,435	2.16
Chemical materials and products	6,827,688	0.70
Leather, leather manufactures and dressed furskins	8,974,871	0.93
Rubber manufactures	19,061,748	1.97
Cork and wood manufactures (excluding furniture)	5,285,120	0.55
Paper, paperboard and articles of paper pulp, of paper or of paperboard	3,992,764	0.41
Textile yarns, fabrics and made-up articles	93,167,979	9.61
Non-metallic mineral manufactures	48,116,031	4.96
Iron and steel	9,804,362	1.01
Manufactures of metals	19,502,330	2.01
Machinery specialised for particular industries	2,744,957	0.28
Metalworking machinery	2,961,009	0.31
General industrial equipment and machine parts	54,436,652	5.61
Office and data-processing machines	59,122,645	6.10
Telecommunications and recording equipment	66,408,382	6.85

Table 8.12 continues.

Table 8.12 (continued)

Product type	A$	%
Electrical machinery and appliances	27,399,183	2.83
Road vehicles (including air-cushion vehicles)	1,235,393	0.13
Prefabricated buildings and fittings	1,120,344	0.12
Furniture and stuffed furnishings	10,451,138	1.08
Travel goods, handbags and similar containers	5,520,841	0.57
Articles of apparel and clothing accessories	34,187,438	3.53
Footwear	19,701,103	2.03
Professional and scientific instruments	1,749,205	0.18
Photographic equipment, optical goods and clocks	7,626,580	0.79
Miscellaneous manufactured articles	74,459,858	7.68
Confidential trade and commodities	40,595,870	4.19
Other items	1,906,549	0.20
TOTAL IMPORTS	969,639,327	100.00

Source: ABS, *Foreign Trade Statistics: 1994–95*. Canberra: ABS, 1995, pp 857–8.

Opportunities exist for Australian businesses to supply plant and equipment for infrastructure development. Thailand's government is in the process of upgrading roads, mass-transit systems and railways, port and airport facilities, and electricity-generation plants. Australian business has the potential to supply equipment and expertise in these priority areas.

Because of Thailand's many environmental problems, such as air, water and noise pollution, deforestation, soil degradation and waste disposal, opportunities are presented for businesses that have environment-management expertise. Lucrative prospects also exist for consumer products because an increasing number of Thais, particularly those in Bangkok, have Australian levels of disposable income.

Due to Thailand's shortage of technically skilled workers and managers, Australian companies are provided with opportunities in education and technical training over a wide range of skills. As Thai industry moves towards more complex, higher value-added forms of manufacture, two areas that will become critical will be vocational training, particularly in electronics, banking, consumer-goods industries and oil and petroleum areas and technological training.

Future prospects

Rapid economic growth and past administrative mistakes have both been responsible for creating and exacerbating a range of geographic, social and environmental problems that the current government is attempting to address. The disparity that exists between incomes, rural problems, poor infrastructure, environment management and improved education and health facilities, have all been targeted for government reform.

Wealth redistribution

Disparity in wealth distribution continues to increase. The upper fifth of Thailand's population accounts for 55 per cent of the wealth whereas the poorest fifth accounts for less than 5 per cent of it. The inequitable distribution is most evident between rural and urban households: fewer than 5 per cent of villagers have monthly incomes greater than US$320 (A$485) whereas almost 60 per cent of Bangkok's residents have incomes in this range.

Thailand's development is also extremely unbalanced. Due to economic activity's concentration in greater Bangkok, millions of workers are drawn from the rural areas except during the planting and harvesting seasons. For most of the year, the northeast, the poorest region, is emptied as labourers migrate to Bangkok for work. Industrialisation has been responsible for sending harvest wages soaring by as much as 70 per cent in four years and even greater urban competition means farmers have problems retaining their labourers. Unless better economic parity is achieved between the urban and rural sectors, potential exists for social conflict.

This mass migration has also been responsible for straining Bangkok's already overwhelmed social services. Politicians have begun to realise that under a democratically elected government, the rural sector is responsible for the return of most national members of parliament. Rural problems have to be speedily addressed if political stability is not to be jeopardised.

Addressing agricultural problems

The government has promised to improve agricultural production through research and technology and promotion of a planned, commercial, capital-intensive approach. Small farm holdings are no longer viewed as being productive. In the past, improvements in agricultural output were achieved through increasing the amount of land under cultivation rather than through increasing productivity. To date, hardly any government financial or planning help has been given to the agricultural sector, despite agriculture's importance for the economy. Thailand is the world's ninth-largest net food exporter and Asia's largest. In the past, the government exploited agriculture through use of taxation and pricing policies in order to extract agricultural surpluses for fuelling industrial development. Thai farmers have also suffered because of low produce prices. The government has to provide incentives for the farmers to either diversify away from low-income commodities or face the prospect of indefinite poverty. Landlessness also contributes to rural poverty. This problem has been neglected for decades and, if it is not addressed, Thailand could follow the example of Taiwan, a former food exporter which is now a food importer.

Improving essential services and infrastructure

Development of efficient and effective infrastructure is a high priority for both Bangkok and the provinces. Thailand is the classic example of manufacturing outpacing infrastructure. In the mid-1980s when the Thai economy took off under the impact of a surge of foreign investment, public spending on infrastructure was about 7.5 per cent of GDP. By 1990 the figure had fallen to 3.5 per cent – the lowest among Thailand's neighbours and the ASEAN members.

Bangkok

Bangkok's traffic problems are infamous. The World Bank reports that as much as 1.7 per cent of GDP may be lost simply due to the hours wasted in time spent on commuting. The World Bank also comments that infrastructure demand is outpacing public resources, thereby threatening to become a 'drag on growth'. Telecommunications, water, roads and services are all overloaded. Unless infrastructure problems are addressed, the frustration currently experienced by foreign investors may translate into businesses locating in rival countries in which infrastructure is better developed.

Over the years, the government has targeted many types of projects for private investment on the principle of build–operate–transfer (BOT). However, because of lack of a cohesive government policy with reference to privatisation of infrastructure projects, foreign investors and financiers are wary of participating in these arrangements. If the government plans to continue with the BOT principle, clearer policies, coupled with firm commitments to investors, will be necessary. Two of the world's most expensive oil refineries are now being developed in Thailand under licences granted to Shell and Caltex and several projects for developing the country's natural gas reserves also depend on private investment. Firm commitments such as pre-agreed taxation rates are vital to these ventures' success. Voter confidence and political stability could also be adversely affected if firm policies are not implemented.

In the provinces

Increasing access to essential services and development infrastructure in order to support expansion into rural areas is a government priority. However, it is difficult for Thailand's government to inspire industries to locate away from the ports because of the provinces' lack of supporting infrastructure. Currently, water and power supplies are inadequate for industry and road and rail services to carry goods to and from the ports. The Eastern Seaboard Development Plan highlights this problem. Although it commenced a decade ago under the Prem Tinsulanon government, it is showing results only now. Infrastructure remains poor, but the opening of Port Laem Chabang has resulted in renewed investment in the eastern seaboard.

Quality-of-life improvement and natural resource protection

Government initiatives designed to improve quality of life and resource protection include increasing the length of compulsory education from six to nine years; support of public health services and improvement of safety standards; preservation of the environment through regulation of air, noise and water pollution.

Education

Thailand has one of South-East Asia's highest literacy rates (90 per cent), the result of having a strong system of compulsory primary-school education. Secondary school education, particularly in rural areas, has lagged behind. For most rural children, education finishes at the end of Year 6. Only 10–15 per cent of provincial children continue secondary schooling, compared with 80 per cent of Bangkok children. Nationwide, this translates to only 35 per cent of twelve- to seventeen-year-old children attending secondary school. The remainder are in the workforce. Although compulsory schooling has now been extended to Year 9, Bangkok children remain strongly advantaged.

Thailand's long-term economic growth is threatened as a result of low secondary-school enrolments. The country lacks an educated, skilled, adaptable workforce. In 1993, the number of graduates for company positions was insufficient: openings existed for 10,000 engineers and technicians but only 2,500 graduates were available. As the economy shifts from having labour-intensive industries to having higher technology ones, this lack could be a critical factor. Export-oriented industry requires higher skill levels and a better educated labour force. Thailand's economic rivals are better equipped: by percentage of children who are enrolled in secondary school, the World Bank ranks South Korea first (86 per cent) and Thailand last (29 per cent). Thailand's closest rival is China (44 per cent). Qualified instructors are also lacking in some of the main skill areas industry requires; maths, science and English curricula have the most shortages. According to the 1993 World Bank report,

> Thai schools are not producing enough knowledgeable workers to satisfy the demands of a more industrialised economy . . . And those with only a primary-school education are increasingly being excluded from the better-paying jobs in Thailand's rapidly expanding manufacturing and service sectors.

The number of public-university places is also inadequate for the level of demand. In 1994, for example, 126,662 school leavers fought for only 29,044 places. Given that education is now compulsory for nine years, this situation could worsen if government planning and financial help does not keep pace.

Health

In Thailand, the greatest threat to economic and social progress is arguably the AIDS epidemic. It threatens to overwhelm the country's health and social welfare systems. In 1991, between 200,000 and 400,000 HIV-positive people were estimated to be among Thailand's population of 57 million. By the year 2000 it is projected this figure will have increased to about four million. One per cent of blood donors and pregnant mothers are infected and 24 per cent of brothel prostitutes carry the virus. This plague's economic consequences are considerable. As well as the obvious health-care costs there is the cost of funerals and mourning rituals, the cost of caring for AIDS orphans and loss of the victims' productive output. In

Thailand over the next decade, most AIDS deaths will be of adults who are in their prime working years. Given that for foreign businesses one of the main criteria for choosing to invest in Thailand is its abundance of cheap labour, the existence of AIDS threatens to alter the Thai economy's attractiveness. Labour shortages in both quantity and quality and high absenteeism rates due to illness, could be very disruptive for companies. Tourism could also be adversely affected if the escalating problem is not addressed.

Since 1989, Thailand's Ministry of Public Health has been conducting tests of various groups engaged in high-risk and low-risk behaviours in an attempt to monitor the spread of the AIDS epidemic. Its surveys have highlighted some disturbing trends. The epidemic continues to grow at an alarming rate and has also spread to the general population, a fact that suggests that many people's behaviours have to change in order for the epidemic's proliferation rate to be reduced.

Education programs have to be resourced by both the government and the private sector for the epidemic to be reduced. Alternatives such as encouragement of rural girls to continue on to secondary education have been successful in aiding cessation of migration to the Bangkok brothels.

Safety standards

To date, Thai industries' safety standards have been woefully neglected. In many cases working conditions are poor, workers receive lower than the minimum wage, and building and safety measures are substandard. A fire that occurred on 10 May 1993 in a toy factory in one of Bangkok's western suburbs highlighted the problem. Two hundred workers were locked inside the factory and were killed. On 13 August 1993, substandard construction and lack of safety measures were responsible for the breakout of a hotel fire in Nakhon Ratchasima in north-eastern Thailand. One hundred people were killed. Unless safety issues are monitored and improved, investment may be adversely affected.

The environment

Deterioration of natural resources and environmental pollution need to be halted in Thailand. The country's most important natural resource is its forests and although the government banned logging of natural forests in January 1993, an estimated 320,000 hectares of natural forest are illegally logged each year. In 1961, when the First National Economic and Social Development Plan commenced, forests covered 53.3 per cent of Thailand's total land area. The figure is now only 15 to 28 per cent, depending on the source. So much destruction has been responsible for upsetting the ecological balance and for affecting agricultural production.

Tourism, which is one of Thailand's main industries, has also been responsible for exerting tremendous pressure on resources and the environment. This is particularly the case with reference to water. Water catchment areas and watersheds have been drastically reduced because of its extensive use in tourist resorts. According to

Dr Apichai Puntasen in the conference paper 'Income Inequality, Thai Rural Poor and "Balanced" Economic Growth', Thailand is now facing a new problem of perpetual drought throughout the country. In addition, Thailand's main rivers are chemically polluted and Bangkok has one of the most dangerous air pollution problems of any capital city in the world. The diminishing availability of drinking water in Bangkok, in particular, is an increasingly urgent problem.

The government has introduced measures in order to force riverside factories and seaside resorts to install waste-treatment plants. Plans also exist for accessing water from the Mekong and Salween rivers and for a series of dams in the north.

The government plans to rejuvenate Bangkok by solving the transport problems, and housing shortages, assisting the growing number of poor and supporting the relocation of industry outside the metropolitan area. Consideration has been given to moving the government bureaucracy outside Bangkok entirely in an attempt to fight congestion and pollution. Laem Chabang, the new port located on the eastern seaboard, Chachoengsao and Chomburi provinces have been mooted as possible choices.

Research and development

Fostering development of science and technology through supporting research and development, encouraging technology transfer and providing scientific and technological services to increase production efficiency, are necessary initiatives if Thailand is to maintain a competitive edge.

In the past, most companies were able to capitalise on cheap labour and tariff protection without having to worry about improving technology to increase productivity. This situation is changing however. Thailand is facing increasing competition from Indonesia, Vietnam and China. Foreign investment has been increasing in these countries because wages are lower and natural resources are abundant. In order for Thailand to maintain its competitive edge, technology transfer and indigenous technological development are essential. Currently only 0.3 per cent of GDP is spent on research and development. Even with the expected increase to 0.75 per cent by 1996, Thailand will continue to lag behind other Asian NICs. Singapore, Taiwan and South Korea spend between 1 and 2 per cent of their GDP on research and development. Yongyuth Yuthavong, the National Science and Technology Development director, says:

> Industries in Thailand are becoming more aware of the importance of technology because their advantages in labour and natural resources are eroding very fast.

The government has commenced a series of programs to bolster the country's scientific and technological capabilities. Planners are focusing much of their attention on improving links between university researchers and engineers and executives in the biotechnology, material-science and electronics sectors.

Barriers to technological development in Thailand include the severe shortage of skilled labour mentioned above and the pattern of economic development over the past decade. MNCs, which dominate export industries, have tended to leave their research and development operations in their home countries. Therefore, although Thai employees of foreign-owned companies may learn to operate hi-tech equipment, they gain hardly any technical knowledge of the products they are turning out. Thai workers also need the education to understand the technology.

Impediments and problems that face Australian investors in Thailand

While there are many opportunities for Australian investment in Thailand, there are also a number of constraints. Culture and language differences can make the Thai market difficult to penetrate. Companies that wish to develop business in Thailand have to invest a considerable amount of time in building networks and gaining an appreciation of Thailand's business culture. Companies are more likely to succeed if they are supported by a local partner who can provide an introduction to the people who influence decisions in the industrial, commercial and financial sectors.[3] This can prove frustrating to businesses used to dealing with the culturally close, traditional markets of Europe and North America.

For foreign investors, an ongoing concern is the *laissez-faire* environment in which Thai business operates. The stock exchange, for example, has a casino-like atmosphere. Speculators and stock manipulators have much more leeway than is tolerated in European markets. Thailand also needs to develop its infrastructure and improve building and safety standards. Other constraints limiting potential investment include the country's high tariff regime, non-tariff barriers (such as a complex commercial licensing system), rules on market entry, restrictive establishment rights and lack of government cohesion in decision making.

Despite these impediments, Thailand offers exciting opportunities for businesses prepared to research the market and build a sound understanding of Thai business.

ENDNOTES

1   Zone 1 includes Bangkok, Samut Prakan, Samut Sakhon, Nakhon Pathom, Notaburi and Pathum Thani.

2   Zone 2 includes Kanchanaburi, Samut Songkhram, Ratchaburi, Suphanburi, Angthong, Ayuthaya, Saraburi, Nakon Nayok, Chachoengsao and Chonburi.

3   See the report that investigates the experiences of a number of Australian companies conducting business in Thailand: Edwards, R, Edwards, J and Muthaly, S, *Doing Business in Thailand: Essential Background Knowledge and First-Hand Advice – A Business Guide*, prepared in 1995 by Monash University's Asian Business Research Unit for the Australia–Thai Chamber of Commerce, Melbourne, 1995.

REFERENCES

Apichai, P, 'Income Inequality, Thai Rural Poor and "Balanced" Economic Growth'. Conference paper presented at the Thailand Update 1993 Conference, The University of Melbourne, 29 October 1993.

Australian Chamber of Commerce and Industry, *Australia and APEC: The Trade Relationship*. Canberra: Australian Chamber of Commerce and Industry, 1995.

Australian–Thai Chamber of Commerce, *Australian–Thai Chamber of Commerce Handbook & Directory*. Melbourne: Australian–Thai Chamber of Commerce Melbourne, 1992.

Board of Investment, *A Guide to Investing in Thailand*. Bangkok: Board of Investment, 1993.

—— 'New Dimensions of the BOI', Bangkok, Board of Investment, in *Promotional Circular*, 1993.

—— *Key Indicators of Thailand*. Bangkok: Board of Investment, September 1992.

Boontanacin, N, 'Thai Economic Policy Under the WTO System', in Il Sakong and Jaymin Lee, *Asia–Pacific Economic Co-operation under the WTO System*. Seoul: Institute of East and West Studies, Yonsei University, 1995, pp 131–56.

Burton, T, 'Keating's Vision Takes Shape', in the *Australian Financial Review*, 15 November 1993.

Corben, R, 'Spread of AIDS Sets Off Economic Alarm', in the *Australian*, 3 December 1993.

Davies, B, *Euromoney Supplement*, March 1994.

Clifford, M and Handley, P, 'Burning Questions: Thai Factory Blaze Gives Investors Pause for Thought', in the *Far Eastern Economic Review*, 27 May 1993.

Department of Foreign Affairs and Trade, *Australian Trade and Investment Development*. Canberra: 1994.

—— *The APEC Region Trade and Investment*. Canberra: Australian Government Publishing Service, 1993.

—— *Country Economic Brief: Thailand – October 1993*. Canberra: Australian Government Publishing Service, 1993.

East Asia Analytical Unit, Department of Foreign Affairs and Trade and Austrade, *Australia's Business Challenge: South-East Asia in the 1990s*. Canberra: Australian Government Publishing Service, 1992.

Economist Intelligence Unit, *Country Profile: Thailand, Myanmur (Burma), 1992–1993*. Economist Intelligence Unit, 1992.

Fairclough, G, 'Spread of Wealth', in the *Far Eastern Economic Review*, March 1995.

—— 'The Knowledge Factor: Thailand Seeks Skills to Keep Its Competitive Edge', in the *Far Eastern Economic Review*, 11 March 1993.

—— 'Missing Class: Problems Loom Over Failure to Educate Rural Poor', in the *Far Eastern Economic Review*, 4 February 1993.

Far Eastern Economic Review, 'Regional Briefing', in the *Far Eastern Economic Review*, 26 August 1993.

Handley, P, 'Thought For Food: Thai Farm Policy Faces Long-term Choices', in the *Far Eastern Economic Review*, 29 April 1993.

—— 'Heart of Darkness: Overcoming Barriers to Growth', in the *Far Eastern Economic Review*, 28 January 1993.

Herderschee, H, *Protection and Exports: A Comparison of Taiwan and Thailand, 1952–87*. Canberra: ANU Press, 1991.

—— *Incentives for Exports: A Case Study of Taiwan and Thailand, 1952–87*. Aldershot: Avebury, 1995.

—— 'Incentives for Exports', in the *ASEAN Economic Bulletin*, vol 9, no 3, March 1993, pp 363–48.

Hewison, K, 'March of Capitalism Brings Little Pleasure', in the *Australian*, 3 December 1993.

—— *Thailand*. Sydney: The Australia–Asia Institute, The University of New South Wales, 1993.

Hirsch, P, *Development Dilemmas in Rural Thailand*. Singapore: Oxford University Press, 1990.

Hong Kong and Shanghai Banking Corporation, *Business Profile Series: Thailand*, sixth edition. Hong Kong: Group Public Affairs, 1990.

Janssen, P, 'Provincial Push Gathers Speed', in *Asian Business*, September 1993.

Keyes, C F, *Thailand: Buddhist Kingdom to Modern Nation-State*. Honolulu: University of Hawaii Press, 1994.

Laothamatas, A, quoted in Tasker, R and Fairclough, G, 'Return to Duty', in the *Far Eastern Economic Review*, 20 May 1993.

—— *Business Associations and the New Political Economy of Thailand: From Bureaucratic Policy to Liberal Corporatism*. Boulder: Westview Press, 1992.

Muscat, R J, *The Fifth Tiger: A Study of Thai Development Policy*. Armonk: M E Sharpe, 1994.

Mechai, V, Obremskey, S and Myer, C, 'The Economic Impact of AIDS on Thailand'. Conference paper presented at the Thailand Update 1993 Conference, The University of Melbourne, 29 October 1993.

Minter, E and Morris, F, *Doing Business with South-East Asia*. Sydney: Minter, Ellison, Morris and Fletcher, 1992.

Neher, C D, 'Thailand in 1987: Semi-successful Semi-democracy', in *Asian Survey*, vol xxviii, no 2, 1988.

Pasuk, P, 'Technocrats, Businessmen and Generals: Democracy and Economic Policy-making in Thailand', in MacIntyre, A and Jayasuriya, K (eds), *The Dynamics of Economic Reform in South-East Asia and the South-West Pacific.* Britain: Oxford University Press, 1992.

Sheehan, B, *Trends in Australia–Thailand Trade, 1980–1991.* Canberra: National Thai Studies Centre, Australian National University, 1993.

Suchint, C, of Baker McKenzie, Bangkok, Thailand, 'Thailand Update – Legal Developments' Conference paper presented at the Thailand Update 1993 Conference, The University of Melbourne, 29 October 1993.

Suphachalassai, S, *Thailand's Clothing and Textile Exports.* Canberra: Institute of Southeast Asian Studies, 1994.

Tasker, R, 'Southern Discomfort: Muslim Separatist Violence Raises its Head Again', in the *Far Eastern Economic Review*, 2 September 1993.

'Paying the Price', in the *Far Eastern Economic Review*, 5 August 1993.

Towie, M, 'Education Anomalies Threaten Prosperity', in the *Australian*, 3 December 1993.

Tuckey, B, 'A Smooth Drive in the Quest for Quality', in the *Age*, 12 February 1994.

World Bank, Thailand Development Research Institute, quoted in Fairclough, G, 'Missing Class: Problems Loom Over Failure to Educate Rural Poor', in the *Far Eastern Economic Review*, 4 February 1993.

World Bank, *World Development Report 1994: Infrastructure for Development*, Oxford University Press, Oxford, 1994.

Warr, P G (ed.), *The Thai Economy in Transition.* Cambridge: Cambridge University Press, 1993.

Yongyuth, Y, quoted in Fairclough, G, 'The Knowledge Factor: Thailand Seeks Skills to Keep its Competitive Edge', in the *Far Eastern Economic Review*, 11 March 1993.

Yoshihara, K, *The Nation and Economic Growth: The Philippines and Thailand.* Singapore: Oxford University Press, 1994.

APPENDIX 8.1: *Australian and Thai representation*

Australian addresses

Australia–Thailand Business Council
PO Box E14
Queen Victoria Terrace
Canberra 2600, ACT, Australia
Telephone: (61 6) 273 2311
Facsimile: (61 6) 273 3196

Board of Investment
Thai Government
Royal Exchange Building
Level 12, 56 Pitt Street
Sydney 2000, NSW, Australia
Telephone: (61 2) 9247 8905
Facsimile: (61 2) 9251 6905

Royal Thai Embassy
Chancery
111 Empire Circuit
Yarralumla 2600, ACT, Australia
Telephone: (61 6) 273 1149
Facsimile: (61 6) 273 1518

Thai addresses

Australia and New Zealand Banking Group Limited
Ninth Floor, Tower A
Diethelm Towers
93/1 Wireless Road
Bangkok 10330, Thailand
Telephone: (66 2) 256 6350/6358
Facsimile: (66 2) 256 6347

Australian Embassy
37 South Sathorn Road
Bangkok 10120, Thailand
Telephone: (66 2) 287 2680
Facsimile: (66 2) 287 2589

Australian Trade Commissioner
Australian Embassy
37 South Sathorn Road
Bangkok 10120, Thailand
Telephone: (66 2) 287 2680
Facsimile: (66 2) 287 2589

Australian–Thailand Business Council
The Thai Chamber of Commerce
150 Rajbopit Road
Bangkok 10200, Thailand
Telephone: (66 2) 225 0086
Facsimile: (66 2) 225 3372

Australian–Thai Chamber of Commerce
889 South Sathorn Road
Yannawa
Bangkok 10120, Thailand
Telephone: (66 2) 210 0217
Facsimile: (66 2) 210 0218

National Australia Bank Limited
Sixteenth Floor, Sathorn Thani Building
90 North Sathorn Road
Bangkok 10500, Thailand
Telephone: (66 2) 236 6016/6017
Facsimile: (66 2) 236 6018

Thai Board of Investment
555 Vipavadee Rangsit Road
Chatuchak
Bangkok 10900, Thailand
Telephone: (66 2) 537 8111
Facsimile: (66 2) 512 0020

Westpac Banking Corporation
Level 24, CP Tower
313 Silom Road
Bangkok 10500, Thailand
Telephone: (66 2) 231 0011
Facsimile: (66 2) 231 0015

APPENDIX 8.2: Australia's Strategic Priorities for Thai Trade and Investment

- Strengthen our market share in traditional mineral, energy and agricultural commodities.
- Improve awareness of Australia as a competitive and reliable supplier of sophisticated manufactures and services.
- Expand trade and investment in new manufactures and related services.
- Identify and promote opportunities for trade and investment in product markets like processed foods and beverages, particularly in regional areas such as the north-east.
- Support Australia's commercial efforts to apply environment technologies and management skills.
- Seek reductions in Thailand's tariff and non-tariff barriers.
- Expand trade and investment in services, particularly in construction, education and professional services.
- Encourage Australian business to take long-term approaches, to find the right partners and to develop consortia, particularly in infrastructure and government projects.
- Increase the numbers and spending of Thai tourists.
- Improve the commercial benefits that ensue from our bilateral aid program, particularly following opening the high profile Mekong bridge.

Source: Department of Foreign Affairs and Trade, *Australian Trade and Investment Development*. Canberra: Australian Government Publishing Service, 1994, p 106.

9

Vietnam

Peter Schuwalow

Introduction

Twenty years after the fall of Saigon (now renamed Ho Chi Minh City), Vietnam is at a critical point in its history. Following decades of war and a crippling economic embargo, positive signs exist that the Vietnamese economy can finally look forward to a brighter future. This country has enormous potential: its economy is now growing at an average of 8 per cent a year, exports are accelerating, and rice production is at an all-time high – quite commendable for a country that continues to be viewed as one of the world's poorest countries. Indeed, some consider Vietnam to be one of Australia's most attractive export markets. This chapter examines some of this potential, through examining the country's geographic setting, political history, economic and financial development and prospects for foreign investment and trade.

The setting

Vietnam extends more than 1600 kilometres down the east coast of IndoChina, from the Chinese-border mountains and the Red River delta in the north, along the Laotian and Cambodian borders, to the fertile Mekong River delta in the south. Although in its extreme north the country is more than 500 kilometres wide, much of its middle section is a relatively narrow strip of coastal land. For a considerable distance it is about 80 kilometres wide, and in the south it expands again to about double that width. Vietnam's total land area is 325,360 square kilometres, and about 75 per cent of it is hill country or mountainous.

The climate is typically monsoon, and the temperature varies considerably according to latitude. In the tropical south, conditions are warm to hot throughout the year and the humidity is usually high. In the north, particularly in the highlands,

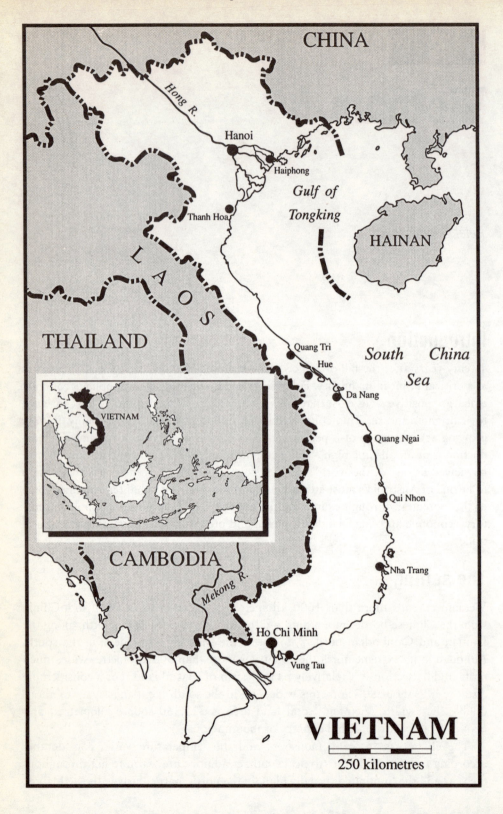

markedly warmer and cooler seasons occur and temperatures are much lower than those at sea level.

In 1995, Vietnam's population was estimated to be 74.4 million, which makes it ASEAN's second-most populous nation. Although about 90 per cent of the people are ethnic Vietnamese, there is a large ethnic-Chinese population (about 3 per cent) as well as a wide variety of indigenous tribal hill peoples and Lao, Khmer and Thais. Therefore, although Vietnamese remains the national language and is spoken throughout the country, there are a number of Chinese and other dialects. Because of the country's French-colonial past, French is the most common second language. English is widely spoken in the south, and Russian is spoken in the north among some middle-level public servants.

Vietnam is a socialist republic, so religion would not be expected to play an important part. However, Buddhism continues to have a major, though probably indirect, influence on the local culture. Although the Roman Catholic Church was the religion of only a small percentage of the population during the French period, it has maintained a small but important presence.

Political history

Because Vietnam's extensive borders are located along an often narrow coastline and important agricultural land exists around the Red Delta in the north and the considerably larger Mekong Delta in the south, the country has frequently been a target for invasion.

In the past, major portions of modern Vietnam have therefore been part of various empires. The middle and south, for example, were at first controlled by the Kingdoms of Champ and Kampuchea respectively. In contrast, the north was subject to Chinese rule from about the second century to 938, when the Chinese were expelled. A history of border conflict with the Chinese in the north and expansion to the south against the Cham and then the Cambodians were thereby commenced. Although Vietnam eventually reached something of its current size by the mid-eighteenth century, civil war from the seventeenth to the eighteenth century hampered its progress.

The country had at first avoided European expansion in Asia, but in 1858 a French–Spanish military force attacked Da Nang following the murder of some Catholic missionaries. In 1859 the French invaded Saigon. By 1867 the French had gained control of much of the south and, in 1883, of the central and north of the country. Vietnam therefore formally became a French protectorate. Along with what is now Laos and Cambodia, it formed what was known as French IndoChina.

The French maintained control of the country until World War II broke out. Although the Japanese were at first allies of France's Vichy government, they stationed troops in Vietnam in September 1940. In March 1945, towards the end of the war, the Japanese took full control but were forced to surrender in August of that year. Although the French planned to resume control of their colony, the Vietnamese declared their own independence on 2 September 1945. This development eventually proved to be the start of a revolutionary and then a civil war that lasted almost 30 years.

During the struggle, the Vietnamese communists – the Viet Minh – led by Ho Chi Minh, became the strongest of the nationalistic anti-French forces. On 7 May 1954 they defeated the French military at the remote north-western junction of Dien Bien Phu and forced the French to withdraw from the north.

Although French-colonial rule soon ended and agreement was reached to have internationally monitored national elections and reunification, conflict between the communists in the north and anti-communists in the south left the country divided along the seventeenth parallel. Nationwide elections planned for July 1956 promised unification. The elections, however, did not take place. The communists retained rule of the north under the leadership of Ho Chi Minh. In the south, although Vietnam's Emperor Bao Dai remained the figurehead ruler, his prime minister, Ngo Dinh Diem, was supposedly in charge. In practice, the south was somewhat more divided and was effectively controlled by a weakly connected coalition of religious and military leaders who looked to the West for help against the potential threat from the north.

Diem moved to consolidate his position on 26 October 1955 by declaring the south the Republic of Vietnam, with him as the first president in Saigon. During this early period, more than one million refugees fled to the south and up to 100,000 communist sympathisers moved north. From 1956, communist guerilla warfare became more evident in the south, and in 1960 various guerrilla groups joined to form the National Liberation Front, or Viet Cong.

In 1961 the US took over responsibility for the military support of South Vietnam, arguing the decision was in the interests of freedom and containment of communism. If communism, particularly Chinese communism, was permitted to move into South Vietnam and the rest of IndoChina (which in fact happened), then it would be able to spread through the rest of Asia and beyond. This 'domino theory' provided the rationale for US's involvement in the region.

Diem's regime became more oppressive as the situation in South Vietnam deteriorated. Large numbers of communists, who were originally from the south, infiltrated back there. Many South Vietnamese officials were assassinated. The US became frustrated with Diem, partly because of its own demands on him but also because it believed his repressive regime was hampering efforts to fight the communists and working against South Vietnam's democratic reform and development. In 1963, due to increasing military pressure from the north and with US's support, the South Vietnamese generals had Diem overthrown and assassinated.

Throughout the 1960s, as the Vietnam War continued to escalate, the Saigon government's problems of corruption and instability continued. The US sought help from its allies; and Australia, New Zealand, Korea, the Philippines and Thailand eventually provided direct support. With reference to Australia, our military advisers were first sent on 29 July 1962 in order to help the South Vietnamese army; in 1965 they were joined by full-scale Australian troop units.

The Viet Cong's Tet Offensive against the South in 1968 was a turning point in the conflict. Even though the US and South Vietnamese armies were able to push back the Viet Cong and regain Hue, the war was now viewed as unwinnable. The US wished to have an honourable withdrawal.

The Tet Offensive placed a new emphasis on the Paris peace talks, the initial phase of which commenced in May 1968. It was commonly believed that the North Vietnamese would not seriously negotiate unless they were faced with considerable military pressure, so the US forces' active participation continued. On 27 January 1973, progress was finally achieved when free and fair elections in South Vietnam were agreed to in return for American troops' withdrawal.

In 1973 the US continued to have a presence in and around South Vietnam even though its troops had all but gone. The US downgraded its aid while the North Vietnamese were simultaneously receiving almost unlimited aid from China and the former USSR. After Saigon fell, on 30 April 1975, many Vietnamese were executed and hundreds of thousands were sent to re-education camps. Up to two million people attempted to escape by sea, and many thousands drowned. Despite these problems, the north called for national elections to be held in April 1976, and on 1 July 1976 the north and south again became one country: the Socialist Republic of Vietnam.

With reunification came an attempt to transform the south from a basically market economy to a planned one. Businesses were nationalised and collectivisation applied to agriculture. In the meantime, trade with the West was greatly restricted due to a US trade embargo. Vietnam's conflict with Cambodia during 1977–80 and border conflict with China in 1979 further hampered the country's progress.

Despite the collapse of many communist regimes in Eastern Europe, the Communist Party of Vietnam remains in full control. There has been some relaxation of social and political controls, but real power has been retained by the party.

Like its more successful South-East Asian neighbours, Vietnam has realised that political stability is a key factor in economic development. It has thus placed emphasis on economic policy reforms rather than political ones. Indeed, while the government encourages debate on economic issues to a certain degree, it strongly rejects dissent in political matters, particularly on the Communist Party's role in Vietnamese society.

In the past, the National Assembly (Vietnam's parliament) sessions were a 'rubber stamp'. However, because the assembly's new, younger and more educated members have gained influence, the institution has become a more meaningful part of Vietnam's political structure. However, despite new members having been elected to the Politburo, the current balance within the party seems likely to continue. The Eight Party Conference in mid-1996 certainly reconfirmed the existing policy of minimum politic reform coupled with a continued drive toward a market economy. This economic reform, however, will continue at its current pace rather than a faster one.

Economic development

Before the mid-1980s economic crisis occurred, Vietnam could be characterised as having a strong command-economy system. For up to a decade after the Vietnam War ended, Hanoi's leaders tried to implement socialism in what was supposed to be a reunified Vietnam. However, the country was plagued with food shortages, starvation and, at times, hyper-inflation. Poverty was and remains a serious problem. A 1995 World Bank report confirmed that Vietnam remains very poor: 51 per cent of its people are estimated to live in poverty. This figure compares with China's 9 per cent, Indonesia's 15 per cent and the Philippines' 21 per cent. Although this situation may not be so obvious in the cities, in which 27 per cent of people live in poverty, it is more obvious in the rural areas, where 57 per cent live in poverty.

In the mid-1980s the national economy was approaching the brink of disaster, and changes were needed. With the death of the Communist Party General Secretary, Le Duan, and the retirement of a number of key officials at the Sixth Communist Party Congress in 1986, the government was restructured, controls liberalised and economic reforms commenced. These were introduced under the policy of *doi moi* (economic renovation).

Since that time, progress has clearly taken place. Over the past six years, annual rice production has more than doubled to 25 million tonnes, which makes it the world's third-largest rice exporter. Coffee, rubber, marine products and offshore-oil exports have all been surging as well. As a result, per-capita income has increased from its 1970 level of US$150 per year to US$230 per year. Despite the tremendous progress that has been made since 1986, Vietnam's future as the 'next Asian Tiger' is by no means assured.

Some communist leaders have not fully committed themselves to the concept of a market-led economy. They have not permitted private enterprise to have free rein, particularly in southern Vietnam, which has attracted a reasonable amount of business interest in recent times. Partners in the country's first oil-refinery venture (a US$1 billion project led by a French company) were informed that the development should take place not in a city but in a quite remote location in the central provinces. Similarly, Coca-Cola was informed it could build a plant only in Hanoi, not Ho Chi Minh City as originally planned. The government is therefore clearly concerned that the benefits of economic development be more evenly spread throughout the country. Another example is Vietnam's largest infrastructure achievement to date: a 1500 kilometre, 500 kilovolt power line. Although the cheaper alternative was to build new capacity in the south, the focus is clearly on diversion of new investment away from Ho Chi Minh City. The south has been advantaged through use of the infrastructure left behind by the US but also through its strong commercial traditions. It shifted to a market economy before the rest of the country meant its obsolete machinery was replaced earlier and its factories became more efficient and productive sooner.

Ho Chi Minh City, the population of which is almost six million, is accelerating ahead of the rest of the country. The south is expanding at an annual rate of 15 per cent and is twice the size of its northern and more remote capital. Foreign investment in the southern region is 40 per cent of the nation's total. Vietnam's 'bread basket', which is responsible for producing between 50 and 60 per cent of the country's agricultural produce, is in the south's adjacent Mekong Delta, and the recently tapped oil wealth is located off the southern coast.

Another problem for Vietnam has been its business environment. In the early 1990s when the IMF indicated that of all the post-communist countries Vietnam was the most progressive, considerably more attention came to be focused on Vietnam as a potential investment opportunity. However, Hanoi administration is considered to be somewhat erratic in its decision making, particularly with reference to decisions that have impacted on foreign companies. Japan, for example, has been very hesitant about investing in Vietnam. This was mainly due to US commercial pressures but Japanese companies also had concerns over local infrastructure and bureaucracy.

With reference to Vietnam's business environment, the country's main concern is that it does not wish to be dominated by foreign firms or governments. Understandably, the Vietnamese authorities will attempt to realise the best possible deal, and wherever possible, foreigners have to operate through joint ventures with State companies. This usually means the local company will put up the land and labour for the project, take a 30 per cent share and play an active role in running the business through having seats on the board, whereas the foreign partners meet all capital and technology requirements.

Having had 10 years of *doi moi* reforms, Vietnam is signalling to the rest of the world that it is prepared to take the next step and introduce more market reforms. Included in this is an overhaul of government structure, which is a legacy of the command-economy era. Thus, on 21 October 1995 the National Assembly approved a new, rationalised government structure with eight ministries merged into three 'super' ones. In terms of foreign investment, the new Ministry of Planning and Investment should streamline approvals, process with local institutions given the power to approve smaller projects; previously all investment had required State Committee for Co-operation and Investment (SCCI) approval. Other changes to be introduced include creation of more efficient foreign-investment procedures, reduction of land tax by 25 per cent, and introduction of a tax-reform package whereby a more modern and efficient tax system is signalled including a special consumption tax. The Ministry of Trade is examining the option of reducing the number of forms and approvals – at present between 12 and 16 – that are necessary simply for importing or exporting goods. With reference to trade reform, Vietnam's most important development has been the country's entry to ASEAN in July 1995. Hanoi officials have already indicated they have agreed to reduce tariffs on imports from the ASEAN countries to 5 per cent by 2006.

Since 1986 when Vietnam's economic reforms were launched, agricultural production has increased by more than 40 per cent, hard-currency exports have grown from US$221 million in 1985 to US$3.6 billion at the end of 1994, per-capita income has risen by 30 per cent, electric-power generation has trebled, and cement production has increased fivefold. These developments have all been responsible for helping to change the basic structure of Vietnam's economy. Although in dollar terms it is growing rapidly, agriculture has come to represent a declining portion of the overall economy: in the short period 1991–93 it has dropped from 39.52 per cent to 29.29 per cent of GDP. Industry, construction and – in particular – services have simply grown much more rapidly.

Table 9.1 Vietnam's GDP by sector, 1991–93

Sector	1991		1992		1993	
	billion of dong	%	billion of dong	%	billion of dong	%
Industry	15,193	19.81	23,956	21.67	29,371	21.51
Construction	3,059	3.99	6,179	5.59	9,423	6.90
Agriculture	30,314	39.52	36,468	32.99	39,998	29.29
Forestry	744	0.97	1,045	0.95	1,476	1.08
Others services	27,397	35.72	42,887	38.80	56,303	41.23
TOTAL	**76,707**	**100.00**	**110,535**	**100.00**	**136,571**	**100.00**

Source: General Statistical Office, *Statistical Yearbook 1993*. Hanoi: Statistical Publishing House, 1993, p 25.

With reference to the government's current five-year plan, economic growth has risen from 6 per cent in 1991 to 8.6 per cent in 1992. In 1993 the growth rate was 8.1 per cent and in 1994 it was 8.8 per cent: 0.8 percentage points above the target that had been set at the start of the year. It is estimated that over the next few years the growth rate will be about 8 to 10 per cent. Infrastructure improvements, a foreign-investment increase, higher education standards, bureaucratic reforms and more adequate legal and financial frameworks will aid the growth's continuation.

Table 9.2 Vietnam's CPI, 1985–93

Year	CPI	Annual change %
1985	100.0	–
1986	590.0	590.0
1987	2,650.0	349.2
1988	11,050.0	317.0
1989	19,550.0	76.9
1990	25,220.0	29.0
1991	46,150.0	83.0
1992	63,594.7	37.8
1993	69,000.2	8.5

Source: Asian Development Bank, *Key Indicators of Developing Asian and Pacific Countries*. 1994, p 29.

As indicated in Table 9.2, in the mid-1980s inflation reached triple-digit figures but by 1990 – due to much tighter control over monetary policy – the inflation rate had been reduced to 29 per cent. Strong economic growth and foreign-currency inflows, and a sharp rise in food prices, which was partly due to the Mekong Delta's disastrous flooding in October 1994, have been responsible for the 1994 inflation rates increasing to an estimated 14.4 per cent. In 1995 the government was already finding it difficult to take the pressure off inflation. Further tightening of monetary policy was therefore likely for late 1995 or early 1996.

In 1994, Vietnam's government had a budget deficit that was equivalent to 4.1 per cent of GDP, compared with 4.8 per cent in 1993. This has continued to be a problem for it, with 1995, at an estimated 4.3 per cent, showing no signs of improvement. About US$150 million had to be raised from international sources in 1995, mainly due to the pressure placed on expenditure for infrastructure works and social welfare programs. On the domestic front, in June 1994, in an effort to fund the deficit, the government issued six-month Treasury bills and three-year bonds for domestic sale. In 1995 a plan was developed to market official bonds for sale abroad, thereby marking the government's first move into international capital markets.

Financial development

Vietnam's financial system has made steady progress towards meeting the needs of a market-oriented economy. Among the achievements are maintenance of positive real interest rates and reduction of inflation to a rate that for transitional economies is competitive. Banks have been given more freedom to determine their own lending decisions. Less reliance is now made on foreign exchange and gold as a means of payment, due to the creation of new payment instruments. Also, because reforms have been made to reserve requirements, the taxation of financial intermediation has somewhat lessened despite remaining quite high.

The banking system continues to be controlled by the State Bank of Vietnam. As Vietnam's central bank it also issues the country's currency – the dong – and provides the government with a range of other banking services. These services are supplemented by the services of four specialised government-owned banks: the Industrial and Commercial Bank of Vietnam, the Vietnam Bank of Agriculture, the Bank for Foreign Trade of Vietnam and the Investment and Development Bank of Vietnam. The last two were at first established for servicing specific aspects of the economy, whereas the first two were created in 1988 from the State Bank of Vietnam's commercial banking branch networks in the urban and rural areas, respectively. Although the firstmentioned two banks' names continue to reflect the earlier specialist roles, the distinction has become somewhat blurred over time.

As Table 9.3 indicates, a number of locally established joint-stock banks also exist, notably the Vietnam Export–Import Commercial Joint Stock Bank. Since 1993, foreign investment has been permitted in this type of institution. Three joint-venture banks that involve ASEAN institutions are also worth noting: the Indovian Bank (Bank Dagang Nasional Indonesia combined with the Industrial and Commercial Bank of Vietnam), the VID Public Bank (Malaysia's Public Bank combined with the Bank for Investment and Development of Vietnam) and the VINASIAM Bank (the Vietnam Bank of Agriculture combined with the Siam Commercial Bank and the Charoen Pokphand group of Thailand). At first, foreign participation was limited to this form of indirect entry.

Table 9.3   Vietnam's financial institutions, 1995

Institution	Number of Institutions
State Bank of Vietnam	1
State-government commercial banks	4
Joint-stock banks	46
Joint-venture banks	4
Foreign banks (19 branches)	17
Credit co-operatives	120
Finance companies	2
Financial leasing companies	3
Insurance companies*	1
Total of Institutions	198

*Although the state-government-owned Boa Viet (Vietnam Insurance Company) has had a monopoly on local insurance, foreign insurers have recently been given permission to open local offices.
Source: Australia and New Zealand Banking Group Ltd, 1996.

Table 9.4   Foreign banks with branches in Vietnam, 1995

Bank	Home country
ANZ Bank[a]	Australia
Bank of America	United States
Bangkok Bank[a]	Thailand
BFCE[b]	France
Banque Indosuez	France
Banque Nationale de Paris	France
The Chinfon Bank[c]	Taiwan
Citibank	United States
Credit Lyonnais[a]	France
Deutsche Bank	Germany
Hongkong and Shanghai Banking Corp	United Kingdom
ING Bank[d]	Netherlands
Malayan Banking Berhad	Malaysia
Shinhan Bank	Korea
Standard Chartered Bank	United Kingdom
Thai Military Bank	Thailand
United Overseas Bank	Singapore

Note 1: [a]The bank has two branches: one in Hanoi and one in Ho Chi Minh City. [b]This stands for 'Banque Francaise du Commercial Exterieur'. [c]Before 1995, this was known as the Cathay Investment & Trust Company. [d]This stands for 'Internationale Nederlanden Bank'.
Note 2: At the time of writing, ABN AMRO Bank and the Bank of China had been given permission to open branches in Vietnam but had not opened. Chinfon Bank had also been granted permission to open a second branch, in Ho Chi Minh City.

A number of foreign banks have also established local representative offices (in December 1995 some 57 offices existed), and more recently, as Table 9.4 indicates, some 19 foreign banks have been permitted to open local branches. In 1993 when the first licences were granted they were restricted to only six banks, of which the Australia and New Zealand Banking Corporation (the ANZ Bank) was one. The ANZ Bank now operates a full branch in Hanoi; and in Ho Chi Minh City and plans to open a representative office in Da Nang.

These and subsequently established foreign branches are permitted to offer a full range of commercial banking services, including savings, current and fixed deposits in local and foreign currencies, business and personal loans and international-trade-finance services such as letters of credit, bankers' guarantees and performance bonds. In practice, though, the new entrants have found business to be difficult. This is because most Vietnamese people are unfamiliar and uncomfortable with Western banking practices (local cheques were introduced only in 1995) and are uncertain about whether to establish arrangements with foreign banks. Foreign investors and joint-venture partners who have local interests, and these parties' expatriate staff members, therefore provide much of the business at first.

According to the July 1995 issue of *Asiamoney*, at the end of 1994 the 13 foreign banks that had operational branches accounted for a combined total of about 7 per cent of total banking assets.

Financial reform in a transitional economy such as Vietnam's includes government financial policies (tax-sector reform and enterprises' financial autonomy), a new approach to monetary policy (particularly interest rates, exchange-rate policies and price stabilisation) and development of an efficient banking system. Although much of this reform has commenced, Vietnam's financial sector has a number of tasks ahead. The system has to raise and allocate resources efficiently, make payments, aid financing of the emerging private sector, firmly promote budget constraint for State enterprises and perform a corporate-governance function in both the private and the public sector. Importantly, although a non-banking sector is starting to emerge, banks remain the dominant financial force and can be expected to continue being the main influence on the financial sector at least until the turn of the century.

Although the banks will doubtlessly retain their dominance, the State-government banks' role may change significantly. As deregulation proceeds in both the financial sector and the real economy, these institutions will be subject to increasing pressure to change. For example, their foreign and joint-venture competitors and their new operations have the potential to offer much more efficient services at lower costs as well as a wider range of new products. Business will therefore become difficult to retain and will be potentially less profitable. In the meantime, as the real-sector reforms are having their impact on other State enterprises, the State banks will again suffer. As in the case of other State-planned countries, the Vietnamese banking system's loan portfolio has been dominated by advances given to State enterprises. Indeed, in 1994 this type of lending comprised about 96 per cent of the State-government banks' loan portfolios. Because State enterprises are typically among the worst affected during a liberalisation period, much State-bank lending is placed at considerable risk. This problem is one the government well realises, and in December 1994 it appointed the ANZ Bank as adviser to the State Bank of Vietnam and as restructurer of that bank's loan portfolio.

If Vietnam expects to increase its financial depth over the next few years it will have to adopt particular measures. Holding of excess reserves at the State Bank of Vietnam has to be reduced, and banking's exemption from paying the 'turnover tax' will mean banks are encouraged to expand. Other measures include further improvements in the payments system and, in order to promote increased confidence in the banking system, risk-asset and audit reviews of the State-owned commercial banks and strengthening of its bank supervision function.

Foreign investment

Foreign investment's role in enhancing Vietnam's economic development has increased in importance since 1992. As Vietnam seeks to realign itself, politically and economically, with market economy governments, it has plenty to offer, including abundant natural resources such as oil and coal as well as a workforce that is predominantly cheap but has a relatively high literacy rate: 90 per cent. Given Vietnam's population of about 74.4 million, it is not surprising that investors are interested in South-East Asia's second-largest country.

The main law relating to foreign investment is the Law on Foreign Investment (FIL), which was enacted in December 1987. A number of amendments have been made to it, the most recent being in April 1993. It is the foundation of Vietnam's foreign-investment policy and addresses foreign investors' areas of concern. It defines foreign investment, set-up procedures, taxation, accounting, foreign exchange, employment of Vietnamese people, visa issue, use of land, technology transfer and royalties.

As the law stands at present, for people who are interested in conducting business in Vietnam, foreign investment is permitted in three forms: business-co-operation contracts, joint ventures and 100 per cent foreign-owned enterprises. Production-sharing contracts have been permitted in the oil-and-gas sector, and in February 1994, BOT (build, operate, transfer) contracts for infrastructure projects were approved. Other main elements of the law include corporate income-tax rates of between 10 and 25 per cent, full repatriation of profits, tax holidays, and waivers on some import and export duties. Expropriation is prohibited. Recent amendments to the law have enabled joint ventures' life to be extended from 20 to 50 years, and some projects are eligible for a licence for up to 70 years.

The government's efforts at attracting foreign investment have been rewarded. As indicated in Table 9.5, total commitments (though not always actual investment) increased to almost US$14 billion between 1988 and 1995. New investment almost doubled: it rose from US$590 million in 1990 to US$1185 million in 1991, US$1995 million in 1992, US$2800 million in 1993 and US$4000 million in 1994. The joint ventures conducted with State companies are the main type of investment. Japan, the largest bilateral trader, has not as yet been very keen to invest in Vietnam and ranked only fifth behind Taiwan ($US2.4 billion) and Hong Kong ($US1. lion). Other Asian countries have increased investment over the past 18 mor. Singapore was in third place, South Korea fourth and Malaysia seventh. Austra ranked sixth. While the US is ranked fifteenth, its investment is growing rapidly an will soon be among the most significant sources. In order of importance, foreign investors' main areas of interest have been heavy and light industry, hotels and tourism, oil and gas, transport and communications, agriculture, finance and banking, and seafood.

Table 9.5 Vietnam's FDI, by major source, January 1988 to March 1995

Country	US$ million	%
Taiwan	2,462.6	19.51
Hong Kong	1,605.0	12.72
Singapore	1,241.6	9.84
South Korea	1,046.1	8.29
Japan	816.0	6.47
Australia	688.3	5.45
Malaysia	619.4	4.91
Switzerland	482.4	3.82
France	479.9	3.80
British Virgin Islands	464.5	3.68
Netherlands	391.6	3.10
United Kingdom	374.6	2.97
Thailand	289.7	2.30
Bahamas	264.0	2.09
United States	227.3	1.80
Bermuda	170.4	1.35
Russia	158.3	1.25
Cayman Islands	120.5	0.95
Indonesia	111.8	0.89
Other countries	607.5	4.81
TOTAL	**12,621.5**	**100.00**

Source: *Vietnam Investment Review*, 1995.

Although Vietnam's economic potential is beyond doubt, bureaucratic restrictions at every level of the economy, corruption and only a basic economic infrastructure continue to make it difficult for the country's new players. Also, the business environment remains underdeveloped: Vietnam continues to be one of South-East Asia's poorest countries. Only a very small proportion of the population has achieved a reasonable level of purchasing power.

Another major problem that faces FDI in Vietnam is lack of qualified staff. In some cases, businesses have been given staff by their Vietnamese partners and have had no control over staff selection. The electricity supply cannot be relied on, especially in the south, and communications, particularly the domestic telephone system, is limited in coverage and reliability. However, the international communications network is excellent.

Despite the many difficulties presented, if foreign companies are prepared to invest 'for the long haul', Vietnam offers considerable potential, because it is strategically located in the Asian region. A key factor is that the Vietnamese people are very determined to improve their standard of living; also, they have a well-educated labour force that is relatively inexpensive.

Many promising opportunities exist, particularly for Australian investors. Talks have already focused on co-operation in the areas of oil and gas, coal, electricity, telecommunications, infrastructure and services – notably in banking, law, accounting, education, tourism and business consultancy. There is potential for more Australian involvement in the major project transmitting northern-generated electricity to the south. Australian firms are also 'in the running' to upgrade Vietnam's roads, bridges and ports.

Foreign trade

Because Vietnam is part of the communist world, its trade used to be largely directed towards other planned-economy countries. It was a member of the Council for Mutual Economic Assistance (the former USSR's version of the EU), and as a result, the former USSR, Poland, Hungary and Romania were among its major trading partners. A US-imposed embargo on trade between that country and Vietnam precluded direct US trade transactions and was responsible for preventing many US MNCs from dealing even through affiliates or third countries. Due to the former USSR's collapse, and lifting of the US embargo on 4 February 1994, Vietnam has already experienced some major changes in its trade relationships, and more changes can be expected.

The most significant change will be caused, at least in part, through Vietnam having become ASEAN's seventh member in July 1995. ASEAN is the world's fastest growing economic group. Its acceptance of Vietnam is motivated by its desire to deal with China's economic resurgence and the need to present ASEAN as being a superior place for foreign investment through increasing the size of its free-trade area. Of concern to ASEAN is the fact that a cloud of uncertainty remains about how Vietnam will adjust its economy to free-trade principles.

Vietnam may find it difficult to match AFTA's tariff-reduction timetable even if it is given extra time to implement it. It has stated its intention to reduce tariffs to 5 per cent by 2003, a timeline that is within the guidelines embraced by ASEAN's other members. ASEAN, though, is aware of the difficulties Vietnam will face during its transition to a more market-oriented economy and has indicated that Vietnam can have until 2006 to phase in its tariff reductions. Considerable domestic resistance could nevertheless come from Vietnam about this issue, particularly within the Hanoi administration, as the time draws near. The government's concern is that opening the economy too quickly might leave its industries vulnerable to imports from its more advanced neighbours as well as accelerate its loss of control over the economy.

In regards to the China issue, ASEAN believes a united front that includes Vietnam will aid in keeping Beijing (China's capital) at arm's length. China's impressive economic performance has been responsible for increasing that country's regional power and it is already claiming the whole of the South China Sea as its territorial waters. If it is successful in its territorial claim, it would immediately become the neighbour of many South-East Asian countries, including Vietnam. In the process, China would gain control of some very lucrative offshore oil and natural gas reserves that have recently been discovered in the area. Vietnam's government is also hoping that by joining ASEAN, more political pressure can be applied to China, thereby encouraging it to agree to holding multilateral negotiations about disputed ownership of the Spratly Islands.

As indicated in Table 9.6 and Table 9.7, petroleum products play an exceedingly important role in Vietnam's trade relations – indeed, they represent the country's major single commodity type for both imports and exports. With reference to other imports, capital equipment and machine parts are also very important in aggregate terms. Among specific commodities, though, a range of consumer-related products continue to feature highly among Vietnam's imports.

Table 9.6 Vietnam's major imports, by product type, 1993

Product type	US$ million
Petroleum products	716
Motorcycles	250
Chemical fertilisers	150
Iron and steel	150
Pharmaceutical products	81
Electrical appliances	70
Cigarette ingredients	60

Source: *Asia 1995 Yearbook: A Review of the Events of 1994*. Hong Kong: Review Publishing Company Ltd, 1995, p 224.

Table 9.7 Vietnam's major exports, by product type, 1992–94

	US$ million		
	1992	**1993**	**1994**
Crude oil	805	861	976
Textiles and garments	221	350	550
Sea products	307	370	480
Rice	418	350	406
Coal	62	84	115
Shoes	–	24	100
Coffee	91	85	98
Rubber	67	70	70
Cashew nuts	41	31	60
Peanuts	32	47	45

Source: Vietnamese Ministry of Trade, 1995.

With reference to exports, Vietnam has been self-sufficient in rice production for some years and is now a major exporter in the world market: it holds third place, after the US and Thailand. Other food items are also important as exports. Only textiles, garments and footwear are important with reference to manufactured goods. As a range of recently established foreign-investment projects commence production, the structure of both Vietnam's exports and imports can be expected to change significantly.

In terms of its trading partners, Vietnam has already experienced some major changes. Although it used to be dependent mainly on trading with other planned economies, those countries are now of minimal relative importance. Since the early 1980s, Japan has been an important trading partner as one of Vietnam's largest import sources, and since 1987, its largest export market. Despite this, Japan has been, somewhat constrained in the types of products it could sell and the type of foreign-investment linkages it could establish with Vietnam, due to informal US-government pressures. Even so, its trading relations with Vietnam have expanded rapidly. Now that the US embargo has been lifted, Japan will doubtless experience even more dramatic growth in its relationship with Vietnam.

Vietnam has experienced rapid growth in exports: in the period 1992–93, total exports increased by 30.6 per cent. Although increased exports to Japan were a major part of this growth, Vietnam's growth in exports to Singapore has been even more impressive: as Table 9.8 indicates, in 1992–93 it almost doubled. Singapore has therefore risen to become the second-largest (10.6 per cent of exports, compared with Japan's 32.2 per cent) market for Vietnamese goods. This growth is, at least in part, a function of Singapore's recent importance in the FDI area, particularly in the development of manufacturing facilities. Improved relations with France have been responsible for that country's return as a major Vietnamese-export market and Taiwan, Hong Kong and China also remain important. Trade with Germany continues to be significant, and at least some of this trade is related to links that Vietnam developed with the former East Germany. As the lifting of the US trade embargo has its effects, the US is expected to rise sharply towards the top of the export-market list. Similarly, the ASEAN countries, which at present account for 17.6 per cent of exports, can be expected to increase in relative importance.

Table 9.8   Vietnam's exports, by country or region of destination, 1987–93

Country or region	US$ million						
	1987	1988	1989	1990	1991	1992	1993
United States	–	–	–	–	–	–	–
Canada	6	8	13	13	11	14	21
Australia	13	17	15	15	24	156	172
Japan	132	178	313	543	602	791	976
New Zealand	–	–	–	–	–	1	1
France	17	11	22	29	43	83	159
Germany	7	12	21	38	91	216	264

Table 9.8 continues.

Table 9.8 (continued)

Country or region	US$ million						
	1987	1988	1989	1990	1991	1992	1993
United Kingdom	–	1	2	2	10	19	30
Africa	1	2	15	24	25	30	31
Bangladesh	–	–	6	–	–	1	1
China	–	–	–	1	10	66	111
Hong Kong	103	123	139	147	157	135	126
India	7	9	115	54	35	62	47
Indonesia	5	6	20	38	79	30	35
Korea	–	–	–	–	37	52	82
Malaysia	13	25	36	41	57	115	86
Myanmar (Burma)	–	–	–	–	–	–	–
Pakistan	–	2	1	–	1	1	2
Philippines	–	–	19	103	42	12	12
Singapore	–	–	–	–	–	118	320
Sri Lanka	–	–	–	11	12	32	37
Thailand	3	8	41	85	106	73	77
Taiwan	–	–	26	51	73	112	140
Eastern Europe	91	108	144	48	44	34	31
Middle East	–	–	1	2	1	2	2
Other countries	21	18	35	61	131	156	255
Total	**419**	**528**	**984**	**1,306**	**1,591**	**2,311**	**3,018**

Source: International Monetary Fund, *Direction of Trade Statistics Yearbook.* 1994, p 429.

Table 9.9 indicates that the US trade embargo did not entirely stop all US exports to Vietnam. Some goods, typically medical and humanitarian ones, continued to be provided. These nominal amounts, though, should skyrocket as Vietnam seeks to re-equip much of its capital goods and infrastructure in the south. Unlike in the area of exports, in which Japan is the dominant player, Vietnam is somewhat more diversified in its import sources. Indeed, in 1993 both Singapore and South Korea were more important: they had 20 per cent and 14.8 per cent of total imports, respectively. Japan occupied third place: it had a 13.1 per cent share. Next in importance were Taiwan, Hong Kong, France and China. The ASEAN group provided Vietnam with 29.5 per cent of the country's total imports; this, though, was mainly a function of Singapore's important role, because the other countries accounted for 9.5 per cent. However, this share will doubtless rise in importance.

Table 9.9 Vietnam's imports, by country or region of origin, 1987–93

| Country or region | US$ million | | | | | | |
	1987	1988	1989	1990	1991	1992	1993
United States	26	17	12	8	4	5	8
Canada	2	4	2	7	17	13	12
Australia	5	12	68	16	44	48	85
Japan	199	213	185	236	239	497	706
New Zealand	1	–	3	–	3	6	11
France	41	56	101	102	117	240	309
Germany	15	18	17	162	81	55	135
United Kingdom	5	4	7	11	13	39	28
Africa	1	5	1	11	1	1	1
Bangladesh	–	–	3	7	1	8	9
China	–	–	–	2	24	117	304
Hong Kong	74	105	129	151	420	1,035	561
India	10	19	12	9	14	20	24
Indonesia	27	21	34	30	155	182	189
Korea	–	–	–	–	219	480	801
Malaysia	4	7	12	7	26	55	151
Myanmar (Burma)	1	1	1	1	1	2	2
Pakistan	–	4	–	1	1	3	4
Philippines	2	14	15	10	22	33	44
Singapore	–	–	–	–	–	427	1,078
Sri Lanka	–	–	–	4	5	–	–
Thailand	5	5	18	20	24	84	127
Taiwan	–	–	8	69	168	306	552
Eastern Europe	143	205	164	53	8	33	35
Middle East	3	3	–	5	5	4	5
Other countries	51	81	50	92	71	122	213
Total	**615**	**794**	**842**	**1,014**	**1,683**	**3,815**	**5,394**

Source: International Monetary Fund, *Direction of Trade Statistics Yearbook.* 1994, p 429.

Trade with Australia

As indicated in Table 9.8 and Table 9.9, Australia has played a small but relatively important role in Vietnam's trade relations. This role increased rapidly during the period 1991–92 when Vietnam's exports to Australia increased by about 550 per cent; in 1992–93 they increased at the somewhat more modest rate of 10.3 per cent. Australia's exports to Vietnam have also grown over this period but not at quite the same magnitude. Australia's relative shares of Vietnamese trade, as indicated in Table 9.10, shows its importance as a destination for Vietnam's exports has varied. It dropped at first in the mid-1980s, only to increase again in 1992; in 1993 it stood at 5.7 per cent. Australia's position as a source of Vietnam's imports has been more varied, which doubtless reflects the success or failure of particular major-commodity-related or infrastructure-related contracts; in 1993, our imports accounted for only 1.6 per cent of total imports.

Table 9.10   Australia's importance for Vietnamese trade, 1987–93

Year	Vietnam's exports Australian as % of total	Vietnam's imports Australian as % of total
1987	3.1	0.8
1988	3.2	1.5
1989	1.5	8.1
1990	1.1	1.6
1991	1.5	2.6
1992	6.8	1.3
1993	5.7	1.6

Source: International Monetary Fund, *Direction of Trade Statistics Yearbook.* 1994, p 429.

To some extent, Australia's foreign investment and trade has benefited from the US trade embargo. We have a large expatriate-Vietnamese community that is familiar with the Vietnamese language and culture. In contrast, the community's American counterpart has been somewhat more constrained, due to the US trade embargo. However, these advantages were reasonably minor in terms of the overall picture, because our major trade has been through more traditional business contacts.

As indicated in Table 9.11, telecommunications equipment is our largest export. This is a function of the Australian government's Telstra and its major telecommunications infrastructure development contracts in Vietnam. Australia's other exports are somewhat more traditional.

Table 9.11   Australian exports to Vietnam for year ended 30 June 1995

Product type	A$	%
Non-fish live animals	33,000	0.02
Meat and meat preparations	697,358	0.46
Dairy products and eggs	5,756,461	3.84
Fish and shellfish	95,536	0.06
Cereals and cereal preparations	7,884,789	5.25
Vegetables and fruit	798,360	0.53
Sugar, sugar preparations and honey	28,057	0.02
Coffee, tea, cocoa, spices and manufactures thereof	1,717,667	1.14
Feed for animals (excluding unmilled cereals)	132,583	0.09
Miscellaneous edible products and preparations thereof	434,209	0.29
Beverages	454,677	0.30
Raw hides, skins and furskins	205,244	0.14
Textile fibres	10,885,324	7.25
Crude animal and vegetable materials	1,579,010	1.05
Petroleum and related materials	2,637,123	1.76
Animal or vegetable oils and fats	441,495	0.29
Chemicals	287,456	0.19

Table 9.11 continues.

Table 9.11 (continued)

Product type	A$	%
Dyeing, tanning and colouring materials	1,142,917	0.76
Medicinal and pharmaceutical products	7,395,248	4.93
Essential oils, perfume and cleansing preparations	1,313,499	0.88
Fertilisers (excluding crude)	35,829	0.02
Plastics	2,589,194	1.73
Chemical materials and products	338,376	0.23
Leather, leather manufactures and dressed furskins	292,660	0.20
Rubber manufactures	42,538	0.03
Cork and wood manufactures (excluding furniture)	250,015	0.17
Paper, paperboard and related products	83,664	0.06
Textile yarns and fabrics	904,499	0.60
Non-metallic mineral manufactures	1,139,134	0.76
Iron and steel	5,416,493	3.61
Non-ferrous metals	6,387,483	4.26
Manufactures of metals	2,275,732	1.52
Power-generating machinery and equipment	1,926,931	1.28
Machinery specialised for particular industries	6,772,112	4.51
Metalworking machinery	596,489	0.40
General industrial equipment and machine parts	6,069,411	4.05
Office and data-processing machines	3,175,034	2.12
Telecommunications and sound equipment	17,203,216	11.47
Electrical machinery and appliances	10,698,919	7.13
Road vehicles	566,534	0.38
Transport equipment	2,217,906	1.48
Prefabricated buildings and fittings	381,243	0.25
Furniture and furnishings	803,647	0.54
Apparel and clothing accessories	183,748	0.12
Professional and scientific instruments	1,447,535	0.96
Photographic equipment, optical goods and clocks	200,928	0.13
Miscellaneous manufactured articles	3,073,194	2.05
Confidential trade and commodities	21,682,709	14.45
Other items	9,371,318	6.25
Total exports	**150,046,504**	**100.00**

Source: ABS, *Foreign Trade Statistics: 1994–1995*. Canberra: ABS, 1995, pp 1819–21.

Australia's imports from Vietnam are somewhat more concentrated: petroleum and petroleum products account for about 68 per cent of the total. Coffee and tea are also important, as are fish and shellfish. The other items, shown in Table 9.12, are somewhat more diverse.

Table 9.12 Australian imports from Vietnam for year ended 30 June 1995

Product type	A$	%
Meat and meat preparations	174,065	0.06
Fish and shellfish	20,365,502	6.90
Cereals and cereal preparations	314,899	0.11
Vegetables and fruit	3,284,669	1.11
Sugar, sugar preparations and honey	50,282	0.02
Coffee, tea, cocoa and spices	40,680,039	13.78
Feed for animals (excluding unmilled cereals)	44,520	0.02
Miscellaneous edible products and preparations thereof	299,622	0.10
Crude rubber (including synthetic and reclaimed)	164,808	0.06
Cork and wood	139,065	0.05
Crude animal and vegetable materials	1,050,346	0.36
Coal, coke and briquettes	1,534,040	0.52
Petroleum and petroleum products	201,584,377	68.28
Fertilisers (excluding crude)	111,619	0.04
Plastics	111,035	0.04
Rubber manufactures	1,208,629	0.41
Cork and wood manufactures (excluding furniture)	498,420	0.17
Paper and paperboard	129,758	0.04
Textile yarns and fabrics	2,300,132	0.78
Non-metallic mineral manufactures	2,417,858	0.82
Non-ferrous metals	932,201	0.32
Manufactures of metals	290,811	0.10
General industrial equipment and machine parts	111,284	0.04
Office and data-processing machines	300,140	0.10
Road vehicles (including air-cushion vehicles)	90,301	0.03
Furniture and stuffed furnishings	703,020	0.24
Travel goods, handbags and similar containers	3,473,350	1.18
Articles of apparel and clothing accessories	5,475,416	1.85
Footwear	5,632,979	1.91
Miscellaneous manufactured articles	1,569,330	0.53
Other items	173,694	0.06
Total imports	**295,216,211**	**100.00**

Source: ABS, *Foreign Trade Statistics: 1994–95*. Canberra: ABS, 1995, pp 962–3.

Future prospects

The basic imperatives that led to disintegration of the command economy, such as collapse of the Eastern planned economies; public pressure for improved living standards; the need for help, improved technology and infrastructure development; and the geo-strategic need to integrate Vietnam into its immediate region, all remain. Vietnam's continued economic reform towards a market-based economy therefore should continue.

It is too early to determine whether Vietnam is a future 'Asian Tiger'. We have every reason to believe that rapid progress is possible over the next 10 years, especially now that the US trade embargo has been lifted and access to international funding sources has been restored. The provisos are that the pace of economic reform has to continue and that Vietnam avoid major political conflicts that would impinge on the country's present high growth rates.

At the time of writing, the indications were that economic growth would continue to expand at about 8 to 10 per cent in real terms over the next couple of years. The most significant growth sources are likely to be continued foreign investment, increased industrialisation of the economy, increased crude-oil output and, due to emergence of a middle class, increased consumer spending in not only Ho Chi Minh City but the whole country.

The hyper-inflation of recent years seems to have been brought under control. Although of concern in the short term, the budget deficit should be offset in the longer term by foreign investment, international help, an improved tax system and continued economic growth. Once the current consumer-demand boom has petered out and new industries begin to develop export markets, the current-account problem should be controllable.

Unemployment, though, is an emerging problem that is not likely to improve due to the existence of a rapidly expanding population. This will be responsible for creating social tensions, thereby placing pressure on the Communist Party and the economic reform process.

REFERENCES

Ashwood, Neil, *Vietnam: A Business Guide*. London: Graham & Trotman, 1994.

Banister, J, *Vietnam: Population Dynamics and Prospects*. Berkeley: Institute of Asian Studies, University of California, 1993.

Beresford, M, *Vietnam: Politics, Economics and Society*, London and New York: Pinter, 1988.

Burke, F, *The Vietnam Business Guide*. Sydney: CCH Publications, 1994.

Champuis, Oscar, *A History of Vietnam: From Hong Kong to Tu Duc*. Westport: Greenwood Press, 1995.

Cleary, P, 'Winning the Peace in Vietnam', in the *Australian Financial Review*, 28 April 1995.

—— 1995 to be Watershed on Future of Economy', in the *Australian Financial Review*, 10 May 1995.

—— 'Vietnam – A Minefield for Foreign Investors', in the *Australian Financial Review*, July 1995.

Cumming-Bruce, N, 'Vietnam', in the *All-Asian Guide*, vol II. Hong Kong: Far East Economic Review, 1992.

Dana, L P, 'Economic Reform in the New Vietnam', in the *Current Affairs Bulletin*, vol 70, no 11, 2 April 1994, p 19.

Department of Foreign Affairs and Trade, *Country Economic Brief – Vietnam, November 1994 and June 1995*, Canberra: Australian Government Publishing Service, 1995.

Dollar, D (ed), *Vietnam: Transition to the Market – An Economic Report*. Washington: United States–Vietnam Trade Council, 1993.

Duicker, William J, *Vietnam: Nation in Revolution*. Boulder, Colorado: Westview Press, 1983.

Dulta, M, 'Vietnam: Marketization and Internationalization of its Economy', in *Journal of Asian Economics*, vol 6, no 3, fall 1995, pp 311–26.

Far Eastern Economic Review, 'Vietnam', in *Asia 1995 Yearbook*. Hong Kong: Far Eastern Economic Review, 1995, pp 219–24.

Fforde, A, *The Institutions of Transition from Central Planning: The Case of Vietnam*. Canberra: National Centre for Development Studies, 1994.

Fforde, A and Seneque, S, *The Economy and the Countryside in Vietnam: The Relevance of Rural Development Policies*. Canberra: National Centre for Development Studies, 1994.

Fforde, A and de Vylder, S, *From Plan to Market: The Vietnamese Economic Transition 1979–1994*. Boulder, Colorado: Westview Press, 1995.

Gates, C L and Truong, D, *Reform of a Centrally Managed Developing Economy: The Vietnamese Perspective*. Copenhagen: Nordic Institute of Asian Studies, 1992.

General Statistical Office, *Statistical Yearbook 1993*. Hanoi: Statistical Publishing House, 1993.

Indochine Project, *Vietnam in 1993: Trade and Investment Review*. Washington DC, 1995.

Jamieson, N L, *Understanding Vietnam*. Berkeley: University of California Press, 1993.

KPMG, *Investment in Vietnam*. Melbourne: KPMG, 1993.

Le, D D, *Economic Reform and Development in Vietnam*. Canberra: Research School of Pacific Studies, Australian National University, 1992.

Leipziger, D M, *Awakening the Market – Vietnam's Economic Transition*. Washington, DC: World Bank, 1992.

Liden, J, 'Vietnam: The Long Anticipation of Rich Rewards', in *Asiamoney*, June 1995, pp 16–23.

Montes, M F, 'Vietnam's Macroeconomic Transition', in *Journal of Asian Economics*, vol 6, no 3, fall 1995, pp 351–66.

Norlund, I, Gates, C L and Vu Cao Dam (eds), *Vietnam in a Changing World*. Richmond: Curzon, 1995.

Quinlan, J P, *Vietnam: Business Opportunities and Risks*. Berkeley: Pacific View Press, 1995.

Richardson, M, 'New Era as Vietnam Joins ASEAN', in the *Australian* 'Asia Business' section, 28 July 1995.

Robinson, J W, *Doing Business in Vietnam*. Rocklin, California: Prima Publishing, 1995.

Schwarz, A, 'Banking: Red Tape', in the *Far Eastern Economic Review*, 27 April 1995, p 68.

Spencer, C, *Australian Business in Vietnam*. Perth: Asia Research Centre, Murdoch University, 1993.

Spencer, C and Heij, G, *A Guide to Doing Business In Vietnam*, Policy Paper 16. Perth: Asian Research Centre, Murdoch University, 1995.

Stewart, C, 'Muoi's Visit Presents Golden Opportunity for Investment', in the *Australian* 'Asia Business' section, 28 July 1995.

Stults, T J and Massa, P J, *How to Do Business in Vietnam*. 1994.

Than, M and Tan, J L H (eds), *Vietnam's Dilemmas and Options: The Challenge of Economic Transition in the 1990s*. Singapore: Institute of Southeast Asian Studies, 1993.

Thyer, C A and Marr, G (eds), *Vietnam and the Rule of Law*. Canberra: Australian National University Press, 1993.

Turley, W S and Selden, M, *Reinventing Vietnamese Socialism: Do Moi in Comparative Perspective*. Boulder, Colorado: Westview Press, 1993.

'Vietnam – War and Peace', in the *Far Eastern Economic Review*, 4 May 1995.

'Vietnam – The Call of the City', in the *Economist*, 4 March 1995.

'Vietnam', in *Journal of Japanese Trade and Industry*, vol 14, no 2, March 1995, p 15.

'Vietnam', in the *Australian* 'Special Survey', 2 September 1994.

World Bank, *Viet Nam: Public Sector Management and Private Sector Incentives*. Washington, DC: World Bank, 1994.

World Bank, *World Economic Development Report*. 1995.

APPENDIX 9.1: *Australian and Vietnamese representation*

Australian addresses

Australia–Vietnam Business Council
PO Box E14, Queen Victoria Terrace
Canberra 2600, ACT, Australia
Telephone: (61 6) 273 2311
Facsimile: (61 6) 273 3196

Embassy of the Socialist Republic of Vietnam
6 Timbarra Crescent
O'Malley 2606, ACT, Australia
Telephone: (61 6) 286 6059
Facsimile: (61 6) 286 4534

Vietnamese addresses

Australia and New Zealand Banking Group Limited
14 Le Thai To Street
Hanoi, Vietnam
Telephone: (84 4) 258 190
Facsimile: (84 4) 258 188

Australia and New Zealand Banking Group Limited
11 Me Linh Square
District 1, Ho Chi Minh City, Vietnam
Telephone: (84 8) 299 319
Facsimile: (84 8) 299 316

Australian Trade Commission
Australian Embassy
79 Ly Thoung Kiet Street
Hanoi, Vietnam
Telephone: (84 4) 258 480
Facsimile: (84 4) 267 982

Australian Trade Commission Office
Third Floor, Seaprodex Bldg
4 Dong Khoi Street
Ho Chi Minh City, Vietnam
Telephone: (84 8) 299 387
Facsimile: (84 8) 291 656

Commonwealth Bank of Australia
Hanoi Business Centre
51 Ly Thai To Street
Hanoi, Vietnam
Telephone: (84 4) 243 213
Facsimile: (84 4) 243 961

APPENDIX 9.2: *Australia's strategic priorities for Vietnamese trade and investment*

- Build on Australia's reputation of being a reliable, technologically advanced and competitive supplier in Vietnam.
- Advance Australia's business interests in markets in which Australia clearly has a competitive advantage:
  - telecommunications
  - infrastructure development
  - minerals and petroleum exploration and development services
  - education services
  - financial and legal services.
- Help Australian commercial interests to access participation in multilaterally and bilaterally funded projects.
- Monitor potential financing arrangements for exports and investment.
- Promote links between Australia's business community and Vietnamese officials and enterprises, particularly through training and development.
- Closely monitor regional competitors' activities and evaluate the implications of these for advancing Australia's economic interests.

Source: Department of Foreign Affairs and Trade, *Australian Trade and Investment Development*. Canberra: Australian Government Publishing Service, 1994, p 118.

10

Marketing in ASEAN

David Watson

Introduction

From a marketing perspective, the ASEAN countries' similarities are more important than their differences. For marketers who seek to sell to ASEAN nations, the key issues are common to all the nations. Because the important differences occur at the level of the individual product or market, they are beyond the scope of a general guide such as this. Readers who are interested in exploring the aspects that are unique to a particular country should consult the sources included in Appendix 10.1.

A key characteristic of ASEAN – particularly Indonesia, Malaysia, Singapore and Thailand – is the economic growth rates its member nations have experienced over the past decade. Growth rates that sometimes have exceeded 10 per cent per year are a cause for both excitement and concern for Australian marketers who are interested in exploiting the opportunities. Although opportunity for handsome rewards ensues from growth of this magnitude, improperly managed marketing can cause problems for unwary people: a long-term strategic view is required. That strategic view will manifest itself in all aspects of the marketing plan, particularly in issues such as product adaptation, representation strategy, pricing policy, channel management, product sourcing and promotional strategy.

Product adaptation

In general marketers recognise that consumers' needs and tastes vary. Often the changes that are made to a product so that local market requirements can be met are quite minor – perhaps all that is required is the making of a small change to formulation so that local tastes can be satisfied. One frequently cited example of this is McDonalds' inclusion of the 'satay burger' on its Singaporean restaurants' menu. In other cases the changes may be more significant. Consumer preferences for laundry equipment such as washing machines, for example, vary from market to market. What is desirable in Australia, in which most consumers live in relatively large, free-standing houses, is very different from what is desirable in Singapore, in which most consumers live in relatively small apartments located in tower blocks. Washing-machine manufacturers should therefore modify their range of sizes and features in various markets.

Other factors such as distribution and purchase frequency can impact on a product's packaging, particularly on each pack's quantity. Although many ASEAN consumers use Western-style supermarkets for many of their grocery needs, they continue to shop at traditional markets for a range of items. This tendency is par-ticularly evident among older consumers and people who live in regional and rural areas. Although daily shopping is partly a social activity in those areas it is also practical, because the people lack the fridge and freezer space necessary for storing a week's worth of food. Those consumers shop for products in quantities that are suitable for one day's worth, or perhaps two days' worth, of meals. Extra-large or family-size packages, which are designed for many Australian consumers' once-a-week shopping strategy, are therefore not appropriate for most ASEAN consumers.

Representation strategy

For Australian companies that wish to market their products in ASEAN countries, a range of representation strategies are available. The strategies vary with reference to not only the effort and expense they require but to their outcomes. The nine strategies that are available are briefly examined in the following section.

Significantly, as they become more involved in exporting, most companies will change their representation strategy at least once. In high-growth markets such as ASEAN's, the representation strategy will almost certainly be changed if the market was incorrectly assessed at first.

If a product that is placed in a market 'takes off', an agency-arrangement strategy is likely to provide neither the exporter nor its customers with enough local support. The wholesaler and the retailers will find it difficult if the company does not hold adequate local stocks, and the consumers will lose confidence, given the lack of local warranty and repair facilities.

A strategy that is based on an import–distribution agreement would enable these concerns to be addressed. However, if market growth is particularly rapid and volume significant, a better and more profitable solution would be to cease exporting and commence manufacture in the target market, through either a manufacture-under-licence (MUL) arrangement or a strategic alliance. If local manufacturing also offers favourable opportunities for entering adjacent markets, FDI – in either a joint venture or a wholly owned subsidiary – may produce significant benefits.

The first difficulty that exporters face when they are examining an ASEAN market is correct assessment of their product's market potential. The second diffi-culty is choosing the most appropriate representation strategy, given the market's growth potential. The third difficulty lies in successfully exiting from an inappropriate representation strategy when the product's true market potential becomes obvious.

Issues when selecting a representation strategy

As suggested, a company's representation strategy has to be adjusted to market and product conditions. Each arrangement has its own advantages and disadvantages. The nine representation strategies are an Australia-based trading company, an Australia-based export agent, market-based import agent, importer–distributor, licensee, representative office, strategic alliance, joint venture, and FDI.

Australia-based trading companies

These companies take title to the goods in Australia and pay in Australian dollars. The manufacturer has neither a role in the marketing nor any opportunity to develop the brand in the local markets. Warranty, repair and maintenance issues are usually the final customer's responsibility.

Australia-based export agents

These agents seek oversees buyers for Australian products and take a commission (usually a percentage of value) on the resultant sales. They never take title to the goods, and they play no role in marketing the products in the target market. It is therefore often in the agent's interests to ensure that the buyer and the seller do not know each other's identity. If this is not the case, the seller has no opportunity to develop the brand locally. Once again, warranty and repair issues are usually the final customer's responsibility.

Market-based import agents

These agents may undertake one of two quite different roles. With reference to the first role, the agent seeks overseas suppliers for a range of the products on behalf of a small group of clients. In this role, the agent charges a commission (usually a percentage of sales value), neither maintains stocks nor takes title to the goods, and plays no role in the local marketing. Warranty, repair and maintenance issues are usually the final customer's responsibility. With reference to the second role, the import agent actively represents the overseas manufacturer's interests, may hold a limited inventory on consignment, and is active in marketing those products. In this role, the import agent may provide some limited product support. Major warranty and repair issues are nevertheless usually referred directly to the manufacturer.

Importer–distributors

Importer–distributors are usually the manufacturer's accredited representative in a particular market. They take title to the goods, maintain stocks and a spare-parts inventory, provide repair and warranty support, and are responsible for and often contribute to the cost of advertising and promotion.

Licensees

Licensees produce products or services under licence from the owner of the product, production process, brand or image. Licence agreements typically involve but are not limited to arrangements for manufacturing products in a particular country through MUL agreements. The licensee obtains particular rights to the product (or production process or brand or image) in return for either an annual licence fee or a royalty from the profits on each unit that is produced. Although for the licensor these agreements are often more profitable than exporting, some countries restrict the value of the royalty payments that are allowable. Also, many companies are wary of licence agreements, because the companies fear they will lose proper control over their intellectual property once it is given to the licensee. For this reason, many licence agreements are structured so that the licensor retains direct control over one or more key stages or processes.

Representative offices

These offices are usually established when sales volumes are low but the unit value of each sale is very high. For example, most aircraft and mainframe-computer manufacturers maintain representative offices in their target markets. The offices are usually responsible for all sales, marketing and public relations activities and for providing direct product support.

Strategic alliances

In these alliances, two or more parties are involved in an activity for the benefit of all participants. Alliances take many forms and may include research and development, raw-materials supply, production, promotion, warranty support and so on. Many alliances are formed for achievement of a particular end and are dissolved when the objective is met. Other alliances are extremely longlasting and may alter over time in order to reflect the participants' changing needs. A strategic alliance's legal form may involve nothing more than a handshake or may entail drafting of extensive contractual documentation, depending on the parties' wishes. Although alliances are becoming more widespread – particularly in ASEAN countries – Australian companies have a poor record of success, in both establishment and maintenance of alliances in the region.

Joint ventures

These ventures involve creation of a separate legal entity in order to exploit an opportunity that none of the parties could realise independently. In ASEAN countries they typically involve supply by the external party of the technology, equipment, expertise and capital, whereas the local party provides land, labour and market access. In some cases, such as in Malaysia and Indonesia, legislation governs much of the relationship between the parties.

Foreign Direct Investment

FDI represents the highest possible commitment to a market, because it involves establishment of a wholly owned business in the target market. Historically, it usually followed a period of strong market growth that was supported by exports from the home country. In many cases, manufacturing success in the target market leads to closure of home-market manufacturing and to goods' importation from the overseas factory.

Channel management and product liability

Channel management is a topic that is closely related to representation strategy. Traditionally, companies that were involved in exporting concentrated on managing the distribution-channel aspects that related to goods' and product information's flow down the channel and money's flow back up the channel.

Although the company's immediate concerns were addressed through use of this approach, under Australian product-liability and consumer-protection legislation it is no longer acceptable. To all intents and purposes, the standards that Australian companies apply when selling their products in ASEAN countries have to be the same as those they apply in Australia. Under section 65F of the Trade Practices Act (Cwlth), it is imperative that as soon as a company becomes aware of a defect in a product it sells that for consumers is potentially harmful, it immediately bring the defect to consumers' notice and recall all defective products that are held in the distribution chain. In the legislation it is also required that the company write to the Minister for Consumer Affairs about the nature of the problem and the action it has taken in order to ensure consumer risk is minimised. If the product is exported, in the legislation it is required that the company separately write to Australia's Minister for Consumer Affairs and each export market's relevant authorities about the defect and the action that has been taken in order to protect consumers. The latter obligation applies regardless of the existence of any relevant law in the export market.

In Australia, because of the distribution channel's short length and the well-developed relationship between the channel members, consumers' concerns and complaints about products are quickly referred to the supplier or manufacturer for appropriate action. In an export market, the distribution channel is longer and the relationships between channel members may not be as well developed. Consumers' concerns and complaints may therefore not travel freely back up the channel to the importer or distributor and from there to the Australian manufacturer. Due to these differences in the information flow, a particular obligation is placed on the manufacturer to address the issue. If a problem comes to light in an export market, a company is required to respond as if the problem had occurred in the home market. If it can be shown that the manufacturer (or representative) knew or should have known of a product defect, and if the manufacturer did not respond appropriately, the manufacturer is potentially liable for any loss or injury the consumer has suffered.

Pricing policy

Although pricing is a key element of any marketing strategy, it causes particular problems in international markets. Australian companies that deal with ASEAN nations benefit from having frequent, relatively cheap air and sea freight services to most destinations. This means that in the selling price, the proportion of international freight charges and insurance is low. However, it does not mean that when the product reaches the consumer in Singapore, Bangkok, Jakarta and so on its price is only marginally different from the price in Australia.

Price escalation is inevitable whenever goods are exported from one country to another. The way in which the escalation occurs is best understood through examining the example provided in Table 10.1.

Table 10.1   Australia's pricing policies for domestic and export sales

Policy	Domestic sales (A$)	Export sales (A$)
Ex-factory price	8.27	8.27
Domestic freight	0.70	0.70
Export documentation		0.45
International freight and insurance charges		1.26
Landed cost		10.68
Import duty (Tariff: 20% of landed cost)		2.14
Price to wholesaler or importer–distributor	**8.97**	**12.82**
Wholesaler's margin (20%)	1.79	
Importer–distributor's margin (25%)		3.20
VAT on importer–distributor's margin (5%)		0.16
Price to retailer	**10.76**	**16.18**
Retailer's margin (50%)	5.38	8.09
VAT on retailer's margin (5%)		0.40
Price to the consumer	**16.14**	**24.67**

For the marketer, the implications of price escalation depend on the market. In some markets, consumers willingly pay the inflated price, whereas in others, because of the costs of simply getting the product to the consumer, the product will be uncompetitive. When this occurs, the marketer can

- simply ignore the market
- reduce the product's ex-factory cost either by
  - marginally costing products that are specifically produced for export
  - redesigning the product in order to reduce its number of features and thereby reduce the price (in Australia, the Mercedes-Benz company adopted this strategy with reference to its 180E model)
- reduce the number of steps in the distribution chain
- enter an alliance with a local firm in order to have the firm assemble or manufacture the product in the target market (the duty payable is thereby often eliminated or reduced)
- directly invest in the market and commence manufacturing there.

Given the ASEAN market's size and the member countries' growth rates, simply eliminating from consideration the region or its individual markets is unlikely to be a realistic solution. The marketer is therefore faced with a series of strategic options that have to be carefully examined.

Many Australian firms have adopted marginal costing in order to get their products into ASEAN markets. The impact of marginal costing can be dramatic, as Table 10.2 indicates.

Table 10.2   Marginal costing of products

Cost item	Standard cost (A$)	Marginal cost (A$)
Materials	3.20	3.20
Fixed costs	1.00	0.00
Additional foreign-product costs	0.00	0.12
Production overhead	0.60	0.00
Total production cost	*4.80*	*3.32*
Domestic marketing costs	2.60	0.00
General and administrative expense	0.87	0.00
Ex-factory price	*8.27*	*3.32*

Had marginal costing been adopted for the costings calculated in Table 10.1, the selling price in the target market could have been A$12.69 instead of A$24.67.

In the early stages of marketing – whether as an aggressive market-entry strategy, a means of providing higher margins to channel members, or a means of finding a use for surplus or seasonal production capacity – marginal pricing seems to offer considerable benefits. However, at best it is a short-term strategy; at worst it is a recipe for disaster. If the target market is small and potential growth is limited, marginal costing may be sustainable. If, though, as in the ASEAN nations' case, the market potential is large and growth is significant, marginal costing can trigger an unwanted crisis for the exporting company. This crisis will occur when, due to export growth, the proportion of marginally costed items that are sold reaches a 'critical mass'. At this level the company has to rely on an ever decreasing proportion of its total production in order to cover fixed costs, production-overhead expenses and administrative expenses. Each additional marginally costed product sold effectively reduces the company's ability to renew its means of production. At this point the company has to decide to either limit its exports or adopt a new production strategy, such as entering into a joint venture, negotiating an MUL agreement or directly investing in fully owned manufacturing facilities in the target market. In a number of cases companies have very successfully established themselves in ASEAN markets through use of marginal costing strategies, only to be forced to either artificially restrict their growth or withdraw from the market altogether.

For companies that adopt marginal costing, additional complications exist. The first complication involves allegations of dumping; the second involves relationships with importers, wholesalers and other channel members.

'Dumping' is when a product is sold in an export market at a price that is lower than the domestic one, plus a reasonable allowance for transport and associated charges. In Table 10.1, the A$3.85 difference between the exporter's domestic-target-market wholesale price is sufficiently large for a supplier in the target market to allege dumping and for a government to commence anti-dumping action against the exporter. Should the dumping charge be proven, the exporter would possibly face stiff financial and/or market-access penalties and any cost advantage from marginal costing would thereby be removed. Overall, the ASEAN member nations have shown themselves to be willing to take whatever action is necessary in order to protect domestic suppliers from overseas competition.

Of more strategic importance than 'anti-dumping' is the long-term damage that is done to a company's relationships with its importer or distributor and wholesalers as well as to other channel members. These relationships can be strained, even irretrievably broken, if, having established itself in a market through use of a marginal costing strategy the company is forced to make drastic alterations in its supply arrangements. Placing artificial supply limitations on channel members when a product is performing particularly well will only be responsible for encouraging the people involved to seek an alternative supplier. If an alternative production or supply arrangement is adopted such as a strategic alliance or an MUL agreement the supply problem may be alleviated. However, establishing a local supply source may also involve adoption of the supplier's distribution strategy whereby the importer or distributor and other channel members who were instrumental in establishing that product in the market are excluded.

In the ASEAN nations, as in other Asian countries, 'connections' (in Chinese, *guan-xi*) are a vital part of all business relationships. The cost of exiting a relationship such as an import or distribution agreement – particularly with reference to a successful product – will involve more than simply money: it will involve protracted negotiations in order to ensure the local parties suffer no 'loss of face'. A poorly managed exit from a relationship can be as devastating as failure to manage entry to a relationship. The 'mythology' of doing business in ASEAN is replete with 'horror stories' about relationships that have gone sour and the negative consequences for the foreign companies that are involved.

Assessing opportunities in ASEAN

With reference to marketing to ASEAN member nations, one of the keys is understanding the nature of the marketplace. As is the case with any grouping of nations, similarities and differences exist whereby once they are recognised, marketing strategies can be produced that can be applied in each market.

If various statistical indicators are examined, such as those shown in Table 10.3, differences are highlighted between not only the ASEAN nations but the ASEAN nations and Australia.

Table 10.3   Australian and ASEAN-nation statistics

Nation	Population (1993 estimate)	Per-capita GDP (US$), 1991	Level of urbanisation (%)	Cities the population of which is greater than one million
Australia	17,800,000	14,662	85	5
Brunei	280,000	16,000	58	0
Indonesia	188,000,000	610	29	5
Malaysia	19,050,000	2,490	42	1
Philippines	65,000,000	740	2	2
Singapore	2,800,000	12,890	100	1
Thailand	58,300,000	1,580	23	1
Vietnam	70,400,000	36	22	3

Source: *The SBS World Guide*. Melbourne: Text Publishing, 1994.

The statistics in Table 10.3 indicate the various levels of urbanisation and per-capita GDP among the ASEAN nations. Although the individual markets might be large, the portion of the population that represents an attractive marketing opportunity is concentrated in a few large cities. Marketers also recognise income levels in most communities are skewed and that a community's affluent members tend to live in urban as opposed to rural areas. This trend is particularly evident in the ASEAN nations, and Singapore is the most extreme example.

An interesting characteristic of the ASEAN nations' affluent members is that as their wealth increases, they become less influenced by their cultural heritage and behave more like wealthy consumers in Australia or other Western nations. These similarities are most evident in areas such as car ownership, use of prestige credit cards and consumption of prestige goods such as cognac and whisky. Similarities also occur in other areas, and the patterns of behaviour and areas of concern are strikingly similar to those in Australia. Table 10.4 and Table 10.5 clearly document the extent of the similarities.

Table 10.4   Per cent of ownership and consumption among affluent people in Australia and the ASEAN nations

Nation	Car	Gold credit card	XO cognac	Premium quality scotch
Australia	91	41	22	44
Brunei	–	–	–	–
Indonesia	96	67	14	21
Malaysia	96	64	32	35
Philippines	88	36	19	31
Singapore	88	77	24	27
Thailand	94	54	22	44
Vietnam	N/A	N/A	N/A	N/A

Note: N/A = Not applicable.
Source: *Asia 1992 Yearbook*. Hong Kong: Far Eastern Economic Review, 1992.

Table 10.5   Affluent Asians' activities and desires

Activities	%	Desires	%
Carrying a mobile phone	46	To have less pollution	65
Travelling first class	67	To have more leisure time	60
Taking a package holiday	59	To have less job stress	36
Eating fast food	60	To have a bigger home	35
Playing sport	86	To have shorter commuting time	24
Mixing with foreigners	87		
Gambling	24		
Singing at a karaoke bar	40		
Using a computer	82		

Source: *Asia 1992 Yearbook*. Hong Kong: Far Eastern Economic Review, 1992.

Understanding culture when marketing in ASEAN

Culture plays a major role in marketing: if the culture is understood the issues that require addressing in the marketing strategy are understood. Although many approaches to defining culture exist, in the approach that is most relevant to marketers, aspects of daily life are grouped into seven areas, or dimensions. The dimensions and what they cover are set out in the Table 10.6.

Table 10.6 Culture's seven dimensions

Dimension	Description	Significance for marketers
Material life	This is what people do in order to earn income. It includes the tools, techniques, methods and processes that are used in a culture in order to produce goods and services. It also governs distribution and consumption of goods and services.	Product Packaging Promotion Distribution
Social interaction	This defines the roles people play in society and the authority and responsibility patterns that exist. It also involves the society's institutional frameworks such as education, marriage and group governance.	Product Promotion Distribution Negotiation
Language	This involves not only the spoken word but communication of time, space, things, friendship and agreements, as well as use of gestures, expressions and other body movements.	Product Promotion Packaging and labelling Brand names
Aesthetics	This is the art, drama, music, design, style, colour, expressions, symbols, movements, emotions and postures that are preferred in a culture.	Product design Packaging design Promotion
Religion and faith	These define outlook on life and life's meaning and concepts in a culture.	Product Promotion Design Negotiation
Pride and prejudice	These refer to sense of self in a culture in relation to other cultures' sense of self.	Product (origins) Promotion Brand names
Ethics and mores	These govern concept of what is right and wrong and how people relate to each other. They particularly impact on negotiation positions and how people handle difficult negotiation situations. They also impact on need to provide inducements so that deals can be completed.	Promotion Negotiation

Source: Adapted from Jain, S C, *International Marketing Management*. Belmont, California: Wadsworth, fourth edition, 1993.

Culture's significance for marketing is clear. What makes culture so important in the ASEAN region is the fact that marketers are faced with a wide variety of cultures – not only between nations but within them. The extent of the region's cultural differences is clearly identifiable in Table 10.7.

Table 10.7   Australia's and the ASEAN nations' cultural elements that are important for marketers

Nation	Major ethnic groups	Main language/s	Religious affiliations
Australia	95.4% European 2.1% Asian 1.1% Aboriginal	English	74% Christian 0.9% Muslim 0.8% Buddhist 0.4% Jewish
Brunei	64.4% Malay 20% Chinese 8.3% indigenous tribal	Malay Chinese	64% Islam 14% Buddhist 9.7% Christian

Indonesia	Ethnically diverse;
	  divisions determined
	  by geography
		Bahasa Indonesia
		Javanese
		Sundanese
		A total of 583 languages
		  spoken in the
		  archipelago
			87% Muslim
			9% Christian
			2% Hindu
			1% Buddhist

Malaysia	59% Malay
	32% Chinese
	9% Indian, Pakistani
	  and Tamil
		Bahasa Malaysia
		Chinese
		Tamil
		English
		Tribal and local
			53% Muslim
			17.3% Buddhist
			11.6% Confucian and
			  Taoist
			8.6% Christian
			7% Hindu
			2% tribal

Philippines	Predominantly Malay	Filipino English Cebuano	92% Christian 5% Muslim 3% Buddhist

Singapore	76.4% Chinese
	14.9% Malay
	6.4% Indian
		Chinese
		English
		Malay
			56% Buddhist and
			  Taoist
			Muslims, Christians,
			  Hindus and Sikhs
			  also represented

Thailand	75% Thai 14% Chinese 11% Other	Thai Chinese Malay English	95.5% Buddhist
Vietnam	Not available	Not available	Not available

Source: *The SBS World Guide*. Melbourne: Text Publishing, 1994.

Promotion

Promotional strategies that are open to marketers in the ASEAN nations are strongly influenced by both culture and availability of suitable media outlets. Culture will determine an advertisement's content whereas the target audience's media preferences will determine media selection. As previously mentioned, culture influences every aspect of marketing. There are cases, though (particularly among affluent people), in which local culture in some ways becomes subservient to the culture of wealth that is almost universal. For prestige products, therefore, few if any changes are necessary in a promotional strategy.

However, for more utilitarian products a more localised approach is necessary. This entails not only developing a campaign that is sympathetic to the community's culture but choosing a media strategy whereby the message is successfully carried to the targeted consumers. In Table 10.8, the ASEAN region's pattern of advertising expenditure is compared with Australia's. The most striking feature is Australia's advertising expenditure as compared with ASEAN's. Even though Singapore's per-capita spending on advertising is more than that of the other ASEAN countries combined, that country spends only about 50 per cent of Australia's amount.

Table 10.8   Australia's and the ASEAN nations' advertising expenditures, 1990

| Nation | Total advertising expenditure | Advertising expenditure per-capita | $US million | | | | | |
			Print	Television	Radio	Cinema	Outdoor transit	Other
Australia	3,548	226.3	1,869.7 (52%)	1,057.9 (30%)	335.2 (9.5%)	63.3 (1.8%)	221.9 (6.25%)	N/A
Brunei	N/A	N/A	N/A	N/A	N/A	N/A	N/A	N/A
Indonesia	286.9	1.6	172.2 (60%)	26.1 (9.1%)	53.3 (18.5%)	4.1 (1.4%)	31.0 (10.8%)	N/A
Malaysia	321.6	18.1	153.5 (47.7%)	130.7 (40.6%)	5.5 (1.7%)	1.1 (0.3%)	26.2 (6.8%)	4.6 (1.4%)
Philippines	N/A	N/A	N/A	N/A	N/A	N/A	N/A	N/A
Singapore	314.7	115.7	200.3 (63.7%)	95.4 (30.3%)	6.6 (2.1%)	1.9 (0.6%)	8.3 (2.6%)	2.2 (0.7%)
Thailand	N/A	N/A	N/A	N/A	N/A	N/A	N/A	N/A
Vietnam	N/A	N/A	N/A	N/A	N/A	N/A	N/A	N/A

Note: N/A = Not available.
Source: *World Advertising Expenditures.* New York: Starch, INRA, Hooper and the International Advertising Association, 1992.

In the various markets, the difference between the expenditure levels and the media chosen is a direct result of the market's level of development. In a mid-1992 study of the Asian region, the ASEAN markets were described as being either affluent or emerging. The characteristics of these two types of market are listed in Table 10.9.

Table 10.9   Characteristics of ASEAN's affluent and emerging markets

Affluent markets	Emerging markets
Singapore	Brunei, Indonesia, Malaysia, the Philippines, Thailand and Vietnam

In an affluent market
• the people
  – are well educated
  – are wealthy
  – live in areas of high population density and therefore represent an effective marketing environment
• a sophisticated distribution network exists in which people are capable of and experienced in handling most consumer products
• level of exposure to Western goods and services is high
• the consumer units are small, wealthy households
• demand for financial, entertainment and other services is increasing
• significant demand exists for imported quality and/or sophisticated products
• brand recognition is generally high.
	In an emerging market
	• the youth markets
	  – represent significant volume opportunities
	  – are experiencing rapid changes in consumption and behaviour norms
	• GDP per capita is low and spending power is therefore low
	• communications and transport networks are less developed, although improvements are rapidly occurring
	• a bias exists towards lower price personal expenditure items and entertainment.

Source: Adapted from Laurant, C R, *The Diversity and Opportunity of Asia*.

However, in these markets a substantial number of wealthy and sophisticated consumers exist whose tastes and consumption patterns are similar to those of the Australian community's corresponding sector.

Although each ASEAN nation offers significant opportunities for Australian companies, the opportunities vary from country to country. The main potential probably remains in specific niches but opportunities for commodity products continue to exist. As is the case with all international marketing, the issues that have to be examined before a market is chosen remain the same: market size, extent of urbanisation, income, access and risk.

REFERENCES

Armstrong, R W, *The Influence of Culture on Perception of Ethical Problems in International Marketing*. Perth: Asia Research Centre, Murdoch University, 1993.

ASEAN Business Directory. Leverett, Massachusetts: Rector Press, 1995.

Asia–Australia Marketing Journal, various issues.

Australia Through the Eyes of Asia: Adding Innovation. Canberra: Australian Government Publishing Service, 1995.

Cooke, I M, *Overseas Marketing from Australia*. Mornington, Queensland: The Australian Institute of Export, 1991.

Dalton, T, *Building a Successful Strategy for Asia: Lessons From Leading Australian Companies*. North Sydney: International Market Assessment Pty Ltd, 1994.

Enderlyn, A, *Cracking the Pacific Rim: Everything Marketers Must Know to Sell Into the World's Newest Emerging Markets*. Chicago: Probus, 1992.

Engholm, C, *The Asia & Japan Business Information Source Book*. New York: John Wiley & Sons, 1994.

Hughes, H and Berhanau, W, 'The Emergence of the Middle Class in ASEAN Countries', in *ASEAN Economic Bulletin*, vol 11, no 2, November 1994, pp 139–49.

Jain, S C, *International Marketing Management*. Belmont: Wadsworth, fourth edition, 1993.

James, D L, *Doing Business in Asia*. Cincinatti: Betterway Books, 1993.

Padget, J (ed), *Hunting With the Tigers: Doing Business With Hong Kong, Indonesia, Korea, Malaysia, the Philippines, Singapore, Taiwan, Thailand and Vietnam*. San Diego: Pfeiffer, 1993.

The SBS World Guide. Melbourne: Text Publishing, 1994.

World Advertising Expenditures. New York: Starch, INRA, Hooper and the International Advertising Association, 1992.

APPENDIX 10.1: *Sources of market information*

Companies that are seeking to investigate business opportunities in ASEAN should consult a wide range of information sources before they commit to a specific course of action.

Depending on the nature of the opportunity, companies may have either primary data or secondary data, or they may have both. Primary data are data that are collected through surveys, focus groups, taste tests and so on, specifically for the company. They are typically time consuming and expensive to collect and analyse but are of very high value as a decision-making aid.

Primary-data collection is best contracted out to market-research companies that have an established record of high-quality research in ASEAN. A number of Australian market-research companies have excellent affiliations in ASEAN and can provide high-quality primary data.

Secondary data are data that have been collected for a specific purpose but that are now available for other people's use. Significant amounts of secondary data are available from a multitude of sources, including those listed in this appendix. The difficulty involved with secondary data is that

- their quality is variable
- they are often biased to reflect a particular point of view
- they are often contradictory
- their original source is omitted or obscure.

Having stated this, it is a fact that using secondary data can quickly isolate the issues and opportunities that have to be subjected to detailed examination. Some important sources of secondary data are listed below.

Trade-show organisers

Exhibitors' and attendees' names and addresses are often available from the show's organisers, for a fee. The lists give an indication of who is active in or interested in the market.

Conference organisers

Delegate lists are often available from conference organisers, for a fee. The lists indicate who is active in or interested in the market.

Commercial research companies

Many companies have been created with the objective of collecting and selling industry-specific and market-specific data. Only a few of the companies that are involved in the activity are listed as follows.

- The Economist Intelligence Unit (a subsidiary of the *Economist* magazine) publishes high-quality country, product and industry reports that are updated on a regular basis.
- Wards, an American publisher, provides a powerful insight into the world automotive industry.
- Pyramid Research, a market-research firm that is based in Cambridge, Massachusetts, specialises in the world telecommunications industry.
- The Gartner Group and Patricia Seybold both specialise in the computer industry.
- Political & Economic Risk Consultancy Ltd publishes *Asian Intelligence*, a fortnightly bulletin about Asian business and politics.

Stockbrokers' reports

Stockbrokers regularly produce detailed reports on individual firms' and industries' investment potential. Although the reports are produced in most countries that have active stock markets, access to them can be difficult.

In the US, though, much of the material is available via on-line computer databases. Because of the US market's size and nature and the important role US firms play in many industries, reports that originate in the US often provide important clues as to what is happening elsewhere in the world.

On-line information services

Reuters, Dialog, Info Line, the Electronic Yellow Pages, CompuServe, Dun and Bradstreet, and Lexus/Nexus, are only a few of the on-line information-services providers that can provide international marketers with access to valuable information.

By 1989 more than 3000 electronic databases were available via information-service providers worldwide, and the number has been growing rapidly since then. Everything from general articles about the economy and firms and industries in the daily and business press, to detailed analyses of individual companies' financial health and industries' short-, medium- and long-term prospects are available on-line.

Trade journals

Trade journals and other industry-specific publications can provide valuable insights into the market. They have information about

- the types of product available
- the activities of actual or potential competitors
- the current state of the market or industry and the prospects in the short to medium term
- companies that are offering or seeking agency or distribution arrangements.

For most markets, journal subscriptions can usually be processed through subscription agencies such as Gordon & Gotch.

Media-services companies

These companies provide tracking and reporting services. For a fee, they will collect and forward to you all the relevant articles, advertisements and advertorial that are published in the press and the relevant stories and ads that are presented on radio and television.

Government agencies

These agencies, such as Austrade and the Department of Foreign Affairs and Trade (DFAT), can also provide valuable information. Austrade maintains a network of more than 70 offices around the world. The offices provide on-the-ground support for exporters and also support trade missions and companies that are participating in trade fairs. For a fee, Austrade can also be commissioned to provide a wide range of market-research services.

DFAT publishes 'country economic Briefs' that provide summary data about particular countries' economic conditions. Also, it regularly conducts seminars in Australia at which ambassadors and other senior embassy staff from Australian missions located overseas talk about their respective post territories' relevant political, economic and trade matters.

The Australian Bureau of Statistics (ABS) and its overseas equivalents collect and manage a vast array of various data. As well as demographic data, the agencies collect data about volume and direction of trade. The data are usually in a common format known as SITC (Standard International Trade Classification), whereby exports and imports are able to be analysed in some detail.

Business-services organisations

Many large legal and accounting firms maintain offices in or have affiliations with firms that are located in markets around the world. The firms often publish information about the markets in which they are active, and you can usually obtain the information by contacting the Australian office. Although information that is available from these sources is often very specific, such as a guide to personal and company taxation in Indonesia, some firms publish more general material, such as a guide to doing business in China.

Financial services organisations

The major international banks and stock exchanges regularly publish business guides that contain valuable information about their home market and other markets. The Hongkong & Shanghai Bank, for example, publishes an excellent guide to doing business in China. Guides can usually be obtained by contacting the local office in Australia.

Stock exchanges are also valuable information sources. They maintain detailed, up-to-date information about the companies that are listed on their boards. Also, the nature and level of activity on a stock exchange can be a good indication of the type of business activity that is occurring or that will occur some time in the not too distant future.

Travel guides

Travel guides that are produced by Lonely Planet, Fodor and other publishing companies are a cheap, reliable source of general but nevertheless valuable information about a country.

Libraries

As well as maintaining their general collections of books, periodicals and audio-visual materials, a number of public libraries provide research services, for a fee.

An example is the Business Information Service of the State Library of Victoria. The services are a valuable, although often under-used resource.

Chambers of commerce

State and regional chambers of commerce, and bilateral chambers such as the Australia–Thailand Chamber of Commerce, may be able to provide insights into the market that are not readily available from other sources.

International agencies

Through its various agencies, the UN collects and distributes a wide range of data. These include information about countries' development and the nature and direction of trade between countries. Agencies such as the World Bank, the Asian Development Bank and the European Bank for Reconstruction and Redevelopment collect data about countries and provide funds for development projects. The agencies can provide valuable data about countries and through their programs are major consumers of products and services.

11

International management and ASEAN

Marilyn Fenwick

Introduction

For a firm, management involves planning, leading, organising and controlling employees' activities so the firm can realise its goals. In international management, an even greater focus on effective communication and effective human-resource management is required. Because Asian work settings are often very different to those in Australia, Australian managers have to be careful that they consider cultural differences that exist in Asia in all aspects of management. In Chapter 11, therefore, the focus is on aspects of expatriate management in an ASEAN context and to address these from an Australian perspective.

ASEAN's cultural environment

In international management research there is ongoing debate about the extent to which culture impacts on work behaviour.[1] It seems that how we work is becoming more similar, due to industrialisation. Because similar technology is used for producing goods and services, similar organisational structures and education systems evolve so that an appropriately skilled workforce can be supplied. Work might be similar, then, but individual, culturally determined differences remain in the way in which people work. Therefore, although Asian countries such as Singapore have adopted many Western business ways, the adaptation may be only superficial. Because deeply held cultural values and traditions endure, cultural differences remain evident at many levels. Ability to manage cultural risk – threat of loss that results from differences in codes of conduct and values between companies and regulators – is critical for success in international trade. In host countries, an important element of cultural risk management is development of an awareness and understanding of the dominant cultures' values and customs. The greater the cultural distance between participating firms' national cultures, the greater the potential loss. Most business practitioners would agree that the cultural distance between Australia and the ASEAN members is great.

Because cultural differences, and therefore distances, exist even within cultures, it is also unwise to assume a lot of similarity exists between ASEAN members. For example, Australian expatriate managers have faced difficulties in their British subsidiaries despite Australia's and Britain's strong traditional links, common language, same dominant religion and same education and legal systems.[2] Other factors such as differences in organisational characteristics may also contribute to the existence of management-style variations.

Keeping these thoughts in mind, cultural differences' impact on international management has to be acknowledged and discussed. In order to effectively manage and conduct business activities in ASEAN nations, managers first have to understand how this culture context impacts on the nations' work-related values. According to Hofstede in the book *Cultures and Organizations: Software of the Mind*, 'the main cultural differences among nations lie in values'. He describes culture as

> 'mental software' – a usually unconscious conditioning which leaves individuals considerable freedom to think, feel and act but within the constraints of what his or her social environment offers in terms of possible thoughts, feelings and actions.[3]

Ethnicity, language and religion are responsible for framing beliefs, attitudes and values. The latter, in turn, are reflected in education, legal and political systems, as well as in the work-related values that influence workplace behaviour.

Through briefly describing the abovementioned cultural influences in both Australia and each ASEAN country, significant differences in ethnicity, religion and language can be highlighted.[4]

Australia

Our country is predominantly Anglo-Saxon. English is the language used exclusively by most of the population. Relatively few Australians are bilingual. The dominant religion is Christianity.

Brunei

The dominant ethnic groups in this country are Malays and Chinese. Malay is the main language, and English is widely spoken. Sixty per cent of the people are Muslim; 14 per cent are Buddhist, Confucian or Taoist; 10 per cent are Christian.

Indonesia

This country is mainly populated by Malay, Chinese and Irianese people. The official language is Bahasa Indonesian (a form of Malay). Twenty-five local languages (mainly Javanese) are used and more than 250 dialects are spoken, which reflects the fact that 13,700 islands form this, the world's largest archipelago. Eighty-seven per cent of Indonesians are Muslim, 10 per cent are Christian, and the rest are Hindu or Buddhist or identify with a tribal religion.

Malaysia

This country is also mainly populated by Malays (59 per cent), 32 per cent are Chinese, and 9 per cent are Indian. English is widely used, and Chinese, Tamil and Iban are spoken by minorities. Fifty-three per cent of the people are Muslim, 19 per cent Buddhist. Christians are a minority among all the races.

Philippines

In this country the population is dominated by Malays, and the minority ethnic groups include Chinese, Americans and Spanish. The national native language is Tagalog; a derivative of this, Filipino, and English, are the official languages. Ninety-four per cent of the people are Christian and 5 per cent Muslim.

Singapore

This country's population is 77 per cent Chinese, 15 per cent Malay and 6 per cent Indian. The national language is Malay, and the administrative language is English. English is also the medium of instruction in most schools. The main religions are Buddhism, Taoism, Islam, Christianity and Hinduism.

Thailand

This country's population comprises 75 per cent Thai and 14 per cent Chinese; the other 11 per cent comprises Malays and indigenous 'hills' people. Buddhism is the dominant religion, and Christianity and Islam are minorities. The national language is Thai.

Vietnam

This country is ASEAN's most recent member. It is the second-most populous member, after Indonesia: 72 million people. Some 90 per cent are ethnic Vietnamese, 3 per cent Chinese, and the rest are mainly from a variety of other IndoChinese ethnic groups. The national language is Vietnamese and the dominant religion is Buddhism. Elements of Indian religion and the three Chinese religions – Mahayana, Confucianism and Taoism – are also evident.

In international management research, differences have been found in work-related values and therefore in work behaviour. With the exception of Brunei and Vietnam, the ASEAN nations were included in Hofstede's 1980 study of a multinational enterprise's employees located throughout 50 countries. Although the study was criticised for failing to account for within-country differences in multicultural countries and for using a population of only one for its sample,[5] it provided an insight into culture's impact on four work-related values. Indeed, in light of earlier comments made about the difficulty of isolating culture's influence, focusing on only one organisation may actually be more helpful. In Table 11.1, Hofstede's work-related values with reference to Australia and ASEAN are summarised.

Work related variables

The power–distance index (PDI)

This refers to a society's extent of acceptance that power is unequally distributed within institutions. For example, in countries that have a high PDI such as Malaysia and the Philippines, employees follow the boss's orders, basing this on hierarchical seniority, and rarely bypass the chain of command.

The individualism value (IDV)

Countries that are relatively high on individualism, such as Australia, value individual achievement and initiative as well as democracy. Countries that are low on individualism, such as the ASEAN members Thailand and Singapore, value harmony, 'saving face' and the group's well-being ahead of the individual's well-being.

The masculinity value (MAS)

In a society, this refers to the extent of prevalence of the traditionally 'masculine' values such as assertiveness, materialism and pragmatism. For example, in relatively masculine societies such as Australia, fewer women occupy senior positions in organisations.

The uncertainty-avoidance value (UAI)

This refers to the extent to which people within a society feel threatened by ambiguity. Of the ASEAN countries, Singapore recorded the lowest UAI score and Thailand the highest; Thai organisations, according to Hofstede, are therefore more likely to adhere strictly to formal rules and procedures. Thai managers therefore have a propensity for making low-risk decisions, compared with Singaporean managers. It is not surprising, then, that Australian managers in Thailand find that their employees prefer not to commence projects that are not clearly defined or possibly beyond their capacity to complete.

Table 11.1 Australia and selected ASEAN nations: four work-related values

Score, and score rank in parentheses

Country	The power–distance index	The individualism value	The masculinity value	The uncertainty–avoidance value
Australia	36 (6)	90 (1)	61 (2)	51 (2)
Indonesia	78 (3)	14 (6)	46 (5)	48 (3)
Malaysia	104 (1)	26 (3)	50 (3)	36 (5)
Philippines	94 (2)	32 (2)	64 (1)	44 (4)
Singapore	74 (4)	20 (4/5)	48 (4)	8 (6)
Thailand	64 (5)	20 (4/5)	34 (6)	64 (1)

*Brunei and Vietnam were not included in the study.
Source: Adapted from Hofstede, G, *Culture's Consequences: International Differences in Work-related Values*. Beverly Hills: Sage Publications, 1980.

Communication

Managers spend most of their time communicating with other people. Effective communication, both between individuals and within the firm, involves not only sending and receiving messages but arriving at shared meanings as a result of this. Culture influences the way in which individuals communicate – the extent of formality, the preferred mode, even who talks to whom, varies not only within but across cultures.

In the *International Handbook of Corporate Communication*, William Ruch outlines key differences in Australian and ASEAN members' communication styles.[6] Generally, Australians are considered to be highly individualistic and are therefore very direct communicators: they tend to say what they mean. The Australian culture is also viewed as being a low-context one with reference to communication. In contrast, collectivist, higher context cultures such as ASEAN ones base communication to a large extent on shared understanding between members of the culture: what is not said but is known through shared cultural membership is often equally as important as the stated message. For example, an Indonesian's or Malaysian's request is unlikely to meet with an open refusal. Rather than say 'no', which will result in a loss of face for both parties, other means are used if the request cannot be granted. People who are 'in the know' understand that direct refusal is impolite, therefore Australians sometimes leave meetings believing their proposals have been accepted when a polite refusal has in fact been intended. The key to establishing effective communication in high-context cultures is being aware of the 'rules' of communication and being prepared to invest time in establishing respect and trust.

Respect for status is highly valued in ASEAN cultures. The different attitude towards status is evident in the content of business cards: whereas Australian business cards tend to be simple and often omit academic qualifications, Asian business cards can be quite different. In Malaysia, for example, the cards may be elaborately detailed in both presentation and content. All academic qualifications are usually presented. In order to reflect status it is also very important that the appropriate title be used. Problems in establishing business relationships can often result from use of an incorrect title. A version of the card should be printed in the host country's dominant language.

With reference to communication, Australians tend not to assume a common understanding. Our first concern is to establish our own identity and what we want from the communication process. In a business context, meeting objectives is generally considered to be more important than establishing a relationship. Australians expect punctuality, spend very little time on small talk, separate business and social affairs, and like to maintain eye contact when speaking with other people. They also rapidly adopt the use of first names. This informality can be particularly offensive in countries in which a large amount of communication formality exists, such as Indonesia, Malaysia and Vietnam. Communication is also more formal in Singapore, Thailand and the Philippines than in Australia.

Communication styles vary between ASEAN countries. In Indonesian firms, for example, personal interaction dominates. Letters begin with 'Dengan hormat' ('With respect'), and respect should always be considered when other people are being addressed. Because the most serious insult is embarrassment of someone else, necessary criticism or disagreement should be handled privately, and laughing at another person's mistakes is very offensive. Apart from handshaking, which is common, physical contact is generally avoided.

In Philippines firms, business follows introductory small talk that is designed to give the host an opportunity to get to know the visitor. The talk may conclude with questions about family and background that for Australians may seem to be too personal. Filipinos are formal and indirect, combine work and social life, confront other people through an intermediary, and value smooth interpersonal relationships. They believe life is determined by fate and that time moves slowly.

Thai firms' communication emphasises respectful vertical relations: the notion of *pen rabiab*, to be 'in good sequential order', is the conerstone of organisational life. Correspondence, for example, has to 'pass many desks' until it arrives at the appropriate superior. Everything takes time, due to deference to rank and authority. Before visiting Thailand you should make appointments well in advance. Business is conducted most smoothly when foreigners provide letters of introduction and work through local representatives.

Although concern for vertical relations is important, consideration should also be made of the informal relationships that exist in some Asian cultures due to family ties and friendships. For example, an Australian discovered that a relatively junior executive, a son of a close friend of an Indonesian firm's managing director (MD), had direct access to the MD by virtue of his father's personal friendship. Unfortunately, business was substantially delayed due to the Australian's adhering to the firm's formal hierarchy. When the MD was unavailable the Australian dealt with the general manager, who respectfully waited for the MD's return, having been instructed not to raise business matters in his communications with the absent MD. During these times, the junior executive had been in contact with the MD on a daily basis and could have raised the issues that required attention.

Human resource management

In the book *Human Resource Management in Australia*, Schuler, Dowling, Smart and Huber define human resource management (HRM) as recognition of the importance of an organisation's workforce in achieving the organisation's goals. This recognition is reflected in the use of several activities and functions in order to ensure human resources are used fairly and effectively for the benefit of both the individual and the organisation[7].

Human resources' role in making international operations successful is critical. As Duerr suggests in the article 'International Business: Its Four Tasks',

> Virtually any type of international problem, in the final analysis, is either created by people or must be solved by people. Hence having the right people in the right place at the right time emerges as the key to a company's international growth.[8]

Broadly speaking, the differences involved in managing human resources in domestic and international organisations have been identified as those in relation to perspective, scope and activities, and risk exposure. Culture determines perspective via basic assumptions, which in turn determine acceptable, feasible behaviours and practices. In international firms, HRM's scope and activities are not only broader; they are different. For example, compensation has the added dimensions of external factors such as personal income taxes and exchange rates. Similarly, risk exposure may extend beyond expatriates' financial safety to their physical safety. According to Dowling and Welch in the article 'International Human Resource Management: An Australian Perspective', international HRM may therefore be defined as interaction of three dimensions: human-resource functions, types of employees, and countries of operation.[9]

Companies may staff their key positions at home and abroad using parent-company nationals (PCNs): an 'ethnocentric' approach. Alternatively, they may appoint management staff abroad from local, or host-country, nationals (HCNs): a 'polycentric' approach. A third option is to ignore nationality and opt for a 'geocentric' approach – selecting the best person for the job, regardless of his or her nationality. The final option is the 'regiocentric' one – moving managers around but limiting the movement to within particular regions. Particularly in the early stages of their internationalisation, many firms rely on managers who have been sent from headquarters to run offshore operations. These managers, citizens of one country who have been sent to live and work in another, are referred to as 'expatriates'. The decision to use expatriates rather than local managers reflects strategic objectives such as the filling of staff vacancies, management development and firm development.[10] In the following section, international human-resource management (IHRM) issues are outlined with reference to Australian expatriates who are living and working in ASEAN nations and with reference to their managers at headquarters.

Performance management of expatriates in ASEAN

According to Hitchcock in the article 'The Engine of Empowerment', performance management is the process of 'translating strategic goals into action, monitoring progress, and rewarding results'.[11] Cannon in the article 'Performance Management: A New Perspective', describes the process whereby core values are converted to standards and whereby vision and behaviour are converted to activities and tasks, with a view to continuous improvement.[12]

Although managers recognise performance management's importance in an environment of increasing rates of change and global competitiveness, establishing performance management has been problematic. This is particularly the case in the international context: problems have been identified both in defining international human resource management's role and in adapting well-established human-resource activities to an international environment.[13] When cultural distance is great, such as that that exists between Australia and ASEAN, these problems may intensify.

Although the performance-management process is linked with all HRM activities, its key functions are in recruitment and selection, training and development, performance appraisal, and compensation. What follows is an overview of these functions in an ASEAN context. Although expatriate performance management is the focus, attention is also drawn to issues that face expatriates who in turn must manage their employees' performance.

Recruitment and selection

Much of the performance research relates to recruitment and selection.[14] Not surprisingly, the researchers have concentrated on attempting to predict whether a manager will be 'successful' if he or she has been given an overseas assignment. 'Success' is defined narrowly as completing an overseas assignment in the time prescribed by the parent company.

When selecting an expatriate for an ASEAN assignment, the decision might be to send a good performer from headquarters. Although selection that is based on successful domestic performance is certainly a starting point, it cannot be considered to be the only criteria. A successful headquarters' or parent company's technical ability and managerial skills is no guarantee of overseas success. Other factors such as cultural empathy, adaptability of both the expatriate and his or her family, positive attitude, emotional stability and maturity, diplomacy, and language skills, also affect performance.[15] Also, in Australia and other Western countries the issue of dual-career couples is increasingly responsible for complicating recruitment and selection activities. A question that is becoming more common is 'Which one of us will put our career on hold?' The question may be particularly relevant if work permits are difficult to obtain for partners or if career women are not favoured due to social mores.

The importance of including the spouse or partner and the family in the selection process cannot be overstated. The spouse's or partner's inability to adjust to the new location has been cited as being a major reason why expatriate assignments ended prematurely for both US and European companies.[16] Recent Australian research also supports the finding that companies have to support the spouse as well as the expatriate.[17] This is a worthwhile investment, because US research suggests expatriates' premature return results in direct losses of between US$55,000 and US$80,000 – depending on location and foreign-exchange rates – in training, relocation, travel and replacement costs.[18]

Also for consideration is an additional set of indirect costs such as the possible damage caused to the relationship with the host-country government, the firm's local employees, and headquarters. For the expatriate, the personal cost of loss of self-esteem is also significant in terms of the person's future performance.

Differences may exist between local recruitment and selection practices and the equivalent practices of the expatriate's headquarters. For example, the Philippines' *padrino* system enables organisations' more powerful people to bring friends and relatives into the firm, irrespective of their effectiveness or qualifications.[19] In contrast, with reference to a study recently undertaken in Singapore, although it acknowledged that large firms were over-represented in the sample, it identified that the reference check, the structured interview and the medical examination were the most popular selection procedures.[20] Australian firms similarly favour interviews and reference checks.[21]

Training and development

Much training and development (T & D) of expatriates focuses on the people's ability to adjust to their new culture. It has been found that language instruction, cultural training and familiarisation with practical (day-to-day) matters are particularly beneficial. This is especially the case when the host culture is significantly different from the home culture, as it is for Australian expatriates in ASEAN cultures. Cross-cultural adjustment definitely influences performance. For expatriates, facilitation of adjustment is responsible for easing their anxiety and disorientation about their new cultural setting – 'culture shock'. Culture shock usually involves four stages.

- *Stage 1*: The tourist, or honeymoon, stage – when the attitude is positive and a sense of excitement and anticipation dominates.
- *Stage 2*: The irritation, or hostility, stage – when cultural differences result in problems to do with day-to-day practical matters and problems at work.
- *Stage 3*: The incremental adjustment stage – when small victories in understanding the new culture occur and acceptance increases.
- *Stage 4*: The biculturalism stage – when the expatriate and his or her family accept and appreciate the local ways and can function well in two cultures.[22]

Each stage's length can vary, and some people never achieve Stage 4. As is the case with domestic T & D, recently undertaken research suggests that expatriate assignments should not be viewed as being separate from carefully planned career development.[23]

Specific T & D needs depend on the assignment. For example, if an Australian is to work for 12 months in Thailand and will largely interact with the Thai people and culture, the T & D should be more rigorous than it would be if the Australian was going to, say, the US for the same amount of time. T & D methods should also vary according to circumstances. The 'immersion approach', for assignments such as the Thai one, involves field experiences, assessment centres, sensitivity training and extensive language courses. In contrast, for an Australian who is to go to the US, what might be sufficient would be a less rigorous 'information-giving approach' that involves area briefings, cultural briefings, and films and books.[24] Many companies now recognise that through a generic set of cultural competencies, expatriates' ability to adjust and to perform effectively will be enhanced, regardless of the specific international location.

In international performance management, a significant concern is the expatriate's loyalty to the subsidiary and headquarters. Although this conflict may potentially also exist between a large domestic organisation's divisions and headquarters, the broader perspective, scope and activities, and risk exposure, differentiate the domestic from the international. T & D may also be responsible for reducing potential for an expatriate to favour the subsidiary's best interests over the best interests of the firm as a whole. T & D activities may also be responsible for minimising the perception of being alienated from the headquarters and thereby for redressing the imbalance in the bond that has been formed with the subsidiary. Ongoing T & D might also aid facilitation of re-entry to headquarters when the overseas assignment is completed.

Care has to be taken with reference to the expatriate manager's training activities for employees. For example, many Western designs might be inappropriate in other settings. Assessment centres are increasingly being used for developmental purposes in Australia; they are also being used in the Philippines but more often as a selection tool. Although the negative as well as the positive feedback is made available to the participants, Philippine employees are not familiar with negative feedback.[25]

Other cultural barriers impact on the exercise of 'assertive, verbal fluency'. In Philippine culture, the *hiya* system prescribes that individuals show deference rather than be verbally assertive. Also, as mentioned earlier, hiring people in authority's friends and family members and placing little emphasis on formal qualifications seems to be an accepted practice in the Philippines. Assessment centres that use quantifiable variables and criteria are therefore in direct conflict with this aspect of Philippine culture.

Performance appraisal

The cultural environment, the job requirements and the expatriate's individual personality characteristics are the three major variables that influence whether an expatriate will succeed or fail.[26] For performance management to be effective, it is essential that all three variables be taken into account. For example, as can be noted in Table 11.2, according to Hofstede,[27] because Australia has a relatively short-term orientation, short-term goals may be emphasised. In contrast, the ASEAN nations, such as Thailand and Singapore, have a longer term orientation. Therefore, an expatriate manager who can develop subordinates but is less proficient at meeting production quotas may receive a different local evaluation depending on whether he or she is assessed by someone who has a long-term or a short-term orientation. Underscoring the comment made earlier about the need to caution against assuming cultural similarity within ASEAN is the fact that the Philippines also has a relatively short-term orientation.

Table 11.2 Australia and selected ASEAN nations*, long-term orientation (LTO) index

Country	LTO score (rank)
Australia	31 (3)
Philippines	19 (4)
Singapore	48 (2)
Thailand	56 (1)

*Brunei, Indonesia, Vietnam and Malaysia were not included in the study.
Source: Adapted from Hofstede, G, *Cultures and Organisations: Software of the Mind*. Beverly Hills: Sage Publications, 1992.

Successful performance may be defined differently, according to the situation of economic or political volatility in which the subsidiaries operate. Expatriates' roles also vary with reference to their assignments.

The performance appraisal is central to performance management. It has two distinct processes – observation and judgement – and two distinct purposes – evaluation and development.[28] Feedback about progress towards goal achievement is recommended in most Western settings. Successful appraisal systems have to satisfy two basic requirements: job relevance, and acceptability to both appraiser and appraisee.[29] However, more than any other HRM function, this activity is often found to be threatening and/or unnecessary by appraiser and appraisee alike.

The extent of this dissatisfaction varies across cultures.[30] For ASEAN societies that have a high power–distance index, giving and receiving feedback can be interpreted as 'loss of face'. This is particularly likely, for example, in the case of an employee's performance problem when the feedback is likely to be critical or negative. If, for example, an Australian manager was required to counsel the sales manager who was habitually late in completing paperwork, most Australian managers would consider it to be appropriate that there be an open and direct discussion of the matter between the manager and the sales manager in the privacy of the manager's office. However, this approach would nevertheless result in loss of face in, for example, the Philippines. There, the most appropriate approach may be to raise the general problem of late paperwork as an issue for the firm as a whole, and to seek the sales manager's input about how the problem might best be solved. This enables the performance problem to be addressed without direct criticism of the individual's performance and causing of embarrassment and loss of face. The issue of who provides the feedback also varies between cultures. In cultures in which face saving is a priority, it may be appropriate to use a third party in order to communicate performance feedback to a subordinate.

Other problems to do with appraising expatriate performance include communication distance, expatriate performance and performance appraisal. The lastmentioned problem involves choice and location of appraisers, the appraisers' relationship to the expatriate, and the appraisers' international experience. Great physical distance, which often exists between subsidiaries and the parent organisation, can result in lack of both meaningful, effective observation and expatriate support and supervision. Opportunities for thorough performance reviews by head office should be planned around these differences.

Compensation

International compensation's objectives are to
- ensure that all categories of international staff receive consistent and fair treatment
- attract and retain people effectively in all areas of operation, according to need and opportunity priorities
- facilitate the cost-effective transfer of international staff
- motivate empoyees.[31]

As is the case with other HRM activities, the broader perspective, scope and activities, and added risk exposure are responsible for the existence of differences between domestic and international management. Expatriates' compensation has been a major challenge for multinational enterprises, because rewarding expatriates involves internal and external equity, taxation and cost of allowances, relocation, housing, and education.[32]

Most companies choose a home-based, host-based or region-based policy.[33] The first approach potentially facilitates the return of the employee to his or her home-country pay rates and standard of living when the assignment is completed. Its two main disadvantages are that if it is used, equity is offered with neither local nationals nor other expatriates at the host location and that it becomes very costly for the firm. The home-based approach is the most common, however, and comprises the base salary, benefits, allowances and taxes. This structure often results in repatriation problems, though, because allowances often inflate expatriate salaries. Because the allowances are removed when the expatriate returns to headquarters, great dissatisfaction is caused for the expatriate, and his or her level of 'reverse culture shock' is increased.

The host-country approach is based on local salary levels and usually involves paying the expatriate in the local currency, as well as expectation of a lengthy assignment (more than five years). Expatriates are expected 'to live on the local economy, rather than attempt to duplicate his or her previous standard of living'.[34] An important performance-management consideration is ensuring expatriates do not financially lose through acceptance of an overseas assignment, movement to another location or re-entrance to headquarters.

The third approach is to pay expatriates who are working in their home regions, for example Australians who are working in ASEAN locations, at levels relatively lower than those for people who are working in regions that are far from home. This approach can also be responsible for reduction of compensation costs but also for provision of equitable compensation to all employees.[35] However, in using it, the existence of small economic and cultural distances within regions seems to be assumed.

Care also has to be taken when home-country compensation practices are being designed or implemented in other cultures. For example, assumptions about motivation can be culturally as well as individually based. Just because individual achievement is valued and rewarded in Australia does not mean ASEAN cultures' members are similarly motivated. Using Hofstede's research as a guide, Indonesian employees (low individualism), for example, would be more motivated in a compensation system whereby the group, rather than the individual, is rewarded.

Conclusion

Managers spend most of their time communicating with other people. Effective communication, both between individuals and within the firm, involves not only being able to send and receive messages but being able to arrive at shared meanings as a result. Australian managers who wish to build successful relationships with ASEAN managers have to appreciate the fact that culture influences the way in which individuals communicate and that it adds 'noise' to the communication process – that is, cultural differences are responsible for increasing the risk of ineffective communication between people.

In managing people across cultural boundaries, an understanding of the differences that potentially exist between cultures in work-related attitudes and values is also required. The international HRM environment's added complexity can be described in terms of varying cultural perspectives, a broader scope, different activities, and greater risk exposure. In this chapter we have discussed aspects of expatriate management – specifically, recruitment and selection, training and development, performance appraisal, and compensation, in the context of ASEAN and from an Australian perspective. Also hopefully provided are some useful insights into the complexities of international HRM for people who are preparing to do business in ASEAN nations but who will not be involved with expatriate management.

Some final words are offered in the form of recommendations made by Oddou,[36] a well-known researcher on international management. Because of the high costs of expatriate failure and a 20 per cent risk of failure, firms should select the people who are most likely to succeed in assignments. The following six questions may be helpful when selecting the best person for the job.

1. How quickly and easily has the employee adapted to expected and unexpected changes in the domestic workplace?
2. How diplomatic and openminded is the employee about attitudes, behaviours and opinions that vary from his or her own?
3. Does the employee enjoy meeting and learning about new people?
4. How self-confident and/or self-reliant is the employee?
5. How supportive and cohesive is the employee's family?
6. Does the employee deal effectively with stress?

When the right person is selected for expatriation, good preparation is essential so that the potential for culture shock on arrival is minimised and the expatriate is helped to perform at the desired level. Companies that are aiming for excellent success rates should provide the following support.

- Clearly specify the performance criteria and ensure the performance-appraisal process is understood and that the domestic and foreign location managers' expectations are consistent with reference to the expatriate's future performance.
- Give full details of all aspects of the compensation package, including all information about the move's implications for taxation.
- For the employee and his or her spouse or partner, provide a field visit to the new location.
- Permit some time reduction in the domestic (home-country) workplace while the expatriate is preparing for the assignment.
- Arrange language training that is directed at day-to-day-conversation competency.
- Offer practical support such as liberal long-distance phonecall privileges and regular contact with the expatriate.
- For the expatriate, carefully choose a mentor at both the domestic and the foreign site.
- Make an organised, strategic effort to reposition the expatriate in a satisfying, rewarding position that uses his or her new skills.

Although remaining cautious in automatically attributing any apparent differences to culture, thereby ignoring intra-cultural and organisational differences, culture cannot be ignored when international operations are being planned and conducted. In international trade with the ASEAN nations, as in any international context, each firm has to develop a management strategy that best meets its internal capabilities and external demands.

ENDNOTES

1 See, for example, Adler, 1986, England and Lee, 1974, and Hofstede, 1980 and 1992.
2 See, for example, research by Barry and Dowling, 1984 and more recently that by Fenwick and Edwards, 1994.

3   Hofstede, 1992.
4   Demographic information is taken from the *Europa World Yearbook*, vols 1 and 2.
5   Ronnen, 1986.
6   Ruch, 1989.
7   Schuler, Dowling, Smart and Huber, 1992.
8   Duerr, 1986.
9   Dowling, Schuler and Welch, 1994.
10 Edstrom and Galbraith, 1977.
11 Hitchcock, 1992, p 50.
12 Cannon, 1992.
13 See, for example, Dowling and Welch, 1988, and Schuler, Dowling and De Cieri, 1993.
14 See, for example, Tung, 1981, Mendenhall and Oddou, 1985, and Mendenhall, Dunbar and Oddou, 1987.
15 Dowling *et al*, op cit.
16 Tung, 1981.
17 De Cieri, Dowling and Taylor, 1991.
18 Mendenhall and Oddou, 1985.
19 Imada, Van Slyke and Hendrick, 1985.
20 Chew and Teo, 1991.
21 Vaughan and McLean, 1989.
22 Oberg, 1960.
23 Dowling *et al*, op cit.
24 Mendenhall, Dunbar and Oddou, 1987.
25 Imada *et al*, op cit.
26 Schuler *et al*, op cit.
27 Hofstede, 1992.
28 Cascio, 1992.
29 Bernardin and Beatty, 1984.
30 Adler, op cit, and Dowling *et al*, op cit.
31 Dowling *et al*, op cit.
32 Crandall and Phelps, 1991, Hodgetts and Luthans, 1993, and Dowling *et al*, op cit.
33 Dowling *et al*, op cit.
34 Crandall and Phelps, op cit, p 31.
35 Dowling *et al*, op cit.
36 Oddou, 1991.

REFERENCES

Adler, N, *International Dimensions of Organizational Behavior*. Boston: PWS-Kent, 1986.

Barry, B and Dowling, P J, 'An Australian Management Style?' in *Australian Institute of Management Research*. Report Number 1. Victoria: Australian Institute of Management, 1984.

Bedi, H, *Understanding the Asian Manager: Working with the Movers of the Pacific Century*. North Sydney: Allen & Unwin, 1991.

Bernardin, H J and Beatty, R W, *Performance Appraisal: Assessing Human Behavior at Work*. Boston: Kent Publishing, 1984.

Black, J, Gregersen, H and Mendenhall, M, *Global Assignments: Successfully Expatriating and Repatriating International Managers*. California: Jossey-Bass, 1992.

Cannon, F, 'Performance Management: A New Perspective', in *Executive Development*, vol 5, no 4, 1992, pp 11–15.

Cascio, W F, 'International Human Resource Management Issues for the 1990s', in *Asia Pacific Journal of Human Resources*, vol 30, no 4, 1992, pp 1–18.

Chen, M, *Asian Management Systems: Chinese, Japanese and Korean Styles of Business*. London, New York: Routledge, 1995.

Chew, I K and Teo, A C, 'Human Resource Practices in Singapore: A Survey of Local Firms and MNCs', in *Asia Pacific HRM*, vol 29, no 1, 1991, pp 30–8.

Crandall, L P and Phelps, M I, 'Pay For a Global Work Force', in *Personnel Journal*, February 1991, pp 28–33.

De Cieri, H, Dowling, P J and Taylor, K F, 'The Psychological Impact of Expatriate Relocation on Partners', in the *International Journal of Human Resource Management*, vol 2, no 3, 1991, pp 377–414.

Dowling, P J and Welch, D E, 'International Human Resource Management: An Australian Perspective', in *Asia–Pacific Journal of Management*, vol 6, no 1, 1988, pp 39–65.

Dowling, P J, Schuler, R and Welch, D E, *International Dimensions of Human Resource Management*. California: Wadsworth, second edition, 1994.

Duerr, M, 'International Business: Its Four Tasks', in *Conference Board Record*, October 1986, p 43.

Edstrom, A and Galbraith, J R, 'Transfer of Managers as a Co-ordination and Control Strategy in Multinational Organizations', in *Administrative Science Quarterly*, vol 22, no 22, 1977, pp 248–63.

England, G W and Lee, R L, 'The Relationship Between Managerial Values and Managerial Success in the United States, Japan, India and Australia', in *Journal of Applied Psychology*, vol 59, no 4, 1974, pp 411–19.

Europa World Yearbook, vols 1 and 2, 1994. London: Europa.

Fenwick, M and Edwards, R, 'Managing the British Subsidiary: Is Cultural Similarity Misleading? The Case of Australian Manufacturers'. Paper presented at the Australian and New Zealand Academy of Management Annual Conference, December 1994, Wellington, New Zealand.

Hitchcock, D E, 'The Engine of Empowerment', in *Journal for Quality and Participation*, vol 15, no 2, 1992, pp 50–8.

Hodgetts, R and Luthans, F, *International Management*. New York: McGraw-Hill, second edition, 1993.

Hofstede, G, *Cultures and Organizations: Software of the Mind*. London: McGraw-Hill, 1992.

—— *Culture's Consequences: International Differences in Work-related Values*. Beverly Hills: Sage Publications, 1980.

Imada, A, Van Slyke, M and Hendrick, H, 'Applications of Assessment Centres Multinationally: The State of the Art, Obstacles and Cross-Cultural Implications', in *Journal of Management Development*, vol 4, no 4, 1985, pp 54–67.

Mendenhall, M, Dunbar, E and Oddou, G, 'Expatriate Selection, Training and Career Pathing: A Review and Critique', in *Human Resource Management*, vol 26, 1987, pp 331–45.

Mendenhall, M and Oddou, G, 'The Dimensions of Expatriate Acculturation: A Review', in *Academy of Management Review*, vol 10, 1985, pp 39–47.

Oberg, K, 'Culture Shock: Adjustment to New Cultural Environments', in *Practical Anthropologist*, vol 7, 1960, pp 177–82.

Oddou, G, 'Managing Your Expatriates: What the Successful Firms Do', in *Human Resource Planning*, vol 14, no 4, 1991, pp 301–8.

Ronen, S, *Comparative and International Management*. New York: Wiley, 1986.

Ruch, W, *International Handbook of Corporate Communication*. Jefferson, North Carolina: McFarland, 1989.

Schuler, R, Dowling, P J and De Cieri, H, 'An Integrative Framework of Strategic International Human Resource Management', in *Journal of Management*, vol 19, no 2, pp 419–59.

Schuler, R, Dowling, P, Smart, J and Huber, V, *Human Resource Management in Australia*. New South Wales: Harper, 1992.

Schutte, H, *The Global Competitiveness of the Asian Firm*. New York: St Martin's Press, 1994.

Tung, R, 'Selecting and Training of Personnel for Overseas Assignments', in *Columbia Journal of World Business*, vol 16, no 1, pp 68–78.

Vaughan, E and McLean, J, 'A Survey and Critique of Management Selection Practices in Australian Business Firms', in *Asia Pacific HRM*, vol 27, no 4, pp 20–33.

12

Trade finance and ASEAN

Michael Skully

Introduction

While ASEAN is clearly an attractive market, potential exporters must have suffi-cient funds to exploit these opportunities. Money is required not only for marketing but for production, and then, in most cases, for some sort of trade credit for the end customer. Although the lastmentioned requirement is usually associated with export or trade finance, in practice exporters require enough money for funding the entire process.

The good news is that these funds are available. As the Department of Foreign Affairs and Trade (DFAT) book *Australia's Business Challenge: South-East Asia in the 1990s* concludes, 'there are few legitimate complaints regarding availability of regular trade finance'. The problem lies in knowing what techniques to use and where to find the funding. This chapter attempts to answ ̖ at least some of the relevant questions. It first provides some of the history of trade and trade finance and how the region's historical background is manifested. In particular, it examines the regional representation of foreign, ASEAN and Australian banks. It then exam-ines the various types of trade finance and the specialised types of export finance and insurance institutions that operate within both Australia and the ASEAN coun-tries. Issues rebated to non-commercial risk and foreign-exchange risk and manage-ment of these are then considered. The chapter concludes with some comments about the growth of technology and the impact of this on export finance.

Definitions

Export finance enables the purchaser to have additional time to pay for the goods or services that have been provided by a seller located in another country. The funds can be provided to the exporter, in which case they are known as 'supplier's credit', and sometimes to the importer in which case they are known as 'buyer credit'. Most of the finance relates to relatively short-term transactions that involve raw materials, consumer goods and non-durable goods. Large-scale transactions that involve capital-good purchases or commodity purchases may be subject to special, longer term financing arrangements that are provided by both private-sector and public-sector institutions.

Exporting to ASEAN countries is in some ways no different from selling a product in Australia. However, ASEAN transactions are typically more difficult to arrange and they definitely incur additional risks, because the buyer is located in another country. The information process is therefore complicated and the potential risk that the transaction will go wrong is thereby increased. For example, exported goods could have arrived overseas only to find the importer has refused delivery. Re-shipping the merchandise to other buyers may be both difficult and costly. Similarly, if the buyer does not pay, more difficulties are often found in collecting the funds, given that the legal system is a foreign one.

As well as these buyer-related or commercial risks, a non-commercial 'country' risk exists that is associated with export transactions. The buyer may be pleased with the goods and willing to pay but unable to do so if the local government places a freeze on, or reschedules, all foreign-exchange remittances and/or repayments. A revolution, war or major natural disaster might similarly make payment impossible. In addition, when the invoice is not denominated in Australian dollars, foreign-exchange risk is involved.

From the exporters point of view it is ideal to get paid for the exports as soon as possible but be able to delay paying for any imports as long as possible. Not surprisingly, the extent to which either position can be demanded depends on each party's relative strength. If the exporter has considerable competition, the buyers can demand what they want. Alternatively, if the exporter is the only supplier, the buyer will have to follow their wishes. The same applies to importing.

In some cases, then, the importer may have to pay the exporter the purchase amount up front, or what is called a 'clean payment'. For an exporter, the payment risk is not only thereby removed, but the exporter may also be provided with some pre-shipment finance. Unfortunately, buyers are not keen to make the clean payment, because they may not get their money back if the goods do not arrive. The exporter therefore has to have a well-established reputation. In practice, these terms are used only for very small orders, for risky clients, or for orders from very risky countries.

The reverse of this, which is when the supplier provides the purchaser with so many days to settle after the shipment or invoice date, is called an 'open account'. Although this is probably the most common type of trade finance, it is also the most risky. If the buyer does not pay, the seller may not be able to recoup the goods or money. Sellers therefore give open-account service only to very large, well-established firms or when a longstanding client relationship exists. As well as depending on competition, open-account funding depends on the supplier's own financial resources, because banks may be unwilling to lend against a transaction that has no obvious security.

A common way to limit the risk to both exporter and importer is through what is called 'documents on collection'. This is when banks become directly involved in the process. The buyer makes payment only when the correct documentation (shipping documents and title to the goods) is presented to the bank. On their presentation, the buyer is required to either pay the amount on the invoice (a 'document-against-payment', or 'D/P' transaction) or undertake to pay by accepting a bill of exchange that is payable on a specified date (a 'document-against-acceptance', or a 'D/A' transaction). This arrangement affords both parties protection, because the seller does not get paid until the buyer receives the documentary title to the goods.

When the buyer is unknown to the seller, a letter of credit is usually involved. This is typically done through a documentary credit that is provided under an irrevocable credit (which cannot be changed without the written agreement of both parties), a revocable credit (which can be changed or cancelled) or a confirmed credit (a bank requests another bank to confirm the irrevocable credit). In ASEAN-related trade, irrevocable credits have traditionally been the most common position (but this is gradually changing). Whether an irrevocable credit is confirmed by another bank depends somewhat on the country, the client and the bank involved. The same applies with reference to whether the exporter will seek export-credit insurance on the transaction, and some banks may require this. Although the specifics of these operations are outside this book's scope, most banks will provide booklets in which the process is discussed in more detail. National Australia Bank's publication entitled *Finance of International Trade*, which is now in its eight edition, is particularly helpful. It should be emphasised that a letter of credit provides protection not only for the exporter but for the bank involved in the transaction. As Rhee (p.2) commented in a 1994 World Bank study,

> [a] confirmed letter of credit (supplemented by pre-shipment finance guarantees and export-credit insurance or guarantees) as collateral is far superior to using physical collateral (such as buildings, land, equipment).

This is a message that some traders may wish to relate to their local bank manager.

Although no specific statistics are available about the way in which Australia–ASEAN trade is handled, some insight can be gained by examining Australia's overall position. As indicated in Table 12.1, Australia imports on an open-account basis more than it exports on one. This is not surprising, because Australia is perceived as having limited 'country' risk. Likewise, many of Australia's major importers (often MNCs) have affiliations with the seller and are therefore effectively party to an intra-group transaction.

Table 12.1   Australian trade transactions by type, 1994–95

Transaction type	% Exports	Imports
Open account	45.37	72.61
Collection	27.54	12.49
Letters of credit	27.09	14.90
Total	**100.00**	**100.00**

Note: The figures are based on the total Australian-dollar turnover in trade transactions that were handled through the Australian branches of the National Australia Bank for year ended 31 January 1995.
Source: National Australia Bank (NAB) correspondence, 1995.

Again, it has to be emphasised that letters of credit are particularly important when the two parties do not know each other or when concerns exist about the buyer's financial 'health'. Another explanation for the growing importance of open accounts is, therefore, that some Australian and ASEAN businesses have come to know each other enough sufficiently to be comfortable in dealing on that basis. Similarly, competition from other traders may have been responsible for forcing this 'trust' to develop, because an open account is the least costly option for potential buyers. Finally, the growing availability of credit insurance could also be a factor.

Discussions with the Export Finance and Insurance Corporation (EFIC) indicate it has experienced a considerable increase in the volume of open-account-style transactions it has been asked to insure. It has responded by adopting an increasingly liberal approach to such policies that cover ASEAN countries (even, to some extent, the Philippines and Vietnam).

Bank finance is usually restricted to relatively short periods, typically not more than 180 days. The banks' involvement, though, is not limited simply to providing documentary credits. Most banks provide a wide range of services in relation to trade transactions. Some banks and other financial institutions also offer their clients international factoring and forfaiting services. The most common bank-related trade-transaction services are listed as follows.

- Bankers' acceptances
- Bid bonds
- Bill discounting facilities
- Bills for collection
- Document collections
- Documentary credits
- Exchange-risk-protection products
- Export-credit guarantees
- Export-marketing finance
- Foreign-exchange transactions
- Letters of credit
- Overdrafts
- Packing credit
- Performance bonds and guarantees
- Pre-shipment and post-shipment finance
- Remittances
- Shipping guarantees
- Short-term loans
- Trust receipts
- Working-capital finance

International factoring is a specialist form of trade finance in which a financial institution purchases the exporter's accounts-receivable. The financier (or factor) assumes the administration of the purchased receivables, and may utilise the services of international associates in the buyer's country to ensure payment. Factoring of the receivables enables the exporter to obtain immediate access to the funds that would otherwise be tied up in the unpaid receivables.

The receivables may be purchased with or without recourse. Receivables purchased 'without recourse' result in the factor assuming the risk of the debtor's inability to pay. Not surprisingly, therefore, in a non-recourse arrangement the financier determines which debtor accounts will be approved for a credit line. The factor will generally charge an administration fee for the purchase of the debts, ranging from 0.5 per cent of factored receivables for a low-workload recourse arrangement and up to 4 per cent for a high-workload non-recourse arrangement. A discount charge would also apply, which reflects the *de facto* interest costs of the period until the debt is paid to the factor.

While factoring is still more common in domestic than international transactions, it does play some role in ASEAN trade. As shown in Table 12.2, Singapore has had the most involvement.

Table 12.2   Factoring in Australia and ASEAN, 1995

Total	No. of companies	Domestic turnover	International turnover	Total turnover
Australia	15	2,300	100	2,400
Brunei	N/A	N/A	N/A	N/A
Indonesia	58	2,730	55	2,785
Malaysia	16	2,000	40	2,040
Philippines	2	17	8	25
Singapore	20	1,900	350	2,250
Thailand	15	1,215	30	1,245
Vietnam	N/A	N/A	N/A	N/A

Note: Turnover figures in US$ million as of 31 December 1995. Number of companies represent Factor Chain International members operating in each country.
Source: International Chain of Factors and Scottish Pacific Business Finance Pty Ltd, 1996.

Whereas factoring traditionally involves short-term finance, forfaiting provides medium-term export finance, generally for capital goods. It entails discounting of buyer-originated trade bills or promissory votes, usually as part of a series of instruments, which are rolled over for periods typically between two and eight years.

As forfaiting's name may suggest, the financier who is providing forfaiting forfeits any right of recourse to the exporter should the buyer not redeem the instruments on maturity. As a result, the financier usually requires that the instruments be supported by a form of bank guarantee or acceptance, called an aval.

Depending on the type of transaction, other types of finance are often available through specialist, often government-owned, export-finance or export-insurance institutions. These are discussed further on in the chapter.

Another *de facto* source of finance that is used in some international trade transactions is countertrade. Although some exporters may view it as being a glorified name for barter transactions (exchange of one shipment of goods for another), countertrade also includes clearing agreements, switch transactions, counterpurchases, buy-backs, offsets and goodwill. Although some scope for barter transactions exists in Vietnam and elsewhere in IndoChina, the other types of countertrade have become more important in ASEAN. This is particularly the case when bidding is being undertaken on major government contracts, particularly defence-related ones. The Malaysian government, for example, promotes proposals for offsets, and to a lesser extent counterpurchases and buy-backs, as part of any major bids. The Thai government, particularly the Ministry of Defence, similarly encourages companies that are making bids to indicate whether any arrangements exist for purchasing Thai products as part of the tender; Indonesia requires this for all public-sector purchases in excess of $500,000 (foreign-aid-funded purchases are exempt). The Philippines extends this requirement for countertrade proposals when capital-goods-import contracts exceed $1 million. Although only a limited number of Australian exporters are directly required to provide countertrade proposals during contracting with ASEAN countries, these requirements means smaller firms might be able to benefit as an end buyer of these ASEAN-produced goods and services. The Australian Countertraders Association is well placed to provide more specific details on these opportunities.

Development of trade and trade finance in ASEAN

Trade within ASEAN is hardly new: historically extensive trading links have existed. Tin from Thailand and Malaysia and spices from Indonesia, for example, were traded throughout the region.

However, this intra-regional trade was dwarfed by the existence of an even greater outside interest in ASEAN products. The Chinese, for example, were among the earlier traders, as were the Indians and Arabs. Although this trade was important with reference to economies and particularly to cultures, it was limited because of the size of the ships involved and therefore the trade each voyage afforded. Transaction costs were high, as were the risks and opportunity costs involved in undertaking longer and more difficult voyages.

Within Europe, trade suffered exactly the same problems. It was not dependent simply on ship building technology; it was dependent on merchants' willingness to face the risks involved in carrying large cargo sizes. If the ship was a smaller one, the merchant could own the ship and much of the cargo. In the case of larger ships, the risk of losing a ship became too high and single merchants could no longer afford to own both the ship and its cargo. As these journeys' length increased, the length of time that merchants' funds were tied up in the cargo also increased, and, naturally, more cargo meant an even greater investment.

The European solution to these problems was to share risks through merchants' shipping their cargo in smaller portions over a range of ships and thereby diversifying their exposure to any one ship sinking. The ship captains posted a notice about where the ship would sail, and merchants wrote what they wished to ship under the ship's name. It is from this 'under writing' that the term 'underwriting', as is now used in insurance, developed.

Even if the ship arrived safely, though, there was no certainty that exporters would receive payment. The larger merchant houses had already resolved this problem by establishing agents in the major trading centres, to hold the export goods' title until the customer paid for the goods. Because each exporter could not afford to establish offices in every city, it was more economical to pay a small fee to other merchants for this service, in return for a major reduction in payment risk.

In Europe, the problem of financing larger amounts for longer periods was similarly resolved, in part, through provision of finance by these same merchant houses, for a fee, to their smaller colleagues. This was typically done through the smaller merchants' issuing of promissory notes (an IOU) on which the larger and better known merchants signed their name. This indicated the larger merchant would accept liability to pay the amount due should the smaller firm, the one that drew up the promissory note, fail to do so. Because these well-known merchants were considered to be financially sound, private investors were often willing to purchase the lesser firms' IOUs, which they would not have done otherwise. It is from these early merchant acceptances of the thirteenth and fourteenth centuries that much of today's trade finance developed.

Many of the larger merchant houses eventually found the finance side of their business to be so profitable that they largely ceased their own trading and instead concentrated on finance. It is from there that merchant banks developed, and from these, part of our modern-day banking system.

When the European traders followed their explorers into the ASEAN region, there was therefore already a well-established practice of financing and insuring for supporting their trading activities, despite the length of the voyages involved.

With reference to intra-ASEAN trade, the problem was that these finance functions were designed almost exclusively to service trade between what was often a real or *de facto* South-East Asian colony and the 'mother' country. Although British, US, Dutch, French and other traders all had some early involvement in these types of finance and trading facilities, the colonial governments gradually ensured that their mother country's trading houses dominated the local business. Gradually, these firms were supplanted by commercial banks. By the late 1800s, commercial banks provided the bulk of the ASEAN countries' trade finance.

Foreign banks

Unfortunately for intra-ASEAN trade, these early banking firms were foreign institutions – usually banks whose head offices were in the mother country. Therefore, although trade finance was certainly available for exports from the colony to the mother country, these institutions were often less keen to support trade with other countries. Indeed, strong commercial incentives existed to retain both sides of the transaction within the bank's own branch network as well as, when possible, to help the home-country customers expand their business. Because colonial business with the mother country was also effectively a form of domestic trade, it had few of the credit information, different legal systems and foreign currency problems associated with truly international transactions. Undoubtedly, many colonial and mother-government administrations also provided strong informal and sometimes formal support for retaining as much trade as possible within the 'family'. Strong institutional reasons therefore existed for trade to be mainly north–south rather than within the region.

Although domestic commercial banks now dominate each ASEAN country's financial sector, the historical emphasis remains responsible for the favouring of developed-country trade, and foreign banks remain important sources of trade finance. Foreign banks are even important in intra-ASEAN trade, and many of them, particularly Citibank and the Hongkong and Shanghai Banking Corporation, continue to be represented within ASEAN better than most domestic ASEAN banks themselves – refer to Table 12.3.

Table 12.3   ASEAN countries' major foreign commercial bank representation,* 1995

Bank	Brunei	Indonesia	Malaysia	Philippines	Singapore	Thailand	Vietnam
Bank of America	–	BR	SB	BR	BR	BR	BR
Bank of Tokyo	–	BR	SB	BR	BR	BR	BR
Banque Indosuez	–	RO	JV/OB	OB	BR	BR	BR
Banque Nationale de Paris	–	BR	OB	OB	BR	OB	BR
Chase Manhattan Bank	–	BR	SB	OB	BR	BR	–
Citibank	BR	BR	SB	BR	BR	BR	BR
Credit Lyonnais	–	JV	–	OB	OB	OB	BR
Hongkong and Shanghai Banking Corporation	BR	BR	SB	BR	BR	BR	RO
Sakura Bank	–	JV	OB	RO	BR	OB	–
Standard Chartered Bank	BR	BR	SB	BR	BR	BR	BR

Note: 'OB' stands for 'offshore branch'; 'BR' stands for 'branch'; 'RO' stands for 'representative office'; 'JV' strands for 'joint venture'; 'SB' stands for 'subsidiary'.
*The representation is of non-ASEAN and non-Australian banks in ASEAN.
Source: Correspondence with respective banks, 1995.

The ASEAN countries have taken differing approaches to bank-licensing. This is particularly the case for the way foreign banks are allowed to operate in a specific country. In the least restrictive mode, foreign banks are allowed to enter (subject to normal prudential requirements) and operate exactly as a local banking institution.

Few countries within the Asia–Pacific region have permitted such free entry. In Australia, for example, foreign banks that seek to conduct retail banking (provide banking services to the general public) have been required to establish locally incorporated subsidiaries. Foreign banks that are willing to restrict themselves to servicing only larger businesses are able to open branches directly. Although the significance of this may not be particularly evident, a foreign-bank branch of a major international bank basically has the full financial backing of the entire banking group. In contrast, a locally incorporated subsidiary has only immediate access to its own capital and reserves and so is much more limited in what it can do. Therefore, in terms operational power after a full branch comes a wholly owned subsidiary, then a joint venture that has some local ownership, then a restricted branch, then an offshore branch, then an agency, and finally a representative office. With reference to trade finance, each of these bank-licensing types is different in terms of the services it provides.

The bank representative office

This is the least useful with reference to trade finance, because it is typically not allowed to conduct any banking business in the country in which it is located. It can, nevertheless, provide business clients with some help in their trading activities. Because these offices serve as their bank's listening and marketing arms with reference to that country, their staff attend the 'right' business functions and attempt to know the 'right' people. They also try to maintain good relations between their bank and banks in that country. A foreign-bank representative office can therefore be a good source of local information and contacts. It can also provide advice on the cost of local trade finance and other trade-related services. Finally, it can also arrange finance through its parent bank or through the parent bank's branches in other countries.

The bank agency

Although in the South-East Asia region the agency is not a common licensing form, it is one step up from a representative office. It typically cannot accept deposits, but it can make loans and often arrange trade finance or help in trade documentation. These agencies used to be a common vehicle through which Australian banks operated in the US.

The offshore bank branch

Although an offshore branch does not have to be physically offshore, its business technically does. In its pure form, all its transactions have to be made between parties who do not reside in the country in which the offshore branch is located; they are therefore not of much direct use in the financing of any local export or import business. Indeed, although this only 'non-resident' activity might not seem to provide much justification for establishing a local operation, it is usually associated with some tax incentives. More importantly, few offshore branches are kept totally offshore: most also have some limited entry into the domestic market. This is particularly the case in Malaysia, Philippines and Thailand. Because these offshore branches are often simply a separate set of accounts within a normal bank office, they are often called 'offshore banking units', or 'OBUs'.

The restricted bank branch

As discussed previously in this chapter, a restricted branch is usually restricted with reference to either the type of business it conducts (it may be allowed only medium to large businesses as clients) or where the business can be conducted (it might be limited to one bank branch), or special permission might be required for additional offices to be opened. In Singapore, for example, no new foreign banks have been able to open additional retail-banking branch offices since 1977. Although this may seem to be extreme, it should be recalled that until Australia deregulated in the mid-1980s no new foreign banks had been allowed in our country from the mid-1940s. Restricted branches are usually allowed to provide most international trade services.

The joint-venture bank and the wholly owned foreign-bank subsidiary

These are typically normal commercial banks that can provide a full range of banking services. The only drawback is that the connection with the parent is not always evident. In Australia, the name of the Bank of Singapore, for example, has not provided much indication that the bank is a subsidiary of the Oversea-Chinese Banking Corporation. These joint-venture banks, subsidiaries, foreign banks and local commercial banks can provide most of the trade services that have been discussed in this chapter, or a close equivalent.

Australian banks

It could have been the case that Australia was similarly well represented in the ASEAN countries. Sadly, though, Australian banks were somewhat undecided about how to approach Asia. Westpac was the most ambitious at first: it had branches, representative offices and investments in local financial institutions (both directly and through AGC), but financial problems at home caused it to sell much of this involvement. The ANZ Bank was the other major player. Through its acquiring of the British colonial bank Grindlays PLC, it gained a considerable branch representation throughout the Asia–Pacific region. Because Grindlays retained much of its earlier trade-finance orientation, ANZ is now probably the best placed of Australia's banking institutions. Indeed, as the ANZ Bank claims in its 1994 *Annual Report* (p. 13)

> access to the local knowledge of the ANZ team in countries such as Vietnam and Indonesia or the market standing of ANZ Grindlays in South Asia, is of particular value to customers seeking to exploit trade opportunities or develop their presence in these markets.

Although the Commonwealth Bank of Australia (CBA) and the National Australia Bank (NAB) have some representation, as indicated in Table 12.4, their level of commitment to ASEAN has not been the same as ANZ's.

Table 12.4   ASEAN countries' Australian bank representation, 1995

Country	ANZ	CBA	NAB	Westpac
Brunei	–	–	–	–
Indonesia	Joint venture	Joint venture	Representative office	Representative office
Malaysia	Representative office	–	Representative office	Representative office
Philippines	Branch	–	–	–
Singapore	Offshore branch	Offshore branch	Offshore branch	Offshore branch
Thailand	Representative office	–	Representative office	Representative office
Vietnam	Branches	Representative office	–	–

Note: BankWest (formerly the R & I Bank) also has a representative office in Singapore.
Source: Correspondence with the four banks, 1995.

Besides offering finance, Australian banks' overseas offices will usually try to help their clients to find suitable local clients or partners. Some banks are more active than others and have dedicated specific computer systems to this role. Once the product and market have been determined, the system will therefore generate a list of contacts from the bank's customers. This overseas awareness is important for the client in another way, too: in the Asian Development Bank's book *Export Finance: Some Asian Examples*, (p. 20) it is stated that

> lack of, or inadequate, information on foreign markets and buyers is viewed as one of the root causes for an anti-export bias among banks.

The bias is that banks that understand overseas markets are more likely to understand export finance. Therefore, if a bank does not seem to be interested, find a bank that is already dealing with the country in question. The more active the involvement, the less difficulty the bank is likely to have in establishing the facilities.

This bias, such as it is, also impacts on the bank's willingness to finance investment in the region. Therefore, as DFAT states in its book *Australia's Business Challenge: South-East Asia in the 1990s*, (p. 6), 'a lack of finance had caused Australian companies to shun Asia as a place to invest'.

ASEAN banks

Today, as restrictions on foreign banks' entry into Australian banking have been relaxed, exporters no longer have to limit their business to Australian banks. An increasing number of ASEAN institutions have established offices in Australia and are seeking export business. The most prominent ones are the Singaporean bank, the Oversea-Chinese Banking Corporation and its Bank of Singapore (Australia) Ltd subsidiary. Although the Bank of Singapore's two major competitors, the

Overseas Union Bank (OUB) and the United Overseas Bank (UOB), also have Australian branches, the Bank of Singapore is the only one of the three banks that is authorised for retail banking; it has branches in Sydney, Melbourne and Perth. Like its two competitors, its main business is aiding its Singaporean and Malaysian customers' investment and trading activities in Australia and helping Australians do business in Singapore and Malaysia.

Table 12.5   ASEAN country banks' Australian representation, 1995

Country	Bank/s	Office location/s
Indonesia	Lippo Bank (Lippo Finance Australia)	Sydney
	Bank Indonesia International	Sydney
Brunei	–	
Malaysia	MBf Bank (MBf Australia)	Sydney
Philippines	Allied Bank	Sydney
Singapore	Bank of Singapore (Australia) Limited*	Sydney/Melbourne/Perth
	Overseas Union Bank (OUB Australia)	Sydney
	United Overseas Bank (UOB Australia)	Sydney
Thailand	–	
Vietnam	–	

*In Australia, the Bank of Singapore is an authorised retail–commercial bank and a subsidiary of the Oversea-Chinese Banking Corporation. OCBC plans to open its own branches in 1996.
Source: Correspondence with the respective banks, 1995.

ASEAN institutions have also become more attractive because the institutions themselves are seeking to increase their share of ASEAN-trade financing. All ASEAN's major banks have taken at least some steps towards increasing their visibility, if not their operations, in their neighbouring countries. Unfortunately, as indicated in Table 12.6, no bank has yet gained full banking access in all the ASEAN countries.

Table 12.6   ASEAN countries' ASEAN bank representation, 1995

Bank	Brunei	Indonesia	Malaysia	Philippines	Singapore	Thailand	Vietnam
Malayan Banking	BR	–	HQ	–	BR	–	–
United Malayan Bank	BR	–	HQ	–	BR	BR	–
Philippine National Bank	–	RO	–	HQ	BR	BR	–
Development Bank of Singapore	–	JV	OB	BR	HQ	OB	–
Oversea-Chinese Banking Corp	–	–	SB	OB	HQ	BR	–
Overseas Union Bank	BR	–	BR	OB	HQ	OB	–
Tat Lee Bank	–	JV	BR	–	HQ	RO	–
United Overseas Bank	–	JV	SB	OB	HQ	–	RO
Bangkok Bank	–	BR	BR	BR	BR	HQ	BR

Note 1: 'BR' stands for 'branch'; 'RO' stands for 'representative office'; 'HQ' stands for 'head quarters'; 'JV' stands for 'joint venture'; 'SB' stands for 'subsidiary'.
Note 2: Indonesia's and Malaysia's banking regulations promote joint ventures and subsidiaries, respectively, rather than direct branches. Other ASEAN banks may have a single representative office or branch elsewhere in ASEAN.
Source: Correspondence with the respective banks, 1995.

Given foreign banks' wide representation and Asian institutions' increased activity in ASEAN trade, it is perhaps not surprising that Australian banks no longer have a *de facto* monopoly on this type of Australian business. Instead, Australians are quite willing to deal with these other institutions when the institutions offer the best price and/or service. As a result, DFAT's 1992 survey of Australian businesses that are active in South-East Asia (*Australia's Business Challenge: South-East Asia in the 1990s,* p. 152) found that

> 72 per cent of respondents used Singaporean financial institutions either solely or in addition to other sources of finance for activities in South-East Asia; 56 per cent did not use Australian institutions.

Trade finance internationally

The emphasis placed on non-Australian institutions is also understandable considering the Australian banks' relative position in the international banking market and, more specifically, their place in international trade finance. With reference to international ranking, the July 1995 issue of the *Banker* (p. 179) reported it had been found that in terms of capital, our four major banks: ANZ, CBA, NAB and Westpac, ranked only ninety-first, sixty-eighth, forty-ninth and sixty-ninth respectively. Similarly, as indicated in Table 12.7, with reference to trade finance only ANZ deserved a mention in the list of the 20 top institutions.

Table 12.7   World trade finance providers, 1994

Provider	Home country
Export–Import Bank of Japan	Japan
Citicorp	United States
WestLB Group	Germany
ABN AMRO Bank	Netherlands
Deutsche Bank	Germany
Union Bank of Switzerland	Switzerland
Societe Generale	France
Barclays Bank	United Kingdom
Banque Indosuez	France
Banque Nationale de Paris	France
Bayerische Vereinsbank	Germany
ANZ Grindlays Banking Group	Australia
Standard Chartered Bank	United Kingdom
Dresdner Bank	Germany
Banque Française du Commerce Exterieur	France
Bank of America	United States
Creditanstalt–Bankverein	Austria
Banca Nationale del Lavoro	Italy
Landesbank Rheinland–Pfalz	Germany
CSFB–Credit Suisse	Switzerland

Source: *Project & Trade Finance*, February 1995.

Domestic finance

Domestic trade finance is also available for Australian exporters' local clients in ASEAN countries. ASEAN's local banks provide a range of import financial services that is much the same as Australia's. Some differences nevertheless exist, particularly in the terms available: some indication is provided in Table 12.8.

Table 12.8   ASEAN countries' private finance for local importers, 1994

Country	Source of finance
Brunei	Unknown
Indonesia	State buyers preferred
	Unsecured terms and long-term cover possible
Malaysia	Usually short-term cover but some long-term possible
Philippines	Short-term cover and secured terms only
Singapore	Most terms
Thailand	Secured terms preferred but some long-term cover also possible
Vietnam	Unknown

Source: *Project & Trade Finance Handbook*. London: Euromoney Publications, 1994.

As well as accessing trade funding from local banks and other financial institutions, some ASEAN countries operate special financial help packages in order to attract foreign investment, particularly if the production is to be exported. These packages are in addition to any tax incentives or regulatory exemptions. Singapore is perhaps the most organised country with reference to financial help and has designated a number of institutions for this purpose.

Some specialist institutions, often government owned, are available for helping Australian businesses that seek to export from either Australia or their operations located in specific ASEAN countries; this typically relates only to exports, not imports. This type of financial help usually comes as either supplier credits or buyer credits. The supplier's credit is provided by the exporter through raising of the funds via bills of exchange or other document-related credit in its own right. In contrast, buyer's credit is finance that is directly provided to the importer by another financial institution, often through a back-to-back loan that is arranged through the exporter's bank. These funds are very often provided at concessional rates.

The degree to which these credits mean either better terms or better interest-rate costs, should have a favourable impact on the success of exporters from that country. Some countries also attempt to blend these concessional funds with commercially priced money (mixed credits), in order to stretch their impact as much as possible. The statistics shown in Table 12.9, though, suggest export finance may not be quite so important as might be thought. Only in Thailand are these facilities significant, and this is because in 1988 the funding mechanism operated through the commercial banking system as a whole rather than through a specialist export–import bank, one of which has since been created.

Table 12.9 Selected Asia–Pacific countries official export credits: 1988 data

Country	Exports credits for 1988 (US$ million)	% of 1988 exports
Australia	649	1.9
Japan	5,314	2.0
South Korea	415	0.7
Malaysia[a]	58	0.3
Thailand[b]	4,015	25.0
United States	8,185	2.5

Note: [a]Malaysia's figures also include guarantees. [b]Thailand's pre-shipment finance comprised 75 per cent.
Source: *Review of Overseas Export Enhancement Measures*. Canberra: Industry Commission, vol 1, 1991, p 50.

The extent to which governments can help with exports finance is limited through international agreement. The OECD Arrangement on Guidelines for Officially Supported Export Credits was specifically established to limit competition between OECD member States, and many other countries also follow its rules. The Arrangement requires that the purchaser pay at least 15 per cent of the contract with cash, set a maximum term of usually 8.5 years and arrange for monthly publication of a schedule of the minimum interest rates that can be offered for selected currencies. These rates are calculated from a base rate (typically the yield, in the secondary market, on a government bond that has a remaining maturity of five years) plus an agreed margin; the latter is currently 0.2 per cent for yen-denominated finance, 0.5 per cent for EU currency and 1 per cent for most other currencies (including the Australian dollar). Specific understandings also exist with reference to financing the export of ships, telecommunications, nuclear-power plants and civilian aircraft. Interestingly, pre-shipment finance and contractual performance guarantees, particularly those provided to small-size and medium-size enterprises, are not covered under the Arrangement and therefore at present may afford a few areas in which some competitive government-provided advantage might be gained.

In practice, the existence of the OECD agreement, combined with the work of GATT (now the World Trade Organisation) and the Berne Union, have provided enough stimulus for some countries to doubt their export-finance programs' effectiveness – in January 1990, Bank Indonesia therefore removed its export subsidies completely. As the bank described it in its 1989/1990 annual report (p. 72), this policy change

> had two objectives, first, to improve the competitiveness of export commodities, and second, to conform to the agreement on the GATT code on subsidies and countervailing duties reached in March 1985, which was aimed at gradually removing export subsidies.

In Australia, for example, EFIC serves as this specialist provider and can lend directly to overseas buyers, or their bank, seeking to purchase Australian capital goods and services. This lending is usually provided when the Australian exporter has to provide credit terms and rates competitive with exporters from other developed countries. When these credit terms and rates represent concessional finance, EFIC is compensated accordingly by the Australian government. Although the specifics depend on the contract conditions, the contract's size, the good sold and the buyer, the finance can involve repayment over a period of between two and ten years.

As shown in Table 12.10, EFIC has counterparts in most ASEAN countries. The rest of this section addresses these country-specific characteristics.

Table 12.10   ASEAN countries' specialist export–import finance institutions

Country	Institution/s
Brunei	–
Indonesia	Bank Indonesia; Asuransi Ekspor Indonesia
Malaysia	Bank Negara Malaysia; Export–Import Bank of Malaysia
Philippines	Bangko Sentral ng Pilipinas; Philippine Export and Foreign Loan Guarantee Corporation
Singapore	ECICS Credit Insurance; Monetary Authority of Singapore
Thailand	Export–Import Bank of Thailand
Vietnam	–

Indonesia

Indonesia has no institution specifically for export finance. Although Asuransi Ekspor Indonesia can provide export-credit guarantees, the funds are usually provided through commercial banks. The central bank, Bank Indonesia, will in turn help the banks (both local and foreign) through a special liquidity-support scheme whereby pre-shipment financing is aided. The scheme is available only when the transaction is supported by a full set of trade documents and is insured through Asuransi Ekspor. Although Indonesia once subsidised its non-oil and gas related exports, these concessions were largely phased out by 1990. Some mention should be made of the government-owned Bank Ekspor Impor Indonesia. Its name would suggest it is a specialist in export–import finance, and although this used to be the case, it is now simply a commercial bank.

Malaysia

Malaysia has two specialist export-finance institutions: the Malaysian Export Credit Insurance Berhad and the Export–Import Bank of Malaysia Berhad (both subsidiaries of the government's Bank Industri Malaysia), as well as a range of commercial bank schemes that are supported through the central bank, Bank Negara Malaysia. As in other countries, short-term commercial bank advances are the most common type of advance. They are often refinanced through Bank Negara

Malaysia's Export Credit Refinancing Scheme, which covers advances of up to 180 days. Typically, these advances are given only after a Malaysian Export Credit Insurance bank-guarantee policy has been obtained, and they are denominated in Malaysian ringgit. The advances are on a concessional interest rate. The Export–Import Bank provides medium-term to long-term export funding (up to 10 years with a two-year grace period on repayments). It will also finance on similar terms up to 70 per cent of the costs of Malaysian joint-venture projects overseas where the venture is at least 40 per cent Malaysian owned and has a 40 per cent Malaysian content in the resulting products. This bank was created in 1995 to enhance Malaysia's exports and provides special medium-term to long-term export finance schemes. It offers both supplier-credit and buyer-credit programs as well as bank guarantees.

Philippines

The Philippines' Export and Foreign Loan Guarantee Corporation and central bank, Bangko Sentral ng Pilipinas, are its two major government-owned specialist providers of export finance. Commercial bank, peso-denominated short advances for export purposes receive some support through a special Bangko Sentral ng Pilipinas Rediscount Facility. This facility will cover advances up to 90 days and includes the possibility of renewing for an additional 90-day period. As with other ASEAN government schemes, borrowers gain directly from the lower interest rates, because a maximum is set on the lending rates allowed under the scheme. As well as the usual commercial bank finance, most banks offer special foreign-currency-denominated finance through their foreign-currency-deposit units (FCDUs). These units were authorised by the Philippines' government to mobilise foreign-currency deposits within the banking system and then lend out the foreign currencies to the clients for periods of up to 360 days. However, most export finance is for much shorter periods. Apart from these major sources, a number of government agencies offer small, very specialised financial help for particular local activities, and export-financing help is sometimes included in this. The most recent edition of Bangko Sentral ng Philipinas's publication *Financing Opportunities Available for Philippine Exporters* details the various options.

Singapore

Singapore's commercial banks provide the country's main funding of exports and imports. However, bank export finance is supported by the Monetary Authority of Singapore's Rediscounting Scheme. This scheme permits banks to rediscount advances made via commercial bills of exchange in support of export of eligible, locally manufactured products. These advances are subject to a price limitation of 1.5 per cent over the effective rate charged the banks under the scheme. The government's ECICS Credit Insurance (formerly the Export Credit Insurance Corporation of Singapore), besides credit insurance, provides concessionary medium-term to long-term fixed-rate export finance for construction of capital equipment. Singapore's construction of ships and oil rigs, for example, is often supported by ECICS funding.

Thailand

Thailand's commercial banks also provide the bulk of that country's export finance. This has typically been of a short-term nature and has been supported, at least in part, through guarantees. The government's Export–Import Bank of Thailand (Thai–Eximbank) permits Thai exporters to provide longer and more favourable terms in order for them to compete with larger, capital equipment exporters. The bank also provides guarantees and credit insurance. In addition, it has assumed the commercial banks' trade-refinance functions that used to be fulfilled by the Bank of Thailand. It fulfils the functions by using its own capital and borrowings from the Bank of Thailand, from domestic sources or from foreign sources. The bank will also finance import of capital equipment or services that are necessary for producing exports or for advancing Thailand's national development. Australia's joint-venture parties in Thailand may be able to use this source when their operations are being created or expanded for export purposes.

Export-financing help is only one of many types of government assistance that are provided in ASEAN countries. Table 12.11 provides some indication of the variety of assistance.

In Vietnam there are no specific specialist trade finance instutions. The Bank for Foreign Trade of Viet Nam (Vietcombank) was once sole provider of foreign exchange and trade finance, but must now compete for business just like other banks.

Table 12.11 Export incentives in selected Pacific Basin countries

Country	Direct subsidies	Credit or insurance	Tax incentives	Export-processing zones	Marketing help	Infra-structure	Investment incentives	Research and development
Australia	S	G	na	na	G	s	s	G
Indonesia	na	G	na	s	G	s	na	na
Malaysia	na	G	G	G	G	G	G	G
Singapore	na	g	G	G	G	G	G	G
Thailand	na	g	s	S	G	S	S	na

Note: 'G' stands for 'generally available'; 'g' stands for 'available'; 'S' stands for 'selectively available'; 's' stands for 'very selective'; 'na' stands for 'not generally available'.
Source: *Review of Overseas Export Enhancement Measures*. Canberra: Industry Commission, vol 1, 1991, p ii.

In Australia, Austrade's International Trade Enhancement Scheme will aid small and medium businesses in exporting with loans of $150,000 to $5 million for six years with the first 3 years interest free and at 40 per cent of the bank rate. These funds are available under special draw down conditions for projects that can justify A$3 million in exports over five years. Similarly, AusAID's special assistance program, the Development Import Finance Facility (DIFF), has supported major high-priority public-sector projects in specified developing countries. Although Indonesia has been a particularly important recipient of this support, the Philippines, Thailand and Vietnam are other ASEAN countries that are especially suitable. DIFF funding will help Australian exporters to match the tied finance and credit finance that is offered by other countries' exporters, through blending AusAID grant money and commercial export credit – typically, that provided by EFIC.

Unfortunately in May 1996, the Australian government announced plans to drop the Development Import Finance Facility as well as the Export Market Development Grant program (a 50 per cent rebate scheme on eligible overseas market development expenses). The problem for the government is the political damage that dropping the at least 52 projects (worth some $1.2 billion) already discussed with the recipient country governments. Similarly, the government's $120 million per annum in savings may well be offset by the possibility of Australian businesses not receiving other government contracts in those countries (particularly the Philippines and Vietnam). The government has since indicated that it might replace the DIFF with a more targeted concessional finance scheme.

Other non-bank trade finance

As mentioned, commercial banks are by the far the Asia–Pacific region's most important source of export finance. Confirming houses, finance companies and the informal financial market may also be important in some countries. However, export finance does not necessarily come exclusively through financial institutions: corporations can provide trade finance themselves.

Japan

The most visible non-financial institutions are the Japanese trading companies such Mitsui and Mitsubishi. They help potential exporters through offering a whole range of direct and indirect support, of which trade finance is only one type. Although these trading companies serve a wide range of customers, they are particularly associated with specific Japanese industrial groups, or *keiretsus*. Although these informal conglomerates' impact has lessened because their members have been able to access offshore sources of equity and quasi-equity, they remain important within the context of Japanese business.

South Korea

Having noted the advantages these trading companies offered, South Korea promoted development of its own version: *chaebol*. Indeed, since 1975 these conglomerates have been granted a special 'integrated trading company' status. More recently, South Korea has tried to encourage its *chaebol* to specialise their activities rather than maintain their more traditional, broad approach to trade.

Taiwan

Although Taiwan attempted to establish a similar type of trading company, the companies never became particularly popular, especially because trade financing for small to medium business was both readily available and cheaper through the banking system. Trading companies are nevertheless important for Taiwan – but the Japanese ones, not the Taiwanese. As Winckler and Lodge (p. 206) explain in their 1989 book, the Japanese know our production and marketing better than we do, and they guarantee our firms a modest profit while assuming most of the risk and appropriating most of the rewards.

Although the abovementioned examples relate to North-East Asia rather than South-East Asia, the trading-company concept has been attractive in the latter region. Most ASEAN countries have formally considered providing special tax incentives or other incentives in order to encourage trading companies to develop locally. Unfortunately, these local versions have not had much impact.

Other risks and their management

Whereas previous sections have discussed the credit risk involved in international trade, more mention is required of the risks of non-payment for non-commercial reasons, as well as of the foreign-exchange risks that are entailed when the trade transaction is denominated in other than Australian dollars.

Non-commercial risks

As mentioned, international trade involves exposure to a range of risks that is much wider than that for domestic transactions. An exporter faces the danger that even if the buyer wishes to pay, the payment may be disallowed or delayed. Not surprisingly, the amount of risk depends on the country involved, and as Table 12.12 indicates, the ASEAN countries rate reasonably well in this context.

Table 12.12   ASEAN countries and funds transfer

Country	Transfer of funds
Brunei	Not available
Indonesia	Delays of up to two months reported
Malaysia	No difficulties
Philippines	Delays, but improving
Singapore	No delays
Thailand	No specific delays reported
Vietnam	Not available

Source: *Project & Trade Finance Handbook*. London: Euromoney Publications, 1994, pp 74–80.

Even so, many exporters prefer to minimise their credit and non-commercial non-payment risks by having export-credit insurance. In Australia, this is available through the government's EFIC. Cover is available for credit terms of up to 180 days, mainly for consumable exports, but it can be extended in accordance with accepted international practice. However, EFIC's policies do not cover the full exposure for commercial risk – instead, like other export-credit insurers, EFIC adopts a risk-sharing principle. Therefore, in the case of, say, buyer insolvency or delay in payment, it will pay only 90 per cent of the loss incurred. This same risk-sharing approach may also apply to EFIC's non-commercial risk cover. When the risk involves reasonably creditworthy markets, EFIC will provide full cover; however, for more risky countries this drops to 90 per cent of the insured amount. Table 12.13 shows the risk profile for selected Asian countries: a ranking of 1 is the least risky.

Table 12.13   EFIC's short-term-market gradings for selected Asian countries, 1995

Country	Grading
Brunei	1
Indonesia	3
Malaysia	2
Philippines	4
Singapore	1
Thailand	2
Vietnam	5
Burma	5
Cambodia	5
Laos	5

Note: EFIC will provide full cover on countries that are ranked 1 to 4 but not for countries that rank 5 and 6.
Source: EFIC, 1996.

In order to ensure its own risks are properly managed, EFIC would like its policies to cover a wide range of countries and therefore prefers clients to insure all their exports, not only specific transactions – otherwise it would find its business was largely limited to covering exports to high-risk countries. However, it will provide special policies for covering single contracts on a one-off basis for periods of, in some cases, up to 10 years, as well as for covering both pre-shipment and post-shipment finance.

As indicated in Table 12.14, most ASEAN countries also have their own local-export-credit insurance organisation. Although few of these organisations are likely to help Australian exporters directly, they will cover Australian–local joint ventures that export from the country in question.

Table 12.14   ASEAN countries' export–import insurance institutions

Country	
Brunei	–
Indonesia	Asuransi Ekspor Indonesia
Malaysia	Malaysia Export Credit Insurance
Philippines	Philippine Export & Foreign Loan Guarantee Corporation
Singapore	ECICS Credit Insurance Ltd
Thailand	Export–Import Bank of Thailand
Vietnam	Insurance not yet available

Source: Correspondence with the five firms, 1995.

Export insurance has become quite important for some aspects of international trade, and as indicated in Table 12.15, each year countries insure millions of dollars' worth of transactions. Japan is by far the Asia–Pacific region's biggest user of this type of insurance: in 1989, its exporters insured US$57.6 billion worth of exports – and that amount accounted for about 21 per cent of the country's total exports. In that year, only Australia, the US and Hong Kong had insurance contracts that reached the 'billion' level.

Table 12.15   Selected Asia–Pacific countries' export-insurance: 1989

Country	Exports insured (US$ million)	% of 1989 exports
Australia	4,741	13
Hong Kong	1,376	2
Indonesia[a]	61	–
Japan[b]	57,559	21
South Korea	298	–
Malaysia	109	–
Singapore	208	–
Taiwan	300	–
United States	4,366	3

Note: [a]Indonesia's figures are for 1988; [b]Japan's figures are for 1987.
Source: *Review of Overseas Export Enhancement Measures*. Canberra: Industry Commission, vol 1, 1991, p 47.

Given the important risk-reduction advantage this type of insurance seems to provide, we might expect the cover's availability to be significant in a country's exporting activities being successful. However, the results seem to suggest no correlation exists between use of export insurance and successful exporting. As the 1991 Industry Commission report, *Review of Overseas Export Enhancement Measures* (p 48) concludes,

> economies that have recently been very successful in terms of export growth (i.e. the Republic of Korea, Singapore and Taiwan) are among the smallest users of export insurance and guarantee facilities.

As well as offering credit insurance, some agencies will insure foreign direct investment (FDI) against non-commercial political risk when an investment is located in its country, or, in the case of EFIC, in other countries. In addition to seeking cover from EFIC and local agencies, Australian businesses that make FDI in less developed countries could seek cover from the World Bank Group's Multilateral Investment Guarantee Agency (MIGA); Indonesia, Malaysia, Philippines and Vietnam are all developing-country members. Its policies cover 90 per cent of the investments' value against expropriation, currency inconvertibility (or transfer risk) and war or civil disturbance. The coverage can be provided for both existing investments and new investments and is arranged to cover periods of between three and twenty years. As of mid-1995, MIGA had written policies for covering risks in Indonesia, Philippines and Vietnam.

Foreign-exchange risk

Currency-risk exposure can be minimised by arranging for the currency's forward purchase or sale. The price for which to buy or sell the foreign currency out of or into Australian dollars is set at the date of the 'contract for delivery at a specified future date'. Usually, an exporter will be converting the foreign-currency proceeds from a sale of goods into Australian dollars, whereas the importer will be converting from Australian dollars into another currency in order to pay for the goods' purchase. Although these forward-exchange contracts can in theory be made to cover any period, in practice most of them involve a period of less than a year and are typically for a much shorter period. Likewise, the more exotic the currency, the shorter – and often the more expensive – the cover available.

Firms that have considerable foreign-exchange exposure might alternatively decide to manage their risk over the exposure's life rather than fix the price when the risk is at first created. This option may be particularly attractive when the exposure seems likely to provide a higher return with reference to Australian dollars or when one currency's interest rates provide a higher return or a lower cost. These treasury-management functions are important in larger firms.

Another alternative is to organise some offsetting liability or asset in the same currency. For example, an exporter, expecting to be paid in some foreign currency, could help to finance the sale by taking out a short-term loan in the foreign currency in question. This advance could help to finance production of the export products and could be repaid from the proceeds of the products' sale. Conversely, an importer could borrow in Australian dollars and convert them into the currency denomination of the goods' purchase; and then pay the supplier, in which case the trade debt remains in Australian dollars.

The decisions as to whether to cover foreign-exchange exposure and how to do this are outside the scope of this book. However, given the Australian dollar's movement against other currencies, some form of foreign-exchange-risk management is essential. Naturally, the Australian dollar's strength or weakness against other currencies varies from currency to currency and from time to time. Nevertheless, it is tempting to try and make a prediction, and Table 12.16 sets out an attempt at this. Only time will tell whether the suggested characteristics prove to be true.

Table 12.16 Australian and ASEAN-country currencies characteristics

Currency	Characteristics
Australian dollar	Often weak, but can be strong according to rising commodity prices or high real domestic interest rates. Viewed as having low political risk.
Brunei dollar	Tied to the Singapore dollar and therefore has the same hard-currency aspects.
Indonesian rupiah	Generally weak, and subject to a government policy of gradual depreciation. Reflects the price of oil and negatively responds to the strength of the yen.
Malaysian ringgit	Moderately weak and used for supporting the government's export drive. Strong local-economic-growth prospects should ensure it strengthens over the longer term.
Philippine peso	Generally weak due to the country's general economic problems and associated political uncertainties.
Singapore dollar	A strong currency that reflects Singapore's economic growth, political stability and government policy of using a strong dollar to limit local inflation.
Thai baht	A much stronger currency in recent years due to the strength of the Thai economy and the baht's use as a *de facto* currency in Laos, Cambodia and Myanmar (Burma).
Vietnamese dong	After years of severe weakness, the dong gained some strength in the early 1990s and is now subject only to gradual depreciation.

Conclusion

This Chapter has considered the main types of export financing, development of trade finance and its related institutions, problems to do with additional risk on non-payment and foreign-exchange-rate movements, and some ideas on how these problems can be managed. The intention has been to show that a wide range of types of export financing exists as well as a number of potential sources from which the finance can be obtained. The best place to start is with the local bank: each bank has its own export-finance specialist who can provide details about what it offers. If the details are insufficient, a copy of one of the bank trade-finance books that are listed under 'References' can be obtained. As Hsuan explained in the 1982 article 'Financing ASEAN Trade' (p. 156), 'there is no lack of resources and capacity in ASEAN to finance foreign trade'. In the mid-1990s this remains the case for ASEAN, and the statement applies equally well to Australia. The resources exist – it is up to Australian traders and investors to use them.

REFERENCES

Anderson, K and Blackhurst, R, *Regional Integration and the Global Trading System*. London: Harvester Wheatsheaf, 1993.

Asian and Australasian Companies: A Guide to Sources of Information. Beckenham: CBD Research, 1994.

Asian Development Bank, *Export Finance: Some Asian Examples*. Manila: Economics and Development Resource Centre, 1990.

Australian Countertrade Association, *Countertrade Review*, various issues.

Ball, J and Knight, M (eds), *The Guide to Export Finance*. London: Euromoney Publications, fifth edition, 1990.

Chen, E, 'Changing Patterns of Financial Flows in the Asia–Pacific Region and Policy Responses', in *Asian Development Review*, vol 10, no 2, 1992, pp 47–85.

Claessens, S, 'Alternative Forms of External Finance: A Survey', in *World Bank Research Observer*, vol 8, no 1, 1993, pp 91–117.

Clarke, T and Bruce, R, 'Trade Finance', in Bruce, R, McKern, B, Pollard, I and Skully, M (eds), *Handbook of Australian Corporate Finance*. Sydney: Butterworths, 1991, fourth edition, pp 368–89.

Commonwealth Bank of Australia, *Financing International Trade: Commercial Banking*. Sydney: Commonwealth Bank of Australia, fifth edition, 1993.

East Asia Analytical Unit, Department of Foreign Affairs and Trade, *Australia's Business Challenge: South-East Asia in the 1990s*. Canberra: Australian Government Publishing Service, 1992.

External Trade Department, *Financing Opportunities Available to Philippine Exporters*. Manila: Bangko Sentral ng Philipinas, 1993.

Financial Business Training, *Documentary Credits Beyond 400 – UPC Updated*. Hong Kong: HongkongBank, 1993.

Gannell, I, 'International Trade Finance', in Skully, M (ed), *International Corporate Finance: A Handbook for Australian Business*. Sydney: Butterworths, 1990, pp 268–92.

Gipson, C R, *The McGraw-Hill Dictionary of International Trade and Finance*. New York: McGraw-Hill, 1994.

Hsuan, O, 'Financing ASEAN Trade', in Swee-Hock, S and Hai, H (eds), *Growth and Direction of ASEAN Trade*. Singapore: Singapore University Press, 1982, pp 154–63.

Johnson, G G, Fisher, M and Harris, E, *Officially Supported Export Credits: Developments and Prospects*. Washington, DC: International Monetary Fund, 1990.

Industry Commission, *Review of Overseas Export Enhancement Measures*. Canberra: Industry Commission, 1991.

International Chamber of Commerce, *Documentary Credits: uniform customs and practice for documentary credits ICC no 500*. Hong Kong: Hongkong and Shanghai Banking Corporation, 1993.

Kirmani, N (ed), *International Trade Policies: The Uruguay Round and Beyond*. Washington, DC: International Monetary Fund, 1994.

—— (ed), *International Trade Policies: The Uruguay Round and Beyond – Background Papers*. Washington, DC: International Monetary Fund, 1994.

Kreinin, M and Plummer, M G, 'Effects of Economic Integration in Industrial Countries on ASEAN and the Asian NIEs', in *World Development*, September 1992, pp 1345–66.

Kuhn, M, *Official Financing for Developing Countries*. Washington, DC: International Monetary Fund, 1994.

National Australia Bank, *Finance of International Trade*. Melbourne: National Australia Bank, eighth edition, 1996.

Naya, S and Imada, P, 'Trade and Foreign Investment Linkage in ASEAN Countries', in Ying, S L (ed), *Foreign Direct Investment in ASEAN*. Kuala Lumpur: Malaysian Economic Association, 1990, pp 30–58.

Project & Trade Finance, *World Export Credit Guide*. London: Euromoney Publications, 1995.

Rhee, Y W, *Trade Finance in Developing Countries*. Washington, DC: World Bank, 1989.

—— 'Key Role for Trade Finance in Transition and Developing Economies', in *World Bank Viewpoint*, October 1994, pp 1–2.

Skully, M, *ASEAN Financial Cooperation: Developments in Banking, Finance and Insurance*. London: Macmillan, 1985.

The Guide to Venture Capital in Asia. Hong Kong: Asian Venture Capital Journal, 1993–94.

Thillainathan, R, 'The ASEAN Financial Sector: A Drag or a Leader', in *ASEAN Economic Bulletin*, vol 12, no 1, July 1995, pp 1–9.

Treasury Centre of Excellence, *Handling Your Bank: A Small Business Perspective*. Melbourne: Australian Society of CPAs, 1994.

United Nations Conference on Trade and Development, *Trade and Development Report, 1991*. New York: United Nations, various years.

Winckler, Edwin A and Lodge, George C, 'Taiwan, 1986: Choices for the Future', in Lindenberg, Marc and Ramirex, Noel (eds), *Managing Adjustment in Developing Countries: Economic and Political Perspective*. San Francisco: ICI Press, 1989, pp 203–23.

APPENDIX 12.1: *Australian and ASEAN-country addresses for specialist sources of trade finance*

Australian addresses

Australian Countertrade Association
31 Mawson Drive
Mawson 2607, ACT, Australia
Telephone: (61 6) 286 2701
Facsimile: (61 6) 286 6924

Australian Trade Commission
Austrade Grants (EMDG)
PO Box 55
World Trade Centre
Melbourne 3005, Vic, Australia
Telephone: (61 3) 9284 3140

Australian Trade Commission
Austrade Loan Program
PO Box 55
World Trade Centre
Melbourne 3005, Vic, Australia
Telephone: (61 3) 9284 3111

Export Finance and Insurance Corporation
Export House
Level 8, 22 Pitt Street
Sydney 2000, NSW, Australia
Telephone: (61 2) 9201 2111
Facsimile: (61 2) 9251 3851

Development Import Finance Facility
Business Co-operation Section
AusAID
GPO Box 887
Canberra 2601, ACT, Australia
Telephone: (61 6) 276 4659
Facsimile: (61 6) 276 4875

Indonesian addresses

Bank Indonesia
Jl Mohammad Husni Thamrin No. 2
Jakarta 10340, Indonesia
Telephone: (62 21) 231 0847
Facsimile: (62 21) 385 5723

Malaysian addresses

Export–Import Bank of Malaysia Berhad
Levels 14
Bangunan Bank Industri
Jalan Sultan Ismail
Kuala Lumpur 50796, Malaysia
Telephone: (60 3) 292 2707
Facsimile: (60 3) 292 7078

Bank Negara Malaysia
Jalan Dato' Onn
Kuala Lumpur 50480, Malaysia
Telephone: (60 3) 298 8044
Facsimile: (60 3) 291 2990

Philippine addresses

Bangko Sentral ng Pilipinas (BSP)
A. Mabini Street
Corner Vito Cruz Street
Malate 1004, Manila, The Philippines
Telephone: (63 2) 50 7051
Facsimile: (63 2) 52 1 5224

Philippine Export and Foreign Loan Guarantee Corporation
Fifth Floor, Executive Building Centre
Corner Puyat Avenue and Makati Avenue
Makati, Metro Manila, 1200 The Philippines
Telephone: (63 2) 818 0316
Facsimile: (63 2) 895 1416

Singaporean addresses

International Factors (Singapore)
C/– ECICS Holdings
141 Market Street
10–00 International Factors Building
Singapore 0104, Singapore
Telephone: (65) 272 8866
Facsimile: (65) 226 2129

Monetary Authority of Singapore
10 Shenton Way
MAS Building
Singapore 0207, Singapore
Telephone: (65) 225 5577
Facsimile: (65) 229 9491

Thai addresses

Export–Import Bank of Thailand
Boon Pong Tower
1193 Phaholyothin Road
Bangkok 10400, Thailand
Telephone: (66 2) 271 3700
Facsimile: (66 2) 271 3029

APPENDIX 12.2: Australian and ASEAN-country addresses for specialist sources of export-credit insurance

Australian addresses

Export Finance and Insurance Corporation (EFIC)
Export House
Level 8, 22 Pitt Street
Sydney 2000, NSW, Australia
Telephone: (61 2) 9201 2111
Facsimile: (61 2) 9251 3851

Indonesian addresses

Asuransi Ekspor Indonesia (ASEI)
JL MH Thamrin, No. 11
Jakarta 10350, Indonesia
Telephone: (62 21) 390 2050
Facsimile: (62 21) 323 662

Malaysian addresses

Malaysia Export Credit Insurance
Bangunan Bank Industri
Levels 12 and 13, Jalan Sultan Ismail
Kuala Lumpur 50250, Malaysia
Telephone: (60 3) 291 0677
Facsimile: (60 3) 291 0353

Philippine addresses

Philippine Export–Import and Foreign Loan Guarantee Operation
Fifth Floor, Executive Building Centre
Corner Puyat Avenue and Makati Avenue
Makati, Metrol Manila, 1200 The Philippines
Telephone: (63 2) 818 0316
Facsimile: (63 2) 895 1416

Singaporean addresses

ECICS Credit Insurance
141 Market Street
10–00 International Factors Building
Singapore 0104, Singapore
Telephone: (65) 272 8866
Facsimile: (65) 226 0939

Thai addresses

Export–Import Bank of Thailand
Boon Pong Tower
1193 Phaholyothin Road
Bangkok 10400, Thailand
Telephone: (66 2) 271 3700
Facsimile: (66 2) 271 3029

13

Legal systems in ASEAN

Alice de Jonge

Introduction

Many factors influence the way in which societies and the legal systems within them develop. Geography, for example, can determine whether a society is land centred – relying on the soil's fertility, or sea oriented – relying on the fruits of the ocean. It is believed that more complex forms of agricultural co-operation and social regulation are more likely to develop in the former than in the latter. Climate, natural resources, language, culture and religion are other important factors that influence development of the formal and informal rules that are found in all societies. If these factors are understood, the context in which a legal system has been born and developed may be understood. In South-East Asia, this understanding can also aid the foreigner in recognising the many diversities of a region that is all too often described and thought of in terms of over-generalised and artificial similarities and unities.

Contemporary South-East Asia's economic, political, linguistic, cultural and demographic diversity is reflected in its legal systems. Historically, the artificial 'national' boundaries that exist between identities such as Malaysia, Singapore and Indonesia played a major part in the creation of fragmented national legal systems, which were developed to serve the interests of diversified societies. Only if this fact is understood can the outsider begin to identify the close relationship that exists between history, ethnicity and politics on the one hand and the regulation and conduct of foreign commerce, investment and commercial dispute resolution on the other. Having this understanding can mean that doing business in the region is an easier, a smoother and a much more pleasant journey to embark on. It can also prove to be invaluable in early identification of warning signals, thereby enabling the Australian partner to take action that is swifter and more appropriate than is often now the case.

In this chapter these matters are addressed on an ASEAN-country basis, covering Brunei, Indonesia, Malaysia, the Philippines, Singapore, Thailand and Vietnam, respectively.

Brunei

Having been a British colony for many years, the tiny Sultanate of Brunei inherited a legal system that is based on English common law. Most of its important legislation can be traced back to UK laws. The Application of Laws Act, for example, expressly incorporates into local law the UK Sale of Goods Act 1893 along with most other UK statutes that govern commercial transactions – statutes that were enacted before 25 April 1951 (the date of incorporation). Laws that govern intellectual property rights are also based on English legislative precedents. In the case of patents, an even stronger link with Britain exists – in Brunei, patent protection stems from a patent's having been granted in Britain; after that granting, patent protection automatically extends to Brunei.

Another British law that applies in Brunei under the Application of Laws Act, is the English Foreign Judgements (Reciprocal Enforcement) Act 1933. Under that Act, which closely resembles Australia's *Foreign Judgements Act* 1991, court judgements that are rendered in a reciprocating country (including Australia) can be registered and enforced in Brunei. The evidentiary and procedural rules for registration of a foreign judgement that is issued by the High Court of Brunei also closely resemble the rules of Australia's High Court.

Although many of Brunei's commercial laws and practices may at first seem familiar to Australians, significant differences exist. In particular, Brunei's legal system – like its economy – is dominated by two essential influences that are not found in Australia's business law. For the foreigner, the first and most obvious difference is the country's Islamic faith; the second difference is the dual nature of the legal system as a whole. Although Brunei's royal family is a dominant force in the country's economy, it is in many cases exempt from the local legal and regulatory restrictions that govern ordinary commercial relationships. Royal-family imports, for example, are exempt from customs inspection and are not recorded in the official trade statistics. Although royal-family economic activities are not recorded in the official national statistics, it seems reasonably certain they account for a significant proportion of total internal and external economic activity. For example, more than 40 per cent of Brunei's demand for live animals for *halal* slaughter is supplied by the government's Australia-based cattle-export company.

The royal family's economic role has to be understood in the context of the country's overall political system. In Brunei, political and legal ideology is based on the concept of the Malay Islam Monarchy (*Melayu Islam Beraja*). This concept, which in July 1990 was outlined by Sultan Hassanal Bolkiah, emphasises that Brunei is a Malay State, that the official religion is Islam and that the government system is an absolute monarchy whereby loyalty to the sultan is demanded. In a legal context, Hassanal is the supreme executive and sovereign. He rules by decree using advice from a Cabinet of eleven ministers and has the power to dispose of all State assets – including land – as he sees fit. He is prime minister and minister for defence, and two of his brothers hold the key ministries of foreign affairs and finance. In this system of government, neither the sultan nor, indeed, any member of Brunei's executive is answerable to any independent parliamentary body – because there is none. The system as a whole can perhaps best be described as hierarchical: the order of legal precedence extends from the sultan and the royal family down through ministers, permanent secretaries, heads of departments and others. People who are in the private sector and who have poorer working conditions and much less prestige are at the bottom of the hierarchy. Even prominent businesspeople can find themselves not even being acknowledged on ceremonial occasions.

Although in 1959 a Constitution was proclaimed that provided for a Legislative Council, the Council was suspended in 1984 on the country's regaining of independence. A state of emergency that was declared after a coup was attempted in 1962 continues to be renewed every two years by the sultan. The sultan has also made statements that emphasise the Bruneian system's proven virtues and Islam's important role in national affairs. A strong tradition exists of deference to the sultan's authority, and in an economy that continues to flourish there seems to be little reason for opposition groups to develop. The citizens at least seem to be generally content with their stable if somewhat authoritarian government system. The people who conceivably have most cause for discontent, given their relative poverty and low social status, are the many foreign workers and stateless permanent residents, who comprise more than 40 per cent of the population. Brunei's 50,000 ethnic-Chinese people have also suffered due to the Hassanal regime's explicit emphasis on Malay ascendency as reflected in the doctrine of the Malay Muslim Monarchy. The ethnic-Chinese are being steadily squeezed out of jobs (and contracts), despite the fact that Brunei is chronically short of labour, and are thereby being squeezed out of the country.

However, as Brunei becomes further integrated in the international economy, the royal family's activities – both locally and internationally – may be subjected to a wider range of regulatory and other restrictions. In 1984, Brunei became a UN member and ASEAN's sixth member. It is a member of the Commonwealth, the Organization of Islamic States Conference, the APEC forum and, since 1992, the Non-Aligned Movement. In November 1993 it became GATT's one-hundred-and-seventeenth member and it is now a World Trade Organisation (WTO) member.

Because of all these developments, Brunei's government is gradually being subjected to the rules, standards and standard-setting procedures that are set by international and regional organisations. As a member of these organisations it also participates in development and supervision of codes that are set out in instruments such as the Convention on the Enforcement of Foreign Arbitral Awards, the Convention which established the International Centre for the Settlement of Investment Disputes (ICSID), the United Nations Draft Code of Conduct on Transnational Corporations, and the APEC Bogor Declaration. These instruments and organisations must surely operate as forces for political, economic and social change in Brunei, a country that is heavily dependent on foreign investment for its future development and prosperity. At the very least, the existence of international standards that govern relationships between government entities and foreign nationals means that investors are provided with an avenue of recourse should arbitrary or unfair treatment occur. In particular, in any government contract, foreign investors should be sure to include an agreement that any dispute be submitted to international arbitration in, say, Kuala Lumpur or Singapore or another neutral body, for resolution under either the ICSID guidelines or another appropriate set of international arbitration rules.

Foreign investors' increasing presence in Brunei (and, conversely, the increasing presence of Bruneian investment abroad) is another force behind recent economic, social and political changes. Signs that change is occurring can be found in, for example, the sultan's 1994 National Day speech. In commemorating 10 years of independence, he stated that a review of the 1959 Constitution would be completed in the near future and would result in 'certain changes' that he was confident his people would be pleased with. Whether this leads to the placing of more emphasis on individual rights and freedoms and on democratic values remains to be seen.

One historical force that is less likely to diminish, though, is the influence of Islam. Throughout the 1990s, the sultan and the government have continued to emphasise Islam's primacy, both as a guide to daily living and as the basis for ethical policy making. Islam is not only Brunei's official religion; it permeates the country's social and economic life. Indeed, the strength of Islamic morality and principles of justice is probably greater in Brunei than anywhere else in South-East Asia. Islamic principles can, for example, often form the basis of commercial transactions. Institutions such as the Islamic Bank of Brunei and the Islamic Insurance Company (both established in 1993) provide Muslims with the opportunity to conduct their financial affairs according to Islamic banking principles, in which charging interest on loans is forbidden. Non-Muslims who seek to operate in Brunei should also be aware of the importance of conducting business negotiations and other commercial activities to ensure there is no conflict with the demands of the Islamic religious calendar. It is also worth noting that imported goods are likely to be scrutinised and excluded for containing substances that offend Islamic sensitivities much more than for containing illegal items. Brunei's religious leaders regularly denounce imported goods that may have been tainted by alcohol, or pork-derived additives, non-*halal* slaughtered beef and other meat products. Goods that have been subjected to this denouncement can be almost impossible to sell in the local market.

Brunei's Economic Development Board has recognised the need to promote foreign investment as a means of stimulating the country's sluggish private sector. Despite the existence of generous tax incentives that are aimed at diversifying the economy away from oil and gas, setting up is rarely cheap or easy. Skilled workers are difficult to find locally, and recruiting workers abroad can mean you have to pay expensive airfares, housing costs and food costs. Brunei's steep charges for freight and telecommunications are another burden, and quick customs approval for exports can be difficult to obtain. The bureaucracy is slow moving, and paperwork should be planned carefully. The local business-day routine is one whereby, in the words of one investor, 'everything has to be settled before 11.30', and an extra burden is thereby added to the obtaining of shipping documents. When viewed in combination with the public sector's importance for the local economy in general, these problems can mean that finding the right (well-connected) investment partner is essential. Some foreigners also state that many Bruneian officials do not want the outside social influences that come with foreign investment. Although one may not experience any overt discrimination, it pays to remember that Brunei is, after all, an Islamic State in which alcohol, *karaoke* and public dancing remain officially banned.

At the same time, however, there is no doubt that the government is currently making a concerted effort to court foreign investment, and a number of highly lucrative incentives have been made available; no personal income tax, no sales tax, payroll, manufacturing or export tax. Pioneer investment incentives are also available to any firm seeking to invest in an industry not previously carried on in Brunei on a commercial scale suited to the country's economic requirements. There must also be a favourable prospect of further developing the industry for export, and it must be one which it is in the public interest to develop.[1] Pioneer companies (which must be limited liability companies) can be granted an extendable company tax holiday of between two and five years, depending on the amount invested, and are also entitled to customs duty exemptions for imported capital equipment. Brunei also has the most flexible attitude to foreign ownership in the region. While joint ventures with local partners are encouraged, there are no restrictions on foreign participation in equity except industries related to national security and a small number of reserved industries. In addition to a number of industrial estates throughout the country which provide modernised infrastructure and business environment, there is also the huge international-standard shipping and warehouse facility at Muara. Finally, there is no doubt that Brunei's strategic position in the heart of South-East Asia remains one of its most promising and attractive features.

Indonesia

Indonesia is the world's most expansive archipelago: it comprises more than 13,500 islands, 6000 of which are inhabited. It has more than 300 identifiable ethnic groups, the members of most of which speak their own distinct language or dialect. At least 250 distinct regional languages have been identified, of which the most widely used (especially in government) is Javanese (despite the fact that the official language is Bahasa Indonesia). All these facts bear repeating, because knowledge of them helps to explain the equally diverse nature of the country's legal system. Historically, this diversity stemmed from the fact that the system developed from many sources.

The first source is Dutch law – the legacy of more than 300 years of Dutch occupation and control. The Dutch civil-law system and Dutch jurisprudence that is rooted in the civil-law tradition were introduced in Indonesia in the seventeenth century, and much of the colonial law continues to apply today. In 1945 on the country's gaining of independence, given the revolutionary context and political turmoil it was decided that a transitional clause be inserted in the new Constitution: that all former existing laws and regulations continue to exist, at least until new ones can be brought in to replace them. However, the replacement process has been slow, and much of the current Civil Code and Commercial Code is seriously outdated. Moreover, a strong Dutch flavour continues to exist in legal training, official court procedures and the way in which judges and lawyers express themselves in court.

Economic-law reform has recently been forced apace by Indonesia's signing of the APEC Bogor Declaration and its acceding to the results of the Uruguay Round of GATT negotiations. Since 1990, existence of a series of deregulation packages has served to improve incentives and bring about an overall liberalisation of foreign investment. A new Bill on investment is currently being drafted in order to replace the Foreign Investment Law 1967 and Domestic Investment Law 1968. The new Bill is aimed at complying with the AFTA, GATT and APEC principles of equal treatment and non-discrimination and will serve to eliminate discriminatory distinctions between foreign investment and domestic investment, to maintain and improve incentives and to simplify foreign-investment procedures.

In early 1995 a new Company Law was enacted that replaced the Company Law that had originated from the outdated (1848) provisions of the Dutch Commercial Code. The new law has long been needed for dealing with modern business practices such as acquisitions and mergers and for providing for elements such as protection of minority-shareholder interests. Intellectual property rights have also been improved and reformed, in accordance with the principles of the Uruguay Round agreement on Trade Related Aspects of Intellectual Property Rights (TRIPS). The Copyright Law 1987 and the Patent Law 1989 provide for compliance with the minimum standards of copyright and patent protection as stated under the 1967 Paris Convention, and the 1971 Berne Convention. Although other areas of protection that are covered by the TRIPS agreement, such as computer programs, are also protected under the Copyright Law, the brevity of the protection's duration has been criticised. At the time of writing, a Bill on industrial design and closed-circuit transmission was also being drafted so that the standards provided for in the 1989 Treaty on Intellectual Property in Respect of Integrated Circuits can be complied with. In relation to trademarks, in 1992 a law on marks was enacted that covers both trade and service marks and replaced the 1961 law that dealt solely with trademarks.

Indonesia's highest law-making body is the *Majelis Permusyawaratan Rakyat* (the parliamentary upper house – hereafter referred to as the MPR), which has 1000 members, 500 of whom are appointed by the president. The 500 members of the *Dewan Perwakilan Rakyat* (House of Representatives – or DPR) form the remainder of the MPR. The president appoints 100 of the DPR members; the other 400 are elected. The MPR is responsible for developing Indonesia's five-year development plans and for making national planning decisions in general. MPR resolutions and decrees issued by the president form the basis of legislation that is enacted by the DPR (the lower legislative body), and that has to be ratified by the president. However, as is often the case in civil-law systems, presidential decrees, MPR resolutions and DPR legislation are typically expressed in vague, general terms. So that they may be implemented, a whole plethora of regulatory instruments are used, including government regulations that are issued by the president (*Peraturan Pemerintah*, or PP), presidential instructions, ministerial decrees, ministerial instructions, ministerial guidelines, and circular letters (all of which have to be in accordance with the 1945 Constitution and MPR policy documents). Especially at the lower levels, the status of rules that have been drafted and 'issued' by senior executives is often uncertain. Problems and uncertainties can also arise if the rules are inconsistent with the internal (often unpublicised) rules of a particular regional authority or non-department agency.

The political concept of *Pancasila*, 'the five principles', has also gained the status of an important legal doctrine and rule of interpretation. The five principles – usually translated as 'belief in One God', 'nationalism', 'humanism', 'democracy' and 'social justice' – are expressly referred to in the preamble to the 1945 Constitution and have been officially interpreted by the MPR. In the national ideology it is required that the principles be referred to by members of the bureaucracy (including judges in their capacity as civil servants of the State), when they are resolving inconsistencies and uncertainties in the law. Legislation and other legal instruments, as well as unwritten legal principles, are (ostensibly at least) also interpreted and applied in accordance with *Pancasila*.

Indonesia's other major source of law is traditional customary law, or *adat*. The relevance of this to any particular case is usually determined by the ethnicity of the people who are involved in the dispute, and a complex body of rules has been developed in order to deal with cases that involve people who are from different ethnic origins. The extent of *adat*'s relevance to any particular case can vary enormously. In many of Indonesia's more isolated rural communities, many people can live out their lives quite happily according to *adat* rules and principles without ever having recourse to the formal legal system. At the other extreme are disputes that involve international transactions, and most of those disputes are now regulated by government legislation that was recently enacted to replace outdated commercial laws or so that wholly new commercial regimes (for example the new Corporations Law and the new Investment Law) could be introduced.

However, the areas in which *adat* law can be relevant for Indonesia's foreign investors and businesspeople are inheritance law and land law. Even a certified title to land that is located in Jakarta's major business districts can be at risk of being claimed by 'owners' who claim they have pre-existing *adat* entitlements to the land. One telling example of the way in which *adat* can be relevant for the foreign investor is the case of Tanah Lot, a famous island temple off the coast of Bali and the site of an Rp400 billion (US$86 million) joint-venture-project proposal. In the proposal, construction of a three-hundred-room hotel, condominiums and a golf course is envisaged on 121 hectares of land that faces one of Indonesia's holiest religious sites. When the provincial government had issued almost all the permits that were necessary for the project's construction, opposition was mounted by local members of Bali's majority Hindu population. When the protesters took their claims to the Hindu Consultative Board, the Board issued a statement: that hotels and other buildings that are erected in the vicinity of *pura*, or temples, should respect the religious norms of *Tri Hita Karana* – a system of geomancy for determining the proper distances to have between sacred and profane objects. The Tanah Lot project would clearly have violated the two-kilometre distance that was required in the Board's *bhisama* (authoritative statement or advice). It has therefore been put on hold while the MPR investigates the matter.[2]

It has been stated that Indonesia is the world's largest Muslim nation. However, this statement has to be read in the context of the nation's geographic, ethnic, cultural and linguistic diversity and resultant religious diversity, as well as in light of its historical development. As more than one writer has observed, what is commonly identified as 'Islamic' today is actually Islam deeply rooted in the rich soils of Hinduism, Buddhism, *adat* and *animism*.[3]

In the formal legal system, Islam's influence has been restricted in that in their jurisdiction the religious (Islamic) courts are limited to matters that involve marriage, reconciliation and divorce. Strictly speaking, *adat* law (over which the district courts and the High Courts[4] have jurisdiction) applies to inheritance and property matters. In practice, though, it is impossible to separate marriage matters from inheritance and property matters, so Islam's influence in family matters extends into the latter areas as well. The way in which this has occurred was succinctly described in 1960 by the Supreme Court when it stated,

> the Supreme Court regards it as clear that in all of Indonesia with respect to inheritance it is essentially the Adat law which applies, which in areas where the influence of Islam is strong contains more or fewer elements of Islamic law.[5]

In Indonesia, any foreign organisation that is unfortunate enough to be caught up in litigation is likely to find itself caught up in attending many court sessions, each of which is interspersed by equally numerous court adjournments. Court procedure is inquisitorial rather than adversarial, and judges may conduct examinations of witnesses and parties as well as supervise prosecutors' investigations. Rights of appeal exist and, given the low court fees involved, have become almost inevitable – indeed, it can often be uneconomical for a losing party *not* to appeal. Litigation of almost any type can therefore last for years before a final and binding judgement is handed down; even then, though, the judgement's execution can be a long, drawn-out process.

The formal procedures of litigation are, however, far less important than the informal influences operating throughout those procedures. It is hard to invest in Indonesia without becoming aware of the 'cronyism' that 'all too often turns into outright corruption',[6] even within the judicial system. Here, the problem has been compounded by the fact that, as bureaucrats, judges receive a low salary which reflects their relatively low status and makes them susceptible to bribery. Even the Minister for Justice, Oetojo Oesman, has admitted the existence of corruption within the judiciary.[7] His comments reflect those of former Deputy Chief Justice Zaenal Asikin Kusumaatmadja, who admitted that judicial power was 'so systematically abused that the justice system was like a business controlled by a "mafia" of Court officials' and that 'bribery was a standard practice, with up to 50 per cent of all Indonesian judges taking bribes'.[8]

It has been suggested, however, that 'Australians involved in Indonesia should look beyond both the formal "black letter" process and the bogey of "corruption" to alternative avenues to settlement when faced with a potentially litigious dispute, instead of dismissing the situation as hopeless'.[9] For the unsatisfactory nature of the formal legal system does not necessarily make it impossible to achieve a fair result. As Indonesian law expert Timothy Lindsey has noted,

> In practice, most Indonesian commercial litigation is resolved not by resort to the Courts, but by alternative dispute resolution. Generally this occurs not through structured mediation, arbitration or conciliation but through informal negotiation, often involving a respected third party with executive or judicial standing.[10]

For the Australian businessperson who prefers a more 'structured' form of alternative dispute resolution, there is arbitration; also a well-established and widely accepted format, particularly when foreign parties are involved. The current locally based commercial arbitration-dispute-resolution centre is the *Badan Arbitrase Nasional Indonesia* (Indonesian National Arbitration Authority – BANI) which was established in December 1977 by the *Kamar Dagang Indonesia* (the Indonesian Chamber of Commerce and Industry – KADIN). The centre was established in order to provide for settlement of commercial disputes of either a national or an international character. The International Chamber of Commerce (ICC) arbitration rules and the United Nations Commission on International Trade Law (UNCITRAL) arbitration clause are commonly favoured by the parties to an international transaction and can be used whenever BANI-based arbitration is chosen. Also, in a number of cases the Supreme Court has demonstrated it will uphold and give effect to arbitration clauses contained in commercial contracts. In 1968 the government ratified the ICSID Convention, the provisions of which were made effective through Law No. 5 of 29 June 1968. Because in the Convention the parties' express consent is required before ICSID Arbitration can occur, investors should ensure an appropriate clause is inserted in all government agreements that relate to their investment. The Investment Law 1967 also contains a reference to arbitration and makes arbitration compulsory if the foreign-investment company is 'nationalised' and the company considers the amount of compensation decided on to be insufficient.

In cases in which arbitration occurs outside Indonesia, enforcement of it can be difficult. Although in 1981 the New York Convention on Recognition and Enforcement of Foreign Arbitral Awards was ratified by presidential decree, because no legislation was implemented for bringing it into effect it was practically impossible to enforce foreign arbitral awards. This situation continued until 1990 when the Supreme Court issued implementing regulations for the 1981 decree. Although it now seems foreign arbitral awards can be enforced, the Supreme Court has demonstrated it can and will refuse to enforce an award if it is one whereby principles of Indonesian public policy are violated.

If a dispute is mediated informally, the parties can make use of the fact that throughout Indonesia, business is based on overlapping networks of relationships; in other words, in business relationships, emphasis is placed on the personal relationship that exists between individuals who are doing business. During the first stages of a relationship, the *process* of negotiation can be more important than the final result that is achieved. Strong personal relationships can help prevent problems or disputes and can also be called on if relationships actually begin to break down. If direct negotiation is unsuccessful as a method of dispute resolution, indirect negotiation can be used as a means of preventing development of any more antagonism or of preventing either party's being forced to 'lose face'. One common way in which this success might be achieved is if a socially eminent and respected third person (for example, a retired judge or an official) trust by both parties, who can help them continue the negotiations, adopt a new approach to the dispute and develop a new solution, often in the form of a mutually acceptable compromise.

Malaysia

As both a federation and a former British colony, Malaysia has a legal system that – superficially, at least – in its overall structure strongly resembles Australia's. The written law comprises

- the federal Constitution and the Constitutions of the thirteen states
- legislation enacted by parliament and the state assemblies, under their respective constitutional powers
- subsidiary, or delegated, legislation that is made by people or bodies, under powers that have been conferred on them by other Acts of Parliament or state assemblies.

Like their Australian counterparts, Malaysia's commonly British-trained judges tend to turn to British and other Commonwealth precedents for guidance and inspiration in their decision making. However, the existence of a number of factors – including the influence of Islamic legal principles, express recognition of customary practices (or *adat*) as a source of law, and the royal familyies' position – has served to create a system that is entirely unique and entirely 'Malaysian'.

The present-day Constitution resulted from a merger between the Federation of Malaya, Sabah, Sarawak and Singapore. When Singapore left the federation in 1965, Malaysia was left with thirteen states, and since that time the federal territories of Kuala Lumpur and Labuan have been created in Selangor and Sabah, respectively. Malaysia's head of state is its king, or *yang di-pertuan agong*, who is elected every five years, on a rotational basis, from among the nine hereditary rulers[11] of the traditional Malay states. Four states (Malacca, Penang, Sabah and Sarawak) are headed by governors, or *yang-di pertua negeri*. A governor is appointed by the king, in consultation with the chief minister of the state in question, for a four-year term.

The nine rulers and the four governors constitute the Conference of Rulers, the main functions of which are consideration of views on matters of public importance and exchanging of views with the federal government.

In the past, royalty's power and influence, and the royal-family members' freedom from control by the courts was a source of controversy. The most recent (1993) confrontation between the government and the rulers led to the introduction of constitutional amendments whereby the royal-family members' various personal legal immunities were narrowed considerably. That incident also served to underline the executive's dominance in the the country's governance.

The executive's dominance in the country's running stems partly from Malaysia's system of constitutional government and partly from the way in which economic planning is undertaken at the federal level. The executive comprises the prime minister and the other Cabinet members, the latter of whom are nominated by the prime minister (from either house of parliament) and formally appointed by the king. The prime minister is also appointed by the king on the basis that he or she is the person who enjoys the confidence of the majority of the *Dewan Ra'ayat* (the lower house, or House of Representatives). Finally, the king also acts on prime-ministerial advice in appointing 32 members to the *Dewan Negara* (the upper house, or Senate). The other 26 members of the 58-member *Dewan Negara* are indirectly elected – two by each of the 13 state legislatures. Because all the state legislatures with the exception of Kalimantan are now controlled by the ruling *Barisan Nasional* coalition that dominates the *Dewan Ra'ayat*, legislative programs that originate in the *Dewan Ra'ayat* have virtually automatic approval from the *Dewan Negara*.

As a result of this structure the prime minister – and through him the *Barisan Nasional* – exercises control over both houses of parliament. In the case of the lower house, for which members are elected from single-member constituencies, the simple-majority electoral system has operated in favour of the *Barisan Nasional* and therefore in favour of the UMNO and its successor, the UMNO *Baru*, which has dominated the coalition since the coalition's formation.[12] The most recent (May 1995) elections resulted in the ruling coalition party's holding 83 per cent of the 180 *Dewan Ra'ayat* seats.

Traditionally, the UMNO government has played a very strong hand in Malaysia's economic-development targets and priorities, which are established under successive five-year plans ('Malaysia Plans'), and in managing the economy through using an associated network of bureaucratic management and administrative controls. These plans have so far been aimed at improving the *bumiputera* population's position in the economy and at protecting key infant industries in the name of industrialisation. Under this system, a number of matters that are of importance for both foreign investors and local businesses are governed by various ministries' policy directives (for example the New Development Policy). Although they are not law, the directives are often incorporated in contracts and are used as decision-making guidelines in government departments as well as in licensing authorities and other statutory authorities. Therefore, the system to a great extent relies on the exercise of administrative discretion in decision making.

An example of this is enactment of the Industrial Co-ordination Act 1975, whereby the MITI was given the power to impose *bumiputera*-shareholding and other conditions on issue or renewal of manufacturing and other compulsory business licences, as well as wide discretion in granting tax and other incentives. Such wide-ranging powers inevitably create scope for nepotism and favouritism in the allocation of shareholding rights and the granting of licences and incentives. Other areas of the regulatory system are similarly responsible for providing government officials with substantial discretionary powers in targeting business incentives and other forms of government support. They have also been responsible for creating an undesirable dependence on government support in a number of industries.

Government members have also entered business in significant numbers, thereby strengthening the government's role in the economy even more. This has stemmed in part from the existence of a deliberate policy of encouragement under which ordinary parliamentarians are remunerated at rates that are noticeably lower than those that are available in the private sector. Ostensibly, this is so that politicians are encouraged to participate in and thereby keep in touch with the problems of ordinary citizens in business, industry and commerce. However, it has also had the disadvantage that politicians have been driven to use means, both laudable and otherwise, of achieving a higher standard of living.

The central planning system has had one major advantage, though: it has aided the implementation of a unified and centrally co-ordinated economic-growth program throughout Malaysia. Even today, one of the Malaysian federation of states' most noticeable characteristics is its many varieties of culture, language, religion, ethnic origin and historical origin. Portuguese, Dutch, Roman Catholic and Protestant influences can be found in Malacca, for example – a legacy of the country's first period of colonial control, from 1511 to the late eighteenth century. Most of Peninsular Malaysia is a 'melting pot' of Malay, Chinese and Indian influences, and Islamic influences are probably strongest in the northern states. With reference to the East Malaysian states of Sabah and Sarawak, Kadazan and Chinese people dominate the former whereas Dayak and Chinese people dominate the latter.

It is these differences that have led to the establishment of a fragmented legal system, a good example of which is the separate legal status that is given to Sabah and Sarawak under the federal Constitution.[13] In the Constitution, a federal division of law-making powers is established in the form of three 'lists'. Under the 'states list', the state governments are given control over Islamic Law and a number of other areas that are viewed as being 'local' matters, whereas under the 'concurrent list', the states share with the federal government a number of other legislative powers. However, should any inconsistency occur, federal law would prevail. A number of extra legislative powers are vested in the state governments of Sabah and Sarawak, including those that relate to religion, the special position of the natives, the national language, the judiciary and emergency powers. The third 'list', the federal one, bears a strong resemblance to a similar list of the Australian federal government's legislative powers that is contained in Australia's Constitution.

A tripartite legal system and system of courts exists. Up until 23 June 1994, the three-tiered common law court structure consisted of the Supreme Court, the highest court in the country; two high courts – one for Peninsular Malaysia's states and the other for the states of Sabah and Sarawak – and the subordinate courts (for example magistrates' courts and sessions courts). However, from late June 1994 this situation has changed, following the making of amendments to the Federal Constitution and enactment of the Courts of Judicature Act 1994. The country's highest court is now known as the Federal Court, underneath which is a new 'Court of Appeal'. Appeals from the two high courts – which have retained their former original and appellate jurisdiction over civil (and criminal) matters – now go to the Court of Appeal, which is presided over by a president and two Court of Appeal judges. Further appeals to the Federal Court are permitted, with the court's leave, in civil matters that involve more than RM250,000.[14]

The states establish the *syariah*, or Islamic courts, of which there are three levels: the Syariah Appeal Court, the Syariah High Court and the Syariah Subordinate Court. In the states of Sarawak and Sabah there is a special court system for dealing with matters that involve questions of native law (*adat*). In Sarawak this system comprises the Native Court of Appeal, the Resident's Native Court, the Native Officer's Court, and the headman's courts. In Sabah it comprises the Native Court of Appeal, the district officer's courts, and the native courts.

A Regional Centre for Arbitration also exists that was established in 1978 in Kuala Lumpur under the auspices of the Asian–African Legal Consultative Committee. The Centre is intended to serve the Asia–Pacific region and operates according to an adapted version of the UNCITRAL arbitration rules. Under a number of co-operative agreements made between the Centre and other arbitration centres located in the region, the Centre offers arbitration facilities under the auspices of the ICSID, the American Arbitration Association and Australia's national institutions such as the Australian Centre for International Commercial Arbitration (ACICA).

In Malaysia, arbitration is regulated by the Arbitration Act 1952 (UK), Order 69 of the Rules of the High Court 1980 and the rules that operate in the various specialised arbitration tribunals. When the arbitration itself occurs outside Malaysia, the resultant award can be enforced in Malaysia under the rules of the widely recognised UN Convention on the Recognition and Enforcement of Foreign Arbitral Awards (the 1958 New York Convention). Because both Malaysia and Australia are party to that treaty, the circumstances in which an arbitral award that has been obtained in Australia can be enforced in Malaysia are essentially similar to those in which an Australian court will enforce a foreign arbitral award under the *Foreign Arbitral Awards (Recognition and Enforcement) Act 1991* (Cwlth).

As a member of the International Convention on the Settlement of Investment Disputes Between States and Nationals of Other States 1965, Malaysia has also enacted the Convention on the Settlement of Investment Disputes Act 1966 and the Arbitration (Amendment) Act 1980. If an ICSID arbitration clause has been inserted in an investment agreement, as a condition of the state's acceptance of ICSID jurisdiction the government can require the foreign investor to first exhaust all available local remedies. Furthermore, in the absence of the parties' agreeing on the applicable law, ICSID tribunals usually apply the law of the host state, together with whatever rules of international law may be applicable. Once obtained, ICSID-tribunal awards have the finality of decisions made by a member country's national courts and are not subject to review by those courts.

Under the revised Civil Law Act 1972, common-law principles that were derived from UK and Commonwealth court decisions form an important reference source for Malaysia's civil courts. A number of UK commercial statutes have also been directly incorporated in Malaysia's legal system. For historical reasons, the laws that govern commercial transactions are now structured along two separate lines. In the Borneo states of Sabah and Sarawak, and the West Malaysian states of Penang and Malacca, the law that is to be administered 'shall be the same as would be administered in England in the like case at the corresponding period'. The 'corresponding period' means 'at the time the transaction was entered into'. With reference to the rest of the federation though, the law that applies is the law that was in force in the UK at the date of incorporation (1956) plus any subsequent, locally enacted legislation.[15] UK legislation that was enacted after 1956, such as the Sale of Goods Act 1979, therefore operates in Penang, Malacca, Sabah and Sarawak but does not apply in the rest of Malaysia, in which the earlier (1893) version of the Sale of Goods Act alone is adopted. It is interesting to note that Australian laws have sometimes also been used as a model. For example, the Malaysian Companies Act 1965 was originally based on the (now repealed) Australian Uniform Companies Code 1961, and Malaysia has also chosen to adopt the Torrens-title land-registration system. More recently, the securities-industries legislation in Malaysia closely resembles the corresponding Australian regime.

Islamic-law commercial principles also influence commercial practices and business organisation. It has been stated that 'Islam in not merely a religion in Malaysia; it embraces the whole of life, encompassing a legal, social and moral order'.

Islam is given constitutional status as the country's official religion, and enjoys express royal patronage by the federation's various state rulers who in their states are guardians of religion. The *yang di-pertuan agong* (supreme ruler of the federation) is the guardian of the states that do not have a ruler: Malacca, Penang, Sabah and Sarawak and the federal territories of Kuala Lumpur and Labuan. Throughout South-East Asia the Malay language has also become the language of Islam as well as the common language of Muslims in Indonesia, Brunei, Singapore, Thailand and other Asian countries.

Prime Minister Dr Mahathir and Finance Minister and Deputy Prime Minister Anwar Ibrahim provide strong leadership for UMNO's progressive Islamic forces. At policy-making level and working 'hand in hand' with many of Malaysia's religious leaders, businesspeople and public-policy planners, Dr Mahathir has been the driving force behind establishment of a government 'think-tank' that is devoted to the integration of Islamic ethics with economic progress. The *Institut Kefahaman Islam Malaysia* (Institute of Islamic Understanding Malaysia – IKIM) was formally inaugurated in 1992, partly due to Malaysian leaders' concern that Islam may be negatively affected in a world of rapid change. The *Institut*'s charter is to redefine Islam's role in the betterment of Malaysia's economic and social interests.

Islam's influence on government policy making is also evident in the (1983) launching of Bank Islam. This was established in order to offer Malaysian Muslims the opportunity to engage in commercial activities without violating Islamic rules against interest earning (*riba*). Since that time, Malaysia has also become the world's first country to introduce a fully fledged Islamic banking system, including a range of sophisticated interest-free instruments and Islamic investment products. Concerned that too many of their clients were switching to Islamic banks, conventional financial institutions are also introducing interest-free banking services, which have proven to be highly competitive. Most recently, a consortium of Malaysian banks that is headed by DCB Bank Bhd launched a fund of more than 200 million ringgit that is specifically aimed at financing *bumiputera* businesses and joint ventures.

As is the case with many of Malaysia's commercial laws, the laws that govern protection of intellectual property rights bear strong resemblance to their original UK laws. The Copyright Act 1987 (as amended in 1990) protects authors of literary, musical and artistic works as well as creators of 'neighbouring rights' such as films, sound recordings and broadcasts. Artistic works are now defined as including computer software. The protection the Act provides is similar to the protection the corresponding Australian Act provides. In the area of trademarks, the Trade Marks Act 1976 came into force in September 1983. Trademarks are protected on their being registered locally. However, the Trade Description Act 1972 remains the single-most effective piece of legislation for combating counterfeiting and passing-off. Under it, the aggrieved proprietor of a trademark (whether it is registered or not) can apply to the High Court for a Trade Description Order, whereby he or she is enabled to lodge a formal complaint with MITI's Enforcement Division. The Division has the power to raid property, seize offending (counterfeited) goods and prosecute an offender.

In Malaysia, patents can be registered under the Patents Act 1983 (as amended in 1986). Registration requirements are similar to the ones that exist in Australia. For inventions that do not satisfy the requirement of an 'inventive step', which is necessary for a full patent to be granted, the Patents Act establishes a 'utility-innovation system' whereby less protection is granted; this is similar to the system that is provided in Australia for petty patents. Although no system exists for processing industrial designs, registration can be sought in the UK under the Registered Designs Act 1949 (UK). On registration, the protection that is provided in the UK by virtue of that registration will automatically extend to all the Malaysian states except Sabah. If no registration exists, the common-law requirements for obtaining a remedy with reference to the common-law tort of passing-off are very similar to those that apply in Australia. The remedies that are available include interlocutory injunctions, delivering-up of the infringing goods, and damages.

The Philippines

As a historical consequence of the Philippines' having been under the rule of both Spain (1565–1898) and the US (1898–1946), the country's legal system is characterised by a mixture of both civil-law and common-law systems. The Civil Code and the Penal Code, for example, are substantially based on Spanish law, whereas commercial law, negotiable-instruments law, taxation law, constitutional law and remedial law are all mainly derived from US law. The Philippine legal profession is also modelled on the US legal profession.

A similar combination of influences is evident in the social sphere: although much of the country's older architecture and a strong Roman Catholic Church remain as reflections of its Spanish origins, the English language and American culture are dominating influences, particularly with reference to young people. The 'picture' is further complicated by the presence of a strong, if small (5 per cent) Muslim population, which is mainly based in Mindanao, Sulu and other southern provinces that are near Borneo.

Under the Philippines' 1987 Constitution, the form of government is 'unitary', and, like the US government system, this is based on separation of powers between executive presidency, bicameral legislature and independent judiciary. The president is the head of state, chief executive of the republic, and the armed forces' commander-in-chief. The president is elected by popular election for a six-year term and is not qualified to be re-elected. Executive powers are even more constrained by virtue of the simple fact that for most administrative policies and programs, legislative underpinning is required, and these therefore depend on Congress's support. In the Constitution there is also an American-style Bill of Rights whereby, unlike the case with the American Bill, emphasis is placed on economic and social (as distinct from civil and political) rights. The Bill of Rights and a number of other constitutional provisions and recognised implied limitations on congressional powers serve to somewhat limit the extent to which Congress is otherwise enabled to 'legislate on any area of activity'.

The bicameral Congress consists of a 24-member Senate, which is elected nationwide, and a House of Representatives, which is largely elected through single-member constituencies (200 members), as well as a possible maximum of 50 members who the president may appoint to represent minority groups. Because party machinery and discipline are not well developed, a situation has resulted whereby administration bills – even when they are non-controversial – often 'languish' on an overloaded legislative agenda. Lack of party cohesion and the detrimental effects of this on administrative effectiveness became particularly evident during the six turbulent years of the Aquino presidency, which began in early 1986 following the overthrow of the Marcos government's martial-law regime.

Senatorial and local elections were first held in 1987, and in May 1992, during the Philippines' first 'free' presidential elections, Corazon Aquino was replaced by Fidel Ramos. Since that time, Ramos has managed to consolidate political support for himself and his party, thereby creating an environment of relative political stability. From the May 1995 elections onwards, the Ramos-led *Lakas*–National Union Christian Democrats (NUCD) party and its coalition partners have dominated the lower house. In August–September 1994, the Administration *Lakas*–NUCD party forged an official alliance with the *Lakas ng Democratikong Pilipino* (Liberal Democratic Party – LDP) in order to field a common ticket for the 1995 congressional elections and to draw up a common legislative program. The government was thereby given a large majority in the Senate which enabled it to deliver the passage of some crucial legislation. Among the laws was included ratification of the Uruguay Round results and enactment of a new law for promoting private-sector participation in construction and infrastructure. The latter was achieved through streamlining of approval procedures and making it possible for the government to guarantee projects in transport, power, telecommunications and other areas that use overseas development assistance funds. The common-ticket agreement was also responsible for ensuring the coalition retained its two-thirds Senate majority from the time the elections were held.

Other important recent developments have included the strengthening of intellectual property rights protection under the Philippine Patent Law as amended (RA No. 165), Presidential Decree No. 49 (Copyright Law) and the Philippine Trademark Law as amended (RA No. 166). The Philippines is signatory to international conventions on intellectual property rights, and the legislation reflects this. The government has also created an inter-agency committee to serve as the central body for formulating policy, monitoring enforcement and orchestrating efforts of the government and private sector to protect IP. Where intellectual property is transferred in the form of a technology transfer agreement (such as a licensing agreement) or technical assistance agreement, these must be registered with the Philippine Technology Transfer Registry.[16]

With reference to law-making powers, the Constitution establishes a system of citizens' initiated referendum, under which any law that is enacted by either Congress or a local government body (provinces, cities, municipalities and *barangays* in rural areas) can be rejected through the holding of a popular referendum. However, this Constitutional provision was not implemented until 1989 (Republic Act No. 6735, 1989); nor, to the author's knowledge, has it been used so far. A more important illustration of the political challenges that face the Ramos Administration lies in the role played by the Supreme Court.

The Supreme Court heads the Philippine judiciary, which also consists of the Court of Appeal, the regional trial courts, metropolitan trial courts, city municipal courts, municipal courts and municipal circuit trial courts. There is also a court that specifically deals with corruption cases (the *Sandiganbayan*). Under a February 1977 presidential decree, in July 1985 Islamic *shari'a* courts were established in the southern Philippines. As in Malaysia, the *shari'a* courts' jurisdiction is confined mainly to family and inheritance law matters. Since that time relations between the judiciary and the government have been testy, mainly because both sides have been subjected to the influences of directly opposed political interest groups.

With reference to Congress and the executive, many civil servants and politicians are members of large, land-owning families and rely on the traditional politics of patronage. Other people are members of a new, professional and business, urban elite that can rely on support from economically powerful colleagues. Senators, who are mostly drawn from prominent families, tend to be prominent lawyers, business-people or former government ministers and senior officials.[17] Despite the proliferation of non-government organisations (NGOs) and 'cause-oriented' groups, virtually no mainstream 'Left' or 'Green' representation exists in either Congress or the Administration. However, this situation has improved since a new system of party listings was introduced that is designed to provide congressional representation for smaller parties.

Public interest groups have, though, used with effect the Supreme Court's experience in constitutional law that has been inherited from the US. In April 1995, for example, a major Ramos project – a computerised lottery – was blocked by the Supreme Court following filing of a complaint by various citizens' groups. Popular opposition to the Ramos Administration's proposal for an expanded value-added tax (VAT) also led to the Supreme Court's granting of an injunction in order to restrain the new tax's implementation. Even after the Supreme Court finally ruled in favour of the legislation, the injunction remained temporarily in place, and one of the government's key tools for broadening the country's narrow tax base was thereby frustrated.

The provinces, particularly the southern islands of Mindanao and Sulu, also represent a potential challenge to central government power. In June 1995, popular Senator Gloria Macapagal-Arroyo proposed that the Senate should debate a Bill proposing that regional autonomy – currently reserved for the Autonomous Region of Muslim Mindanao – be extended to the whole country. Although unlikely to be implemented, the proposal for extending economic and administrative powers to other regional provinces is one which, like the senator herself, commands considerable popular appeal.[18]

A bilateral trade co-operation agreement between Australia and the Philippines came into effect in 1979. The Philippines signed a double taxation treaty with Australia and a memorandum of understanding on trade and investment and memorandum of understanding on science and technology in January 1989. Officials meet annually at the Philippine–Australia Joint Commission Meeting (JCM) in order to discuss policy issues to do with bilateral and multilateral trade. The Australian government has also actively helped the Philippines' trade-promotion efforts through aid funding under the Trade and Investment Promotion Service (TIPS). Locally, the government has taken a number of steps towards broadening foreign ownership in Philippine businesses under the Foreign Investments Act (FIA) 1991.[19]

A Council of Investments has been set up to assist foreign investors to obtain necessary approvals from the Securities & Exchange Commission (SEC) which registers all corporations in the country. Foreign investors who invest in more than 40 per cent of the equity of a Philippine corporation or partnership must secure prior approval of the Philippine SEC. SEC approval is also required for a foreign firm to establish a branch office in the Philippines. Registration with the Philippines' Board of Investment (BOI) is needed to qualify for incentives under the Omnibus Investments Code (Executive Order No. 226, enacted in 1987). Under the Investments Code, various incentives are granted to investors in industries considered pioneer, or in activities which are not pioneer but 60 per cent of the production of which is exported. Additional incentives for exporters are provided for under the *Export Development Act* of 1994. These include a number of tax incentives as well as customs duty preferences and exemptions.[20]

The Philippine Chamber of Commerce and Industry has also established a Committee on Conciliation and Arbitration for arbitrating, on a voluntary basis, commercial disputes that involve its members. For arbitration purposes it also acts as the national committee in the Philippines, under the ICC Rules of Conciliation and Arbitration. Rules specifically for voluntary arbitration of civil disputes are contained in the Arbitration Law. A Construction Industry Arbitration Commission also exists. The Philippines is a member of the Convention on the Settlement of Investment Disputes Between States and Nationals of Other States 1965 and a party to the New York Convention on the Recognition and Enforcement of Foreign Arbitral Awards 1958. The Philippines has also become a full member of the Multilateral Investment Guarantee Agency (MIGA) so that foreign investments entered through this agency are now insured against risk associated with host government restrictions on currency conversion and transfer, expropriation law, revolution or civil disturbance.

Singapore

The former British colony of Singapore achieved internal self-government in 1959. It became a State of the Federation of Malaya in 1963 but seceded in 1965. As a former British colony it has inherited a legal system that is based on the British common-law system – a mixture of case law and legislation. By virtue of the Second Charter of Justice, as at 27 November 1826 all UK statute law is automatically part of the law of Singapore. In addition, the Civil Law Act 1979 provides that all commercial cases that arise in Singapore are to be governed by whatever English common law and statute law is current at the time of the case's arising unless a contradictory law on the same issue exists in Singapore. Most major commercial laws that are passed in England therefore also apply in Singapore, including, for example, the Sale of Goods Act 1979 (UK). The recently enacted Application of English Law Act 1993 (Chapter 7A) limits the effect of the Charter of Justice and the Civil Law Act somewhat. It outlines the English Acts to be applicable in Singapore and effectively excludes the application of all other English Acts. Most of the important UK legislation previously in force relating to commercial law is preserved, including both the UK Sale of Goods Act 1979 and the UK Carriage of Goods by Sea Act 1992.

Other important commercial legislation has also been modelled along Australian lines: the Land Titles Act, for example, is modelled on the *Real Property Act 1900*

(NSW) as amended. Chapter 50 of the Companies Act and the securities-industries legislation are both closely modelled on the equivalent Australian legislation. As was the case in Australia until 1986, the Privy Council in London remains the final court of appeal for civil cases. Singaporean judges therefore continue to tend to look towards English cases for guidance. Particularly in the taxation-law and company-law areas, though, an increasing tendency exists to also look towards Australian and US case law.

The 1965 Constitution (as modified in 1980) provides for a parliamentary system of government that is based on the Westminster model. There is a unicameral house of parliament that comprises 81 elected members and (at present) six nominated members of parliament (NMPs) from the business community, the legal and medical professions and community organisations. Although NMPs may speak on any issue before the house, they have limited voting rights. The parliament is elected for a five-year term through universal and compulsory adult suffrage.

In 1991 the Constitution was amended to provide for the president's election by the citizens of Singapore and for the president's being vested with specific veto powers that relate to, *inter alia*, appointment of key executive personnel, investigations into corruption, and internal security detentions. On 28 August 1993, the president was for the first time elected by registered voters rather than being appointed by the parliament.

In his or her capacity as head of state, the president technically appoints the prime minister and Cabinet – a role that is similar to that of Australia's Governor-General. Executive powers lie with the prime minister and Cabinet members, who are directly responsible to parliament.

The People's Action Party (PAP) has dominated Singapore's parliament since first being elected to power in 1959. In the 1991 elections it won 61 per cent of the vote, and it holds 77 of the 81 elected seats in parliament. The party's basic strategy has been substitution of administration for politics: State and party are intertwined, and meritocratic recruitment into both the party and the public service has served to minimise dissent and create of a public-service workforce that is committed to the party's goals.

As is the case with most of the ASEAN countries, a strong relationship exists between the government and business through government-linked companies (GLCs) and statutory boards. The government owns or controls 450 companies and about 40 companies are owned by the statutory boards; more than 100 companies compete with the private sector. However, unlike in other countries, this has not – so far, at least – resulted in inefficiency and bureaucracy. Levels of taxation – both direct and indirect – are high, and in the past, emphasis was placed on direct forms of taxation. Since April 1994, though, the government's having introduced a 3 per cent GST seems to have been signalling a fundamental shift in fiscal policy from direct to indirect forms of taxation. High revenue levels, combined with a strong belief in social planning and provision of social welfare services, have been responsible for Singapore's public spending levels being among Asia's highest. Moreover, the combination of adequate funds and a strong (even oppressive) system of supervision, control and accountability have been responsible for creation of GLCs and statutory boards that are among the region's most efficient and corruption free.

The Constitution provides for an independent judiciary that comprises the Supreme Court, subordinate courts and the Privy Council. The subordinate courts comprise district courts, magistrates' courts, juvenile courts, coroners' courts, and the Small Claims Tribunal.

The system of appeals arising from Subordinate Court decisions was restructured in 1993. A new, single, permanent Court of Appeal was created to replace the previously existing Court of Appeal and Court of Criminal Appeal. The restructured Supreme Court includes the Court of Appeal and the High Court, and a new tier of appeal judges is appointed from among current High Court judges. Professor Jayakumar, the Minister for Law, has indicated that because of the creation of the new Court of Appeal, the right of appeal to the Privy Council may in due course be reviewed with a view to its eventual removal.[21]

At present, though, it remains the case that an appeal from a decision made by the appellate court may, in civil proceedings, be brought before the Judicial Committee of the Privy Council in London. This can only be done if, before their case is heard by the appellate court, both parties to the proceedings have consented, in writing, to be bound by the decision the Privy Council makes.

The legal profession's structure is similar to that of most Australian states. The profession is fused – that is, once a person has been admitted, he or she may practice as both an advocate (or barrister) and a solicitor, and the profession is largely self-regulating. Judges are appointed by the president, acting on the advice of the prime minister in consultation with the Chief Justice. English is the court proceedings' official language.

Enforcement of foreign judgements is governed by the Reciprocal Enforcement of Foreign Judgements Act (as revised in 1985) – a piece of legislation that is almost identical to Australia's *Foreign Judgements Act 1991*. For example, the requirements for registering a foreign (including Australian) judgement are the same as those that apply in Australia. Applications for registration and enforcement are made to the High Court. Once a judgement is registered, it has the same effect, and is subject to the same rules of enforcement and so on, as if it had been issued by the High Court itself.

The Arbitration Act supports and regulates arbitration. In it, terms that may be implied into arbitration agreements are prescribed and the procedure for arbitration is provided.

The Singapore International Arbitration Centre (SIAC) is a non-profit organisation that in March 1990 was incorporated as a public company limited by guarantee. It commenced operations in July 1991 and now provides a high-quality alternative to formal court procedures, particularly now that local lawyers are gradually becoming more familiar and more comfortable with arbitration procedures.

Simple arbitration rules that are nominated by the parties can be used. The SIAC has also developed its own set of arbitration rules for clients to make use of, and these are largely based on the UNCITRAL rules and the rules of the London Court of Arbitration, with some modifications. A panel of eminent foreign arbitrators who offer their services to the centre has been established and completed.

Singapore's government is in the process of developing a new arbitration law that will most likely be along the lines of the UNCITRAL-model law on arbitration. Meanwhile, as of March 1992 the government has amended its laws to allow foreign lawyers to appear in international arbitrations that are held at the SIAC, with the proviso that in cases in which Singaporean law applies, the foreign lawyer has to appear with Singaporean counsel.

An added bonus is that in another country, enforcement of arbitral awards is usually easier than enforcement of a foreign judgement. In August 1986 Singapore became a party to the New York Convention on the Recognition and Enforcement of Foreign Arbitral Awards 1958. By virtue of that Convention, SIAC awards are enforceable internationally across 80 countries including the UK and the US.

For Singapore, the Convention on the Settlement of Investment Disputes Between States and Nationals of Other States 1965 (ICSID) came into force in November 1968. The country has enacted the Arbitration (International Investment Disputes) Act 1968 in order to make the Convention's provisions effective there.

Apart from copyright law, the system for protecting intellectual property is very much linked with that of the UK. In the area of copyright protection, in the past it was important that Singapore was not yet a party to the Berne Convention. However, since 1987, under a bilateral treaty that was signed by Australia and Singapore, works that are subject to copyright in Australia have been automatically protected under Singapore's Copyright Act 1987. That Act was developed with Australian help and is very similar to Australia's *Copyright Act 1968*. In Singapore now, because the country is a party to the Uruguay Round TRIPS agreement, Berne Convention standards of protection apply to all works that originate from a GATT or WTO member nation.

Designs are protected in Singapore on their being registered in the UK. Trademark registration is also possible; marks that are not registered can nevertheless be protected, based on the common-law tort of 'passing off'. Likewise, the common law that relates to protection of trade secrets is recognised by a Singaporean court.

A new Registrar of Patents was established in February 1995 under the Patents Act of 1994 (Chapter 221). Any inventor, joint inventor, or other person entitled to the whole of the property in an invention in Singapore under any law or treaty may now apply to the Registrar for the grant of an invention patent in Singapore. Singapore is a signatory to the 1883 Paris Convention for the Protection of Industrial Property. Singapore is also a member of the Patent Co-Operation Treaty signed at Washington on 19 June 1970, and the new Patents Act contains provisions giving effect to that treaty. Part XVI of the new Act provides that any international application for a patent made to the International Bureau under the terms of the treaty which designates Singapore shall be treated as an application made under the Act for an invention patent in Singapore. Transitional provisions also ensure that previously granted and existing patent registration certificates and applications under the UK

Patents Act 1949 or 1977 and/or the (now repealed) Registration of United Kingdom Patents Act (Singapore) shall continue in force.

For investors seeking simply to explore the markets in Singapore and the region, and promote customer contact, an ideal vehicle is the representative office, set up under the auspices of Singapore's Trade Development Board (TDB). If and when a decision is made to enter into business in Singapore, an application can be made to either set up a branch office or to incorporate in Singapore. The branch office is particularly suitable for short-term projects, as it can be easily deregistered. Two resident agents must be appointed to be responsible for the company's compliance with the *Companies Act*. One requirement under this Act is that two sets of financial statements must be submitted annually – one in respect of branch office operations in Singapore, and one in respect of the parent company. Foreign companies may also establish a subsidiary, with or without local participation, as a private limited company in Singapore. Public limited companies may also be formed where the number of members exceeds 50, or when required by relevant legislation (merchant banks, for example, must operate through a public company).[22]

Thailand

In Thailand, the only ASEAN nation that does not have a history of foreign-colonial domination, the beginnings of a formal legal system were established in 1868, during the reign of King Chulalongkorn. A Ministry of Justice was created in 1892, and the four basic codes were adopted several years later. The four codes – the Civil and Commercial Code, the Criminal Code, the Civil Procedure Code and the Criminal Procedure Code – are based on continental Europe's (civil-law) tradition of codification. The codes' content was drawn from the laws of countries that have codified civil-law systems (for example, France, Switzerland and Germany), countries that have essentially common-law systems (for example, England) and Thailand's traditional law.

Thailand is a constitutional monarchy, and the 1991 Constitution is the highest source of law. Under the Constitution, the king's executive powers are exercised by a prime minister and a council of ministers. The Constitution also provides the king with the emergency power of issuing decrees that are deemed necessary for protection of national security or prevention of a disaster.

In the Constitution, an elected lower house and an appointed upper house are allowed for. The king appoints members to the upper house on the advice of the prime minister, who also heads the Cabinet. Bills that are introduced in the House of Representatives become law once they have passed both houses of the National Assembly, have been signed by the king and have been published in the *Government Gazette*. In exercising their executive powers, government ministers and other executive members also have the power to make laws through issuing regulations.

As is the case in most civil-law systems, major pieces of legislation tend to be drafted in broad terms and to set out basic principles rather than specific rules. This legislation necessarily depends on passing of other special laws in parliament and/or issuing of a number of detailed regulations before it can be effectively implemented. This is certainly the case in the commercial law area, in which most types of activity are governed by a proliferation of special laws and regulations; an absolute maze is thereby created for the unwary foreigner to become lost in.

Thailand's civil service is responsible for implementing laws and regulations. This responsibility, together with the service's law-making powers, helps in ensuring that the effectiveness of most laws, including commercial laws, is highly dependent on administrative discretion. However, more administrative powers and functions are exercised at the civil service's lower levels than is the case in a number of neighbouring Asian countries, and this in turn tends to be responsible for distancing many administrative actions from undue political influence. Private corruption has been a problem in some areas, though – most noticeably in the police force.

A three-tier judicial system exists. At the top of the hierarchy is the Supreme Court (the *Sarn Dika*), which is the final court of appeal in all civil, bankruptcy, labour, juvenile and criminal cases.

The Court of Appeals (the *Sarn Uthorn*) has appellate jurisdiction in all civil, bankruptcy, juvenile and criminal matters. Throughout the country, appeals from all 'courts of first instance', except the Central Labour Court, come to this court. The Court of Appeals is divided into a number of divisions that cover various jurisdictions.

The courts of first instance (the *sarn chunton*) include the Central Labour Court, the Civil Court, the Criminal Court, the Magistrates' Courts and the provincial courts. Although separate juvenile, labour and tax courts exist, no separate courts exist for administrative-law matters. Discussions have recently taken place at government level about establishing a court of administrative review. In Thai law, all cases are decided by judges and no provision exists for trial by jury.

In 1995–96 the government proposed establishment of an intellectual property court. This new court would be able to build on the work that has already been done by the Ministry of Commerce's intellectual property department – a department that was established in 1992 for training specialist judges and police officers to enforce intellectual property laws. Should the proposal be successfully implemented, Thailand might soon become South-East Asia's first country to have this type of court, and the court's existence would serve to mitigate Thailand's previously poor record for respecting foreign intellectual property rights.

The problem has not been that the country lacks adequate legislative protection for intellectual property, because those laws have existed for several years. There is the Patents Act 1979, which, has now been supplemented due to Thailand's having acceded to the Uruguay Round TRIPS agreement. There is also the Copyright Act 1978, which affords foreign copyright works the internationally accepted standards of protection that are set down in the Berne Convention. Although the 1978 law left undecided the question of protection of computer software, that loophole was closed in March 1995 when Thailand's latest copyright legislation came into effect. With reference to trademarks, under Thailand's Trademarks Act 1931, amended in

1961, registration and protection of marks closely follow the UK model. The Act provides protection for both trademarks and service marks as well as for certification marks, and it also establishes a registration system for licensing agreements. Penalties for infringement have also recently been increased.

The problem has been that in the Thai legal system, enforcement of legal rights can be notoriously difficult. Legal proceedings that are initiated in a Thai court can be long, complex and frustratingly 'opaque'. Because of Thailand's non-confrontationist legal culture, it is also difficult for law-enforcement officials and court personnel to recognise that someone who seems to be simply selling goods for a living is in fact breaking the law. Allegations that police officers and other officials have to be paid 'incentives' to enforce the law have also been common.

Thailand has been described as 'a society of relationships . . . not a society of law'.[23] In this context it is perhaps not surprising that informal mechanisms are by far the most effective means of resolving commercial disputes. In this area, Thai people's respect for courtesy, calmness, seniority and experience is responsible for guaranteeing the strength of, and integrity within, alternative dispute-resolution mechanisms. A number of institutions also serve to strengthen the integrity and honesty of arbitrators who are retired members of the legal profession and other senior individuals who may be turned to for help during resolution of a dispute.

An institution of this type is the Thai Bar Association which was established in 1914. Its members include judges, prosecutors, practising lawyers, professors and other people. High status is attached to the position of judge, and examinations for entering the judiciary are notoriously difficult. The presence of the Thai Bar Association, the high status that is attached to the judiciary and the contact that is regularly made between members of the Association also help to guarantee maintenance of standards among members of the legal profession.

Current investment laws allow foreign investment via a sole proprietorship, partnership, private limited company or public limited company. In addition, joint ventures, branches of foreign corporations, representative offices and regional offices may be utilised in some cases. To date, the most popular form of business organisation for major projects has been the private limited company, but with the enactment of the Public Limited Companies Act and the Securities and Exchange Act in 1992, only public limited companies may issue shares to the public and apply for listing of shares on the Stock Exchange of Thailand. Restrictions on the percentage of foreign equity ownership of commercial banks, finance companies, commercial fishing, aircraft, commercial transport, commodity export, mining and other enterprises exist under various laws, Cabinet policies, trade association regulations etc. Investors in permitted areas may apply to the Board of Investment to be granted incentives and promotion. Conditions may be imposed upon promoted projects including minimum capital investment, minimum Thai share participation, training of labour and using locally sourced raw materials.[24]

The law recognises three types of arbitration: arbitration in court, which is governed by the Civil Procedure Code; arbitration out of court, and foreign arbitration, both of which are governed by the Arbitration Act 1987. Since 1967 a set of rules has also existed that was drafted by the Thai Chamber of Commerce in conjunction with ESCAP and is known as the Thai Commercial Arbitration Rules (TCAR). The TCAR provide for a permanent Commercial Arbitration Committee that comprises 17 members, seven of whom are appointed by the Thai Chamber of Commerce and 10 of whom are appointed by the foreign chambers of commerce that are located in Bangkok; the president of Thailand's Board of Trade is the chairperson.

Although Thailand has not adopted the UNCITRAL Model Law on International Commercial Arbitration 1985, the rules may be adopted in the country in connection with an international arbitration case, both inside and outside the court. In addition, the Board of Trade subscribes to the ICC rules and has entered into arbitration agreements with its counterparts in Japan, South Korea and India.

Foreign arbitral awards can be recognised and enforced in Thailand if they are governed by a treaty, convention or international agreement to which Thailand is a party and only to the extent that Thailand is committed to be bound by them. Both Australia and Thailand are party to the New York Convention on the Recognition and Enforcement of Foreign Arbitral Awards 1958. Most arbitral awards that are issued for settling of disputes between nationals from these two countries will therefore be governed by that Convention and can be recognised and enforced in Thailand.

Vietnam

Vietnam has been exposed to three major legal systems: Confucian, French and socialist. Before French colonisation commenced in 1859, the country was largely governed on Confucian principles, as laid down in the Le Code, the Nguyen Code and other codes. Although the villages, which were more influenced by animist and Buddhist viewpoints, had some economic freedom, civil and criminal legislation were regulated by imperial bureaucrats. The French introduced the Commercial Code and the Civil Code, which were very much based on the codes of the colonial authority's home country. Written in French, the codes applied only to Europeans and French-speaking Vietnamese people. As was the case with French political control, the French legal system became more established in the south, where the codes remained in force until 1975.

After September 1945, when Ho Chi Minh declared Vietnam to be independent, little was done in order to develop the legal system; this remained the case during the three decades of almost continuous warfare that followed. The codes were abolished in the north in 1954. Land-law-reform legislation that was enacted in the late 1950s and early 1960s was strongly influenced by China. By July 1976 when unification was achieved between the north and the south, Soviet legal thought was the main influence.

Unified Vietnam has retained its socialist political system, under which the Communist Party of Viet Nam holds firm control of the government. Under the Law on Organisation of the Government of the Socialist Republic of Vietnam 1992, the government (currently headed by President Le Duc Anh) is the executive body of the National Assembly and Vietnam's highest administrative body. The government's main functions include promulgating resolutions and decrees and presenting draft laws to the National Assembly and draft ordinances to the National Assembly's Standing Committee.

The National Assembly is the only body in which the power to amend the Constitution and pass laws is vested. When the National Assembly is not in session, the National Assembly's Standing Committee can be empowered to pass ordinances in order to deal with urgent matters. Decrees are made by the government, whereas the individual ministries are usually confined to issuing circulars, instructions and decisions. Ministers, and those Heads of state-bodies who have ministerial status, also prepare (usually in conjunction with the Ministry of Justice) draft legislation in their area of responsibility; the draft legislation is then submitted to the National Assembly, for debate and promulgation. However, in all cases draft legislation has to be vetted by the National Assembly Legal Commission, the task of which is to ensure that all legislative proposals before the Assembly are in accordance with the Constitution and are consistent with existing legislation.

In Vietnam's legislative system a multi-tier approach has therefore been adopted. It comprises many levels of legislation, from laws (Acts) and ordinances, decrees and ministerial regulations, to circulars, decisions and directives that are issued by the people's committees and other lower level government organs. It is required that documents that have the force of law, which have been promulgated by the government, the prime minister, a minister or Head of a state organ who has ministerial status, be published in Vietnam's *Official Gazette* (*Cong Bao*). All legal documents are written in Vietnamese. An English translation of more than 200 laws that relate to foreign investment in Vietnam exists in the form of a loose-leaf service that is jointly published by the State Committee for Co-operation and Investment (SCCI) and the law firm Phillips Fox.

Since the late 1980s, the National Assembly has been allowed to play a greater role in policy making and politics, as part of the government's new *doi moi* (renovation) economic philosophy. The philosophy and the new managerial rather than controlling role the Communist Party has thereby been given are clearly reflected in the 1992 Constitution. Therefore, although the Constitution provides for the machinery through which electoral democracy functions, it also serves to confirm the Communist Party's place at the helm of national leadership. With reference to the economy, Vietnam's new one is described in the Constitution as 'a multi-sector economy in accordance with the market' that nevertheless has to remain firmly 'based on state management and socialist orientations'. For foreign investors, what is more reassuring is constitutional acceptance of the private sector and the fact that nationalisation of national assets that are held by foreign interests is expressly guaranteed against.

The country's first elections since achievement of reunification in July 1976 were held in July 1992. Although non-party candidates were permitted to stand for election, candidates had to be endorsed by the Vietnam Fatherland Front, an umbrella body for mass organisations. The elections' result was that the party's authority was confirmed, but many new and younger candidates were also elected. Some of those newer, younger members were actively involved in the dissent that developed before the party's mid-term conference was held in late 1993. Criticisms of the conference's draft report and emergence of several underground papers that urged a quick transition to a multi-party political system were responsible for prompting the party leadership to send all party members a warning not to associate with forces 'opposing socialism'.[25]

By the time the conference finally took place, from November 1993 to 24–25 January 1994 – having been postponed for three months – its atmosphere was calm and formal. The 'tightrope' consensus that was reached between reformists and party-controlled centrists is clearly reflected in the final wording of the controversial political report and in the nature of the 20 new members who were finally chosen for the 161 member central committee. Nine of the new members are provincial party leaders from economically fast-moving southern provinces, who it is stated, were included in order to balance northerners' traditional dominance in the party's upper echelons.[26] With reference to the political report, its wording contains a clear rejection of political pluralism, a commitment to 'a socialist-oriented market mechanism under state management' and an equally strong commitment to continuation of reforms towards establishment of a market economy.[27]

As a reflection of the challenges (and tensions) that exist in politics and the economy, Vietnam's challenge in the area of law is to marry socialist legal jurisprudence with a legal system that is attuned to the requirements of the emerging mixed-market economy. The law and the legal system have undergone major changes over the past two decades, during which Vietnam's law makers have drawn on a wide range of laws for their inspiration. In the 1978 *doi moi* legislation (for example, the Foreign Investment Law of 1978), a clever adaptation of Chinese laws was displayed. More recently, French, Anglo-American and, frequently, East Asian laws have been a source of legal inspiration. However, Vietnam's laws are increasingly reflecting the country's social, political and economic conditions.

The Ministry of Justice was re-established in the early 1980s, having been disbanded for 20 years. As a ministry its importance has recently increased as Vietnam moves from a command economy to a market-based economy. Although much work remains to be undertaken in developing Vietnam's legal infrastructure in order to support this development, it is evident that the country is in the process of creating both a more comprehensive legal environment and a more independent style of judiciary.

In October 1992 the National Assembly passed the Law on Organisation of People's Courts, which in late 1993 was proclaimed as amended. This law provides for a greater measure of judicial independence through changing of the procedure under which judges are appointed: instead of being elected for a five-year term by the local people's councils, they are now appointed by the State president. The law also provides for substantial increases in judges' remuneration and, more importantly, ensures that they are no longer paid by the local people's councils, but are now paid by the national government.

Under the abovementioned 1993 law, the court system comprises the Supreme People's Court, which is Vietnam's highest court and is directly accountable to the National Assembly; the local people's courts, which are supervised by the Supreme People's Court; and military tribunals. The Supreme People's Court is headed by the Chief Justice, whose term of office runs concurrently with the National Assembly. The court itself currently comprises the Council of the Supreme Court Justices, the Committee of Judges, the Central Military Court, an economic court, a criminal court, a civil court and three appeals courts.

At the lower levels of the court hierarchy, provincial courts deal with civil, economic and criminal matters whereas district courts deal with only civil and criminal matters. The 1993 decision to establish, in provincial courts and in the Supreme People's Court, economic courts that were to operate as part of the existing judicial system was an essential step in ensuring that economic reforms have substance through the introduction of appropriate legal reforms. As Vietnam becomes increasingly drawn into the new international economy, through its ASEAN membership and its possible future membership of the APEC forum and the WTO, this process will become even more important. In particular, it will aid the country's being brought within the purview of the various international legal regimes that cover trade liberalisation, investment protection and intellectual property protection.

Vietnam is neither a signatory to any of the international treaties that deal with intellectual property protection nor a WTO member. In late 1994 the National Assembly Standing Committee issued the Ordinance on Copyright which, although it provides a measure of copyright protection, falls short of the protection that is offered through international conventions. Copyright protection in Vietnam is extended if the work is registered within 30 days of its original publication. The extent to which protection exists if the work is not registered is not entirely clear. The ordinance covers computer software and audiovisual work, but although it mentions 'musical works', it is not clear whether this covers sound recordings.

With reference to investment, in September 1991 Australia and Vietnam entered into an Investment Promotion and Protection Agreement. In 1992 the two countries also signed an agreement through which double taxation is avoided and fiscal evasion is prevented with reference to income taxes. Although Vietnam has not ratified the 1958 New York Convention on the Recognition and Enforcement of Foreign Arbitral Awards, it is reportedly proposing to do so in the near future. However, even if ratification does occur, it is likely to be some time before effective mechanisms for the Convention's implementation can be put into place.

The Law on Foreign Investment in Vietnam (LFIV – adopted by the National Assembly on 29 December 1987 and revised in 1990 and 1992) is currently the sole law providing any means for establishing a long-term corporate presence in Vietnam. Joint stock companies and limited liability companies as provided for under the 1991 Company Law remain off-limits to foreign investors. The four most important forms of foreign investment under the LFIV are joint venture companies (JVCs); business co-operation contracts; enterprises with 100 per cent foreign-owned capital and build-operate-transfer projects. The establishment of any of these forms of 'Foreign Investment Enterprise' (as they are known) requires a business and investment licence issued by the State Committee for Co-operation and Investment.

Other forms of establishing a presence in Vietnam include the representative office and various contractual arrangements (such as technological co-operation and licensing arrangements) that do not fall squarely within the ambit of the Law on Foreign Investment. More recently, foreign companies have been allowed to establish branch offices in Vietnam in some industries. Managerial control is one of the most difficult issues facing foreign investors in Vietnam. For example, the provisions on joint venture companies in the Law on Foreign Investments require that decisions be approved by at least two-thirds of the JVC board of management, with some important decisions (such as those relating to production and business plans) requiring unanimous approval. Despite the difficulties, however, the future seems bright, with the government intent on a course of continual improvement in both the legal system and the economy.[28]

Conclusion

Globalisation has become the buzz-word of the 1990s. For the ASEAN nations as much as for Australia, globalisation is a fact, and its increasing demands pose new questions in law as much as in other fields. In particular, globalisation is providing the impetus for the development of what could well prove to be the early stages of a truly international legal regime in international trade and commerce.

At the regional level, the process of harmonising product standards, customs procedures and other areas of regulation in trade and investment is now well underway. The process of harmonisation is a slow one. It also tends to proceed more smoothly amongst smaller groupings of countries. Not surprisingly, the processes of harmonisation and cooperation are most advanced between Australia and New Zealand under the CER agreement; less advanced amongst the ASEAN member countries under the AFTA provisions, and hardly begun between the 18 APEC member countries.

Development of regionally and internationally recognised rules and standards can help to promote peaceful and stable economic activity across international borders. This development relies not only upon debate and agreement in international and regional forums, but also upon cooperation between individuals from different nations. Lawyers, politicians, bureaucrats and businesspeople all have a part to play in understanding each other's business practices, culture, society and legal system. Achieving mutual understanding, trust and respect across national and cultural borders can be a difficult, and often frustrating process. It can also, however, be highly rewarding for all concerned.

ENDNOTES

1 Prehn, Eileen, 'Brunei Darussalam' in *Asian Business Review*, April 1966, pp 48–9.

2 Lindsey, T C, At the Crossroads: Globalisation, Social Change and Commercial Law Reform in Indonesia. in Attorney-General's Department, *Twenty-first International Trade Law Conference* (Attorney General's Department, Canberra, 1995) 305.

3 See, for example, 'Islam: Coming in from the Cold?' in Schwartz, Adam, *A Nation in Waiting: Indonesia in the 1990s*. Allen & Unwin, 1994; 'Adat and Islam' in Hooker, M B, *Adat Law in Modern Indonesia*. Kuala Lumpur: Oxford University Press, 1978, pp 91–110; and Howell, Julia Day, 'Indonesia: Searching for Consensus' in Caldarola, Karl, *Religion and Societies: Asia and the Middle East*. Berkeley: University of California Press, 1972, pp 102–34.

4 The high courts are located in most provincial capitals, and deal with appeals from the district courts.

5 Hooker, M B, *Adat Law in Modern Indonesia*. Kuala Lumpur: Oxford University Press, 1978, p 101, citing Decision Regn. 109 k/Sip/1960.

6 McBeth, John, 'The Year of Doing Business'. *Far Eastern Economic Review*, 1 September 1994, pp 70–2.

7 Lindsey, T C, 'Paradigms, Paradoxes and Possibilities: Towards Understandings of Indonesia's Legal System', in Taylor, Veronica (ed), *Australian Perspectives on Asian Legal Systems*. Law Book Co, 1996.

8 Ibid. at p 18; citing 'Oetojo admits legal abuses in the judicial system', *Jakarta Post*, 12 December 1994; 'Dishonest judges threatened with tough action', *Jakarta Post*, 7 January 1995; and Mulyalubis, T, 'Solid legal systems required for free market', *Jakarta Post*, 23 December 1994.

9 Lindsey, T C, 'Paradigms, Paradoxes and Possibilities: Towards Understandings of Indonesia's Legal System', in Taylor, Veronica (ed), *Australian Perspectives on Asian Legal Systems*. Law Book Co, 1996.

10 Ibid.

11 Known as the *raja* in Perlis, the *yang di-pertuan besar* in Negeri Sembilan, and the *sultan* in Malaysia's seven other states (Johore, Kedah, Kelantan, Pahang, Perak, Selangor and Trengganu). The two territories of Kuala Lumpur and Labuan are under the direct control of the federal government.

12 Unlike Australia's preferential voting system, Malaysia's electoral system operates to ensure that a candidate who obtains, say, 5500 votes in a four-cornered fight out of a total of 20,000 cast, is declared the winner, regardless of the fact that a majority of votes (14,500) was in fact cast for the other three candidates.

13 This was the result of the demands for 'special protection' that were made by the Borneo states as a condition of their entering the federation. It was argued that this protection was required due to the special needs and interests of the two states that arose because of their extremely poor level of economic and political development. These demands resulted in a constitution whereby the two states were given a range of legislative powers wider than the range of powers vested in the Peninsular Malaysia states.

14 Appeals to the Federal Court lie unconditionally in constitutional cases or in criminal matters that originated in the High Court, or in other cases with the Federal Court's leave when a question of importance is involved. In addition, the Federal Court has original jurisdiction over all constitutional questions that are referred to it by the High Court, and over disputes between the federation and a state, and over disputes between states.

15 Nineteen fifty-six is the date of the coming into force of the Civil Law Act.

16 Rosabel Socorro Teston Balan, 'Philippines', in Cusick, M and de Mesa, S (eds), *The Asian Investment Law Directory 1995*. Asia Law and Practice Ltd, 1995, pp 131–3.

17 In the 1960s Marcos era there was increasing poverty and income inequality and, consequently, civil unrest. Martial law was introduced in 1972. Although martial law was lifted in 1981, democratic rights were not restored until February 1986 when the 'People's Power Revolution' brought Corazon Aquino to power.

18 *Far Eastern Economic Review*, 8 June 1995, p 12.

19 In the Foreign Investments Act 1991, foreign-equity restrictions were removed for enterprises that export at least 60 per cent of their total production. The Act also allowed for 100 per cent foreign ownership in enterprises that serve the local market, except in areas that are identified under a 'negative list', whereby a maximum of 40 per cent foreign ownership is allowed. The negative list was reviewed in 1994, and the number of industries that are subject to restrictions was reduced. Government proposals for more reform include abolition of the current minimum-capital requirement for foreign investors, opening-up of retail trade and more reduction in the number of areas that are included in the negative list.

20 Cusick, M and de Mesa, S (eds), *The Asian Investment Law Directory 1995*. Asia Law and Practice Ltd, 1995, pp 131–3.

21 International Legal Services Advisory Council, Attorney-General's Dept, *Legal Services Country Profile: Singapore*. Canberra: Australian Government Publishing Service, 2nd edition, 1993, p 7.

22 Sherylene Wang, Alban Tay Mahtani and De Silva, 'Singapore', in Cusick, M and de Mesa, S (eds), *The Asian Investment Law Directory 1995*. Asia Law and Practice Ltd, 1995, pp 139–44.

23 Commerce Minister Amaret Sila-on, 'Moderator's Comments on Culture and Environment in Thailand: Symposium on the Siam Society' (1989), as cited in Thomas N O'Neill III, 'Thai Copyright Law, Economic Development and International Trade', in *International Law and Politics*, vol 24, 1992, pp 1131 and 1167.

24 Chandler and Thong-ek Law Offices, Bangkok, 'Thailand', in Cusick, M and de Mesa, S (eds), *The Asian Investment Law Directory 1995*. Asia Law and Practice Ltd, 1995, pp 157–63.

25 On the eve of the conference, the central committee drafted four new members to the *politburo*, thereby expanding it to a record 17 members. Of the four, only the foreign minister Nguyen Manh Cam has a university degree. The other three are steeped in Marxism–Leninism and are considered to be opponents of acceleration of the reform process.

26 An example is Le Mai, the deputy foreign minister, who is in charge of US relations. Another member, the leader of a State-owned electronics firm located in Hanoi, became the first businessperson to be elected to the committee.

27 Likewise, party leader Do Muoi, the prime minister Vo Van Kiet and other senior leaders have refused to be drawn into any dialogue on political issues or human-rights questions, while they simultaneously provide a distraction for popular frustration by strongly attacking corruption, smuggling and graft among party and government members. Both high-level and lower level officials have been targeted – and caught.

28 Frederick Burke (Baker & McKenzie), 'Vietnam', in Cusick, M and de Mesa, S (eds), *The Asian Investment Law Directory 1995*. Asia Law and Practice Ltd, 1995, pp 165–73.

REFERENCES

Cusick, M and de Mesa, S (eds), *The Asian Investment Law Directory 1995*. Asia Law and Practice Ltd, 1995.

Far Eastern Economic Review, *Asia Yearbook 1996*. Review Publishing Co, 37th edition 1996.

International Legal Services Council, Attorney-General's Department, *Legal Services Country Profile: Indonesia*. Canberra: Australian Government Publishing Service, 1994.

International Legal Services Council, Attorney-General's Department, *Legal Services Country Profile: Malaysia*. Canberra: Australian Government Publishing Service, 1994.

—— *Legal Services Country Profile: The Philippines*. Canberra: Australian Government Publishing Service, second edition, 1995.

—— *Legal Services Country Profile: Singapore*. Canberra: Australian Government Publishing Service, second edition, 1993.

—— *Legal Services Country Profile: Thailand*. Canberra: Australian Government Publishing Service, 1995.

—— *Legal Services Country Profile: Vietnam*. Canberra: Australian Government Publishing Service, 1995.

Taylor, V (ed), *Australian Perspectives on Asian Legal Systems*. (in press, Law Book Co. due late 1996).

14

Taxation planning and ASEAN

Andrew McNicol

Introduction

Because foreign-investment opportunities and trade opportunities are driven by profitability, it is not surprising that many traders and investors concentrate on only the profitability aspect of their transactions. If a business is successful, though, profits will arise and their taxation treatment will become an important issue. It is therefore not uncommon to find – when it is too late – that had a different structure or transaction sequence been chosen, the end taxes that were payable either in Australia or overseas might thereby have been greatly reduced. This chapter argues that many problems of this type can be avoided if proper care is taken before the transaction or investment is formalised. After first discussing the need for tax planning, some of the general principles of the Australian taxation system, double-taxation agreements, the individual ASEAN countries' taxation characteristics, the way in which foreign-sourced income is taxed in Australia and, finally, the workings of Australia's various anti-avoidance provisions are considered.

The need for taxation planning

Any Australian investor who is contemplating trading with or investing in ASEAN first has to know how Australia's Income Tax Assessment Act (Tax Act) and its associated legislation will affect that investor. An investor also has to understand the particular foreign country's taxation and business system. An Australian investor especially has to understand

- taxation of foreign-sourced income (under Australian tax law) that is derived by an Australian resident
- the foreign country's taxation system

- the effect of any international agreements whereby the Australian tax law that is applicable to the resulting foreign income is modified.

Tax planning is essential before international business or investment is conducted with ASEAN countries; indeed, proper tax planning may mean the difference between the project's economic success or failure.

Because an Australian investor is rarely an expert on ASEAN taxation, professional advice about the income-tax consequences of his or her decisions should be sought. In Australia, most major law and accounting firms can help Australian investors who are planning to invest in ASEAN countries as well as provide personal contact with associated firms or businesses located in the relevant ASEAN country. Although this professional advice is usually expensive and not always tax deductible, it may be very cost effective in the long run. Many banks that have foreign operations in ASEAN counties may also have valuable local contacts.

Tax planning may aid determination of issues such as the following.
- The investment vehicle – for example branch, subsidiary company, group of companies, partnership or joint venture
- The mode of investment – debt or equity
- Cash flow – the ability to repatriate profits and/or capital in the most tax-effective way
- Use of investor assets – for example trademarks, capital equipment and specialist staff
- Use of 'tax holidays' – many ASEAN countries grant tax concessions to particular types of investment. Singapore, for example, has many tax incentives that are designed to foster and expand specific local industries
- Remuneration of Australian employees who are sent to work in ASEAN operations
- The appropriate investment sector – for example, manufacturing, real estate, building and construction, and service industries
- The price that is paid or payable by entities who have common control or ownership of goods and services that are produced or acquired by them.

This advice cannot be taken in isolation; it has to be integrated in the investor's long-term and short-term commercial objectives. For example, a trust or joint venture whereby the investors' after-tax return is maximised – a long-term objective – may be totally inappropriate given the investors' other commercial requirements. Similarly, most ASEAN countries restrict foreigners' investment and may require foreigners to use a particular investment structure. This, in turn, may have significant tax implications for an Australian investor. Indonesia, for example, usually requires that foreign investment be made in an Indonesian company that is ultimately controlled by Indonesian residents. Therefore, although a joint venture or trust structure may be very tax effective for the Australian investor, it is totally unsuitable due to Indonesia's foreign-investment requirements.

Likewise, foreign investment by a group of companies may not be appropriate, because in the Philippine, Indonesian, Malaysian, Singaporean and Thai tax systems – unlike in the Australian system – 'grouping' of corporate profits and losses for income-tax purposes is not allowed.

Ability to repatriate capital as well as profits is also significant in a long-term-investment strategy. However, this may be limited due to the non-resident being restricted to selling his or her business interests only to residents of the country in which the investment is located.

In recent years the Australian Taxation Office (ATO) has directed significant resources towards ensuring that international transactions comply with Australia's taxation laws. In August 1995 it published *International Transfer Pricing: Minimising the Taxation Risks in International Associated Party Dealings*. That document sets out guidelines for international transactions whereby the parties are related – for example where an Australian holding company with an overseas subsidiary supplies raw materials and technical expertise to the subsidiary company.

The general principles of Australian taxation

The federal government's power to impose income tax is granted in section 51(ii) of the Australian Constitution. The Income Tax Assessment Act is the statute through which income tax is imposed, including a tax on realised capital gains.

Australia's taxation system is based on a self-assessment regime, therefore the taxpayer has to determine the quantum of

- assessable income, including foreign-sourced income
- allowable deductions
- exempt income (income not subject to Australian tax)
- classes of foreign-sourced income and losses
- foreign-tax credits
- taxable income
- tax payable.

In the self-assessment regime it is assumed that the taxpayer has the knowledge necessary for solving a tax problem – or at least the ability to recognise a problem. Failure to have this basic skill means the taxpayer would be exposed to paying non-deductible tax penalties should assessable income be omitted, deductions prove non-allowable or tax credits are not available.

Two fundamental concepts underpin the Australian taxation system: 'residence' and 'source'. Australia imposes income tax on an Australian resident's worldwide taxable income, irrespective of the income's source. Non-residents are taxed only on their Australian-sourced income.

Section 6(1) of the *Tax Act* defines 'resident' as including

(a)   a person, other than a company, who resides in Australia and includes a person:

   (i)   who resides in Australia unless the Commissioner is satisfied that the person's permanent place of abode is outside Australia

   (ii)   who has actually been in Australia, continuously or intermittently in Australia, during more than one half of the year of income, unless the Commissioner is satisfied that his usual place of abode is outside Australia and that he does not intend to take up residence in Australia

(b) a company which is incorporated in Australia, or which not being incorporated in Australia, carries on business, and has either its central management and control in Australia, or its voting power controlled by shareholders who are residents of Australia.

'Taxable income' occurs when the assessable income exceeds the allowable deductions – see section 48 of the Tax Act. The converse, a 'tax loss', can be carried forward to be deducted against the taxpayer's assessable income in subsequent income-tax years.

For the purposes of the Tax Act, 'income' includes trading income, dividends, interest, royalties, and amounts 'in the nature of income'. Also realised net capital gains have to be included in assessable income where the asset giving rise to the gain was acquired or deemed to have been acquired after 19 September 1985.

Non-capital expenses that are incurred in the gaining of assessable income (current or future) are usually deductible against that income. In contrast, capital expenses are not usually deductible unless the Tax Act specifically makes them deductible. For example, in section 54 a deduction is allowed for depreciation, that is, physical or technological obsolescence of plant and equipment that are used (or are installed ready for use) for producing assessable income.

Taxing of Australian residents' foreign-sourced income has undergone significant legislative change since 1985, and the system is now one of the world's most comprehensive (if not most complicated) systems. In addition, this income may be subject to any applicable double-tax agreement (DTA) Australia has signed with the country in which the foreign income is sourced. The significance and effect of DTAs is discussed in the next section. These foreign-sourced-income rules apply to any income that is derived by Australian investors in ASEAN countries.

Before 1 July 1987, foreign-sourced income that was derived by Australian residents was treated as exempt income in Australia provided such income was taxed at source. However, since that date the federal government has progressively legislated to create a comprehensive taxation regime for foreign-sourced income. Today, an Australian resident who has overseas investments may, depending on a number of variables, be taxed on foreign-sourced income on either a remittance basis or an accrual basis. Usually, where the foreign income is taxed at source and is also taxable in Australia, the Australian resident will be permitted to have a credit in Australia for the foreign taxes he or she has paid.

With reference to foreign-sourced income, in the Tax Act it is required that any expenses that are incurred in the deriving of it be deductible only against income of the same class – see section 160AFD(9). In the Tax Act – see section 160AFD(8) – assessable foreign-sourced income is divided into four classes, as follows.

1. Interest income other than interest that is derived from banking or similar business.
2. Passive income – including royalties, rents, annuities and capital profits.
3. Offshore-banking income.
4. All other assessable foreign income.

If the foreign-income deductions exceed the assessable foreign income, the resultant loss is quarantined and cannot be offset against Australian-sourced income. However, this can be carried forward to be offset against assessable foreign income of the same class – see section 79D of the Tax Act – that is derived in future years.

The legal principles that apply to taxation of foreign-sourced income that is derived by Australian residents are discussed in more detail as follows.

Double-taxation agreements (DTAs)

Australia has entered DTAs with most of its economic trading partners, including the ASEAN countries, of which Brunei is the only exception.

A DTA is a legal agreement that is made between two countries whereby taxation of income that is derived in either country by residents of either signatory country is regulated, double-taxation problems are avoided and tax evasion is prevented.

A DTA usually covers the following issues.

- Residence and source
- The meaning of the term 'permanent establishment'
- Taxation of income from
  - real property
  - business
  - shipping and air transport
  - associated income
  - dividends
  - royalties
  - interest
  - independent personal services
  - employment income
  - directors' fees
  - entertainers (including athletes)
  - pensions and annuities
  - government services
  - students
  - other income
- Elimination of double taxation
- Tax credits
- Exchange of information

Australia's DTAs are integrated in domestic law through the *Income Tax (International Agreements) Act 1953*, the inclusion of section 4 in which means the Act will override Australia's domestic-tax law, notwithstanding any inconsistency between the Acts in question. For example, if a taxpayer is deemed to be a resident of both countries that are covered by the same DTA, the taxation issue will be resolved by the so-called 'tie-breaker' rule in the DTA. See, for example, paragraphs 2 and 3 of Article 3 of the Australia–Singapore DTA.

In DTAs, tax on particular classes of income such as royalties, dividends and interest is limited when such income is derived by a resident of one country and is taxed at source – see, for example, paragraphs 1 and 2 of Article 10 of the Australia–Singapore DTA, whereby the Singaporean or Australian tax on royalty income that is sourced from one country to a resident of the other country is limited to 10 per cent of the gross royalty. Furthermore, when the foreign-sourced-royalty income is assessed in the recipient's country of residence, the recipient, as entitled under Article 18 of the Australia–Singapore DTA, can claim a tax credit for this withholding tax.

In all DTAs, a key concept is the meaning of the term 'permanent establishment', or place of business. If a resident of one country has a permanent establishment in another country, all business profits that are associated with the establishment will be subject to tax in the country in question.

Significant variations exist between Australia's DTAs. In determining the consequences of doing business with any country, having knowledge of the way in which domestic tax laws are modified due to the existence of any relevant DTA is essential.

ASEAN countries' taxation systems

The countries ASEAN comprises cover a wide geographic area with very diverse histories, languages, religions and social systems. This diversity is also reflected in their government systems, including the systems for tax collection and revenue-law enforcement.

The Australian investor who is trading in an ASEAN country or acquiring a business interest there first has to know something about its taxation and business environment. This knowledge can be readily acquired from people who have first-hand experience of doing business in the country in question. These people can be found in the country's law and accounting firms that have Australian associations, and many banks can provide similar help.

Knowledge of the cultural aspects involved in doing business in an ASEAN country is a particularly critical factor for doing business in any ASEAN nation. This knowledge can be used in a variety of ways in order to help the Australian investor. It includes knowing the right question to ask at the appropriate time and knowing the basic etiquette with reference to dress standards, eating and addressing local businesspeople and government officials such as tax collectors. In the following summaries the seven ASEAN countries' tax systems are outlined. The rates of tax noted below may be subject to change by the respective ASEAN country.

Brunei

Brunei does not have a DTA with Australia. No personal income tax is imposed under Brunei's domestic law. A 30 per cent income tax is imposed on limited companies that derive income that has a Brunei source, and income from petroleum operations is also taxable. Although there is no capital-gains tax, profits from assets that are purchased for resale at a profit may be taxable.

Although Brunei imposes import duties and customs duties on a range of goods, various items are exempt from the duties – particularly imported foods.

Indonesia

Indonesia signed a DTA with Australia in 1992. Indonesian residents are taxed on their worldwide income but are taxed on a cash basis with reference to foreign-sourced income. Tax credits are allowed for foreign taxes that are paid on this income. Realised capital gains are also taxed as ordinary income. Tax losses can be carried forward for up to eight years in respect of mining and agriculture. Other losses can be carried forward for up to five years.

A tax resident of Indonesia is a person who is present in the country for more than 182 days in a tax year (1 January to 31 December) or who intends to reside in the country.

The maximum corporate tax rate is 30 per cent. The maximum individual tax rate is also 30 per cent. Indonesia's government offers special tax incentives for investment in particular industries and for businesses located in specific geographic areas. The incentives include an exemption for customs duty for capital equipment, spare parts and raw materials.

In Indonesia's DTA with Australia, the tax that is payable on the following classes of income is limited to the percentages shown.
- Interest: 10 per cent
- Dividends: 15 per cent
- Royalties: 10 per cent to 15 per cent

Indonesia imposes a 10 per cent VAT that is calculated by referring to the goods' sale value. It also imposes stamp duty and land tax.

Fringe benefits such as non-cash benefits that are provided to employees are not taxable.

Malaysia

Malaysia signed a DTA with Australia in 1980. Its residents are taxed on their worldwide income. Capital gains are taxed when the gain relates to land or buildings or to a company that owns land or buildings; the gains are taxed at a rate of between 5 per cent and 20 per cent.

For taxation purposes, a resident is a person who is present for more than 182 days in the tax year (1 January to 31 December). The tax rates for individuals and companies are different: there is a flat 30 per cent corporate rate and a progressive individual rate up to a maximum of 32 per cent.

Malaysia's government offers special tax incentives for investments in particular industries and for businesses located in geographic areas. These include additional deductions for research-and-development expenditure, some export expenditure and industrial expansion.

In Malaysia's DTA with Australia, the tax that is payable on the following classes of income is limited to the percentages shown.

- Interest: 10 per cent to 15 per cent
- Dividends: nil (provided company profits have been fully taxed)
- Royalties: 15 per cent

Malaysia imposes a sales tax of between 5 per cent and 15 per cent of the goods' sale value. It also imposes stamp duty and land tax.

Although fringe benefits such as medical benefits and amounts that are paid as home leave are not taxable, other fringe benefits are concessionally taxed.

Philippines

The Philippines signed a DTA with Australia in 1979. Although Philippine residents are taxed on their worldwide income, tax credits are allowed for any foreign tax that is paid. Capital gains are taxed when the gains relate to shares or real property.

The tax rates for individuals and companies are different: there is a flat 35 per cent corporate rate and a progressive individual rate up to a maximum of 35 per cent.

The Philippines' government offers special tax incentives for investment in particular industries and for businesses located in specific geographic areas. For example, for investment in pioneer projects, income tax may be exempted for up to six years and capital-equipment imports may be exempted from excise duty.

In the Philippines' DTA with Australia, the tax that is payable on the following classes of income is limited to the percentages shown.

- Interest: 15 per cent
- Dividends: 15 per cent to 25 per cent
- Royalties: 15 per cent to 25 per cent

The Philippines imposes a VAT, customs and excise duties, stamp duty, land tax and various local taxes.

Singapore

Singapore signed a DTA with Australia in 1969. Its residents are taxed on their accrued Singaporean-sourced income and on foreign income when it is received in Singapore. A Singapore resident can claim a tax credit with reference to foreign taxes on the foreign income. Realised capital gains are not taxed.

The tax rates for companies and individuals are different: there is a flat rate of 27 per cent for companies and a progressive individual rate up to a maximum of 30 per cent. Non-residents are subject to a maximum tax of 30 per cent, and employment income that is derived by non-residents is taxed, subject to any relevant DTA, at 15 per cent when the person is employed in Singapore for between 60 and 183 days.

For income-tax purposes, a resident has to be physically present in Singapore or employed in Singapore for at least 183 days in the tax year (1 January to 31 December).

Singapore's government offers special tax concessions for particular industries and for businesses located in specific geographic areas. For example, there is an investment allowance and a double-tax deduction for some research-and-development expenses. Industries that have been granted 'pioneer industry status' are taxed at a rate of 15 per cent.

In Singapore's DTA with Australia, the tax payable on the following classes of income is limited to the percentages shown.

- Interest: 10 per cent
- Dividends: nil (provided the profits have been fully taxed in Singapore)
- Royalties: 10 per cent

Singapore also imposes stamp duty, an energy-conservation tax, petrol duty, a tourism-promotion-fund levy and an entertainment tax.

Although fringe benefits are usually taxed, home-leave benefits and accommodation benefits are taxed concessionally.

Thailand

Australia signed a DTA with Thailand in 1981. Although Thai residents are taxed on their worldwide-employment income, irrespective of where the income is deemed to have been paid, other foreign-sourced income is taxable only when it is remitted to Thailand. Capital gains are not taxed, but profits on the sale of assets that are acquired for resale at a profit are taxed as ordinary income.

The tax rates for companies and individuals are different: there is a flat 30 per cent company rate and a progressive individual rate up to a maximum of 37 per cent. For income-tax purposes, a resident has to be physically present in Thailand for more than 183 days in the tax year (1 January to 31 December).

Thailand's government offers special tax concessions for particular industries and for business located in specific geographic areas. For example, there are customs concessions for imported machinery and raw materials, as well as tax holidays of up to eight years for particular investors.

In Thailand's DTA with Australia, the tax that is payable on the following classes of income is limited to the percentages shown.

- Interest: 10 per cent to 25 per cent
- Dividends: 10 per cent to 20 per cent
- Royalties: 15 per cent

Thailand imposes a VAT on goods and services that are consumed in Thailand. It also imposes a municipal tax, stamp duty, a signboard tax and property taxes.

Fringe benefits are taxable as ordinary income.

Vietnam

Australian signed a DTA with Vietnam in 1992. Vietnamese residents are taxed on their worldwide-employment income, irrespective of where the income is deemed to have been paid. This income includes 'ordinary income' – salary, wages and other employee-related remuneration. Gifts, lottery winnings and transfer fees are also taxed as income; the receipts are called 'irregular income'. Different tax rates apply for residents and non-residents.

For income-tax purposes, 'resident' includes a person who is physically present in Vietnam for more than 183 days in the year following his or her arrival; the tax year is 1 January to 31 December.

The tax rates for companies and individuals are different. Companies are subject to a 'profit tax' that is applied at the standard tax rate, the preferential tax rate or (an) 'other' tax rate. The rate that is applied depends on the economic activity that is undertaken. For example, infrastructure developments in remote areas incur a 10 per cent tax whereas profits from oil and natural gas activities are taxed at a rate in excess of 25 per cent (the appropriate 'other' rate is negotiated between the company and the Vietnamese government). When the company is not subject to the 'other' tax rates, the general 25 per cent rate applies. Vietnamese citizens and permanent residents are taxed on their regular income using a sliding scale that has a maximum rate of 60 per cent. Irregular income such as gifts is taxed on a sliding scale that has a maximum rate of 30 per cent.

Vietnam has legislated to impose tax on capital gains that are realised on transfer of an interest in a joint-venture project.

Vietnam's government offers special tax concessions by way of preferential profit tax rates, tax exemptions and tax incentives for BOT projects.

In Vietnam's DTA with Australia, the tax payable on the following classes of income is limited to the percentages shown.

* Interest: 10 per cent
* Dividends: 10 per cent to 15 per cent
* Royalties: 15 per cent

Other taxes Vietnam imposes include the following.

* A turnover tax that ranges between 1 per cent and 40 per cent.
* A special sales tax that ranges between 15 per cent and 100 per cent.
* Import duties and export duties that are determined by the nature of the goods.
* A withholding tax on profit remittance that ranges between 5 per cent and 10 per cent.
* A royalty tax with reference to exploitation of natural resources that is determined by output volume.

Australian taxation of foreign-sourced income

Introduction

Taxation of foreign-sourced income that is derived by an Australian resident is regulated by complex legislation, and the record-keeping requirements are onerous. Furthermore, the arrangements have undergone significant and comprehensive legislative reform.

Before 1 July 1987, for tax purposes this income was usually exempt – see section 23(q) of the Tax Act – provided it had been taxed at source; however, the exemption was abolished on that date. Although foreign-sourced income was thereafter taxed in Australia, credit was given for foreign taxes that were paid with reference to the income. Some employment income that was subject to tax at source and other specific receipts remained exempt, though.

From 1 July 1990 onwards, taxation of foreign-sourced income has become significantly complicated due to the introduction of CFC legislation, FIF legislation, non-resident-trust-estates legislation and complementary provisions whereby particular foreign-sourced income was exempted. This legislation and these provisions are explained as follows.

Exemptions

In the Tax Act, particular classes of foreign income are exempted from Australian tax. Of the exemptions listed as points 1 to 5 as follows, points 2 to 5 have to be understood in conjunction with the CFC and FIF legislation.

1. Foreign-sourced-employment income is exempt from Australian tax when the foreign employment is for more than 91 days and is taxed at source – see section 23AG.
2. An Australian company's foreign-branch business profits are exempt from Australian tax, provided the profits are derived via a permanent establishment located in a 'listed country' (a country that has a tax regime similar to Australia's), are not 'designed concessional income' (income that is subject to concessional tax treatment in the country of source) and are subject to tax in any listed country – see section 23AH.
3. Receipt of foreign-sourced income that has previously been subject to Australian tax by way of attribution pursuant to Part X of the Tax Act – see section 23AI – is exempt from Australian tax.
4. Non-portfolio dividends that are paid by a company that is a resident of a listed or unlisted country are exempt from Australian tax. A non-portfolio dividend is a dividend that is paid to a company when the company has at least 10 per cent of the voting power of the foreign company that pays the dividend – see section 23AJ.
5. Income that has previously been taxed under the FIF provisions – see section 23AK – are exempt from Australian tax.

Foreign-tax credits

Australia's foreign-tax-credit provisions are contained in Division 18 of Part III of the Tax Act: 'Credits in Respect of Foreign Tax'. The right to claim a foreign tax credit is subject to any relevant DTA that may limit the credit available for certain classes of income.

When foreign-sourced income is taxable in Australia, the taxpayer will usually receive a credit for any foreign taxes that are paid with reference to the income. In the Tax Act it is required that the Australian resident 'gross up' the foreign-sourced income by the amount of foreign tax that is paid and then claim a credit for the foreign tax against the Australian income-tax liability. For example, if A$200 of interest income (income that is not effectively connected with a trade or business that is undertaken via permanent establishment of an Australian-resident company located in Singapore) is derived in Singapore by an Australian-resident company, according to Article 9.1 of the Australia–Singapore DTA the Singapore tax on the income is limited to not more than 10 per cent of the gross interest. The Australian resident therefore receives A$180 (A$200 *less* [A$200 @ 10 per cent]).

The Australian-resident company is then assessed as follows.

Gross foreign-sourced income (A$180 + A$20)	= $ 200
Australian tax payable @ 36 per cent	= $ 72
Less Singapore tax credit	= $ 20
Net Australian tax payable	= $ 52

Under Division 18, the foreign-tax credit is limited to the lesser of

> the amount of that foreign tax, reduced in accordance with any relief available to the taxpayer under the law relating to that tax, or . . . the amount of Australian tax payable in respect of the foreign income.

See section 160AF(1)(c) and (d).

If an Australian-resident company derives foreign-sourced income of A$200 that is taxed at 50 per cent in the country of source and Australia's company-tax rate is 36 per cent, the excess tax credit of A$28 (A$200 x (0.50 − 0.36) cannot be claimed as a refund against other income tax liabilities. However, the Australian-resident company can carry forward this credit for up to five years to be offset against future foreign income of the same source.

Not all foreign taxes paid give rise to foreign tax credits. For example, in the definition of 'foreign tax', in section 6AB(2) of the Tax Act 'unitary tax' and 'credit-absorption tax' are specifically excluded. In Income Tax Ruling IT 2507, the foreign taxes are listed that are, in the Commissioner's opinion, 'foreign taxes' within section 6AB(2). The ASEAN-country taxes that are listed are set out in Appendix 14.1. IT 2507 does not list any foreign taxes with respect to Vietnam.

When self-assessing his or her liability with reference to foreign income, an Australian resident has to complete the following five steps.

1. Ascertain the amount of foreign tax that has been paid.
2. Gross up the foreign income actually received by the amount of foreign tax that has been paid.
3. Adjust the gross foreign income by deducting any expenses incurred in the deriving of the income and any carry-forward foreign tax losses that the taxpayer may elect to offset against the income. The residual amount is referred to as the 'net foreign income'.
4. Calculate the average rate of Australian tax that is payable (a flat rate of 36 per cent for a company) and apply this to the 'net foreign income'.
5. Deduct the foreign-tax credits from the Australian-income-tax liability.

Foreign losses

As mentioned, when an Australian resident incurs foreign losses, section 79D provides that the losses are deductible against neither Australian income nor foreign-sourced income of a different class. These losses are carried forward to be offset only against foreign income of the same class.

Accruals – controlled foreign companies (CFCs)

The underlying purpose of Part X of the Tax Act ('Attribution of Income in Respect of Controlled Foreign Companies') is the taxation of Australian residents who earn foreign income through foreign companies they controlled when the income was taxed neither in the country of source nor at tax rates that are comparable with Australia's. Although Part X's intent is clear, its application may be complicated, costly and time consuming.

If a CFC eventually repatriates the attributable income (income that is attributed to, and taxed in the hands of, the Australian shareholder), the shareholder is relieved of paying any more tax, because in section 23AI, dividends that are paid to an Australian resident out of income when the income has been subject to attribution are treated as exempt income. The extent to which these dividends are paid from attributed income is determined by 'attribution-tax accounts' that are maintained by the Australian taxpayer.

Of particular importance when the CFC rules are being applied is determination of the following.
- Whether an Australian taxpayer has a 'controlling' interest in a CFC
- The CFC's residence, in particular whether the CFC is resident in a listed country (a country that is listed in the CFC regulations) or an unlisted country
- Whether the CFC derives income that passes the 'active income' test.
  A company is a CFC if
- it is not a 'Part X Australian resident' (basically a company that is an Australian resident as defined in section 6(1) of the Tax Act)
- any one of the three control tests is satisfied.
  The three 'control tests' are as follows.
1. Do five or fewer Australian residents (and their associates) beneficially hold more than a 50 per cent interest (either directly or indirectly) in the company?
2. Does a single Australian entity (and any of its associates) beneficially hold more than a 40 per cent interest in the company *unless* the company is actually controlled by non-resident entities that are unrelated to the Australian entity?
3. Is the company controlled by five or fewer Australian entities and/or their associates?

For Part X's purpose, a 'listed country' is a country that is viewed as having a tax system that is comparable with Australia's. Schedule 10 of the Income Tax Regulations sets out the 'listed countries' for Part X's purpose and includes all the ASEAN countries except Vietnam.

In Division 8 of Part X, an active-income exemption is also provided. If a CFC passes the 'active-income test', attribution has to apply to only some CFC income, if any.

A company will pass the 'active-income test' if it meets the following five criteria.

1. It exists at the end of the statutory accounting period and it was a resident of a listed country or an unlisted country at all times during the period.
2. It has maintained accounts that have been prepared in accordance with commercially accepted accounting principles and in which a true and fair view of the company's financial position is given.
3. It has complied with the substantiation requirements of section 451(1), that is, that its 'general accounting records' correctly record and explain the company's acts and operations during the period. These records have to be retained by the taxpayer in accordance with section 462. They should contain the particulars of all transactions, calculations and other circumstances that are relevant to application of the CFC provisions. The records have to be retained for the later of at least five years after they were prepared or for five years after completion of the transactions that gave rise to them.
4. It at all times undertook a business in the country in question.
5. Its 'tainted-income ratio' for the period is less than 0.05.

'Tainted income' is passive income and income from sales and services that are referrable to associates of the CFC, Australian residents or permanent establishments in Australia. 'Passive income' covers dividends, interest, royalties and so on, that is, income that can be readily transferred between countries.

Foreign-investment funds (FIFs)

In order to complement the CFC rules, the Australian government introduced Part XI of the Tax Act, for taxing the increase in value between periods of an Australian resident's interest in an FIF.

Although an FIF can be a foreign company or a trust, the FIF rules apply only when the Australian resident has a passive investment, as opposed to control.

As is the case with the CFC rules, an exemption exists for 'eligible activities'; that is, the exemption is an active-business exemption.

Accruals – non-resident-trust estates

Division 6AAA of the Tax Act is an avoidance provision for income that is derived by non-resident trusts the assets of which were acquired from Australian residents. Division 6AAA may apply on a property's or service's transference to a non-resident trust on or after 12 April 1989. If, for example, an Australian resident transfers assets to a discretionary-trust resident in Malaysia, under Division 6AAA the income can be 'attributed' to the transferror – the Australian resident.

Anti-avoidance provisions and international trade

The Tax Act also covers profit shifting from Australia to other countries. The provisions apply to transactions undertaken by an Australian resident who is trading with an ASEAN country.

Sections 38 to 43

In sections 38 to 43, calculation of taxable profits in Australia is regulated for when a business is conducted both in and out of Australia, for an Australian importer who manufactures goods in South-East Asia. In these sections, the Commissioner is given the power to deem profits as having an Australian source. In doing so, he or she considers factors such as the following.

- Manufacture, production or purchase of goods in one country and the goods' sale in another.
- The successive steps of production and manufacture in various countries.
- Making of contracts in one country and the contracts' performance in another country.

Division 13

From 27 May 1981 onwards Division 13 has been a specific anti-avoidance provision for countering non-arm's-length transactions whereby the shifting of profits and consequently of income-tax liabilities is made possible between countries. The Commissioner is thereby given discretion to substitute an 'arm's-length consideration' with reference to the supply of 'property' under an 'international agreement'. For example, an Australian exporter sells goods to an overseas affiliate at less than market value or transfers the goods for no consideration at all. Alternatively, Division 13 could apply if an Australian resident was to purchase goods from an overseas supplier at an inflated price. For this purpose, 'property' is widely defined to be

- a 'chose in action' (a right that is enforceable by law, for example a contractual right)
- an estate or any interest in property
- any right to receive income
- services.
  If Division 13 is to be applied the following factors are required.
- Supply or acquisition of 'property' under an 'international agreement'.
- The Commissioner's forming of an opinion that Division 13 should apply due to
  - any connection that exists between the parties to the international agreement (or any other relevant factor)
  - the fact that the parties to the international agreement were not dealing at 'arm's length'.

- Consideration for the supply or acquisition of the property was less or more than on the consideration that would have been payable in an 'arm's length' transaction.

In section 136AC, an 'international agreement' is defined as being an agreement whereby

- a non-resident supplies or acquires property via an agreement otherwise than in connection with a permanent establishment that is conducted in Australia by the non-resident or
- a resident who is undertaking business outside Australia is supplied with or acquires property via the agreement in connection with that business.

When the Commissioner is applying Division 13 in order to substitute an 'arm's length' consideration for supply or acquisition of property, the Commissioner may adjust the taxpayer's assessable income or allowable deductions. In section 225 of the Tax Act, specific penalties of up to 50 per cent of the tax that has been avoided are also provided.

Part IVA

From 27 May 1981 onwards, Part IVA of the Tax Act has been the Commissioner's general anti-avoidance provision. It is limited by neither any other sections of the Tax Act nor the *Income Tax (International) Agreements Act 1953*.

In Part IVA the Commissioner is enabled to cancel a 'tax benefit' that arises from a 'scheme'. This may involve assessment of income that is otherwise excluded or denial of deductions that result from the scheme.

A 'scheme' is defined very widely to include any agreement that is written or unwritten and whether or not the agreement is enforceable. A 'tax benefit' is an amount that is not included in assessable income or a deduction that would not have occurred but for existence of the scheme.

In Part IVA it is required that the Commissioner (or a court) conclude, using eight criteria – see section 177D – whether the person/s who undertook the scheme did so in order for the relevant taxpayer to obtain a tax benefit. If the section 177D criteria are met, the tax benefit can be cancelled. The eight section 177D criteria are listed as follows.

1. The way in which the scheme was entered into or undertaken.
2. The scheme's form and substance.
3. The time at which the scheme was entered into and the length of the period during which the scheme was undertaken.
4. The result, in relation to operation of the Tax Act, that would, except for Part IVA, be achieved through the scheme.
5. Any change in the relevant taxpayer's financial position that has resulted, will result or may reasonably be expected to result from the scheme.
6. Any change in the financial position of any person who has or has had any connection (family, business or of any other nature) with the relevant taxpayer, this being a charge that is referrable to the scheme.

7. Any other consequence for the relevant taxpayer or for any person mentioned in point 6.
8. The nature of any connection (family, business or of any other nature) between the taxpayer and the person referred to in point 6.

Part IVA may be applied either in conjunction with a more specific anti-avoidance provision such as Division 13 or in its own right. Because Part IVA is not limited by the Income Tax (International) Agreement Act, the Commissioner can use it when transactions involve international dealings.

Conclusion

Taxation of Australian-resident income that is sourced in an ASEAN country is determined by the domestic taxation laws of both Australia and the ASEAN country in question, as modified by any existing international tax treaties.

The taxation issues that are associated with any foreign-investment project that is undertaken by an Australian resident may be a critical factor with reference to the investment entity's legal status and the project's overall profitability. Although taxation should not necessarily be the driving force behind any investment decision, ignoring the relevant income-tax issues may be an act of negligence. Expertise in identification of the tax issues that are relevant to any investment proposal is readily available through various Australian law and accounting firms and other professional advisers. Accordingly, a wise trader or investor would seek this advice.

REFERENCES

Asia and Australasia Tax Summaries. Singapore: Coopers & Lybrand, various issues.

Australian International Tax Agreements. North Ryde, New South Wales: CCH Australia Limited, 1982.

Australian Taxation Office – Corporate Communications Branch, *International Transfer Pricing: Minimising the Taxation Risks in International Associated Party Dealings*. Canberra: Australian Government Publishing Service, 1995.

CCH Australia – CCH International, *International Tax Planning Manual*. Corporations 1 and 2. North Ryde, New South Wales: CCH Australia Limited, 1985.

Cox, T, *Investment in Asia: Foreign Taxation and Regulatory Issues*. Twenty-eighth South Australian Convention Paper. Taxation Institute of Australia Convention 25–27 March 1993.

Hamilton, R and Deutsch, R, *Guidebook to Australian International Taxation*. Redfern, New South Wales: Legal Books, 1984.

Horwath International, *International Tax Handbook*. North Ryde, New South Wales: CCH Australia Limited, 1990.

Lehmann, G and Coleman, C, *Taxation Law in Australia*. Chapter 10. Sydney: Butterworths, fourth edition, 1996.

Minter Ellison Morris Fletcher – Solicitors, *Doing Business in South-East Asia: A Guide for Australian Business*. Melbourne, 1992.

Tax Planning International Review. London: Tax Management International, 1994.

Taxation Institute of Australia, *Cross-border Chaos: International Tax – A Wide-reaching Scrutiny of Problems, Solutions and Opportunities*. New South Wales Intensive Seminar, 29–31 October 1992.

APPENDIX 14.1: *Creditable taxes in the ASEAN countries*

Brunei

- Income tax
- Petroleum-income tax

Indonesia

- Income tax (*pajak penda patan*)
- Company tax (*pajak perseroan*)
- Withholding tax on interest, dividends and royalties (*pajak atas bunga dividen dan royalty*)

Malaysia

- Income tax and excess-profit tax
- Supplementary-income taxes (that is, tin-profits tax, development tax and timber-profits tax)
- Petroleum-income tax
- Real-property-gains tax

Philippines

- Income tax imposed by the government

Singapore

- Income tax

Thailand

- Income tax
- Petroleum-income tax

Vietnam

IT 2507 does not list any foreign taxes with respect to Vietnam.

15

Future directions

Ron Edwards

Introduction

The preceding 14 chapters described the way in which many of Australia's recent gains in international markets, especially for manufactured goods, have been based on exports to our ASEAN neighbours. Much more is possible, but links have to be strengthened with each ASEAN country, and these have to incorporate political, social and cultural ties as well as economic ones.

Historically, Australia has had close relations with Singapore and Malaysia, colleagues in the British Commonwealth. Similar British-colonial heritages have been helpful because they have resulted in the formation of familiar social and business institutions for visiting and expatriate Australian businesspeople. On the surface, at least, it seems Australia's relations with Indonesia are even stronger. It is certainly true that the federal government has worked hard towards ensuring a close business partnership exists with Australia's nearest ASEAN neighbour. At least with reference to investment, Australia's relations with Brunei also seem to be excellent, and relations with Thailand and Vietnam are most promising and will continue to develop.

In short, Australia has developed reasonably good relations in the region, which is fortunate, because Australia's economic future seems to be closely linked with that of the ASEAN countries. This position is true regardless of whether Australia ever becomes an ASEAN member or APEC evolves into an effective trade group.

While it is dangerous to make predictions about Australia's future economic relations, it is appropriate that a book such as this do just that. This final chapter therefore considers what ASEAN has done so far with reference to economic integration, the role APEC may play in the region's affairs, and the possibility of Australia becoming an ASEAN member in its own right as well as the impact this might have on Australia's trade relations. In the final section, some first-hand advice is passed from companies that are already operating in South-East Asia to those who are planning to follow the same path.

ASEAN and economic integration

ASEAN has a long history of reaction to outside forces and events. Its birth in 1967 resulted from fear of communist aggression. Creation of the ASEAN Preferential Trading Arrangement in 1977 and of the AFTA proposals in 1987 were ASEAN's reaction to the economic integration that was occurring in Europe and North America. More recently, ASEAN reacted to the likelihood – at the time – that GATT's Uruguay Round of tariff reductions would be ineffective. In each case its response has been the establishment of a new structure for integration or co-operation. Unfortunately, the structures have not proved to be particularly effective in achieving the specific aims; they were definitely steps in the right direction, but only steps. In this section there is an explanation of the way in which, in the past, individual members' apparent self-interest led at best to a watering-down of co-operative arrangements and at worst to the arrangements' non-implementation. In the ASEAN countries, neither standard of living nor level of trade has been significantly improved directly due to these government-led schemes.

For the ASEAN countries, attempts at developing and implementing meaningful preferential tariff arrangements have been fraught with problems, and although there is reason to expect ASEAN will resolve some of the problems with AFTA, the group's latest attempt at economic integration has to overcome many obstacles. For example, some member countries continue to be influenced by highly protectionist economic views. It has only been the pressure of competition from a more integrated Europe, the threat of increased competition from NAFTA and the existence of a low-wage China that have caused these interests to agree to a more genuine free-trade arrangement under AFTA. Whether this new arrangement, which at present enjoys some political momentum, maintains its current level of support from member governments remains to be seen. Led by Indonesia, member countries have already developed long exclusion lists for goods in 'sensitive' industries – goods that will be exempt from the enhanced competition that is coming from fellow ASEAN countries.

Powerful domestic forces continue to work towards retention of the currently high level of tariffs and other import barriers, even against imports from fellow ASEAN members.

- First, protectionism is profitable for the protected industries. When the preferential tariff cuts begin to impinge on profitability, as they inevitably will, the people who have influence will apply pressure upon governments for assistance. Political will may start to wither.
- Second, some ASEAN governments are restricted in gaining access to revenue because of narrow and sometimes ineffective taxation systems – a common characteristic of developing countries. In these circumstances, tariffs can provide a very effective and relatively inexpensive method of revenue raising for much

needed public services. Until the governments have reliable and efficient alternative sources of revenue, they will be reluctant to implement all the agreed tariff cuts on intra-ASEAN trade.

- Third, ASEAN lacks the level of geographic and political cohesiveness that is enjoyed by the EU and NAFTA. Because ASEAN's members are mostly island or peninsula nations, their ways of thinking about mutual interests vary. Being European or North American has, so far, had much more substance than being an ASEAN citizen, and this may be responsible for limiting the extent to which governments can convince electorates to make sacrifices in the name of ASEAN solidarity.

- Fourth and finally, the ASEAN member countries' various circumstances will continue to be responsible for posing problems. For example, Singapore applies a near-free-trade policy. Importers in high-tariff ASEAN countries will be encouraged to source imports from outside ASEAN, through Singapore, in order to pay the low Singaporean customs duty. Consequently, internal customs barriers will be required so that goods from Singapore can be checked to be of ASEAN origin and therefore deserving of preferential tariff rates. Complex rules of origin will need to be implemented and policed when goods have a mix of ASEAN and non-ASEAN input.

Despite the plethora of summits, ministerial meetings, partner-nation dialogues and other recent examples of consultation, the multitude of tensions and rivalries that have traditionally characterised the South East Asian countries' bilateral relations have not been fully resolved. Thailand and Malaysia are at present in dispute about fishing territory; boats are being impounded and fishing folk held. Thailand and Myanmar (Burma) are also disputing fishing rights as well as responsibility for border control, especially with reference to the movement of drugs. Singapore and the Philippines have fallen out over Singapore's treatment of Filipino workers; the hanging of a Filipina maid has been the most damaging event in recent times. The Philippines, Vietnam and Malaysia dispute each other's claims to the Spratly Islands, as do China and Taiwan. The leaders of Malaysia and Indonesia seem to be in continual rivalry for the mantle of pre-eminent regional 'statesman'.

Although these disagreements are significant for the parties involved, they are reasonably minor when considered from a regional viewpoint. Indeed, ASEAN's major achievement has been the giving of added weight to regional interests in global forums. Through their speaking with one voice, members have had much more impact than would have been possible from a range of single, independent, mainly small, poor countries. For example, The ASEAN countries have been able to negotiate as a group with the EU about its trade-restricting measures, as well as in the Uruguay Round of multilateral trade negotiations. ASEAN has also aided development of much greater personal ties and understanding in the South-East Asia region.

Happily, almost in spite of government-inspired integration schemes, and with the exception of the Philippines, the ASEAN countries have made significant economic progress in recent times. In fact, according to the World Bank, Thailand had the world's fastest economic growth (8.2 per cent per year) in the decade 1984–94.

Singapore had the equal-third fastest growth: 6.9 per cent per year. Indonesia and Malaysia were close behind. The forces that have been responsible for promoting this growth are likely to continue to apply. In reviewing chapters 3 to 9 it is demonstrated that policies for promoting exports, attracting FDI, liberalising trade, deregulating industry and developing each country's physical and human infrastructure – rather than participation in specific government inspired projects – have been the core of ASEAN's economic success.

Regardless of the existence of formal, government-administered arrangements and despite the abovementioned obstacles, the ASEAN economies will undoubtedly become more integrated over time. Four powerful forces will be responsible for promoting this process, and these are discussed as follows.

The ASEAN member countries' increasing integration in the global economy

Although this may take many forms and can be quite intangible, it is important in its effect on economic development. For example, most ASEAN members offer preferential tariff arrangements to MNCs that are prepared to make commitments to export, train local people or locate in prescribed districts. Those companies are entitled to import raw materials and other inputs free of import duty. MNCs account for a major part of many ASEAN countries' manufacturing industry. In 1992, for example, the stock of inward FDI as a percentage of GDP stood at 56 per cent for Indonesia, 39 per cent for Malaysia and 75 per cent for Singapore. These figures compare with an average figure of 7.4 per cent of GDP for APEC as a whole and serve to confirm the MNCs' importance in ASEAN's development. Consequently, an expanding segment of ASEAN trade, trade that is conducted by MNCs, is already enjoying zero or reduced tariffs.

North-East Asian MNCs are particularly important in this process and have contributed greatly to ASEAN's economic growth. In fact, much of that growth has directly resulted from trade and investment links with North-East Asia's industrial powerhouses. In any review of ASEAN trade and investment, the growing importance of, in particular, Japan, China, Taiwan, Hong Kong and South Korea is demonstrated. As these countries' companies develop pan-Asian supply strategies and production strategies, the ASEAN countries will increasingly become integrated with North-East Asia and thereby be more integrated with each other. ASEAN integration will therefore be subsumed in Asian integration as a result of corporate strategies rather than political ones.

The influence of ethnic-Chinese business networks

Historically, some ASEAN countries, including Malaysia and Thailand, sought to circumscribe Chinese entrepreneurship in their communities, intending to give special advantage to local ethnic populations. This policy stance has now been softened, and the Chinese have come to dominate business. They account for 6 per cent of South-East Asia's population, but control more than 70 per cent of the region's corporate wealth, and account for 86 per cent of the region's known billionaires. In Indonesia, for example, although they account for only 3.5 per cent of the population, they control 68 per cent of the 300 top conglomerates. Increasingly, Asia's ethnic-Chinese-controlled conglomerates are treating the region as one large market and are moving towards dominating its important industrial sectors. For example, the commercial raising, processing and fast-food distribution of poultry in Indonesia, Singapore, Thailand, Brunei and Malaysia is substantially controlled by only three overseas-Chinese MNCs. Many other examples of Chinese entrepreneurship are emerging, to the betterment of regional development and integration.

The sheer pressure of economic growth

Whenever domestic resources or markets are insufficient to meet business demands, private decision makers 'reach over borders' to satisfy their needs. A good example of this was Singaporean economic activity's 'spillage' into neighbouring Indonesian and Malaysian provinces during the late 1980s and early 1990s. Although the area has been dubbed a 'growth triangle' by government, it is driven by private, commercial demand in Singapore, which is scarce in land and labour. Singaporean capital has funded labour-intensive and land-intensive projects in these neighbouring countries' low-wage and low-rent provinces. The process will continue – currently underdeveloped parts of Indonesia and Malaysia will become metropolitan Singapore's rural, manufacturing and perhaps residential zones. It will continue regardless of the extent of government schemes – assuming no new administrative barriers are erected.

The concept of growth triangles became popular during the early 1990s and has been described in chapters 3 to 9. However, with reference to the Singapore–Johor–Riau triangle the 'triangle' image is misleading insofar as the commercial ties that exist between Riau and Johor are minimal. The important ingredient in this linkage's success is not government policy makers' geometric imagination; it is Singaporean businesspeople's energy. The critical role for government is to remove the administrative and political forces that limit the energy spreading across political borders.

The shifting of political forces away from protectionism

As the more modern, outward-looking sectors grow, and in particular grow at a rate more rapid than that of the rest of the economy, they will attract resources away from the older, inward-looking, protected industries. Those industries' profitability will be reduced accordingly. As the outward-looking sectors gain in economic importance they should also gain in political influence, most likely at the protectionists' expense. ASEAN-member governments should therefore be increasingly able to support the concept of open regionalism and thereby expand their trade.

In summary, the ASEAN market will become more integrated due to North Asian and other MNCs' pursuit of pan-Asian strategies, the similar activities of home-grown companies that are working together in order to pursue regional market opportunities, and economic activity's spillage from growth centres into comple-mentary parts of neighbouring countries. Combined with an expanding ASEAN membership, competition from other regional trading blocs should serve to further reduce the impact of single-country, protectionist lobby groups. All these develop-ments will work to diminish the commercial importance of political boundaries between the ASEAN countries. Because of the existence of these forces, the likeli-hood that proponents of the AFTA movement will win out is increased. In these cir-cumstances, national governments may decide that latent protectionism only serves to separate their countries from the region's dynamic nature and is therefore harmful to national interests. The political and economic environment is therefore more likely to support a genuine reduction in intra-ASEAN trade barriers, and this should foster economic integration.

If AFTA achieves a genuine and significant reduction in trade barriers, what will be the effect on the ASEAN economies? In the article 'Production and Trade Effects of the ASEAN Free Trade Area', Imada states that liberalising intra-ASEAN trade in manufactures would lead to greater specialisation and increased intra-ASEAN trade. Additional trade would be created within the group as previously protected producers decline and as imports are diverted from outside the group to inside sup-pliers, aided by the discriminatory tariff cut. The changes will be responsible for generating significant trade-balance effects. The more efficient, lower tariff, manu-facturing countries – Singapore and Malaysia – will increase their intra-ASEAN exports by more than their imports, whereas high-tariff Thailand will experience a large deterioration in its intra-ASEAN trade deficit. The real key lies in how much intra-ASEAN trade barriers are genuinely removed and whether trade-liberalisa-tion-policy changes outside the region have an equal if not greater impact. In a real sense, the accelerated removal of intra-ASEAN tariffs has been driven by the prospect that tariff cuts required by the Uruguay Round agreement and in APEC commitments will eventually supersede them.

APEC and ASEAN

Although Australia wishes to develop closer ties directly with ASEAN, it is also developing ties indirectly through its APEC membership. It has to be remembered that the idea of APEC originated in Canberra at a 1989 dialogue meeting between the then six ASEAN-member countries and Australia, Canada, Japan, South Korea, New Zealand and the US. Other countries have joined APEC since then but both Australia and ASEAN can take credit for its conception.

How much free trade this group will achieve is by no means certain. APEC's 1994 Bogor Declaration confirmed that each of its 18 member countries would achieve open markets by 2010 for developed countries and 2020 for developing ones. However, Malaysia subsequently stressed that the Declaration was a voluntary commitment, not a legal obligation. Because of this 'back-pedalling', some doubt is raised about whether all APEC members will in fact deliver on their Bogor promises. The view that each nation will demonstrate its responsibility by holding to the Declaration's principles is perhaps optimistic. To date, Malaysia has been viewed as being a maverick, uncomfortable with APEC but unable to change the group's direction and being forced, at the end of the day, to endorse the group's 'consensus'.

Although APEC dates from only 1989, some of its problems are similar to those that face AFTA. A general agreement exists that trade and investment should be promoted in the region through liberalisation, but exactly how this is to occur is a somewhat more difficult issue. The Osaka meeting left member countries free to develop their own Action Plans. Delays in opening highly protected industries will cause frustration and annoyance among other members. This is likely.

Indeed, some parts of Japan's and other member country's industry are strongly opposed to the Bogor Agreement. Another difficulty is that APEC's membership includes some of the region's poorest countries, which may not wish their markets to be opened to developed-country competition. Similarly, some developed APEC countries, including Japan, do not wish their entire domestic markets to be opened to imports from poor, low-wage APEC members. This is not surprising: Japan has done astonishingly well in Asia's emerging markets without having any help from APEC and has no motivation to help other developed countries to become more effective competitors. It therefore remains protectionist through informal barriers to imports. It has fought hard to resist US pressure to open its car and rice markets, despite demands made by the WTO. Regardless of its commitments to the contrary at Bogor and Osaka, Japan is likely to resist opening its agricultural market. China, Taiwan, Malaysia and South Korea may follow the same path.

Despite commitents to comprehensive liberalisation in Osaka, when it comes to implementation of tariff cuts and delivery of free, open markets, Malaysia may seek special treatment for its car industry, Thailand for its agriculture, and so on. The potential exists for any success in retention of trade barriers to be responsible for encouraging other countries to pursue equivalent policies. If this occurs, it would be required that AFTA and APEC become negotiating forums similar to GATT. However, these organisations do not have the resources to support lengthy, detailed negotiations – as were witnessed in GATT's Uruguay Round of trade negotiations. If concessions become significant, they may foreshadow the demise of the group.

In many countries, informal trade barriers are reflected in the different standards of living and attitudes towards consumer protection. A free-trade area can approach the issue of consumer protection in one of two ways: it can seek to develop a common set of international product standards and testing procedures or require each member to accept products that have met product standards in their country of origin. The former method can be slow and very expensive. APEC is at present developing a number of approaches to this issue. It is working to align standards to existing international standards. It is also pursuing a 'reciprocal' approach. Under such an arrangement, Japanese and Australian safety authorities would be under pressure to accept goods that are imported from fellow APEC members. This is likely to be strongly opposed by Japanese and Australian consumer groups if they fear that weaker standards have been applied and they will pressure their governments to protect consumer interests. Any success on their part will result in what fellow APEC members will interpret as the creation of 'informal trade barriers' and may thereby lead to retaliation.

APEC offers other potential problems for ASEAN members. The more developed members mainly commenced their industrialisation process by focusing on labour-intensive products for export – particularly textiles, footwear, clothing and toys. Economic success has been responsible for raising wages, and those industries are progressively shifting to lower wage sections of Asia. IndoChina and China will increasingly offer competition and potentially win markets for those products. Vietnam is already putting forward serious competition. APEC membership will largely preclude use of protection in order to nurture these and other important industries during the early stages of industrialisation.

APEC therefore provides another avenue for Australia's participation in regional trade and development, even if at present APEC remains at an early stage of its history. Many of the problems that have beset ASEAN since its formation are yet to be solved by APEC. Australian businesspeople would therefore be wise to view with some caution the promised, additional opportunities that may flow from APEC.

Australia and ASEAN membership

It was in 1993 that Thailand first suggested Australia join AFTA, but not all ASEAN's members were keen on the idea. Malaysia's prime minister, Dr Mahathir, was quick to remind us that Australia is not part of Asia. Although this is certainly true in an historical, an ethnic and a cultural context, things are changing. Even Dr Mahathir allows the idea that we might become more Asian in the future.

In any case, ASEAN's membership is likely to continue to grow. In the 1967 Bangkok Declaration it is stated that ASEAN is open for participation by all states in the South-East Asia region that subscribe to the Association's aims, principles and purposes. Discussions between ASEAN and the IndoChina countries, about full membership, have been pursued since 1994. When the ASEAN leaders met in Bangkok in December 1995, one step towards IndoChinese membership was taken. The leaders agreed to the concept of holding a regional leaders' meeting and informal annual meetings of the seven ASEAN countries plus three other nations – Myanmar (Burma), Cambodia and Laos: the 'ASEAN 10'. Indeed, Laos has indicated its intention to join in 1997, and Cambodia and Myanmar hope to join by 2000. For Cambodia, the main obstacle is its volatile internal political situation. However, equivalent problems in Myanmar have not precluded that country's membership negotiations. Unlike the major Western powers, the ASEAN members have not shunned it – they are more accepting of the ruling junta's treatment of political opponents. Political and economic reform should eventually lead to Laos, Cambodia and Myanmar joining ASEAN, thereby creating an economic group of 450 million people.

However, once ASEAN incorporates these 10 South-East Asian states, its capacity for continued geographic growth will be limited. Papua New Guinea is one obvious potential member, because it has already signed the ASEAN Treaty of Amity and Co-operation. The second-most obvious member countries would be China or India. However, these countries are much too large for ASEAN to absorb, even in its expanded form, without some major economic changes being the result. Because of ASEAN's ongoing concern about China's territorial ambitions, concern that is reinforced by China's claim over the Spratly Islands in the South China Sea, a significant barrier to political closeness is also posed. It is likely, when that point is reached, that ASEAN may direct its attention southward towards Australia.

Australia has good reason to promote this development. As was discussed in Chapter 2 and elsewhere in this book, ASEAN has grown in significance as an export market for Australia and is a particularly important market for manufactured exports. This trend is likely to continue, making ASEAN an even more important market in the early twenty-first century. In the paper 'Impact of Growth in South-East Asia on Australian Trade', Vlachos reveals that ASEAN's demand for Australian exports is strongly linked with income levels in the ASEAN nations. Although this is true for all the ASEAN countries, the relationship is particularly strong with reference to Singapore and Thailand, where a 1 per cent rise in income leads, respectively, to a 2.18 per cent rise and a 2.06 per cent rise in demand for Australian exports. As noted previously in this chapter, those two countries had the world's fastest and third-fastest growth rates in the decade 1984–94. Whatever ASEAN's economic-growth rate proves to be – and most analysts expect it will remain prodigious – it will be responsible for generating a more than proportionate increase in imports from Australia, assuming Australian business remains at least as competitive as it is now.

In Vlachos's paper, the importance of remaining price competitive is also highlighted. The author shows how ASEAN demand for Australian exports is highly responsive to price changes. In these circumstances, a price rise will lead to a more than proportionate decrease in the quantity of Australian exports that are demanded. Price reductions, which will perhaps be achieved through either microeconomic reform in the Australian economy or greater efficiency within firms themselves, will pay off in increased export revenue.

The ASEAN economy is likely to continue providing expanding opportunities to Australian businesses if they are competitive with others seeking the same business. Through infrastructure development, be it Thailand's Southern Seaboard Development Program or Jakarta's public-transport expansion, opportunities are offerered for building-product suppliers, architects, engineers and construction companies – areas in which Australian business has already made inroads. However, Australian businesses should be cautious and take great care to research individual markets before committing themselves. Although many of the ASEAN countries are growing rapidly, it cannot be assumed that each market will grow at the same rate, that existing competition will permit an additional player to enter or that foreign firms will have access to the whole, or even to part, of these markets.

For example, although much has been said about Australia's potential to become 'Asia's food basket' – and good opportunities certainly exist in some food and fibre markets – many markets are well covered by highly competitive local companies or MNCs. Furthermore, traditional types of bulk-food products may not be the ones in which Australia is competitive. Opportunities may exist for processed foods, but there again the demand is often for highly processed types of traditional food rather than for Western products. In addition, highly processed goods tend to be subject to levels of protection in ASEAN countries that are higher than those that apply to lower-value-added goods.

The growing size of ASEAN's middle class has been discussed in the preceding chapters. Although those people clearly have more Western-like consumer preferences, the products they demand (for example, clothing) may be readily supplied by local firms, or the existence of different tastes may mean standard Western products lack appeal. For example, in the Philippines, US hamburger restaurants have proved to be popular places for young people to meet but it is common for the same young people to go over the road to local hamburger shops in order to eat.

Another example of a difficult field for foreigners to enter is distribution. A number of Australian companies have been successful in Europe and the US in this field. However, because of the peculiarities of ASEAN cities' road systems, bulk, refrigerated transportation is inappropriate. In the narrow, crowded streets of Asia's capital cities, the practice of transporting food in small vans or even on the back of bicycles is much more appropriate than using the transportation methods with which Australian firms are competitive. Another issue, one that has importance in many industries and many parts of Asia, is that distribution services are often viewed as being the province of ethnic minorities. Governments may move to prevent foreign competition in industries if social dislocation may result. These and other factors have to be weighed before any Australian firm makes significant commitments to new markets in the ASEAN countries. Too many foreign firms have entered the market, performed poorly and eventually been forced to leave, whereas more thorough research would have revealed the dangers that eventually caused the downfall.

First-hand advice

In a book of this nature it is appropriate to emphasise advice from businesspeople who are working in the field. Although the following advice was supplied by Australian managers during interviews conducted in Thailand, it is more widely applicable both within ASEAN and beyond – a point that is attested to by the managers themselves. Because Thailand is considered to be one of the more difficult ASEAN countries for expatriates, Australian managers who have succeeded in that country are certainly well qualified to give advice, explain strengths and weaknesses and relate mistakes and successes. They advise that:

- 'You need defined goals and a business plan.' The venture into the ASEAN market should be the outcome of a company's well-defined and articulated mission. In the business plan, the mission should be operationalised and all potential obstacles addressed.

- The market should be thoroughly researched. 'Ensure there is a market. Just because a product does not exist does not mean there is a market for it'; 'When the market has been confirmed and the venture is to proceed, the parent company must supply appropriate support over the long termbacking of your company and the time to get things done.'

- The plan has to incorporate an effective market-entry strategy. The managers emphasised the importance of 'becoming a local business': 'You need to immerse yourself in the market.' This was sometimes eased through joint venturing with a local partner: 'It's very important to have a good joint-venture partner'; 'Our partner helped overcome the cultural and political problems.' However, successful immersion in the market does not stop at choosing the joint-venture format – it has to be translated into the firm's internal organisational structure: 'Have a localisation plan'; 'Do not apply the company culture without adaptation.'

- The company has to be empathetic with the cultural context in which it operates. In fact, cultural empathy and management experience in the industry were ranked equal as the most important factors in determining whether management was successful in Thailand: 'Understand the culture'; 'Familiarise staff with the social and cultural factors.' This advice applied to both employee relationships and client relationships. One manager, who was in charge of a large operation in Bangkok, exemplified the importance of cultural empathy in marketing by citing the case of a lost customer:

> Young John, an Australian, decided to come to work one Sunday, when the business was closed. He wanted to get a few things ready for the week. It was blazing hot and incredibly humid so he wore his shorts and thongs. A fair thing for an Aussie on his day off. Unannounced, a major client turned up and was introduced to John. He was very polite but he took exception to John's casual dress. He could be our best customer today but we only get a small portion of his business. That day spoiled it for us.

Another manifestation of lack of cultural understanding was failure to recognise the strengths of Thai staff and to respond appropriately: 'People are an asset'; 'They are hardworking people.' Australian managers sometimes offended their staff, though, by not returning their loyalty: 'Thais are far more dedicated, serious and loyal than Australians and far more sensitive.' Treating them in a casual or dismissive way causes staff members to become disaffected and less productive.

- If operating through an import agent, special care has to be taken to choose a good one and then to maintain a close working relationship: 'There have been too many cases of goods [that were] beyond their "use-by" date or in bad condition [being] supplied to retailers by sloppy agents. Too often the goods are placed inappropriately in the supermarkets'; 'Be generous with your agents if you want them to look after you.'

- Flexibility and capacity to adapt to a new cultural and physical environment were essential aspects of good management in Thailand. This meant managers could not expect tasks to be completed in the time they might be completed in Australia: 'Have an open mind. Business is frustrating. Nothing is easy'; 'Don't expect things to be done quickly. The notion of speed in Australia does not apply'; 'You must be able to cope with brick walls.'

In general, although Australia's management practices were found to be appropriate in Thailand – even to be a strength – modification was required in order to accommodate the cultural differences. Australians tended to be too 'production' or 'technology' focused, giving insufficient attention to 'people' relationships and insufficient time to establishing networks. Cultural insensitivity meant 'unspoken messages' were often not picked up. It meant Thai politeness was sometimes misinterpreted as being subservience. Australians who responded in a patronising or arrogant way caused offence.

All in all, the participating managers were enthusiastic about doing business in Thailand and urged more Australian companies to 'take the plunge' – to make a long-term commitment by establishing businesses in the country. Although firms from many countries were already well established, great scope remained for new entrants: 'It's hectic and vibrant,' but 'it's not too late!'

The way ahead

That Australia's relations with ASEAN are a function of a range of political (internal and external), cultural and historical factors is not in question. It is not simply a matter of 'straight economics'. Furthermore, it is not simply Australia's relations with ASEAN and specific ASEAN members that matter, but also Australia's relations with other countries in and outside the Asia-Pacific region. Given this environment, Australia's trade policy towards ASEAN has to be multi-faceted in order to be successful. Australia has to place emphasis on bilateral, regional and multilateral relations.

Indeed, much of Australia's relationship with ASEAN may develop not as a function of direct Australian-government efforts but more indirectly. Each of the 'ASEAN Six' (not Vietnam) countries is also a member of the APEC forum, which has the potential to become a very important regional force. Similarly, the individual ASEAN countries are also members of the WTO; again, that institution's operations could quite possibly have an impact much greater than that of any bilateral trade negotiation Australia may attempt to have.

Although it is somewhat more indirect, the impact of NAFTA and the EU – to the extent they give regional trade groupings more importance – could also help drive ASEAN to value links with Australia – particularly one that included the current CER pact with New Zealand more highly. Indeed, Australia's September 1995 success in initiating a regular annual meeting of the trade ministers of Australia, New Zealand and the seven ASEAN-member countries was achieved through a CER–ASEAN negotiation rather than through a strictly Australia–ASEAN arrangement.

If Australia adopts an outward-looking economic policy at home, a liberalising approach in bilateral economic relations with specific ASEAN countries, and an international perspective at the WTO, it may well encourage ASEAN neighbours to do the same.

In an economic context, Australia is already very much part of Asia. Australia will become even more so as the ASEAN members continue to make gains in their economic development and thereby become more interested in Australia as both a tourist destination and a source of imports. Whether or not Australia becomes part of Asia culturally is less clear. Certainly, the number of Asian people in Australia's capital cities, as well as evidence of their entrepreneurship, is both remarkable and refreshing. However, Australian businesses should not restrict themselves to an ASEAN or even an Asia-centric outlook, as important as these regions might be. It may be useful to borrow the environmentalists' aphorism 'Think globally; act locally' as being the best guide for Australian businesspeople. 'Acting locally' clearly means actively participating in markets located in Australia's neighbourhood, but it must not stop there. Experience and networks in Asia should be used as a springboard to enter global markets. Much opportunity remains to be pursued in specific niche markets in the developed, mature economies of Europe, the US and Japan. Also, the South American and Indian subcontinent countries have been pursuing, at different rates, the market-opening and market-liberalising path that has worked so well for Asia.

New opportunities and a welcome from governments await firms the are prepared to make long-term commitments. The first stage is to ensure the product is competitive in world markets. If the firm is able to match or better the world's best for quality, cost and service and is confident these can be improved at least as quickly as can its rivals, it can aspire to becoming international. With reference to this, international market trends suggest a singleminded focus on cost minimisation and mass production of undifferentiated products, whereby an extreme division of labour is applied in production, is not likely to lead to competitiveness for countries that are at an advanced stage of industrialisation. Instead, firms that seek competitiveness through superior-quality goods and service and superior capacity to innovate are likely to prevail.

The next stage is development of an internationalisation strategy. This should be built around core business strengths that have to be sufficient to prosper in international markets in the long run. The cultural context of international business has to be accepted. Fashion and 'flavour of the month' management strategies should be resisted, and the strategy should be dynamic – growing in breadth, sophistication and capacity with each new experience. In each transaction the company's reputation should be protected. Every supplier–customer relationship should be respected and nurtured as an essential element of the company's core strength. In each new foreign venture the home business should be strengthened, thereby creating synergies that make the business more than the sum of its parts.

If these apparently obvious homilies are adhered to, the business will evolve from being a purely domestic operation into being an Australian operation that has foreign activities, and finally to being an international company that is capable of viewing global markets, resources and organisational structures as a single construct. When the notions of 'local' and 'global' become fused, the firm becomes truly international.

All this will certainly take time, and if this chapter – and indeed this book – could be ended with a message, it is that Australia must be patient. Although Australia has shown considerable improvement over recent years, much remains to be done. If Australia can co-operate with ASEAN and work more closely on mutual economic development, Australia will achieve its goals all the more quickly.

REFERENCES

Acharya, A, *A New Regional Order in South-East Asia: ASEAN in the Post-Cold War Era*. London: International Institute for Strategic Studies, 1993.

Acharya, A and Stubbs R (eds), *New Challenges for ASEAN. Emerging Policy Issues*. Vancouver: UBC Press, 1995.

Ariff, M, *The Role of ASEAN in the Uruguay Round: Opportunities and Constraints*. San Francisco: ICS Press, 1993.

—— 'Open Regionalism a la ASEAN', in *Journal of Asian Economics*, no 5, September 1994.

Blomqvist, H, 'ASEAN as a Model for Third-World Economic Co-operation?', in *ASEAN Economic Bulletin*, no 10, July 1993, pp 52–67.

Bora, B and Findlay, C (eds), *Regional Integration and the Asia–Pacific*. Melbourne: Oxford University Press, 1996.

Davis, B, 'ASEAN Members Tie Trade Knot', in *Australian Business* magazine, August 1994, pp 130–3.

Deardorff, A V and Stern, R M, 'Multilateral Trade Negotiations and Preferential Trading Arrangements', in Deardorff, A V and Stern, R M (eds), *Analytical and Negotiating Issues in the Global Trading System*. Ann Arbor: University of Michigan Press, 1994.

East Asia Analytical Unit, Department of Foreign Affairs and Trade, *Overseas Chinese Business Networks in Asia*. Canberra: Australian Government Publishing Service, 1995.

Edwards, R, Edwards, J and Muthaly, S, *Doing Business in Thailand: Essential Background Knowledge and First-hand Advice*. Melbourne: Thai–Australian Chamber of Commerce, 1995.

Elek, A, 'Trade Policy Options for the Asia–Pacific Region in the 1990s: The Potential of Open Regionalism', in Garnaut, R and Drysdale, P, *Asia–Pacific Regionalism*. Pymble, New South Wales: Harper Educational, 1994, pp 212–17.

Fukusaku, K, Plummer, M and Tan, J (eds), *OECD and ASEAN Economies: The Challenge of Policy Coherence*. Paris: OECD, 1995.

Garnaut, R and Drysdale, P (eds), *Asia–Pacific Regionalism*. Sydney: HarperCollins, 1994.

Imada, P, 'Production and Trade Effects of the ASEAN Free-trade Area', in *The Developing Economies*, no.31, March 1993, pp 3–23.

Motoi, G, 'APEC and Japan', in *Journal of Japanese Trade and Industry*, no 5, 1995.

Park, I, *Regional Integration Among the ASEAN Nations: A Computable General Equilibrium Model Study*. Westport: Prager, 1995.

Pomfret, R, 'ASEAN: Always at the Crossroads'. Paper delivered at the Australian Conference of Economists, Adelaide, September 1995.

Sundqvist, U, *New Technologies in the 1990s: A Socioeconomic Strategy*. Report of the Group of Experts on Social Aspects of New Technologies. Paris: OECD, 1988.

Tan, J L H (ed), *Regional Economic Integration in the Asia–Pacific*. Singapore: Institute of Southeast Asian Studies, 1993.

Vlachos, L, 'Impact of Growth in South-East Asia on Australian Trade'. Paper delivered at the Australian Conference of Economists, Adelaide, September 1995.

Index